MEANING AND METHOD

Meaning and method

ESSAYS IN HONOR OF HILARY PUTNAM

Edited by
GEORGE BOOLOS

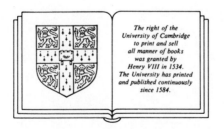

The right of the
University of Cambridge
to print and sell
all manner of books
was granted by
Henry VIII in 1534.
The University has printed
and published continuously
since 1584.

CAMBRIDGE UNIVERSITY PRESS

CAMBRIDGE

NEW YORK   PORT CHESTER   MELBOURNE   SYDNEY

Published by the Press Syndicate of the University of Cambridge
The Pitt Building, Trumpington Street, Cambridge CB2 1RP
40 West 20th Street, New York, NY 10011, USA
10 Stamford Road, Oakleigh, Melbourne 3166, Australia

First published 1990

Printed in the United States of America

Library of Congress Cataloging-in-Publication Data
Meaning and method: essays in honor of Hilary Putnam / edited by
George Boolos.
p.   cm.
ISBN 0-521-36083-8
1. Philosophy.   2. Putnam, Hilary.   I. Putnam, Hilary.
II. Boolos, George.
B29.M436   1990
100 – dc20
90 – 31040
CIP
British Library Cataloguing in Publication Data
Meaning and method: essays in honor of Hilary Putnam.
1. Philosophy
I. Boolos, George   II. Putnam, Hilary
100

ISBN 0-521-36083-8 hardback

Contents

Preface   *page* vii

List of contributors   viii

• 1   The source of the concept of truth   1
      MICHAEL DUMMETT

  2   Facts that don't matter   17
      CATHERINE Z. ELGIN

  3   Has the description theory of names been refuted?   31
      JERROLD J. KATZ

  4   Substitution arguments and the individuation of beliefs   63
      J. A. FODOR

• 5   Meanings just ain't in the head   79
      MICHAEL DEVITT

  6   Semantic anorexia: on the notion of "content" in cognitive
      science   105
      LOUISE ANTONY

  7   Can the mind change the world?   137
      NED BLOCK

  8   Realism, conventionality, and "realism about"   171
      RICHARD BOYD

  9   Invidious contrasts within theories   197
      LAWRENCE SKLAR

 10   Mathematics and modality   213
      HARTRY FIELD

 11   Ontological commitment: thick and thin   235
      HAROLD HODES

12 The standard of equality of numbers   261
    GEORGE BOOLOS

13 Doing what one ought to do   279
    RUTH ANNA PUTNAM

14 Closing up the corpses: diseases of sexuality and
    the emergence of the psychiatric style of reasoning   295
    ARNOLD I. DAVIDSON

15 Perception and revolution: *The Princess Casamassima* and
    the political imagination   327
    MARTHA NUSSBAUM

16 Human rights, population aging, and intergenerational equity   355
    NORMAN DANIELS

Preface

The essays in this collection were written for Hilary Putnam, and expressly for this volume. The branches of philosophy in which they lie are all areas in which Hilary has taken an interest, but they do not exhibit that thematic unity so much beloved of publishers. A volume containing both a discussion of the relations between arithmetic, set theory, and the theory of types and a historically informed account of the concept of sexual perversion, however, cannot be expected to be unified in any significant way.

Although the diversity of philosophical subject matter contained in this anthology certainly reflects the breadth of Hilary's intellectual interests, it does so imperfectly. There is no essay on the theoretical foundations of quantum physics, a field to which Hilary has made significant contributions. There are essays in and on logic, but no essay here deals either with hierarchy theory, a branch of logic in which three of the contributors to the present volume wrote Ph.D. theses under Hilary's supervision, or with his work on Hilbert's tenth problem, which, along with that of Yuri Matiyasevich, Martin Davis, and Julia Robinson, culminated in its final solution.

Dear to the editor's heart, but also unmentioned elsewhere in this volume, is Hilary's greatest *practical* contribution to philosophy: the founding, in 1963, of the graduate program in philosophy at MIT. Dick Boyd and I were two of its first four graduate students; Jerry Katz and Jerry Fodor were assistant professors in the department then. Ned Block is now the program's chairman.

Almost all of the other authors were students or junior colleagues of Hilary's. (The demands of two babies and a colicky university prevented Paul Benacerraf from being a contributor, to Hilary's, his, and my great regret.) A number of us regard Hilary's work, including his teaching, as the most important influence on our intellectual lives. Indeed, we cannot conceive what sorts of philosophers we might have been had we not known him. It is thus not gratitude we feel towards Hilary so much as love.

GEORGE BOOLOS

Contributors

LOUISE ANTONY
Department of
  Philosophy
North Carolina State University
Raleigh, N.C.

NED BLOCK
Department of Linguistics
  and Philosophy
Massachusetts Institute of
  Technology
Cambridge, Mass.

GEORGE BOOLOS
Department of Linguistics
  and Philosophy
Massachusetts Institute of
  Technology
Cambridge, Mass.

RICHARD BOYD
Sage School of Philosophy
Cornell University
Ithaca, N.Y.

NORMAN DANIELS
Department of Philosophy
Tufts University
Medford, Mass.

ARNOLD I. DAVIDSON
Department of Philosophy
University of Chicago
Chicago, Ill.

MICHAEL DEVITT
Department of Philosophy
University of Maryland
College Park, Md.

MICHAEL DUMMETT
New College
Oxford
England

CATHERINE Z. ELGIN
Harvard University
Cambridge, Mass.

HARTRY FIELD
School of Philosophy
University of Southern California
Los Angeles, Calif.

J. A. FODOR
Department of Philosophy
Rutgers University
New Brunswick, N.J.
and
The Graduate Center
City University of New York
New York, N.Y.

HAROLD HODES
Sage School of Philosophy
Cornell University
Ithaca, N.Y.

JERROLD J. KATZ
The Graduate Center
City University of New York
New York, N.Y.

RUTH ANNA PUTNAM
Department of Philosophy
Wellesley College
Wellesley, Mass.

MARTHA NUSSBAUM
Department of Philosophy
Brown University
Providence, R.I.

LAWRENCE SKLAR
Department of Philosophy
University of Michigan
Ann Arbor, Mich.

1

The source of the concept of truth

MICHAEL DUMMETT

Hilary Putnam began his 1976 John Locke Lectures on "Meaning and Knowledge" by observing that "the nature of truth is a very ancient problem in philosophy". It is certainly a problem that has greatly preoccupied Putnam himself; in my opinion, he is an outstanding member of that minority of philosophers who have grappled with what makes the problem so intractable. It is not this problem that I intend to address in this essay, however, but, rather, an antecedent question, namely: how do we ever come by the concept of truth?

If the concept of truth is as central to the content of a thought as Frege maintained, and as Wittgenstein, after him, maintained in the *Tractatus*, how is it that there is uncertainty about its application? The most striking example of such uncertainty is the still unresolved question concerning the truth-conditions of indicative conditionals of natural language. For Frege, for the *Tractatus* and, indeed, for Davidson, any difference about the conditions under which a statement should be accounted true must reflect a difference in the interpretation placed upon it, or in the thought it is taken to express. Yet, surely, the philosophers who engage in disputes about indicative conditionals all understand such conditionals in exactly the same way; what they disagree on is how the concept of truth ought to be applied to them. How, if Frege and the rest are right, could any uncertainty arise about this, given agreement in practice about what the conditionals mean?

Only the boldest of philosophers – Ryle, for instance – have attempted to resolve the problem of indicative conditionals by denying that they admit assessment as true or false at all; but this has been a thesis frequently advanced concerning other large classes of utterances that we should normally classify as statements. There is, however, an important distinction to be made between such claims, according to whether the utterances of the given class are admitted to be informative or not. A straightforward emotivist account of ethical statements, for example, does not allow any informative content to such an utterance as "Rape is wicked": according to it, such an utterance merely registers an attitude that the speaker has to rape. By contrast, Hilbert's way of construing arithmetical propositions involving quantification over all natural numbers concedes to them a great deal of informative content: it merely denies that they are statements assessable as true or false. Suppose that "A( )" is a decidable predicate of natural numbers. For any particular natural number, say 103, the proposition "A(103)" is then uncontroversially an informative statement. The existential proposition, "For some n, A(n)", is taken by Hilbert to be an incomplete communication of any particular such instance: one is entitled to enunciate it if one knows of any specific number of which one can show that it satisfies the predicate "A( )". So understood, the utterance of an existential proposition obviously conveys information: there is no specific statement that one who accepts the utterance as justified is in a position to assert, but the justification requires the speaker to be in a position to assert some one of an infinite range of informative statements. The same holds good, on Hilbert's account, of the utterance of the free-variable form "A(x)", or, what is the same, of the form "For every n, A(n)" with an initial universal quantifier. Such an utterance is justified if the speaker has an effective means of arriving, for any given natural number n, at a proof that it satisfies the predicate. We can view this as another kind of incomplete communication. Someone who cited a specific effective means of finding a proof of each instance of the proposition would be making a particular kind of informative statement, even if it should be classified as a metamathematical statement rather than an arithmetical statement proper. One who merely enunciates the universally quantified proposition is making an incomplete communication of such a metamathematical statement. Here the informative character of the utterance is even less in doubt, since one who accepts the utterance as justified is now in a position to assert each of infinitely many arithmetical statements, namely the instances of the quantified proposition.

Why, then, on Hilbert's view, are such propositions not to be classed as genuine statements, true or false? Plainly because the condition for someone to be entitled to make any such utterance is inseparably connected with his own cognitive position: lacking such an entitlement does not provide an entitlement to enunciate any alternative proposition. The mere fact of not being in a position to cite a true instance of "A(n)", for instance, does not entitle anyone to assert the negation "Not A(x)" of the free-variable statement, which would be tantamount to asserting "For every n, not A(n)"; and likewise, the mere fact of lacking any means of showing, for each n, that "A( )" applied to it, does not entitle one to assert "For some n, not A(n)". Hilbert assumed that the sentential operators are to be explained by the two-valued truth-tables: for this reason, an arithmetical proposition involving unrestricted quantification over the natural numbers cannot be subjected to such operators, if the outcome is to be a meaningful statement. Such a proposition is to be explained in terms of what justifies an utterance of it, not in terms of the conditions for its truth and falsity; although informative, it is therefore not a statement proper, and the operations of negation, disjunction and conditionalisation cannot be applied to it.

The intuitionists in effect accepted the Hilbertian characterisation of the meanings of the existential and universal quantifiers, but denied that statements formed by means of them were incapable of being subjected to negation or the other sentential operators. For them, it was necessary only to explain the sentential operators in the same manner, rather than by truth-tables: that is, to give the meanings of the sentential operators by specifying, for each operator, what would justify the assertion of a statement of which it was the principal operator. With all the logical constants explained in this same manner, rather than by a stipulation of the conditions for the truth or falsity of statements involving them, there would be no obstacle to forming by their means statements of indefinitely high complexity.

There are two components of the intuitionists' claim: (1) that an intelligible use of all the logical constants could be attained by an explanation along these lines; and (2) that our existing use of the logical constants ought to be explained in this way, or, at least, (2a) that *one* of our existing uses of them should be so explained. (1) is incontestably plausible within mathematical discourse; whether it is plausible when extended to empirical discourse is less clear. The case to be made for (2a), when applied to negation, is far from negligible. For a linguistic practice involving the making of claims, to be assessed as justifiable or unjustifiable, rather than as true or false, must still involve a recognition of the incompatibility of claims. The claim to be able to cite a number to which the predicate "A( )" applies is, for example, incompatible with the claim to have a means of showing, for any given number n, that the predicate does not apply to it; and any workable linguistic practice involving the making of such claims must incorporate a recognition of this incompatibility. For this reason, such a practice has, as it were, a place already prepared for the introduction of a non-classical negation, according to which the negative utterance "Not B" expresses a second-order claim to be entitled to make a claim incompatible with the claim that would be made by the utterance of "B". Such a negation would easily be recognised as having the characteristics of intuitionistic negation. For instance, it would easily be seen that "Not: for some n, A(n)"

was equivalent to "For every n, not $A(n)$"; but that from "Not: for every n, $A(n)$", "For some n, not $A(n)$" would not follow.

For the present, however, this is a side-issue: our immediate concern is with the picture of the genesis of the concept of truth supplied by Hilbert's discussion of the quantifiers. The concept of truth is born from a more basic concept, for which we have no single clear term, but for which we may here use the term "justifiability". We have seen that, even if we operate with the classical conception of a large class of utterances that constitute assertions of statements with determinate truth-conditions, we shall still need to acknowledge that not all informative utterances belong to that class. Other informative utterances may be classified, not as assertions of statements, but as expressions of claims: statements are to be assessed as true or false, but claims as justified or unjustified. Such claims are clearly illustrated by Hilbert's account of arithmetical propositions involving unrestricted quantification. The claim may be justified by the speaker's ability to cite a true statement from some large range, or by his possessing an effective means of establishing the truth of any given statement from such a range, or, as on the intuitionistic interpretation of the conditional, to establish the truth of some one statement, given any means of establishing that of a certain other statement. In these cases, the condition for the justification of a claim has been formulated in terms of the truth of certain statements; but it does not follow that the notion of the truth of a statement is prior to that of the justifiability of a claim, since the conditions could just as easily have been formulated in terms of the justifiability of certain other claims (as the intuitionists would insist that they should be).

From this it is clear how it is possible that a certain form of statement, such as the indicative conditional, should be well understood, and yet disagreements arise about its truth-conditions. What is well understood, and what is sufficient for grasping the use of that form of statement in practice, is the condition for an assertion of it to be justifiable. More exactly, such an understanding of it does not yet require it to be construed as a statement, nor an utterance of it as an assertion, in the strict sense in which the terms "statement" and "assertion" were used above. Such an understanding amounts to a mastery of the use of that form of sentence to express a claim. That does not rule out its being taken as amounting to a statement with determinate truth-conditions, since an assertion is a particular species of claim; but it leaves it open whether it can be so construed, and, if so, what its truth-conditions should be taken to be.

Why, then, if this is how things are, do we need the notion of truth, or that of a statement, in addition to those of justifiability and the expression of a claim? Hilbert's treatment of arithmetical propositions once more supplies the answer. We are here setting aside non-informative uses of language, such as questions, requests, commands and so forth, and concerning ourselves only with informative utterances, whether assertions or expressions of claims. To understand the use of a given sentence, considered as used on its own to make a complete informative utterance, we need only consider it as the expression of a claim: we need to know what counts as justifying such an utterance, and we need to know no more than this. If, however, we interpret any of the sentential operators of our language as truth-functional, we shall need to attribute more to the meaning of the sentence than the condition for the justifiability of an utterance of that sentence on its own, if we are to understand the result of applying any such operator to the sentence. For Hilbert, it was just because we can associate with a quantified arithmetical proposition only justification-conditions, and not truth-conditions, that we cannot intelligibly apply negation or any other sentential operation to it. If, then, we have in the language sentential operators which we construe as truth-functional, or as partly truth-functional, we must interpret sentences to which they are applicable as having determinate truth-conditions.

A sentential operator may be called partly truth-functional if the justifiability of an utterance involving that operator requires, for its formulation, mention of the truth or falsity of at least one of its subsentences. An operator's being taken as even partly truth-functional, in this sense, is sufficient to force us to regard any sentence capable of occupying that position as endowed with conditions for its being true or false.

To speak more exactly, all this has been expressed the wrong way round. The concept of truth is far from being wholly a construct of theoreticians. Philosophers who discuss how the concept should be applied to the indicative conditionals of natural language are engaging in a theoretical discussion: it is just because we do not have any intuitive conception of how it should be applied to them that disputes arise over the matter. The philosophers who engage in such disputes are therefore asking how best the concepts of truth and falsity should be applied to such utterances in order to construct a semantic theory faithful to actual linguistic practice, one that derives the use we make of sentences of our language from a specification of their truth-conditions. But the concept of truth is not an invention of theoreticians: it is an intuitive notion with which we operate in natural language; and our linguistic practice is in part guided by our apprehension of conditions for the truth or falsity of what we say. We cannot be said intuitively to regard any sentential operators as truth-functional, since that is a theoretical notion: ordinary speakers do not need, and can rarely pause, to ask which connectives yield sentences whose truth-value depends only on those of their subsentences. Still less can we be seen as intuitively regarding particular sentential operators of natural language as partly truth-functional: for this is not even a familiar theoretical notion (and, as such, awaits further explanation). Rather, it is the existing use of certain operators, which we learn as we acquire our language, that prompts us to form an intuitive conception of the *truth* of sentences to which they can be applied, as opposed to the justifiability of an utterance of such a sentence on its own. This occurs when an operator is used in such a way that the condition for the justifiability of an utterance involving it could not be framed in terms only of the justifiability of certain of its subsentences; we are then compelled to form a pre-theoretical notion of what it is for such a subsentence to be objectively true or false, independently of whether an utterance of it on its own would be justifiable or not.

At least if we subsume tenses to sentential operators, the point is easily illustrated by the future tense. We have two distinct uses of the future tense – what may be called the future tense proper, and the future tense expressing present tendencies. The latter is exemplified by the sentence, "There was going to be a meeting, but it will not now take place"; the former by "They are thinking of cancelling the meeting, but I feel sure it will take place"; to this one might add, "I have said all along that there was going to [or: would] be one". What establishes the difference between these two uses of the future tense? More precisely, what allows room for a differentiation between them? The use of a simple sentence in the future tense, considered as uttered on its own, could not allow us to discriminate between the two uses: for such an utterance will be justifiable if and only if the tendencies prevailing at the time of utterance are for events to occur as stated. One way of distinguishing, however, is by the behaviour of the associated compound past-future tense "was going to . . . ", which we may view as the result of applying the past-tense operator to the original future-tensed statement. Another way is by the behaviour of a conditional whose antecedent is (tacitly) in the future tense. Usually, the antecedent is taken as being in the future tense proper: in a sentence like "If you go into that room, you will die before nightfall" (which, when translated into Italian, say, would have a future-tensed antecedent), the event stated in the consequent is predicted on condition of the truth of the antecedent (construed as in the future tense proper), not of its justifiability; otherwise stated, on its truth when understood as being in the future tense proper rather than as in the future tense that expresses present tendencies. But the distinction between the two ways of construing a future-tensed sentence, and hence between the truth and the justifiability of an utterance of it on its own, arises only because of the behaviour of more complex sentences formed from it: conditionals of which it is the antecedent, and sentences with compound tenses.

This thesis must be distinguished from a related one for which I argued in my article of 1959 on "Truth". There I claimed that the rationale for recognising certain forms of sentence as violating the principle of *tertium non datur* rested solely on the behaviour of such sentences as subsentences of complex ones, never on the use of them when uttered on their own. This is to say that, given concepts of truth and falsity, the incentive for regarding certain sentences as being, in certain circumstances, neither true nor false is always to achieve a means of systematising their behaviour as constituents of more complex sentences, usually by a tacit or explicit appeal to a three- or other many-valued semantics. Here I am making a stronger claim, namely that the very concept of the truth of a statement, as distinct from the cruder concept of its justifiability, is required only in virtue of the occurrence, as a constituent of more complex sentences, of the sentence by means of which the statement is made.

Which operators compel us in this way to replace the conception of justifiability by the more refined concept of truth? "And" plainly does not: the linguistic effect of uttering a conjunction of two sentences is barely distinguishable from that of uttering the two sentences in succession, each as a complete sentence. "Or" is a more promising candidate, but by no means a compelling one. Certainly, its ordinary use in natural language could not be captured by a straightforward intuitionistic explanation, to the effect that a disjunctive utterance "A or B" is justified just in case either the utterance of "A" or that of "B" would be justified; but a more complicated explanation might be given without appealing to the concept of truth. We must first recall that a non-classical negation can readily be introduced in terms of justifiability alone. The utterance of "A or B" may now be thought of as expressing a conditional claim to be able to justify the claim "A", given a justification of "Not B", or, conversely, to justify the claim "B", given a justification of "Not A": this is, in effect, to take the logical law *modus tollendo ponens* as giving the basic meaning of disjunction.

Given such an argument for dismissing the claims of the connective "or" to prompt us to recognise the concept of truth in addition to that of justifiability, it would seem natural to dismiss the claims of the connective "if" on similar grounds. It lies to hand, after all, to explain "if" in intuitionistic style: the utterance "If A, then B", so understood, would express a conditional claim to be able to justify the claim "B", given a justification of "A"; this would be to take the law *modus ponendo ponens* as giving the basic meaning of the conditional. The fact is, however, that such an explanation would signally fail to fit the use of "if" in natural language.

Some may feel sceptical that there is any such difference between "or" and "if", as used in natural language; and it is not a major part of my thesis that there is. If someone accepted the general lines of my argument, but held that our use of "or" as effectively prompts us to form the concept of truth as does our use of "if", he would do little damage to the argument as a whole. The interpretation of "or" proposed above in effect equates "A or B" with "If not A, then B, and, if not B, then A", understood intuitionistically, a rendering of course weaker than the ordinary intuititionistic interpretation of "A or B". On this interpretation, various statements would fail to be logically true that are classically so: for instance, "Either for some n, B(n), or, for every n, not B(n)". It is, however, arguable that the use of the standard logical constants in natural language embodies a great part, though not the whole, of classical logic. Perhaps everyday linguistic practice is not coherent in this regard, that is to say, not systematisable: perhaps classical laws that would be intuitively rejected as invalid are nevertheless derivable from laws that would be intuitively accepted. However this may be, it remains plausible that the classically valid schema cited above would be recognised by the speakers of natural language as logically compelling, and this calls in question the proposed interpretation of the "or" of natural language.

Such an argument exposes an ambiguity concerning the basis on which the connective "if" was rated a better candidate than "or" for being one whose use prompts us to form the concept of truth. We are seeking to discern the genesis of this concept. The thesis that I have been maintaining is that, for a mastery of the simplest part of linguistic practice, a grasp of the concept of truth, however implicit, is not required, but only of the coarser concept of justifiability; but that the more refined concept is needed in order to master the use of certain means of forming complex sentences from simpler ones. The problem is, then, to seek an understanding of how the use of certain linguistic constructions forces us to refine the concept of justifiability so as to arrive at that of truth. It is no part of this thesis that the concept of truth is spurious or redundant: we really do have such a concept, and Frege was not far off target in saying that truth and falsity are known, "even if only implicitly, to everyone who ever makes a judgement". A little more accurately, we may say that an implicit grasp of the concept of truth is required for construing certain utterances as assertions of statements rather than mere expressions of claims.

Now, once we have the concepts of truth and falsity, it is open to us to interpret such a connective as "or" truth-functionally; and it is unsurprising that we should at that stage be disposed to accept logical laws relating to it that are classically, but not intuitionistically, valid. Our doing so will then properly be called part of the practice governing the use of that connective in natural language; but it does not follow from this that it was the use of that connective which originally prompted us to form the concept of truth. Our mastery of common linguistic practice is, of course, acquired in stages. At a stage when we are implicitly operating only with the notion of justifiability, and not yet that of truth, we can, still without needing to form the latter notion, learn enough of the use of "or" to be able to utter disjunctive sentences appropriately, and to respond appropriately to disjunctive utterances of others. At that stage, we shall have only an imperfect grasp of the use of "or" in natural language, but one whose imperfection is unlikely yet to be apparent to us. Only after we have acquired the concepts of truth and falsity shall we be able to perfect our knowledge of the conventional use of the connective "or"; but, despite the imperfection of our knowledge at the earlier stage, it was not our introduction to the use of disjunctive sentences that *forced* us to form the concept of truth. What forces us to do so is the use of conditionals. Although there is indeed a way of understanding conditionals that can be explained in terms of justifiability, rather than of truth, it does not yield even a plausible approximation to the actual use of conditionals in natural language; and that is why it is their use that forces us to form an implicit notion of truth.

As already remarked, it is of minor importance whether or not I am right to think that the use of disjunctive sentences does not, of itself, have this effect: it is very clear that the use of conditionals does so. A conditional assertion is justified provided the speaker can offer a conditional justification of the consequent, but the condition under which the consequent needs to be justified is the *truth* of the antecedent, not the existence of a justification for it. We have already seen that this holds good when the antecedent is in the future tense; but it holds equally in all other cases, for example, when the antecedent is an existential sentence. In themselves, existential statements are like disjunctions. The fundamental justification for an existential claim is the ability to cite a specific instance. It is only after we have come to regard existential sentences as carrying truth-conditions and hence as expressing assertable statements that we acknowledge indirect demonstrations of existential statements; as with disjunctions, this exemplifies the extension of a primitive use by appeal to a truth-conditional conception of content. But a conditional whose antecedent is an existential sentence "For some x, $A(x)$" cannot be interpreted in terms of the primitive notion of the justifiability of an utterance of the antecedent on its own: to justify the conditional assertion, we must be able to justify the consequent, not on the assumption that we can *cite* an object of which the predicate "$A(\ )$" holds good, but on the weaker assumption that there *is* such an object, known to us or not.

It is precisely because occupancy of the position of antecedent of a conditional constitutes that context which most clearly demands that a sentence be regarded as having truth-conditions rather than merely justifiability-conditions that it is the context invariably chosen by those, notably Peter Geach, who wish to appeal to the occurrences of sentences of a given class as subsentences of complex ones in order to refute a philosophical thesis that sentences of that class are not even informative. Geach holds that the admissibility of ethical sentences as antecedents of conditionals suffices to disprove the emotivist interpretation of them: according to him, such a sentence as "If lying is wrong, then it is wrong to get your little brother to lie" (his example) would be unintelligible unless the antecedent, "Lying is wrong", were a full-fledged assertoric sentence with determinate truth-conditions. The cogency of this argument is uncertain, since it is open to the emotivist to claim that a non-truth-functional explanation of conditionals of this particular type would be in place: in the present setting, we need note only that the selection of this particular context – as antecedents of conditionals – to be that in terms of which the argument is stated reflects the peculiar power of the context to demand interpretation in terms of truth-conditions.

It is now clear why it is that philosophers, who perfectly well understand indicative conditionals, as used in natural language, nevertheless find themselves involved in disputes about when they are properly to be called "true". The reason is that we possess no intuitive conception of truth for indicative conditionals. And the reason for that is that nothing in our actual use of such sentences forces us to form such a conception; and, more particularly, that we hardly have a use for conditionals whose antecedents are themselves conditionals, that is, for conditionals of the form "If, if A, then B, then C". They are not, indeed, completely ruled out. In particular, if "C" is a logical consequence of "If A, then B", for instance if "C" is "If not B, then not A", such a conditional would be accepted as making an intelligible and correct claim. In general, however, we should attach no clear content to an indicative conditional whose antecedent was itself an indicative conditional; and this is the same as to say that, while we understand what claim a speaker makes by enunciating an indicative conditional, we have no definite conception of what condition must hold for such a conditional to be true, independently of anyone's reasons for believing it true.

Many claims and counter-claims have been made on behalf of Tarskian truth-definitions that have little to do with Tarski's original intentions. Indeed, it is unclear whether his own later estimation of the significance of such a truth-definition did not diverge considerably from his original intentions; in any case, so much has been said on the subject without deference to Tarski's own views that we may here leave aside the question what those views were. It is frequently conceded that a Tarskian truth-definition does not tell us much about the concept of truth; but it is even more frequently claimed, on behalf of such a definition, that, by yielding what Davidson calls T-sentences for sentences of the object-language, it at least determines the application of the predicate "true" to them. It is, however, clear that it is powerless to do even that in any intuitively doubtful case. If this were not so, the problem of the condition for the truth of an indicative conditional could be very rapidly cleared up: we should need to note only that such a sentence as "If Anna is coming from Cambridge, she will pass through Bedford" is true if and only if, if Anna is coming from Cambridge, she will pass through Bedford. But this helps us not at all. We shall readily grant one half of the biconditional, namely that, if the sentence, "If Anna is coming from Cambridge, she will pass through Bedford", is true, then, if Anna is coming from Cambridge, she will pass through Bedford. But that half will not tell us when the sentence *is* true. To learn that, we shall need the other half of the biconditional, to the effect that if, if Anna is coming from Cambridge, she will pass through Bedford, then the sentence, "If Anna is coming from Cambridge, she will pass through Bedford", is true. But such a stipulation does not help us, precisely because we do not know how to interpret conditionals of the form "If, if A, then B, then C".

We may, quite accurately, express this as follows. The conditional "If, if Anna is coming from Cambridge, she will pass through Bedford, then the sentence, 'If Anna is coming from Cambridge, she will pass through Bedford', is true" constitutes one half of the relevant T-sentence; let us call such a conditional a T'-sentence. The T'-sentence purports to lay down a condition under which the sentence, "If Anna is coming from Cambridge, she will pass through Bedford", is true. We can grasp what this condition is, however, only if we know the condition for the truth of the antecedent of our T'-sentence. But this antecedent is precisely the conditional "If Anna is coming from Cambridge, she will pass through Bedford", whose truth-condition we are trying to establish: hence we are no further on. Of course, the same might be said of the specification of the condition for the truth of any sentence whatever, if expressed in a metalanguage that includes the object-language. Normally, however, the fatuity of the procedure, considered as a means of *specifying* the condition for the truth of the sentence of the object-language, is partly disguised from us by the fact that we already have an intuitive conception of the condition for its truth, a conception closely connected with our use of conditionals of which that sentence forms the antecedent.

It would be a mistake to suppose that there is some effective means of passing from the justifiability-condition of an assertion to the truth-condition of the statement asserted. Still less would it be right to think the transition is of a nature that someone with a tacit grasp of the notion of a justifiable assertion is already equipped to understand. On the contrary, the transition is a major conceptual leap. Nevertheless, the general principle that governs it is clear to anyone who has made that leap, as we all did at an early stage in our acquisition of our mother-tongues. We suppose given a sentence an utterance of which is understood as expressing a claim, a claim taken as justified provided the speaker is able to demonstrate that he possesses a certain cognitive ability. This sentence is now to be used in contexts which demand that a truth-condition be attached to it. What will this condition be? Save, of course, in the special case in which the sentence relates overtly to the cognitive state of the speaker, it must be a condition independent of the speaker's cognitive state (or of anything else peculiar to him), and relating solely to some state of affairs obtaining independently of our knowledge. In general, it will consist in the maximal such state of affairs the obtaining of which would be guaranteed by a justifiable claim expressed by the utterance of the sentence. Thus the utterance of an existential sentence expresses a claim to be able to cite a specific instance: if the claim is justified, the maximum that it guarantees, independently of the speaker's cognitive state, is that there should be such an instance, whether known or not. Since an ability to demonstrate any one instance would establish that the claim was justified, the condition for the sentence to be *true* will then be the truth of at least one of them. The condition for the truth of a universally quantified sentence is similarly arrived at from the condition for the justifiability of a claim expressed by uttering it. Again, the condition for the truth of a sentence in the future tense proper is the bare residue that remains when we prescind from the speaker's possession of inductive grounds or grounds in his own intention for the claim expressed by enunciating it, namely the occurrence of the event predicted, independently of the existence of any means of foreseeing it.

The adoption of the concept of truth does not, of course, render that of justifiability otiose; but, in an obvious manner, it makes the latter dependent on the former: an assertion will now be regarded as justifiable provided the speaker was in a position to know, or had good grounds for believing, that the statement asserted was true. The effect is sometimes conservative, sometimes not; that is to say, it sometimes preserves the original notion of justifiability, and sometimes extends it. It is conservative over sentences in the future tense: it remains the case that intention and inductively based causal principles form the only basis for prediction, and so the justification for asserting a future-tensed statement must be the same as that for a predictive claim. It is also essentially conservative over universal quantification. On the other hand, the availability of the notion of truth leads to an extension of the conditions for justifying an existential assertion. The acquisition of the concept of truth automatically generates the concept of falsity. The essence of the concept of truth is that a statement is conceived as being true or otherwise independently of the speaker's cognitive state and of human cognition generally, in virtue of an objectively existing reality; and this conception provides of itself for the recognition of just one condition that must obtain if the statement fails to be true, namely its being false. Given the notions of truth and falsity, and the interpretation of universal quantification as logical product and existential quantification as logical sum, a justification for denying a universally quantified statement must count as a justification for asserting the existential quantification of the negation of the predicate; and so an indirect justification of an existential statement must be admitted alongside the primitive direct justification.

If the foregoing account of the genesis of the concept of truth is correct, what follows? The account is not concerned with the *explicit* introduction of the concept: it has nothing to say about the use of the word "true" in the language. It is concerned, rather, with a prior implicit grasp of the concept, that is to say, with the creation of a *place* for it to occupy. According to this account, our mastery of the most primitive aspects of the use of language to transmit information does not require even an implicit grasp of the concept of truth, but can be fully described in terms of the antecedent notion of justifiability. But comparatively more sophisticated linguistic operations, and, above all, the use of compound tenses and of conditional sentences, demand, for a mastery of their use, a tacit appeal to the conception of objective truth; and so we have, in our conceptual furniture, a place exactly fitted for that concept as soon as it is explicitly introduced.

This is why any critique of the concept is so fiercely resisted. If it were merely a tool of theorists attempting to devise a semantic theory adequate to account for our existing linguistic practice, it would not appear so indispensable. The same would hold good if our possession of the concept of truth consisted solely in our ability to employ the word "true" within the language, for a large part of the use of that word can indeed be explained simply by appeal to the equivalence principle, that, for any statement "A", "It is true that A" is equivalent to "A". But the concept is neither of these things. Rather, it is deeply embedded in our implicit grasp of the use of our language: not, admittedly, of its most primitive part, but of forms of expression learned at a comparatively early stage, long before we explicitly apply any theoretical notions to our language or the practice of using it. It is for this reason that a criticism of a truth-conditional account of meaning, and, with it, of a realistic interpretation of our language, appears so threatening to the entire conceptual framework of our thinking.

For all that, the account here proposed is no *defence* of the concept of truth, realistically conceived. It does not attempt to explain in what a speaker's grasp of the condition for the truth of a statement consists, nor provide any answer to the charge that any formulation of such a condition begs the question whether it is coherent to attribute to anyone a grasp of such a condition. It simply contends that our linguistic practice cannot be fully described in terms of the notion of justifiability, and that, in achieving a mastery of it, we appear to be compelled to adopt the conception that to most of the informative sentences of our language (though not, for instance, to indicative conditionals) are associated determinate conditions for their truth that obtain independently of our knowledge or abilities.

That has no suasive power against anyone convinced that the concept of truth which, in this way, we tacitly acquire is nevertheless spurious. A tacit acquisition of the concept consists in gaining a mastery of a use of sentences a systematic account of which requires explicit use of the concept. As observed above, its tacit acquisition involves a conceptual leap; but, just because this is so, it is open to challenge. In general, a concept whose acquisition demands a conceptual leap is vulnerable to sceptical attack. Our acquisition of the concept of infinity involves just such a leap; and, for that very reason, no compelling refutation can ever be offered of a radical finitism whose proponents purport not to understand what it means to say that there are infinitely many things of a certain kind, whether natural numbers or stars. Likewise, the view may be consistently maintained that the leap required for a tacit attainment of the concept of truth takes us, not on to firm ground, but into a chasm. That is what, for mathematical statements, the intuitionist holds, and what, for statements of all kinds, the verificationist holds: we are under an illusion that we have acquired a genuine concept or have mastered a coherent linguistic practice.

Thus an intuitionist will not be dissuaded by its being pointed out that the practice of classical mathematicians is not wholly explicable in terms of constructive proof, but rests, instead, upon a conception, tacit or explicit, of the objective truth or falsity of mathematical statements, independently of our capacity to prove or refute them. He knew that already: that is why, rejecting such a conception as untenable, he believes that a just understanding of the meanings of mathematical statements demands a revision of classical practice. Now, although intuitionistic mathematics contains several profoundly subtle ideas, the connection between meaning and justification that it proposes for mathematical statements is peculiarly simple. So simple a connection could not plausibly be suggested for empirical statements: there has to be some definite conceptual advance, some genuine increase in the sophistication of our linguistic practice, that corresponds to the conceptual leap. But what may be called generalised verificationism, or possibly generalised constructivism, must argue that this advance need not be a leap. The concept which corresponds to the full-fledged realist notion of truth, but which, on this view, is the most we are entitled to, is indeed more refined than the straightforward concept of justifiability; but it will still be one that can be explained, even if in a complex and subtle way, in terms of justifiability, and so requires no leap to attain.

In this essay, I have taken no sides in this dispute, either as restricted to mathematics or as extended to other areas of discourse. In several writings, I have addressed the issue because it is my firm conviction that the concept of truth requires more explication by defenders of a truth-conditional account of meaning, and of a realistic conception of the relation between thought and the world, than it has yet received from them; until such an explication is supplied, their views are still unacquitted of the incoherence with which their critics charge them. Here I have sought only to diagnose the deep entrenchment in all of us of a realistic conception of truth, which explains the fanatical commitment of its philosophical defenders and the sense which its critics have of flying in the face of common sense.

2

Facts that don't matter

CATHERINE Z. ELGIN

Responsibility for the indeterminacy of translation is usually assigned to Quine's behaviorist assumptions. Quine prides himself on the connection.[1] Chomsky, Searle, and others castigate him for it, charging that indeterminacy amounts to a *reductio ad absurdum* of linguistic behaviorism.[2] But despite this broad consensus, it is unwise to assume that indeterminacy and behaviorism are so intimately related. For arguments developed by Hilary Putnam show that indeterminacy of translation and its consequences, inscrutability of reference and ontological relativity, survive the repudiation of behaviorist restrictions.

This resilience is unexpected, for univocality seems easy to achieve. The more exacting a standard, the fewer and more uniform its compliants. To foreclose the possibility of mutually incompatible translation manuals seems only to require a suitably demanding standard for translation. Easier said than done. It follows from Putnam's arguments that even criteria expressly designed to eliminate indeterminacy are not up to the task.

Putnam does not take his arguments to have this effect; he constructed and employed them to serve other ends. My goal here is to show that they support and extend the indeterminacy thesis. The endurance of indeterminacy in the face of sustained efforts to eradicate it suggests that it is integral to language. If so, it must be accommodated, rather than repudiated, by any adequate semantics.

Quine's detractors do not dispute the accuracy of the behaviorist's findings or the reliability of his methods. They contend, however, that the methods are unduly restrictive, capable of disclosing but a narrow range of relevant facts. There is, they insist, more to a language than meets the ear. The problem is to determine what more there is, and to secure epistemic access to it. That achieved, they maintain, translation will be determinate. This is doubtful. If Putnam is right, translation manuals that answer to all identifiably relevant facts can still conflict.

©Catherine Z. Elgin, 1990. I am grateful to Jonathan Adler, Nelson Goodman, and Israel Scheffler for comments on an earlier draft of this essay.

Quine, of course, purports to have shown this already. For he contends that all identifiably relevant facts are facts about verbal behavior and dispositions to verbal behavior. And his discussion plainly accommodates these. Still, his methodological parsimony may render his demonstration suspect; for scruples such as his might easily obscure facts that bear on the case. Putnam, though, is generous to a fault. He allows appeal to intentions and intensions; to functional states and possible worlds; to essences, properties, and causal powers. But even Putnam's prodigality is not unbounded. He insists that our theory, however extravagant its apparatus, must be consonant with actual language use. It may supplement or underwrite, but it cannot conflict with usage. This seemingly modest requirement turns out to be far more restrictive than anyone originally supposed.

I

The problem of radical translation arises when a linguist sets out to construct a translation manual for a totally alien tongue.[3] Having nothing else to go on, he must glean the meanings of native utterances from observed verbal behavior.

He starts by correlating utterances with conspicuous local events, translating them as sentences we would utter or accept in the circumstances. 'Gavagai!', being emitted as a rabbit hops by, is tentatively translated as 'Rabbit!' Translations are offered provisionally. Further investigation may convince the linguist that 'Jack rabbit!' or 'Cottontail!' translates 'Gavagai!' better than 'Rabbit!' does. By trial and error, he zeros in on a sentence we would accept when and only when similarly situated natives accept 'Gavagai!' Such a sentence has the same stimulus meaning as 'Gavagai!'

Normally a speaker will assent to any sentence he is prepared to volunteer. So, having discovered the stimulus meanings of some native sentences, the linguist can identify native signs of assent and dissent by seeing how his informants respond to native sentences he volunteers under plainly appropriate and under plainly inappropriate stimulus conditions. Then, by treating those signs as rough approximations of 'true' and 'false', he can identify truth-functional connectives, stimulus synonymy, stimulus analyticity, and stimulus contradiction.

But the marks of stimulus analyticity and stimulus contradiction, invariable assent and dissent, are unspecific as to subject matter. And stimulus-synonymous sentences, though they coincide in circumstances of acceptability, need not agree about anything else. 'George Bush is vice president' and 'Ronald Reagan is president' are stimulus synonymous for anyone disposed to accept both if either, and to reject both if either. So stimulus synonymy does not establish sameness of meaning or reference. No more than stimulus analyticity or stimulus contradiction does it afford a basis for correlating native terms with English ones.

Nor does stimulus meaning. The correlation of his locution with 'Rabbit!' does not demonstrate that the native is committed to the existence of rabbits. For concurrence of verbal response does not demonstrate agreement about what is being responded to. So from their agreement, it does not follow that the linguist and his informant are, or take themselves to be, talking about the same thing.

Thus far the linguist's problems have been purely inductive, a business of inferring generalizations on the basis of limited evidence. Further investigation may disconfirm his findings. And generalizations that are never disconfirmed may yet be false, since they can conflict with usages he happens never to encounter. Such is the scientist's lot. Still, as much as any other empirical scientist, the linguist is entitled to confidence that his highly confirmed results reveal facts of the matter – the actual verbal dispositions of speakers of the language.

But induction can take him no further. To identify native terms and their referents, to settle questions of individuation, the linguist must resolve native sentences into repeatable components and map those components onto his own words. This requires resort to analytical hypotheses.

To be adequate, a system of analytical hypotheses must yield translations that conform to linguistic behavior. The difficulty is that this requirement is too easily met. "Rival systems of analytical hypotheses can fit the totality of speech behavior to perfection, and can fit the totality of dispositions to speech behavior as well, and still specify mutually incompatible translations of countless sentences insusceptible of independent control."[4] That being so, Quine concludes, nothing favors one of the rivals over the rest. There is no fact of the matter.

II

Quine may seem a bit hasty here. The linguist's inability to determine more of the language without recourse to hypotheses does not show that there is nothing more to determine, or that his hypotheses are "analytical" rather than substantive. So we might, like Chomsky,[5] take a translation manual to be an empirical theory that seeks to explain linguistic behavior by means of conjectures about underlying, psychologically real, semantic facts. In that case, a translation manual is correct just in case it answers to those facts. Since theories in linguistics, as in any science, are underdetermined by evidence, it is no surprise that conflicting, evidentially adequate translation manuals can be constructed. Nevertheless, Chomsky believes, the semantic facts, accessible or not, make one manual right, the others wrong.

Were the field linguist's predicament just an occupational hazard, Chomsky would be on strong ground. For we have found no reason to think theories of language less factual than other theories. But the problem of radical translation begins at home. In learning their native tongue, children have no more to go on than the linguist does. Like him, they resolve complex linguistic constructions into repeatable elements and recombine those elements to generate new constructions. Their efforts, like his, are tested against the verbal behavior of competent speakers. And they count as competent when their utterances conform to community standards.

If a linguist could go wrong through misidentifying or misclassifying the components of a language, so could a seemingly fluent native. Her error, like the linguist's, would be undetectable, since she shows every sign of linguistic competence. But her failure to resolve utterances of her interlocutors into, and construct her own utterances out of, the language's real elements would mean that she does not speak the language. The impeccability of her verbal behavior would not reduce the charge against her.

Surely this conception of competence is untenable. To speak English requires no more than consistently speaking as English speakers do. And however idiosyncratic her processing, our native, by hypothesis, does that. Nor can translation be expected to delve deeper than competence does. There is no fact of the matter of meaning beyond what linguistic behavior discloses, because meaningful speech is nothing more than good linguistic behavior. Language is deeply superficial.

But if there is no fact of the matter about what my language means, there is no fact of the matter about what I mean in speaking my language. For I can mean only what my language equips me to mean. It follows that whether I mean 'rabbit' or 'rabbit stage' when I say 'rabbit' is indeterminate; whether I refer to rabbits or rabbit stages, inscrutable; whether I am committed to the existence of rabbits or rabbit stages, absolutely unintelligible.[6] A more counterintuitive result is hard to imagine.

But what is counterintuitive is not necessarily wrong. To undermine Quine's conclusion requires discrediting his argument. Its defect, Searle contends, lies in its mistaken adherence to a requirement of publicity: by restricting the data base to publicly certifiable evidence, Quine deprives the linguist of a rich lode of semantic information – namely, what each of us knows from his own case.[7]

According to Searle, it is perfectly plain to me that by *'rabbit'* I mean 'rabbit', not 'rabbit stage' or 'undetached rabbit part'. And such plain facts demonstrate that indeterminacy does not infect my idiolect. Moreover, like cases should be treated alike. So, barring evidence to the contrary, I am entitled to infer that it is equally plain to each other speaker of my language that by *'rabbit'* he means 'rabbit' too. Since a language consists of the idiolects of its speakers, the validity of such inferences secures determinacy of meaning and reference across the home language. In English then, 'rabbit' means 'rabbit' and refers to rabbits. Finally, it is plain to me that by *'lapin'* I mean 'rabbit'. Since like cases should be treated alike, I can infer that such first-person facts are equally plain to other translators. It follows that translation is determinate. Any bilingual is equipped to refute the indeterminacy thesis by generalizing from his own understanding of the languages he speaks, appealing only to the uncontroversial principle that like cases should be treated alike.

If Searle is right, indeterminacy of translation, inscrutability of reference, and ontological relativity derive entirely from an impoverished methodology that unjustifiably prohibits appeal to plain and plainly relevant psycholinguistic facts. So Searle maintains what Quine denies: that meanings are psychologically real and are epistemically accessible to the agent by means of introspection.

Such disagreements are notoriously difficult to resolve, for each party is convinced that his adversary begs the question or misses the point. Without a shared basis for settling disputes, positions may harden, and arguments disintegrate into name calling across an ever-widening abyss of mutual incomprehension. So rather than pit Quine directly against Searle, I want to consider whether Searle's method, if we use it, is sufficient to generate his conclusion. Arguments drawn from Putnam show that it is not.

III

Imagine a planet, Twin Earth, exactly like Earth but for the absence of H_2O and the presence in like quantities of XYZ, a complex chemical with water's phenomenal properties and ecological functions.[8] So similar are the two chemicals in their manifest characteristics that they can be distinguished only by sophisticated scientific tests. Suppose further that on Twin Earth, each of us has a nearly identical twin who speaks

Twenglish, a dialect very close to standard English. In Twenglish, however, XYZ is called 'water'; H_2O is not.

My twin and I are ignorant of chemistry, so our uses of 'water' are indistinguishable. 'Water' functions in her deliberations, conversations, and responses to the environment just as it does in mine. Moreover, owing to our ignorance, our psychological constitutions are indistinguishable as well. The plain facts that she introspects are no different from those I introspect. Each of us can sincerely affirm

> By '*water*' I mean 'water'.

But she does not refer to H_2O; nor I to XYZ. Although our psychological states are indistinguishable, the referents of our terms are not. Reference then is not determined by what is in the head. So the plain facts Searle invokes are powerless to disclose it.

Nor can they fix meaning, as another divergence in dialects demonstrates. Twenglish speakers use 'beech' when English speakers use 'elm', and use 'elm' when English speakers use 'beech'.[9] So Twenglish speakers would say

> The beech was struck by lightning

when English speakers would say

> The elm was struck by lightning.

I cannot tell a beech from an elm; nor can my twin. My twin and I know vaguely that both are large, deciduous trees and realize that they are trees of different kinds. But nothing in our understanding of the words or their objects differentiates beeches from elms. Nevertheless, my twin and I comprehend beech-talk and elm-talk, and use the terms competently – if uninformatively – in daily life.

Because of our ignorance, my "idea" of a beech is the same as my twin's; my disposition to use 'beech', the same as hers. Each of us can sincerely affirm

> By '*beech*' I mean 'beech'.

Nevertheless, our meanings differ. For my affirmation is in English; hers, in Twenglish. Nor is the fact that we speak different languages disclosed by differences in our psychology. For English and Twenglish coincide in our idiolects. They diverge only in the usage of our more knowledgeable compatriots. The first-person perspective avails me nothing; the plain facts it purports to disclose neither determine what I mean nor afford me a secure basis for generalization.

The moral of Putnam's fiction is this: we often don't know what we mean or what we're talking about, but our linguistic competence is none the worse for that.

Introspection thus cannot disclose mental determinants of meaning. But science sometimes reveals what self-scrutiny conceals. So before abandoning the search for meaning in mind, we should consider the claims of cognitive science.

Fodor contends that the meaning of a word derives from its mental counterpart, a symbol in the "language of thought".[10] Locutions answering to the same mental representation are alike in meaning and in reference, and perform the same functions in their respective languages. Locutions whose meanings and referents differ correspond to distinct mental representations and play different semantic roles. So from the fact that 'rabbit' and 'rabbit stage' are not coextensive, it follows that their mental counterparts are distinct. The correct translation of 'gavagai' may then be 'rabbit' or 'rabbit stage' or neither; but it cannot be both. For terms are intertranslatable only if they answer to the same mental representation; otherwise their meanings diverge. If this is correct, translation is determinate; for a fact of the matter determines whether two expressions correspond to the same mental representation. Any residual uncertainty about 'gavagai' stems from our ignorance, not from a deficit in semantic facts.

The mental representations cognitive science hypothesizes are inaccessible to introspection. So we have no direct evidence of them. Nevertheless, theorists maintain, we should acknowledge their reality because they are central to a fruitful, powerful, explanatory theory. We should recognize the facts cognitive science appeals to for the same reason we recognize the recondite facts of physics – because they are sanctioned by successful science.

Cognitive scientific theories, like physical theories, are underdetermined by evidence. So perhaps we cannot say whether 'rabbit' or 'rabbit stage' correctly translates 'gavagai'. Still, our problem is merely epistemic. If the facts of cognitive function settle the issue, then whether we can ascertain it or not, the meaning of 'gavagai' is as determinate as any fact of physics.

But Putnam's thought experiments tell equally against cognitive science's solution. I cannot distinguish beeches from elms, so in my idiolect 'beech' and 'elm' perform the same function. If linguistic function is determined by cognitive function, the mental counterparts of my terms must be functionally equivalent as well. Since mental symbols are individuated by their function, functionally equivalent mental symbols are identical. But I resolutely deny that 'beech' and 'elm' mean the same thing. I am convinced that their meanings differ, even though I have no idea what the difference is. Nothing in my mind then determines what I mean by 'beech' or by 'elm'. Moreover, since my twin's ignorance aligns with my own, we remain psychologically indistinguishable. Nevertheless, she does not mean by 'beech' what I do. Whether the contents of the mind are determined by self-scrutiny or by science, Putnam's fantasy demonstrates that meanings are not in the head.

IV

In his recent critique of realism, Putnam extends the insight behind his Twin Earth examples.[11] In "The Meaning of 'Meaning'" he showed that nothing in the mind determines meaning; his later work demonstrates that nothing outside it does either. It follows from the Löwenheim-Skolem Theorem (hereafter, the LST) that the axioms of a first-order theory have multiple models in a given domain. Number theory, for example, has numerous set-theoretical models. Nothing in the theory, its models, or the relation of theory to model differentiates the "standard" or "intended" model from "nonstandard" or "unintended" ones; in each model, the formal properties and relations among the natural numbers are preserved. So logic is powerless to identify *the* set-theoretical equivalents of the natural numbers. Each model supplies *a* system of equivalents; but logic provides no basis for favoring one over any of the others.

Putnam's critique rests on the recognition that the LST is indifferent to considerations of content. Any first-order theory, regardless of subject matter, admits of multiple models in a given universe. So a language, being formalizable as a first-order theory, has numerous models in the world. And although the compliants of a term under each interpretation are determinate, selection of any particular interpretation as the bearer of reference is formally indeterminate.

Must multiplicity of models threaten univocality? If meaning and reference are settled by intended interpretation, and if it is determinate that some one interpretation is intended, the existence of unintended models may be a matter of indifference.

But intention is a mental state. A speaker can intend no more than she has in mind. And Putnam's original thought experiments demonstrate that disparate interpretations answer to the contents of a mind. So a speaker's intention cannot determine a unique interpretation of her words. If, for example, she has no idea that H_2O differs from XYZ, she hasn't got what it takes to intend one rather than the other by 'water'. Both referents accord equally with what she has in mind. There is then no such thing as *the* intended interpretation of a speaker's words. Numerous interpretations conform to her intention. So even if we allow intention to constrain interpretation, indeterminacy is not eliminated.

What should we make of the multiplicity of models? Ordinarily, we invoke model theory to explicate the relation between a syntax and a field of reference. If the formalization of a language is just a regimentation of its syntax, the resulting indeterminacy is innocuous. That syntax does not determine semantics is hardly worth worrying about. But the LST's indifference to content means that Putnam's argument applies even when we construe language more broadly. A comprehensive theory of the language *as used* – incorporating patterns of utterance and inference, dispositions to verbal behavior, even statements of the "plain facts" Searle appeals to and the "semantic facts" favored by cognitive science – admits of multiple models. Enriching our conception of language amounts to adding axioms to our theory. Its models become correspondingly more complex. But broad theories as well as narrow ones, complicated structures as well as simple ones, admit of multiple models. So we cannot elude indeterminacy simply by appealing to a more robust conception of language.

Still, an interpretation that is formally indeterminate is not necessarily wholly indeterminate. Our inability to fix a unique interpretation of number theory may derive from the austerity of our means. Mathematics restricts itself to formal methods; and formal methods are inadequate to the task. But interpretation of a language is bound by no such restrictions. Perhaps we can rectify things by introducing extratheoretical constraints that determine a direct empirical or metaphysical connection between language and its objects. If so, the additional facts that secure reference are facts about the speaker's relation to the world.

The empiricist hope lies in subjecting interpretation to operational as well as theoretical constraints.[12] If the correct interpretation is the one that links terms with their compliants, evidence about those compliants should favor that interpretation. Then interpretations that do not answer to the evidence can safely be excluded. Our evidence consists in correlations between particular utterances (our so-called observation sentences) and observed events. Once we adopt such a constraint, interpretations that fail to correlate these utterances with the corresponding events are untenable.

But even if the requisite correlations can be established, they cannot serve as the conduit for reference. For statements of the correlations, like other sentences, are open to multiple interpretations. Moreover, many available correlations connect observation sentences with observationally indistinguishable events. We cannot tell whether 'Gavagai!' signals rabbits or rabbit stages just by looking, since there is no discernible difference between rabbits and rabbit stages. Observation then cannot settle the reference of 'gavagai'.

This is not to say that operational constraints on interpretation are undesirable. It is surely reasonable to require admissible interpretations to correlate observation sentences with observable events. But since those events cannot be individuated apart from language, such constraints cannot be construed as genuinely extratheoretical. They do not escape the indeterminacy that derives from the LST.

Nor can causality serve as the conduit.[13] Unless 'cause' has a determinate reference, a sentence like 'Rabbits cause us to have a word for rabbits' cannot fix the reference of 'rabbit'. But 'cause', like every other word, admits of multiple interpretations. Along with the rest of our claims, causal judgments map onto the world in many ways, yielding divergent models that satisfy our operational and theoretical constraints. Causal statements are part of the structure that requires interpretation, not mechanisms that supply interpretation.

Causal theorists might reply that this response misses their point: the causal theory of reference contends that causality determines reference, not that causal discourse does. Putnam shows, at most, that evidence gleaned from causal discourse does not suffice to identify causality. Nevertheless, causality is a determinate metaphysical relation, and the model bearing that relation to our language determines what our words refer to. The reference of 'gavagai' is then determined by a causal fact of the matter, even if that fact is woefully underdetermined by our evidence. Our inability to discover certain facts does not show that those facts do not obtain.

According to a causal theory then, encounters with rabbits rather than rabbit stages (or with rabbit stages rather than rabbits) cause the natives to have the word 'gavagai' in their vocabulary. If so, rabbits must affect speakers in ways that rabbit stages do not. It's hard to see what difference there could be. So it's hard to credit rabbits with causal powers that rabbit stages lack.

The difficulty is not just epistemic. For the attempt to divorce causality from causal discourse is doomed. Causality is whatever relation the verb 'cause' refers to. So long as the reference of 'cause' is indeterminate, so is the relation of causality. If the causal theory of reference is true, then under one admissible interpretation, rabbits in the vicinity cause the natives to have a word for rabbits; under another, rabbit stages in the vicinity cause them to have a word for rabbit stages.

Under the first then, 'gavagai' refers to rabbits; under the second, it refers to rabbit stages. The reference of 'cause', like that of 'gavagai' and 'refers', is determinate within an interpretation, indeterminate apart from one. Since the causal theory of reference cannot secure an independent, univocal interpretation of 'cause', it affords no escape from indeterminacy. The world then does not determine the reference of natural kind (or any other) terms.

V

If terms with the same meaning are coextensive, indeterminacy of translation follows directly. If the extension of 'gavagai' is indeterminate, that 'rabbit' does nor does not have the same extension as 'gavagai' is equally indeterminate. There is no fact of the matter.

But we needn't detour through Putnam's critique of realism or accept the thesis that intension determines extension to arrive at this result. For, although he does not explicitly acknowledge it, Putnam's argument applies directly to relations between languages. A translation manual is a function modeling one language in another. Every language admits multiple models in any other. And neither the models themselves nor their relations to the original language or to one another determine which of them preserves meaning. Each English model of the native language reflects native patterns of utterance and inference.

  Smerd gavagai, drok gridnip

is reflected in one model as

  If something is a rabbit, that thing is an animal

and in another as

  If some stage is a rabbit stage, that stage is an animal stage.

Each correlates native observation sentences with stimulus synonymous English ones. In the first,

  Gavagai!

is correlated with

  Rabbit!

In the second, with

  Rabbit stage!

In each, native statements of introspectively plain fact are mapped onto English statements of equally plain fact.

Kroq '*gavagai*' ygrup 'gavagai'

maps onto

By '*rabbit*' I mean 'rabbit'

in the first; and onto

By '*rabbit stage*' I mean 'rabbit stage'

in the second. And so on. Since all satisfy our criteria for an adequate translation, there is no basis for saying that exactly one among these models captures *the* meaning of the native tongue. Each of the models can provide a translation manual. But the translations supplied by the various manuals are incompatible. Translation is indeterminate.

It follows that the introduction of a 'language of thought' or a 'deep structure', far from alleviating the problem of radical translation, simply provides another instance of it. For the prelinguistic child's task is then the same as the field linguist's. Each seeks to map initially alien utterances onto a language he already has – the linguist, onto his home language; the child, onto his innate language of thought. And as we have seen, the same evidence is available to both. So the child, endowed with a language of thought, is no better off than the linguist. A spoken language admits of multiple models in such a psychological structure, each with an equal claim to be the determinant of meaning.[14] Moreover, none can be singled out as causally responsible for the generation of surface locutions, since 'cause' is not univocal. The term 'gavagai' no more has a unique mental counterpart than it has a unique English one. Translation, whether into the language of thought or by means of the language of thought from one spoken language to another, remains indeterminate.

Linguistic competence is not the ability to articulate antecedently determinate ideas, intensions, or meanings; nor is it the ability to reproduce the world in words. We have no such abilities. It consists, rather, in mastery of a complex social practice, an acquired capacity to conform to the mores of a linguistic community. It is neither more nor less than good linguistic behavior.

The additional facts that Quine's critics credit derive their status as fact from an interpretive scheme or translation manual.[15] Being products of interpretation, they cannot supply independent constraints on interpretation. Facts they may be, but not facts of the matter philosophy of language concerns.

Notes

1 W. V. Quine, "Indeterminacy of Translation Again," *Journal of Philosophy* 84 (1987), p. 5.
2 Cf. Noam Chomsky, "Quine's Empirical Assumptions," in *Words and Objections*, ed. Donald Davidson and Jaakko Hintikka (Dordrecht: Reidel, 1969), pp. 53–67; John Searle, "Indeterminacy, Empiricism, and the First Person," *Journal of Philosophy* 84 (1987), pp. 124–7.
3 W. V. Quine, *Word and Object* (Cambridge, Mass.: MIT Press, 1960), pp. 26–79.
4 Ibid., p. 72.
5 Chomsky, "Quine's Empirical Assumptions," pp. 53–67.
6 W. V. Quine, "Ontological Relativity," *Ontological Relativity and Other Essays* (New York: Columbia University Press, 1969), pp. 47–8.
7 Searle, "Indeterminacy," pp. 123–46.
8 Hilary Putnam, "The Meaning of 'Meaning'," *Mind, Language, and Reality* (Cambridge: Cambridge University Press, 1975), p. 223.
9 Ibid., pp. 226–7.
10 Jerry Fodor, *The Language of Thought* (Cambridge, Mass.: Harvard University Press, 1975).
11 Hilary Putnam, "Models and Reality," *Realism and Reason* (Cambridge: Cambridge University Press, 1983), pp. 1–25.
12 Ibid., pp. 8–9, 15–17.
13 Ibid., pp. 17–18.
14 Fodor (p. 73) recognizes that translation from a programming language to machine language is indeterminate. But despite his computational model of mind, he does not seem to appreciate the implications of this for human languages. See also his "Fodor's Guide to Mental Representation," *Mind* 94 (1985), p. 96.
15 Catherine Z. Elgin, "The Relativity of Fact and the Objectivity of Value," in *Relativism: Interpretation and Confrontation*, ed. Michael Krausz (Notre Dame: University of Notre Dame Press, 1989), pp. 86–98.

3

Has the description theory of names been refuted?

JERROLD J. KATZ

I

It is widely believed that the description theory of names has been refuted. In this essay I hope to show that the belief is false and that there is a version of the theory which is true. The fact that recent criticisms, particularly Kripke's, do refute the most popular versions of the theory has led many philosophers to conclude that all plausible versions have been eliminated, leaving only those not worth bothering about.[1] I want to show that, to the contrary, this criticism has served as a winnowing process, leaving the one plausible version of the theory.

There are definite signs that the description theory of names was thrown out too hastily. For one thing, none of the anti-descriptivist arguments in the literature is even formulated in such a way as to cover everything that counts as a description theory. It could be, of course, that, collectively, the criticisms manage to refute all versions of the theory, but, then again, there is nothing in the literature purporting to establish this.

For another, there are indications that there may be no replacement that will do the work of the description theory. The puzzles about identity statements, vacuous reference, and substitution into opaque contexts, which Frege introduced the description theory to solve, reappear once senses are dispensed with in favor of the view that the reference of proper nouns is direct. How can sentences like "George Orwell is George Orwell" be analytic or trifling while ones like "George Orwell is Eric Blair" are not? And how can sentences like "George Orwell is not George Orwell" be contradictory while ones like "George Orwell is not Eric Blair" are not? Or how can a name like "Santa Claus," which has no sense or reference, be meaningful and

I wish to thank a number of people for helpful comments, especially Richard Mendelsohn but also Jawad Azzouni, Alan Berger, Robert Fiengo, Paul Horwich, Takashi Yagisawa, Arthur Collins, the students in my fall 1987 seminar at the Graduate Center, and my audiences at Columbia University, North Carolina State University, Oxford University, and Birkbeck College.

contribute to the meaning of sentences? How can atheism, if true, even be formulated? Or why is it that someone can believe "George Orwell wrote *1984*" but not believe that "Eric Blair wrote *1984*"? The answers that today's Millians have given can hardly be hailed as solving these problems once and for all.

Kripke claims that his puzzle about belief is a problem for everyone, on a par with the Liar paradox.[2] It would be comforting for contemporary Millians if responsibility for the problems they are up against could be spread around. But Kripke is wrong to claim that his puzzle is a problem for everyone; it isn't a problem for description theorists, since they reject Mill's view of proper nouns. In Kripke's puzzle, the names from the true non-trivial identity statement "London is Londres" occur as subject, respectively, of the complement clauses in the sentential forms "Pierre believes that *S* is *P*" and "Pierre believes that *S* is not *P*." Since "London" and "Londres" are assumed to have no sense to contribute to the meaning expressions containing them, there is nothing to distinguish the objects of belief in the sentences which result from replacing the occurrences of *S* with "London" in one sentential form, replacing the occurrence of *S* with "Londres" in the other, and plugging in the same predicate for the occurrence of *P* in each form. We get the puzzle when, in order to avoid besmirching Pierre's epistemic reputation, we try to explain how the resulting sentences can have different truth-values.[3] Since description theories explain this straightforwardly, Kripke's puzzle is another example of the Fregean problems which return once Frege's posit of senses is withdrawn. The puzzle is not forced on us unless we are forced to adopt the view that proper nouns have no sense. If I am right that we are not forced to adopt this view, the proper parallel for Kripke's puzzle is not the Liar paradox – that is indeed a problem for everyone – but something like the Third Man paradox, which is a problem only for those holding a mistaken philosophical view.

I readily concede that Kripke's arguments are forceful, and even that they have largely been successful against the versions of the description theory at which they were directed. As will become clear, I am not sympathetic to description theories that derive from Frege's treatment of proper nouns and his overall semantics. I even think that his treatment of proper nouns can be shown not to be adequate as an intensionalist solution to the problems for which it was proposed. The following seems to me a conclusive reason against Frege's treatment being a solution. On that treatment, proper nouns have ordinary senses like the sense of "the most famous of Plato's students." Hence, there ought to be examples of synonymous proper nouns as there are synonymous common nouns. But, given any case of two proper nouns which are synonymous, say, "George Orwell" and "Eric Blair," the true identity statement formed from them, *viz.*, "George Orwell is Eric Blair," which has, say, the semantic structure 'the author of *1984* is the author of *1984*', will be analytic or trifling. As a consequence, the identity statement "George Orwell is Eric Blair" becomes indistinguishable in cognitive value from the identity statement "George Orwell is George Orwell." Therefore, Frege's explanation of why identity statements with the different names escape triviality collapses.

An adequate intensionalist solution requires a treatment of proper nouns on which different proper nouns cannot be synonymous. The basic problem with Frege's treatment of proper nouns is that it is transferred without alteration from his treatment of common nouns, and as a consequence, no distinction is made between the semantics of proper and common nouns. The Millians are right to insist on a distinction between them, but, as I shall argue, wrong to distinguish them by depriving proper nouns of sense. I will argue that the proper distinction is in terms of an essential difference in the kinds of senses that proper and common nouns have.

II

Description theories will be understood here in the broadest way consistent with how they are generally understood in philosophy. A theory of the semantics of proper names is a description theory just in case it claims that proper names have a sense and that their sense is somehow necessary to fixing their reference. No constraint is put on putative senses of proper nouns or on the role of senses in fixing reference. This ensures both that descriptivists' options are not illegitimately restricted and that anti-descriptivists' arguments do not leave descriptivists in a position to claim that those arguments overlook senses of some exotic sort.[4]

Our question is, accordingly, whether every description theory in this sense falls prey to some argument against description theories or whether there is some description theory which does not fall prey to any. The importance of this question is hard to overestimate. The semantics of proper names is a central topic in the work of Frege, Russell, and Wittgenstein, and it has continued to be central in the analytic tradition stemming from their work. The question is an important component of the issue between intensionalism and extensionalism, one which, since Quine, has been critical for the attempt to naturalize epistemology. For descriptivism *is* simply intensionalism

applied to names: intensionalism claims that nearly all expressions in
natural language have sense as well as reference, and descriptivism
claims that proper nouns are no exception. Thus, extensionalists are
perforce anti-descriptivists, though, of course, anti-descriptivists need
not be extensionalists. If the descriptivist position can be refuted, the
scope of intensionalism is substantially restricted, whereas if a version
of the description theory can be vindicated, intensionalism receives
substantial support.

Currently, the theory of direct reference is the most prominent
challenge to intensionalism in the area of names.[5] The theory can, of
course, be intensionalist in connection with common nouns and other
aspects of sentence structure, but, in connection with names, it is
inherently extensionalist. Its principal claim is that the semantic value
of a name is nothing over and above the object it denotes: the reference
of a name is not mediated by sense, but is direct. Direct reference
theorists are the contemporary advocates of Mill's view on proper
nouns, though many part company with him on the issue of whether
common nouns all have sense.

Philosophical support for the theory of direct reference comes from
Kripke's arguments in "Naming and Necessity" together with similar
ones of Donnellan's and Putnam's, as the leading proponents of the
theory are the first to acknowledge.[6] Since Kripke's arguments are the
significant ones in the case of names, I will only touch on Donnellan's
and Putnam's arguments. Elsewhere I have dealt at length with Donnellan's and Putnam's discussions of intensionalism.[7] I will focus on
Kripke's arguments against description theories of proper nouns and
ignore his arguments in the case of common nouns. His arguments in
the case of common nouns are essentially the same as Putnam's.
Kripke's concern demon cats rather than robot cats, reflecting a taste
for Isaac Bashevis Singer over Isaac Asimov.

Kripke's arguments target what is essentially Searle's version of the
description theory.[8] Thus, it is appropriate to say something first about
Searle's theory of names by way of a preliminary. But there is a more
important reason for starting with Searle, namely, that this enables me
to identify, at the outset, what I see as the real problem which has
frustrated intensionalist attempts to develop a theory of the semantics
of proper names.

Searle's principal contribution to the discussion of proper names was
to implement Wittgenstein's suggestion that the notion of a description
might be loosened up to try to get around counterexamples to the
Frege-Russell version of the description theory like his "Moses" cases.[9]
This flanking move, embodied in Searle's version of the description

theory, came to be generally viewed as the only recourse description theorists had left to them. As a result, Kripke's refutation of Searle's version of the theory was seen as removing the description theorist's last hope.

But this scenario disposes of the description theory too quickly. The thought that Searle's version of the theory is the description theorist's last hope is based on Searle's diagnosis that Frege's and Russell's notion of a description is too tightly constrained by a "rigid sense-reference" approach to language.[10] I think that this is exactly the opposite of the truth. My own diagnosis of the trouble is rather that the sense/reference distinction in previous description theories is not nearly rigid enough. Searle's diagnosis is like criticizing a floppy splint on a fracture for being too rigid, and his remedy is like making the splint floppier. Searle's approach is not a radical step toward a solution, but simply a more egregious form of the attitude that has been the heart of the problem all along. The problem is that intensionalists from Frege on failed to draw a sharp enough sense reference/reference distinction.

III

Searle's own version of the description theory is designed to express his belief that proper names are connected with characteristics of the objects to which they refer only "in a loose sort of way."[11] (1) asserts

(1) Aristotle never existed

[that] a certain number of conventional presuppositions, descriptive statements, of referring uses of "Aristotle" are false. Precisely which ... is not yet clear, for what precise conditions constitute the criteria for applying "Aristotle" is not yet laid down in the language.[12]

Thus, on Searle's theory, a statement of the form "Aristotle is such and such" entails that a sufficient number of the "conventional presuppositions," "descriptive statements," associated with the name "Aristotle" are true of a unique individual who is the referent of the name.

Kripke recognized that loosening things up in this way still leaves us with a theory that contains a component of earlier versions of the description theory. He saw that Searle's theory offers basically the same account of reference as earlier versions in the special case where speakers have, in effect, only one "descriptive statement" for a name, and hence, Searle's theory is subject to counterexamples of the same kind. The Gödel-Schmidt case is such a counterexample. In that case a sufficient number of the descriptions are true of the unknown mathematical genius Schmidt and false of the famous mathematical fraud Gödel, since, in that case, there is, in effect, only the one description "the discoverer of the incompleteness of arithmetic." But as Kripke claims, it is Gödel, not Schmidt, to whom we refer when we say, "Gödel never ate a Big Mac."[13]

Kripke bases this claim on an appeal to intuition, offering no backup argument. Some philosophers who claim not to have his intuition reject his claim. I share Kripke's intuition, and furthermore, think there are arguments to back up his claim.[14] I can't fully develop them here, but one illustration will serve to show that his claim need not rest on intuition alone. Let us suppose "Gödel" has the sense of "discoverer of the incompleteness of arithmetic." If so, we would expect this sense to enter the compositional meaning of expressions containing "Gödel," and accordingly, we would expect them to have sense properties and relations reflecting the presence of the sense. In particular, we would expect an expression in which "Gödel" is modified by "discoverer of the incompleteness of arithmetic" to be redundant in the manner of syntactically complex expressions containing common nouns such as "the king who is a monarch" or "free gift." But the expression "Gödel who discovered the incompleteness of arithmetic" is not redundant. In contrast to "the king who is a monarch," its modifier provides new information, information that discriminates the Gödel in question from the other Gödels. This *reductio* argument supports Kripke's claim that "Gödel" does not have the sense of "discoverer of the incompleteness of arithmetic."[15]

Insofar as there is nothing special about the name "Gödel," it has been supposed that Kripke's argument in the Gödel-Schmidt case can be generalized to provide an argument against any name having a sense. But this supposition overlooks the fact that the prospect for such an argument depends as much upon the likeness of the other senses to the sense of "discoverer of the incompleteness of arithmetic" as it does upon the likeness of other names to the name "Gödel." A general argument would have to show that the sense of "discoverer of the incompleteness of arithmetic" is representative of every type of sense.

Although "Gödel" is a perfectly representative name, senses like 'discoverer of the incompleteness of arithmetic' are not perfectly representative senses. There is one type of sense that is sufficiently different to call into question the prospects for generalizing Kripke's argument. These are what I will call "meta-linguistic" senses, that is, senses whose content represents a relation between a proper name and its bearer(s).[16] The meta-linguistic sense of a name "*n*," in contrast to senses like 'discoverer of the incompleteness of arithmetic', contains a concept uniquely representing the grammatical form of the proper noun *"n"* itself and a concept representing the name relation.

There are three advantages of the meta-linguistic conception of the senses of names that warrant our seriously considering it. The first advantage is that the meta-linguistic conception overcomes Frege's failure to draw a distinction between the senses of proper and common nouns. On this conception, the difference is that the senses of proper nouns, unlike the senses of common nouns, essentially involve a concept representing the proper noun itself and a concept representing a name relation. The second advantage, which derives from the first, is that this conception of the sense of proper nouns implies that no two different names are synonymous: the senses of *"n"* and *"m"* differ in that the former contains an *"n"*-representation, whereas the latter contains an *"m"*-representation. Hence, a version of the description theory in which names have meta-linguistic senses cannot undercut the Fregean approach to distinguishing true identity statements of the form '$a = a$' and '$a = b$' in the way Frege's own version of the description theory does.

The third advantage is that meta-linguistic senses are immune from *reductio* arguments such as the one just used to back up Kripke's intuition. Unlike ordinary senses, meta-linguistic senses do not disappoint us with respect to expected sense properties and relations of expressions in which a clause with the sense modifies the proper noun that it is supposed to be the sense of. The expression "Gödel who has the name 'Gödel'" smacks of redundancy. Imagine someone saying to you, "Gödel has the name 'Gödel.'" Your reaction is likely to be a puzzled "Huh?"; New Yorkers might respond with "So what else is new?" In contrast, this would not be the reaction to hearing the non-redundant "Gödel discovered the incompleteness of arithmetic." Moreover, you wouldn't have a puzzled reaction even if you already knew that Gödel made the discovery, since you would think the speaker doesn't know you know the fact about Gödel. In the case of "Gödel has the name 'Gödel,'" you couldn't think that the speaker doesn't know you know the fact about Gödel because the speaker assumes you do in his or her use of "Gödel" as the subject of the sentence.

IV

Let us call a description theory which says that proper nouns have a meta-linguistic sense a "meta-linguistic description theory." To be sure, Kripke considers such theories. He gives three arguments.[17] One is a Gödel-Schmidt type argument. Another is a circularity argument. And

the third is a modal argument. The task facing us in this section is to
show that none of these arguments can be turned into a general
argument against all meta-linguistic description theories. I will try to
show this by exhibiting a meta-linguistic description theory that is
immune to all three arguments. In the following sections, I will turn to
Searle's criticisms of meta-linguistic description theories and to the
theory of direct reference.

The version of the meta-linguistic description theory that Kripke
criticizes is Kneale's theory, which gives the sense of a proper name in
terms of the concept expressed by the verb "call."[18] Kripke's first
argument against Kneale is that Kneale's theory predicts that sentences
like (2) will be analytic or trifling, but, in fact, they are not. As Kripke

   (2) Socrates is the individual called "Socrates"

points out, (2) could be false. Socrates might not have been called
"Socrates." He might have been called "Snub Nose" or "Mr. Gadfly."
Kripke's second argument is that Kneale's theory violates a plausible
non-circulatory condition: it tells us too little "to be a theory of
reference at all":

We ask to whom does he refer by "Socrates" and then the answer is given as,
well he refers to the man to whom he refers. If this were all there was to the
meaning of a proper name, then no reference would get off the ground at all.[19]

Although these are good arguments against Kneale's theory, they are
not good arguments against other meta-linguistic description theories.
Such theories differ from one another in terms of the concept they use
to express the relation between a name and its bearer(s). Thus, different meta-linguistic description theories can be obtained by choosing
verbs or linguistic predicates other than "call." For example, one might
choose "pet name of," "Christian name of," "pen name of," "nick-
name of," "code name of," "stage name of," or "cover name of,"
Different choices will express different relations between a name and its
bearer, and hence, different meta-linguistic description theories.

Of course, any of the predicates just mentioned will give us a
meta-linguistic description theory that is vulnerable to an argument
parallel to Kripke's first against Kneale's theory. But there is one
predicate which gives us a theory that will not be vulnerable. To see
why, note that the admittedly vulnerable theories have the feature that
the sense they ascribe to names involves not only the relation between a
name and its bearer but also some property over and above this
relation. In the case of the verb "call," the property is, roughly speaking, that members of the bearer's community address him or her by that

name. In making such a further property part of the condition for something being the bearer of a name, a meta-linguistic description theory buys into the traditional description theory, thereby acquiring its vulnerability to counterfactual cases in which the bearer lacks the property. Kripke's argument that Socrates might not have been so called exploits this vulnerability.

Only a theory formulated in terms of the bare name relation does not buy into the traditional description theory in this way. Kripke's first argument doesn't work against such a theory because the argument is specifically tailored to exploit the contingent applicability of properties like 'is called such-and-such', and these properties can fail to apply independently of the satisfaction of the bare name relation. A proper noun can be the name of something in spite of the fact that it is never used to refer to the thing. One example is orthodox Jews who are prohibited from pronouncing God's name, much less using it to refer to its bearer. Thus, this argument of Kripke's is not a general argument against meta-linguistic description theories because there is no clear application of it to theories framed with just the concept of the bare name relation.

In earlier works, I presented such a meta-linguistic description theory.[20] I shall refer to it here as the "pure meta-linguistic description theory," or "PMT" for short. Informally, that theory used the verb "bears" to state the name relation, since the application of such a verb involves nothing beyond the meta-linguistic condition that something is the bearer of the name.[21] My specific proposal was, roughly speaking, that the sense of a proper noun "n" is 'the (contextually definite) thing which is a bearer of "n." '[22] Even as it stands, this formulation makes it clear that PMT avoids arguments parallel to Kripke's argument against Kneale's theory. Since, on PMT, the sense of a proper noun involves no predicate beyond the bare name relation, PMT does not predict that (2) is analytic or trifling. It agrees with Kripke that such a sentence is synthetic in virtue of entailing a claim about the speech behavior of the Athenians in Socrates' community. Rather than (2), PMT predicts that sentences something like (3) are analytic.[23]

(3) Socrates is something which is a bearer of "Socrates"

Turning to Kripke's second argument, it might seem that the very bareness of PMT's name relation, which permits it to escape Kripke's first argument, makes it especially vulnerable to Kripke's circularity criticism. The thought is that, insofar as PMT's descriptions lack even the paltry reference-fixing information that descriptions in Kneale's theory have, Kripke's second argument applies with even greater force to PMT than it does to Kneale's theory. But this thought misconstrues both PMT and Kripke's circularity argument. Kripke is quite explicit that violation of his non-circularity condition is a matter of the offending theory telling us too little "to be a theory of reference." But, since PMT is (part of) a theory of sense, not a theory of reference, the argument does not apply to PMT.

Here we have the first instance where making a sense/reference distinction sharper than Frege's pays off. On Frege's notion of sense, the distinction between sense and reference is compromised by making reference determination the essential element in the definition of sense. On our notion of sense, there is no compromise because sense is defined as the aspect of the grammatical structure of expressions and the sentences that determines their meaningfulness, meaninglessness, synonymy, antonymy, analyticity, redundancy, ambiguity, and so on. Hence, on PMT, the information in senses is responsible only for determining their sense properties and relations of proper nouns, not for determining their referential properties and relations. Therefore, while it is true that, on PMT, the senses of proper nouns, by themselves, tell us too little to explain how their reference is fixed, this is no more an objection to PMT than it is an objection to grammars that, by themselves, they tell us too little to explain how speakers produce utterances. Since the absence of an account of how reference is fixed is no criticism of a theory whose goal is to account for the senses of proper nouns, Kripke's second argument is also inapplicable to PMT.[24]

We come now to Kripke's modal argument. In "Naming and Necessity," he remarks that "although the man Nixon might not have been the president, it is not the case that he might not have been Nixon (though he might not have been called 'Nixon')."[25] As it stands, this is far from a general argument that proper nouns have no sense, but it has seemed to some that the modal intuition behind these remarks can be developed into such a general argument. Our task is to show that this intuition does not provide an argument that proper nouns do not have even the minimal sense PMT ascribes to them.

The modal intuition behind Kripke's argument is that "called 'Nixon'" and other meta-linguistic properties are not relevantly different from properties like 'is the president' and others that traditional description theories employ. They are all contingent properties. This being so, meta-linguistic properties, too, will lack a strong enough connection to the bearer(s) of the name across possible worlds. Hence, it doesn't matter what contingent property one chooses to formulate the sense of "Nixon" – choose any meta-linguistic property whatever –

there are possible worlds in which Nixon exists but does not have that property. Since it is impossible that Nixon might not have been Nixon, but possible that he not have the name "Nixon," the predicate "named 'Nixon'" does not provide a sense that is analytically connected with "Nixon." Since, "named 'Nixon'" is the weakest predicate on which to base the claim that names have sense, it follows that names do not have sense.

These considerations can be recast as an argument explicitly directed against PMT. Since, on PMT, "bearer of 'Socrates'" expresses the sense of "Socrates," we can replace the second occurrence of "Socrates" in (4) with the synonymous expression "bearer of 'Socrates.'" The

(4) Socrates might not have been Socrates

replacement gives us (5). But, while (4) is false in the manner of "Nixon

(5) Socrates might not have been a bearer of "Socrates"

might not have been Nixon," (5) is true in the manner of "Nixon might not have been the president" or "Nixon might not have been called 'Nixon.'" We can imagine no circumstances in which *Socrates* isn't Socrates, but can easily imagine ones in which he was never the object of the appropriate baptismal ceremony. However strongly we associate people with their names, we do not think of their name as one of their necessary properties. But if (4) and (5) have different truth-values, they cannot be synonymous as PMT requires, and so, "Socrates" cannot have even the minimal sense PMT ascribes to it.

What makes this argument seem persuasive is that it does show that even the weakest meta-linguistic predicate is too strong to be the sense of a proper name. What makes the argument fail as it stands is that this is not enough for the conclusion that proper nouns have no sense. All that validly follows is that either "Socrates" does not have the minimal senses that PMT ascribes to it or else its sense does not take the form of a predicate. Without a premise to the effect that the sense of meaningful nouns in a natural language has the semantic form of a predicate, it is not clear how the argument shows that proper nouns do not have the minimal sense that PMT ascribes to them. Of course, simply not having the semantic status of a predicate is not, by itself, enough to show that they have sense. But before we can see why Kripke's argument does not prevent names from having sense, we have to see what semantic structure PMT takes the sense of a name to be.

Along with syncategorematic elements, natural languages contain categorematic elements. Proper nouns, as well as common nouns, belong to one class of categorematic elements, substantives. Verbs and verbal phrases belong to the other class, predicates. The sense of a proper noun may involve predicates – just as the sense of a predicate may involve substantives – but their semantic class is substantive. The members of such a semantic class are restricted to one of the two major roles in propositional form, that is, terms or predications. Senses of proper nouns can stand alone in term position, but not in predication position, and the senses of verbs and verbal phrases can stand alone in predication position, but not in term position.[26]

This brings us, by a new route, to the familiar distinction between the "is" of identity and the "is" of predication. The "is" flanking substantives is identity, and "is" flanking a substantive and a predicate is predication. The contrast between the identity and predication senses of the copula is illustrated by the ambiguity of (6). (6) has an identity

(6) John isn't my friend

sense on which it says that John and my friend are different people, and it has a predicational sense on which it says that John is no friend of mine.[27] The identificational sense of (6) presupposes that I have a friend but leaves it open whether John is a friend of mine, whereas the predicational sense of (6) leaves it open that I might be entirely friendless. Consider another type of case. (7) also exhibits both copula

(7) Smith is B(b)lack

senses. Is the speaker of (7) commenting on Smith's race, or saying that Smith is the infamous master spy Black? The ambiguity is present as well in (8). Is the speaker of (8) saying that the object in question

(8) It is G(g)old

is gold in material or in color, or announcing the famous Talmudic scholar Gold? On the former senses, (7) and (8) assert that Smith or it possesses a certain property, while on the latter, they assert that Smith or it is identical with a certain person. Note that it would be absurd to say that the predications are about two objects, but not at all absurd to say that the identity assertions are.

PMT that says that the name "Socrates" is synonymous with the substantive "the (contextually definite) thing that is a bearer of 'Socrates,'" not with predicates like "bearer of 'Socrates,'" and further, it says that the copula in the sentences in question is the "is" of identity. Hence, something essential to PMT's account of the sense of "Socrates" is lost in the very first step of the argument, the step of replacing the substantive "Socrates" in (4) with the predicate "bearer of 'Socrates.' " The predicate "bearer of 'Socrates' " contains neither the determiner that provides the concept of definite reference nor the head noun whose content provides the concept of a substantive. As a consequence of the substitution, the semantic structure of the basic unmodalized sentence is changed from an identity statement to a predicational statement. Were the semantic structure of (4) preserved in the substitution, the result of the substitution would not be a modalized predicational statement like (5), but a modalized identity statement like (4).

Even so, why shouldn't there still be a difference in truth-value? The substitution of a substantive can be responsible for the difference in truth-value like that in the case of (4) and (5). I shall argue that this is because the substitutions also change semantic structure, but that substitutions that conform to PMT's account of the sense of proper nouns do not change semantic structure and do not give rise to a difference in truth-value. To see this, we have to see how the loss of the concept of definite reference in the step from (4) to (5) entrains the loss of the required strength of referential connection across possible worlds.

Consider the similar substitution that takes us from (9) to (10):

(9) Necessarily that bachelor is that bachelor

(10) Necessarily that bachelor is an unmarried man

The fact that (9) and (10) have different truth-values is clearly no ground for saying "That bachelor is that bachelor" is not analytic. (9) is true, as (4) is false, because, once the reference of the subject of the internal sentence is fixed, the description under which it has been referred to is, as it were, shed. Thus, in determining the applicability of the predicate "is an unmarried man" in (10) with respect to counterfactual circumstances, once we have pinned down the object fo predication – i.e., once we have hold of the thing itself, *viz.*, *that* bachelor – it is as if the particular concept 'bachelor' used in getting to him had never been around. Hence, there will be possible worlds in which the internal sentence is false because what we have hold of is a married man.

On PMT, the legitimate substitution would takes us from (9) to (11).

(11) Necessarily that bachelor is that unmarried man

Here the demonstrative determiner involves the concept of definiteness that affords the required strength of referential connection across possible worlds. Turning to substitutions for "Socrates" in (4) that PMT

would allow, we now want to see what it is about the definite determiner in them that similarly affords the required strength of referential
connection. Consider (12), which is an approximation to the result of an

(12) Socrates might not have been the thing which is a bearer of "Socrates"

acceptable substitution. (12) is not a fully explicit formulation of semantic structure of a sentence that PMT would take to be synonymous with
(4) because (12) does not fully explicate the intended sense of (4). This
can be seen from the fact that, in connection with (12), it is possible to
ask "What thing?" or "Which thing?" The same is true of (13). We can

(13) Aristotle is the thing that is a bearer of "Aristotle"

even question the second occurrence of "Aristotle" in (14). The problem with these less-than-explicit formulations is analogous to using

(14) Aristotle is Artistotle

"John came home and he had dinner" as a way of saying that John
came home and had dinner. Strictly speaking, the sentence type allows
the possibility of disjoint reference.

But, though a possibility, it is clearly an assumption of the whole
philosophical discussion of identity sentences that they are taken on the
coreferential interpretation. Indeed, sentences like (14) and Kripke's
own example "Nixon might not have been Nixon" are understood on an
intended sense where the occurrences "Nixon" are coreferential. Not
only do our discussions in philosophy understand a sentence like (14) to
express a true identity statement, but, even outside philosophy, we
normally use them in this way. We do not interpret (14) as, for example,
expressing a false statement identifying the ancient Greek philosopher
with the recent Greek shipowner. The normal interpretation is that
some Aristotle (typically the philosopher) is *that* Aristotle.[28]

The coreferential interpretation involves an anaphoric relation between the sense of the first occurrence of the proper noun and the
sense of the second occurrence on which the latter is constrained to
take on the same reference as the former. There is no possibility of
giving an account of this relation here. A serious account would require
a grammatical formulation of identity sentences that explicates the
structure of the anaphoric relation and explains how the contextual
definiteness in the sense of a proper noun is realized situationally in
sentences with a single occurrence of the noun, but parasitically for
occurrences in sentences like (14) having more than one occurrence.
But the character of the referential constraint imposed by an anaphoric

relation can be informally conveyed by expressing the intended sense of (14) as the sense of (15). (15) makes explicit the anaphoric connection that, according to PMT, is an essential part of the semantics of the

(15) Aristotle is the self-same Aristotle

identity sentences with which we are concerned.

Given this explication of the semantics of such identity sentences, an acceptable substitution for "Socrates" in (4) gives something like (16).

(16) Socrates might not have been the self-same bearer of "Socrates"

(16) is only approximate because it omits the indefinite element in PMT's account of the sense of proper nouns. (I will discuss it below.) But (16) captures semantic structure, which even (12) failed to capture, and which, for present purposes, is critical. It is clear that (16) differs from (5) in virtue of the substituted expression in the former being both a definite nominal and having an anaphoric relation to the subject. Being a definite nominal means that the expression can refer rigidly, and having an anaphoric relation to the subject means that it takes on the reference of that proper noun. In contrast, the substituted expression in (5), lacking this semantic structure, has an extension that varies across possible worlds, and hence, in some of them its extension will not include the extension of the subject. Thus, (16) is a necessarily false statement just as is "Nixon might not have been Nixon," whereas (5) is a true statement like "Nixon might not have been called 'Nixon.' " Hence, the attempt to apply Kripke's modal argument to PMT fails.

It is worth mentioning that standard description theories cannot secure immunity from Kripke's argument by introducing the same anaphoric relation. It accomplishes nothing to introduce this relation into a sentence containing an alleged sense of a name constructed with descriptive predicates beyond the bare name relation. This is because, as Kripke's examples show, in some possible worlds these further predicates will not apply to the bearer of the name, and the sentence will be false in those worlds. For example, since it is possible that Aristotle never taught Alexander, the sentence "Aristotle is the self-same teacher of Alexander" is false in some possible worlds.

V

Having shown that PMT is not refuted by Kripke's arguments, I now want to show that there is linguistic evidence that PMT provides the right senses for proper nouns. I already cited some of the evidence, for example, that PMT explains the fact that no two different proper nouns are synonymous. Further evidence, similarly deriving from the ability of PMT to explain sense properties and relations, is the following. Consider, for example, sentences like (17) which are counterparts of stan-

(17) Socrates is the self-same thing which is a bearer of "Socrates"

dard analytic sentences such as "Bachelors are unmarried men." Like analytic sentences with common nouns as their subject, if (17) makes a statement, then, in virtue of the very semantics of statement making, it is guaranteed to make a true one. That is, in the same way that the sense of "bachelor" fixes its referent as unmarried men, the sense of "Socrates" fixes its nominatum as a contextually definite bearer of "Socrates"; hence, insofar as the truth condition of (17) is that the nominatum of the subject be the nominatum of the nominal in the copula phrase, the condition is automatically satisfied whenever there is a nominatum of the subject.

Further, the denial of (17), namely, (18), is self-refuting. For let us

(18) Socrates is not the self-same thing which is a bearer of "Socrates"

assume that (18) is true. Part of this assumption is the claim that the grammatical subject of (18) names some Socrates (say, the Greek philosopher). But, then, he is a self-same bearer of the name "Socrates," and hence (18), which denies this, is false. Finally, (19) and (20) are the

(19) There are two female Sidneys in the audience

(20) There are two females who are bearers of "Sidney" in the audience

same in meaning. Such synonymy relations are directly predicted on the account of the sense of proper nouns in PMT. These examples show that we have an evidential basis for ascribing PMT-type meta-linguistic senses to proper nouns; namely, doing so enables us to explain sense properties and relations like analyticity, contradiction, and synonymy.

VI

Thus far, I have concentrated on sense. Now I have to say something about the relation of sense to reference. This is necessary both in order to provide background for my examination of Searle's criticisms of meta-linguistic description theories and to state properly the thesis that I want to oppose to the direct reference theorist's claim about the reference of proper nouns.

As indicated, I reject Frege's conception of the relation of sense to reference because it compromises a completely sharp distinction between sense and reference with disastrous results for intensionalism. As a consequence of accepting Frege's definition of sense as the mode of determination of the referent and its corollary that sense determines reference, intensionalists, and hence, descriptivists, have been unable to reconcile analytic necessity in language with contingent possibility in the world. Putnam's and Kripke's well-known arguments make this amply clear. But, in fact, intensionalists need not accept Frege's definition of sense and its corollary that sense determines reference. I observed, in connection with Kripke's circularity argument, that the semantic theory of which PMT is part eschews Frege's definition of sense, employing instead a definition that makes no use of the concept of reference, and as a consequence, does not accord sense the role of determining reference. Because sense is defined on this theory as an aspect of grammatical structure, analyticity can be defined in terms of *sense* containment without the implications for *extensional* containment that Frege's definition has. Since the claim that "CATS are animals" is analytic is merely the claim that the sentence exhibits the appropriate sense containment, there is no claim that, in the use of language, the extension of "cat" must be within the extension of "animal." Thus, linguistic analyticities do not exclude contingent possibilities; in particular, Putnam and Kripke examples, which refute Frege's theory, are merely cases of reference to robots and demons under the false description 'feline animal'.[29]

Since I think proper nouns, like common nouns, have sense, in addition to rejecting the extreme position that sense determines reference, I also reject the extreme position that the reference of proper nouns is fixed without sense. I endorse a middle position in which sense plays the weaker but nonetheless necessary role of *mediating* reference. This is to claim that, although senses do not provide all the information for fixing the reference of proper nouns, they provide information that is indispensable. Mediation involves two related functions: sense is the criterion for literal uses of language and the starting point in all uses.[30]

Literalness is calling a spade a spade. A literal use is one in which the referent is called by its right name. What makes a word the right name for a thing is that the thing fits or conforms to the meaning of the word in the language. Consider two examples. If an employee at a packing-house says, "I made hamburger out of them," referring to steers just processed, the use of "hamburger" is literal. In contrast, if a chess player, referring to his or her opponents, says, "I made hamburger out of them," the use of "hamburger" is non-literal. Note that in the case of the first utterance, but not the second, it is possible to reply, "You bungler, you were told to make steaks." The word "hamburger" is the right name for the stuff processed in the packinghouse because "hamburger" means 'ground beef', and that is precisely what the stuff is. But the word "hamburger" is not the right name for badly trounced chess opponents. That is not what they are.

Literalness is, as it were, conformity to the letter of semantic law. The semantic law stating the relation between expression type and its sense(s) provides the criterion that determines which uses of its tokens are literal. Roughly speaking, the sense of a token is literal in case the sense is the sense of its type, and a referent of the token is literal in case the sense of the token is literal and the referent belongs to the extension of that sense.[31] Another way of saying this is to say that the reference of an (unambiguous) expression type – or the *type-reference* of an expression – is the extension of its sense, and that the criterion for a literal application of a token of the type is that the referent of the token belongs to the type-reference.

The type-reference of the common noun "hamburger" encompasses all the hunks of hamburger in the domain of the language, and hence the application of a token of "hamburger" is literal just in case its referent is one or more of those hunks. The type-reference of a proper noun is the collection of its bearers, in a sense that I will make clear just below. An application of "Hitler" to the Nazi dictator, Hitler, is literal because he is a member of the type-reference, while an application of "Hitler" to one's dictatorial dean is not. We refer to Hitler by name, but we do not so refer to the dean.

Sense is the starting point in the use of language because it sets the problem for the speaker's employment of contextual information. This is well illustrated in the way semantic and pragmatic factors mesh in the literal use of proper names. Given PMT's account of the sense of a proper noun *"n"* as 'the (contextually definite) thing that is a bearer of *"n,"*' the senses of proper nouns involve both an element of *definiteness* and an element of *indefiniteness*. The indefinite element accounts for the widely recognized fact that a proper noun, as a linguistic type, is associated with multiple bearers. For example, "London" refers to London, England, to London, Ontario, London, Ohio, and to potentially other Londons as well. I will use the term "name-bearer correlation" to refer to such a pairing of a name with a bearer. The type-reference of a name is the collection of the bearers in all the name-bearer correlations for that name.

On PMT, there can no more be an ambiguous name than there can different names that are synonymous. Multiple name-bearer correlations for a name represent multiple reference, not multiple sense. This implication of PMT also seems confirmed by the facts of natural language. In genuine ambiguity, a word has two or more different senses in the language, so that an ambiguous expression is paraphrasable by non-synonymous expressions. For example, the two senses of the ambiguous word "sister" are paraphrasable as "female sibling" and "member of a female religious order." But what are the non-synonymous paraphrases for a proper name, say, "John Smith"? It is absurd to say that "John Smith" is as many ways ambiguous as there are John Smiths. (Note that we don't say "chair" is millions of ways ambiguous because there are millions of chairs.)

Most speakers typically know only a few John Smiths, if they know any, and know the correlations pairing "London" with London, England, and London, Ontario, but probably not, say, the correlation pairing it with London, Ohio. In general, speakers know only a few name-bearer correlations for a particular name, and moreover, such knowledge is not at all uniform over the speech community. Its variability from speaker to speaker is a consequence of its not being part of the speaker's knowledge of the language, that is, the knowledge a speaker has *qua* speaker of English. Speakers cannot exploit their knowledge of English grammar to determine the multiple bearers of "London" as they can exploit it to determine the multiple senses of "sister."[32]

The indefinite and definite elements in the sense of proper nouns together pose a selection problem for speakers. The definite element requires that a token of a singular proper noun refer to a unique, contextually specified, one of is multiple bearers – and, in the case of a plural proper noun like "the Londons I have seen," to a unique *n*-tuple of them. The existence of multiple correlations for the same name forces the speaker to apprise the members of his or her audience of the particular correlation for them to use in fixing the reference of the name, so long as the intended correlation is not obvious, say, because the bearer is so famous or is the focus of the conversation. The definite element forces the speaker to choose a means of making the bearer in the intended correlation contextually definite. Speakers can compensate for their intended referent's insufficient fame by conveying contextually appropriate individuating information in various ways; the speaker may simply point, or express the information linguistically, saying, for example, "Eliot the novelist, not the poet." It is in connection with solving this selection problem that Kripke's circularity condition comes in.

The sense of a name remains the starting point in non-literal uses of language. This is because intended non-literal use piggy-backs on literal use. The meaning communicated in the intended non-literal use of a token is a departure from the literal meaning of its type in the language. The destination, we may assume, is the meaning of some other type. In order for the hearers to reach the destination, the speaker must chart a course for them from a specified point of departure on a common map of linguistic types. The speaker's use of a token of a linguistic type specifies the point of departure, and the hearers must start with the meaning of the type and its type-reference. They must then follow the pragmatic directions the speaker uses to chart their course to its final destination, the non-literal reference of the token. Consider again the case of a professor who uses "Hitler" to refer to the tyrannical dean. The professor starts with the sense of "Hitler" in the language and the relevant name-bearer correlation and, by analogy, transforms this name-bearer correlation into one in which the dean is in Hitler's place. The professor's colleagues start with the same sense, figure out its literal referent Hitler, and then, on the basis of their knowledge of the pragmatics of the situation and of Hitler's tyrannical nature, infer the speaker's analogy to the dean, thereby identifying the dean as the intended referent.

Even a sketch of the role of sense in reference as brief as this makes it clear that my approach really is to firm up what has traditionally been a flabby sense/reference distinction. One aspect of the process has been to sharply separate questions of the semantics of the language from questions of the pragmatics of its use. The former concern linguistic types and are answered on the basis of theories of the aspect of their grammatical structure that is responsible for properties and relations like sameness of sense, multiplicity of sense, opposition of sense, and redundancy of sense. The latter concern linguistic tokens and are answered on the basis of theories of the contextual reasoning that enable us to communicate with tokens of linguistic types.[33]

Given such a sharp sense/reference distinction, sense can only have a mediational role in reference. But it must have such a role because pragmatic reasoning depends on information in senses to provide a criterion of literal use and initiate such reasoning.

VII

In his well-known paper "Proper Names," Searle criticizes meta-linguistic description theories on the grounds that "the force of 'Aristotle' is greater than the force of 'identical with an object named "Aristotle"'", for not just any object named 'Aristotle' will do. 'Aristotle' here refers to a particular object named 'Aristotle', not any."[34] There is an equivocation in this argument's use of the term "force." It can mean 'semantic force' (i.e., power to affect sense) or 'referential force' (i.e., power to affect reference). Taking the term "force" in the sense of semantic force (and adjusting for the descriptions that PMT requires), the argument fails because there is no reason to say the forces are different. Moreover, Searle's comments about the reference of the name and the description are beside the point in connection with semantic force, as can be seen from the fact that synonymous expressions, and even one and the same expression, can refer to different things. Alternatively, taking "force" in the sense of referential force, which is clearly how Searle takes it, the forces of the proper name and description can well be different, especially as Searle is assuming a use of "Aristotle" on which the speaker is specifically referring to the philosopher (hence, not any Aristotle will do). But now the argument fails because, since PMT is a theory of sense, it is irrelevant whether the (referential) force of "Aristotle" is greater than that of the description.[35]

Another problem with the argument is that it is illegitimate to compare an application of "Aristotle" to the philosopher – note that Searle observes that we wouldn't challenge the assertion of (1) by citing the proprietor of a Greek restaurant in Hoboken – with the range of possible applications of the description "identical with an object named 'Aristotle.'" A comparison of a particular token reference with the reference of a type is an "apples and oranges" comparison, as can be seen from the fact that such comparisons could be used to show that the force of "bachelor" is greater than that of "unmarried man." The extension of a type will typically be greater than the extension of one of its literally used tokens, since the former contains all the things to which tokens of the type can refer in literal uses, while the latter contains only a narrow portion of this extension.

Searle has more to say about proper names in his recent book *Intensionality*.[36] He begins his discussion by dismissing out of hand all versions of the description theory that hold that proper nouns have a sense in the language, that is, all theories on which it is a fact about the grammar of proper nouns – over and above the facts about how speakers use them – that they have a sense expressible in words. He claims that "the real issue" is "emphatically not" one having to do with such theories. This is a really surprising claim, but the reason he gives for it, that he doesn't know of anyone who ever held such a theory, is, if anything, even more surprising.[37]

It is surprising on two counts. First, it is perfectly obvious that Frege held the theory, that Mill argued against it, and that, for better or worse, controversies about the theory are to be found throughout the literature. We even have it on Searle's own testimony that Frege held such a theory! Somehow forgetting he has just denied that anyone ever held the theory, Searle contradicts himself by criticizing Frege for holding that "semantic content was always in words, specifically definite descriptions, and that the description gave a definition or sense of the name."[38]

Second, it doesn't matter in the slightest whether a theory has ever actually been held. Since when has the existence of adherents been a necessary condition for a theory to be true? And if a theory is true, it should be held. Searle seems to be operating on the dubious methodological principle "Don't consider theories if no one holds them."

Intensionality provides no new argument against grammatical versions of the description theory like PMT, but it does invoke some of Searle's old arguments. However, those arguments do not work without the assumption that there are no facts about sense over and above facts about the use of utterances. Searle would be entitled to this assumption if his dismissal of theories that claim there are such facts were acceptable, but as we have seen, it is not. Let us see how the arguments he invokes fare without it.

Searle reminds us that, in *Speech Acts*, he presented a case in which the speaker's only "identifying description" is "simply the ability to recognize the object."[39] However, saying that a proper noun of English has a sense in the language paraphrasable by a description does not deny that a speaker here or there might identify the referent of an utterance by visual recognition alone. The situation is parallel in the case of common nouns. The lexicographical claim that "judge" means 'public officer invested with authority to determine litigated questions' is not overturned by the example of some bag person who recognizes judges by their black robes and elevated courtroom seat.

Searle also reminds us that he used the same circularity argument that Kripke uses in "Naming and Necessity."[40] This is true. But, as I explained, the argument is irrelevant to a theory like PMT, which concerns the sense of proper nouns rather than their reference. As observed just above, fulfilling the requirement to provide contextually appropriate individuating information is a responsibility of the speaker. The speaker has to enable his or her audience to zero in on the chosen name-bearer correlation. Circularity is a sin of the speaker's, committed in the use of a name, when the speaker fails to communicate because the information he or she has relied on to make the intended bearer contextually definite does not succeed without the audience already having information sufficient to make the bearer contextually definite.

Kripke's and Searle's strictures against circularity are thus relevant to the pragmatics of reference fixing, not the semantics of nouns.

Finally, Searle reiterates the criticism that if one says that the sense of a proper noun "X" is "called X," then "one might as well say that part of the meaning of 'horse' is 'called a horse'. It is really quite amazing how often this mistake is made."[41] Even a brief look at the details of grammatical versions of the description theory shows that there are straightforward grounds for *not* carrying a meta-linguistic analysis of proper nouns over to common nouns. PMT provides an intensional criterion for accepting or rejecting hypotheses about sense structure. The criterion uses the familiar idea of maximizing explanatory power and economy, where explanation, in the present case, concerns sense properties and relations of sentences like (17)–(20) and economy is simply Ockham's razor.

We saw in Section V that this criterion can provide evidence for PMT's ascription of meta-linguistic senses to proper nouns. Now I want to show that it can also provide evidence for *not* ascribing senses like 'called "horse"' to common nouns like "horse." The rationale is that, by not making such ascriptions, we avoid false or uneconomical elements in the explanation of sense properties and relations. For instance, were we to ascribe such a sense to "horse," we would have to say that "horse named 'Horse'" is redundant when it is not. Some horses might have the name "Horse" just as Tarzan's young son has the name "Boy," but few, if any, do. The expression "horse named 'Horse'" is significant, informing us that the horse in question does not have an ordinary horse-name like "Dobbin." Correspondingly, "horse not named 'Horse'" is not contradictory, and is true of the vast majority of horses. Also, unlike (19) and (20), "There are two female horses on the ranch" and "There are two females (female horses) named 'Horse' on the ranch" are not synonymous. Finally, even if there were no such positive evidence, a hypothesis ascribing the meaning "named 'Horse'" to the sense of "horse" would be trimmed away by Ockham's razor because it explains no sense properties or relations not already explained by components of the meaning of "horse" like 'animal', 'mammal', 'solid-hoofed', and so on.

VIII

Before concluding the discussion of Kripke and Searle, I want to make clear that adopting PMT sacrifices none of their significant contributions to the study of naming. This is because PMT concerns sense and semantics, while their contributions concern reference and pragmatics. For instance, nothing I have said challenges Kripke's notion of rigid designation. From PMT's perspective, the notion is fundamentally a pragmatic concept. Although there is a grammatical source in the sense of proper nouns for the fact that they refer rigidly (i.e., the definite element in their sense), only tokens can refer rigidly. Rigidity couldn't be a feature of linguistic types, for the sense of a proper noun, which is independent of the information supplied by a context, is only schematic. The only reference a proper name can have is type-reference, but this, being unconstrained by the information that individuates a particular name-bearer correlation, is not reference as such.

There is reason to think that Kripke also takes the view that rigid designation is a pragmatic notion although he perhaps wouldn't put it this way. In explaining rigid designation, he says, "When I ask whether [a table I have in my hands] might have been in another room, I am talking, by definition, of *it*."[42] Rigidity thus seems to depend on particular features of uses of language, particularly, the speaker's intention to refer to something in virtue of its being the indicated bearer in the chosen correlation, the special authority of the speaker as the source of the communication, and relevant aspects of the context. In Kripke's question about whether the table might have been elsewhere, the token (i.e., Kripke's utterance of "table") takes on constant reference across hypothetical situations on the basis of his intention *qua* speaker to pick out the table in question and the obligation of the audience to honor the intention. This obligation arises from the directionality of the communication process: it is the speaker's intended meaning that is being conveyed *to* the audience. Hence, their assignment of referents in factual and counterfactual situations alike must respect his or her intention.[43]

Kripke's ideas about baptismal ceremonies and historical transmission also fit naturally in pragmatics. Baptismal acts create new name-bearer correlations. One precondition for a baptismal act is that there is no prior correlation between the name and prospective bearer, and the result of the act is existence of a correlation between them. Such acts are speech acts, creating correlations in the same way that promises create obligations. The concepts of name and bearer are part of the language itself, expressed as senses of its words, just as the concept of promising is.[44] But the application of proper names, particularly, the act creating a name-bearer correlation, as well as the transmission of information about such acts to speakers without firsthand knowledge, depends largely on extra-linguistic conditions.

Searle's contributions, too, are preserved in PMT. This is because his contributions are also matters of how speakers use their language. Searle's notion that communication with a proper name requires that a sufficient number of a set of descriptions be true of its bearer fits quite nicely into my sketch of the pragmatics of names in Section IV. His notion specifies one of the ways that the speaker can make the bearer in his or her chosen name-bearer correlation contextually definite. Further, Searle's stress on the primary role of the speaker's intention in communication agrees completely with the role I assigned to communicative intentions in Section 6. This is no coincidence. Searle's long and dedicated efforts on behalf of the importance of communicative intentions were responsible for my coming to appreciate their central role in language use.

IX

Taking the theories of Frege and Searle as the best versions of the description theory, direct reference theorists saw Mill's view that proper nouns have no sense as the only way to escape the dangers of Fregean extremism. Mill's view seemed to them forced on anyone who appreciates the thrust of Kripke's arguments. Their mistake was to suppose that Frege's and Searle's theories are the best intensionalists can do and, on this supposition, to think that Kripke's and other criticisms of those theories generalize into arguments that refute every version of the description theory. In this essay, I have tried to show that this mistake lies behind the myth that the description theory of proper names has been refuted.

I presented a middle position between Frege's extreme position on which the sense of a name is supposed to determine its reference and Mill's extreme position on which sense is supposed to play no role in fixing the referent of a name. I sketched a version of the description theory on which names have senses that are informationally rich enough to enable us to formulate and defend the claim that sense mediates reference, though not so rich as to get us in the trouble that Frege's senses got his theory in. Thus, PMT and the semantic theory of which it is a part can at least be recommended for avoiding the perils of the two extremes. Kripke's and Putnam's arguments, together with those of Wittgenstein and Mill before him, reveal the dangers in the Fregean extreme. The refractoriness of the cluster of problems about identity statements, vacuous reference, and substitution into opaque contexts reveals the danger in the latter extreme.[45]

PMT dissolves this cluster of problems because it preserves the core
idea of Frege's solution that proper names have a sense. On PMT's
account of the meta-linguistic senses of proper nouns, the senses of the
same proper nouns are the same, and the senses of different proper
nouns are different. Therefore, there is an immediate explanation
of the triviality of (21) and informativeness of (22). (21) expresses the

(21) George Orwell is George Orwell

(22) George Orwell is Eric Blair

analytic proposition that the thing which is a bearer of "George
Orwell" is the thing which is a bearer of "George Orwell," whereas (22)
expresses the synthetic proposition that the thing which is a bearer of
"George Orwell" is the thing which is a bearer of "Eric Blair."
Similarly, it doesn't follow from the fact that King George wanted to
know whether the contextually definite bearer of "Walter Scott" was
the author of *Waverley* that the king wanted to know whether the
contextually definite bearer of "Walter Scott" is the contextually definite bearer of "Walter Scott."

PMT provides a simple and elegant solution to the problem about
which, as has become clear, the direct reference theory has nothing
helpful to say – the problem of names without bearers, particularly, the
problem of explaining the semantics of sentences in which such names
are the subject of predications of existence or non-existence. PMT's
account of the sense of names applies straightforwardly to referentless
names, and so easily explains the semantics of such sentences. On PMT,
the claim of atheism can be formulated straightforwardly as the claim
that the contextually definite bearer of "God" does not exist, where
contextual definiteness is secured on the basis of the individuating
information in the theist's notion of a supreme being.[46]

The problem posed by the substitution of different but coreferential
names into sentences like (23) dissolves straightforwardly. The fact

(23) Someone knowing no literary trivia nonetheless knows that _____ .

that the truth-value changes on the substitution of statements such as
(21) and (22) into (23) is explained by the already explained fact that
(21) is trifling and (22) is informative. Kripke's puzzle about belief
dissolves in the same way, since it is merely a variant of this problem.
Pierre believes the proposition 'the thing (city) which is a bearer of
"Londres" is pretty' and also the proposition 'the thing (city) which is a

bearer of "London" is not pretty'.[47] Since the propositions are consistent, there is nothing to besmirch his epistemic reputation. Finally, I have already shown how PMT can account for the synonymy of sentences like (19) and (20), for analytic sentences like (17), for contradictory sentences like (18), and generally for the sense properties and relations of other sentences containing proper nouns.[48]

If my arguments for PMT in the previous sections work, the philosophical motivation for the theory of direct reference disappears. If that happens, the issue returns to the cluster of Fregean problems. Since the theory of direct reference does not provide satisfactory solutions for them, if PMT's solutions, the weight of argument should shift in favor of a non-Fregean intensionalism built around PMT.

Notes

1 S. Kripke, "Naming and Necessity," in *Semantics of Natural Language*, ed. D. Davidson and G. Harman (Dordrecht: Reidel, 1972), pp. 295–308.

2 S. Kripke, "A Puzzle About Belief," in *Meaning and Use*, ed. A. Margalit (Dordrecht: Reidel, 1979), pp. 239–83.

3 It is, moreover, easy to create more such problems. We get a closely related problem by introducing predicates ascribing incompatible properties, and then trying to explain, without besmirching Pierre's epistemic reputation, how the sentences can both be true. Another problem is the following sentences can have different truth-values: "Some people wonder whether Carl Gustav Hempel and Peter Hempel are two people" and "Some people wonder whether Carl Gustav Hempel and Carl Gustav Hempel are two people."

4 It is common, as the term "description theory" itself suggests, to also take description theories to claim that a proper noun is synonymous with a meaningful description. Strictly speaking, this condition is too strong because it assumes that languages have the expressive power to provide a descriptive phrase for each sense that is or might be the sense of a proper noun. Since the assumption could fail, the overall formulation could turn out to be sufficient but not necessary. I do not intend to make anything of this possibility, but mention it only to explain why I chose a formulation that omits the condition.

5 I am not claiming that Kripke himself takes his arguments to refute a descriptivist position. See *inter alia* his comment in Kripke, "Preface" in *Naming and Necessity* (Cambridge: Harvard University Press, 1980), p. 20, fn. 20.

6 In D. Kaplan, "Demonstratives," unpublished ms., March 1977, Kaplan records his debt to Kripke as well as to Putnam and Donnellan.

7 I have argued that their criticisms of intensionalism do not apply to non-Fregean forms of the position, that is, ones that do not define sense in terms of reference or claim that sense determines reference. See J. J. Katz, *Cogitations* (New York: Oxford University Press, 1986), pp. 32–35, and also Katz, "The Domino Theory," *Philosophical Studies* (in press), and *The Metaphysics of Meaning* (Cambridge: MIT Press, in press).

8 J. R. Searle, "Proper Names," *Mind*, (1958), pp. 166–73; reprinted in *Readings in the Philosophy of Language*, ed. J. Rosenberg and R. Travis (Englewood Cliffs: Prentice-Hall, 1971), pp. 212–22.

9 L. Wittgenstein, *Philosophical Investigations*, 3rd ed. (Oxford: Basil Blackwell, 1967), section 79.

58   JERROLD J. KATZ

10 "Proper Names," p. 217.
11 Ibid., p. 217.
12 Ibid., p. 215.
13 "Naming and Necessity," pp. 295–98. Searle's response to Kripke's counter-example (see J. R. Searle, *Intentionality* [Cambridge: Cambridge University Press, 1983], p. 251) changes the case from the one Kripke raised to one in which the agent in the referential act employs the further description "the man called 'Gödel' in my linguistic community or at least by those from whom I got the name." But it is not open to Searle to switch to a case less difficult for him to handle. It is up to his critic to choose the case. Searle might try to claim that Kripke's case is not a possible case unless the further description is included. But it is clear such a claim couldn't show the case to be impossible, since one can easily imagine various ways in which the further description might be inaccessible. For instance, the agent might simply not think about the source of the name or might have read Kripke's discussion of Kneale's theory and be unwilling to touch the further description.
14 For example, see J. J. Katz, "The Neoclassical Theory of Reference," in *Contemporary Perspectives in the Philosophy of Language*, ed. P. A. French, E. E. Uehling, Jr., and H. K. Wettstein (Minneapolis: University of Minnesota Press, 1977), pp. 103–24.
15 Note also that, whereas expressions like "the king who is a commoner" and "fully clothed nude" are contradictory, the expression "Gödel who did not discover the incompleteness of arithmetic" is not. Such arguments from sense properties and relations are the "*other* arguments" to which Kripke refers in Kripke, "Speaker's Reference and Semantic Reference," in *Contemporary Perspectives in the Philosophy of Language*, p. 23, fn. 12. He is right in saying that I thought those arguments "tell against the description theory even as a theory of meaning." However, I now think I was too hasty. The reason for this change will emerge in the course of this essay.
16 W. Kneale, "Modality, De Dicto and De Re," in *Logic, Methodology, and Philosophy of Science*, ed. E. Nagel, P. Suppes, and A. Tarski (Stanford: Stanford University Press, 1962), pp. 622–33, and "The Neoclassical Theory of Reference," as well as my earlier paper "A Proper Theory of Names," *Philosophical Studies*, 31 (1977), pp. 1–80.
17 Kripke's criticism of Kneale's claim that his theory is the only one that can explain why "Socrates is called 'Socrates'" is trifling is a different matter; see "Naming and Necessity," pp. 283–4. I will consider the criticism below in connection with a similar point of Searle's.
18 Ibid., pp. 283–6.
19 Ibid., pp. 284.
20 "A Proper Theory of Names," "The Neoclassical Theory of Reference," and recently, Katz, "Why Intensionalists Ought Not be Fregeans," in *Truth and Interpretation: Perspectives in the Philosophy of Donald Davidson*, ed. E. LePore (Oxford: Basil Blackwell, 1986), pp. 59–91.
21 I use the relation 'x is a bearer of y' rather than 'y names x' for reasons indicated in note 46. I leave it open whether the relation is primitive or definable. Further, my account follows the classical grammatical distinction between *proper nouns* and *general nouns*, where the former denotes an individual without expressing anything about its character and the latter denotes an individual on the basis of something about its character common to other individuals (but without reference to them as occurs with *collective nouns* like "army" or "audience").
22 I say "roughly speaking" because this formulation is only a convenient approximation. It requires amplification, and ultimately, formalization in a technical notation designed to make sense structure fully explicit. I have refrained from using technical apparatus from linguistics here, but this, of necessity, means that the concise non-technical formulations I have used are incomplete. One example of why PMT would need a linguistic presentation is in connection with the synonymy of sentences like "Einstein the musicologist wrote nothing on relativity" and "The musicologist who is a bearer of 'Einstein' wrote nothing on relativity." We need a recursive mechanism to explain how the semantic structure of the substantive to which 'bearer of "n"' is

attributed assimilates other attributions in the compositional process. There is no special problem here, but this obviously recursive structure needs to be worked out in a formalized account of compositional sentence meaning. For a discussion of a linguistic treatment of modification, see J. J. Katz, C. Leacock, and Y. Ravin, "A Decompositional Theory of Modification," in *Actions and Events: Perspectives on the Philosophy of Donald Davidson*, ed. E. LePore and B. P. McLaughlin (Oxford: Basil Blackwell, 1985), pp. 207–34.

23 It should be noted that (3) itself is only a first approximation to a sentence of the kind that PMT predicts is analytic. The respects in which it falls short of a full formulation become important when we turn to Kripke's modal argument.

24 There is also no straightforward definitional circularity either, since PMT's account of the sense of a name does not use the name but only mentions it, or, in more technical formulations, presents it in terms of a grammatical description.

25 "Naming and Necessity," p. 270.

26 Of course, a verb within quotation marks or suffixed with "tion," as in "creation," is not standing alone.

27 R. Fiengo, "Indexing and Reference," in preparation.

28 There are two ways to think of this interpretation of identity sentences. One is as ambiguous between a non-coreferential sense and a coreferential sense in which the second occurrence of the proper noun is anaphoric to the first. This is like the senses of "John came home and he, John, had dinner" and "John came home and some other male had dinner." The context of the discussion disambiguates them in favor of the coreferential sense. Such sentences may also be thought of as having a single sense that leaves it open whether the occurrences of the proper nouns are coreferential. This is like the sense of "John came home and someone, maybe John and maybe another male, had dinner." For our purposes, nothing hangs on the choice between these alternatives, since it concerns, not the nature of coreferential semantic structure in which we are interested, but only how that structure is assigned, whether by disambiguating or by making the sense more specific.

29 The overall semantic theory to which PMT belongs makes a special point of denying that sense determines reference. This denial together with the theory's purely grammatical definition of sense enables the theory to escape the objections to which Frege's theory succumbs, e.g., those in "Is Semantics Possible?", reprinted in H. Putnam, *Mind, Language, and Reality* (Cambridge: Cambridge University Press, 1975), pp. 137–52, and Putnam, "The Meaning of 'Meaning,'" in *Minnesota Studies in the Philosophy of Science*, vol. 7 (Minneapolis: University of Minnesota Press, 1975), pp. 131–93. For discussion, see *Cogitations*, "The Domino Theory," and *The Metaphysics of Meaning*.

30 If I am right, the theory of direct reference is deficient not only in failing to account for the sense of proper nouns in the language, but also in failing to consider the ways in which reference is mediated by sense in linguistic communication. Although my discussion here is confined to proper names, to avoid unnecessary quibbles, I should note that Kaplan claims that terms of the form 'd-that[the so-and-so]' can have a full-blown sense and that indexical terms can have a partial sense and still be directly referential. See "Demonstratives." I find this mysterious. Either the claim contradicts the basic thesis of the theory of direct reference, or else contradiction is avoided by an explication of "direct reference" that, in allowing sense a limited mediational role in reference, robs the theory of the thesis that sets it apart from other theories and makes it philosophically significant. Either way, the claim undermines what is special, and hence interesting, about the theory of direct reference.

31 This statement is much simplified. See *The Metaphysics of Meaning*, Chapter 2.

32 Further, that knowledge of name-bearer corrections is extra-linguistic knowledge is implicit is our earlier distinction between the multiple reference of proper nouns and the ambiguity of common nouns. Other considerations confirm the extra-linguistic nature of such knowledge. The recluse who knows no correlation for the vast majority of the names in English is not for this reason a less fluent speaker of English than the

social butterfly who knows many correlations for a large class of names. Rip Van Winkle's linguistic fluency didn't diminish as a consequence of the disappearance of many name-bearer correlations during his long slumber. Also, English speakers living in isolated places will typically have sets of name-bearer correlations with little or no overlap with English speakers living in other isolated places, but this is not, by itself, grounds for supposing they speak different dialects.

33 I have had in mind the accounts of pragmatics in H. P. Grice, *Studies in the Way of Words* (Cambridge: Harvard University Press, 1989), and D. Wilson and D. Sperber, *Relevance* (Cambridge: Harvard University Press, 1986), but nothing hangs on this. The semantics to go with such pragmatic accounts is found in Katz, *Propositional Structure and Illocutionary Force* (Cambridge: Harvard University Press, 1980).

34 "Proper Names," p. 215.

35 PMT addresses the traditional issue between Mill and Frege about the sense of proper names. On my view, both were right and wrong: Mill was right to deny the attributive character of names but wrong to think that, as a consequence, the reference of names cannot be based on sense; Frege was right to assert that the reference of names is based on sense but wrong to think of the basis as determination and wrong to think of senses as non-metalinguistic. See J. S. Mill, *A System of Logic* (London: Parker, Son, and Bourn), and G. Frege, *Philosophical Writings of Gottlob Frege*, ed. M. Black and P. Geach (Oxford: Basil Blackwell, 1952), pp. 56–78.

36 *Intentionality*, pp. 231–61.

37 Ibid., pp. 232–3.

38 Ibid., p. 244.

39 Ibid., p. 233.

40 Ibid., pp. 242–3.

41 Ibid., p. 243. Note that, in "Naming and Necessity" (pp. 283–4), Kripke criticizes Kneale by observing that "Horses are called 'horses'" is trifling. I shall assume that Searle's "called a horse" is intended to be essentially the same description as Kripke's.

42 "Naming and Necessity," pp. 272–3, and also p. 268.

43 The ease of access to such ostensive definitions within pragmatic approaches to reference explains why one can easily rigidify definite descriptions and why such rigidification does not meet the challenge of Kripke's modal argument. Such rigidification, which takes place in the use of language, produces some rigid description tokens among all the tokens of a description type alleged to express the sense of a name. But there will be other tokens that the modal argument can make use of to show that the description type cannot be synonymous with the name.

44 A theory of illocutionary force information as an aspect of the sense structure of sentences is presented in *Propositional Structure and Illocutionary Force*.

45 Proponents of the theory of direct reference have, of course, not ignored these difficulties, but their attempts to overcome them have not been successful. See my study "Names Without Bearers," in preparation.

46 Various objections have been made to the meta-linguistic treatments of referentless names. One turns on the fact that some proper nouns (e.g., "Clark Kent") have not only uses where they name an actual person but also uses on which they do not (e.g., "Lois Lane doesn't know that Clark Kent is Superman"). To account for this fact, we can say that some of the name-bearer correlations for "Clark Kent" relate the name to real people with that name, while another relates it to the fictional character. In the latter case, the semantics and pragmatics work in the same way only with respect to the possible world introduced by the pretense of the fiction. Another objection turns on the implausibility of treatments that put existence claims in the form of an assertion that a name has a referent. I agree that such solutions are implausible. For this reason, I do not analyze a sentence like "Socrates exists" as an assertion about the word "Socrates." The focus in PMT conception of the sense of a proper noun is on the bearer, not the name. The issue of how to understand "exists" is, of course,

another question, but on one way of understanding it, "Socrates exists" can be analyzed as asserting that the contextually definite bearer of "Socrates" is among the things in the actual world. Some aspects of these questions are discussed in *Cogitations*; a full discussion appears in "Names Without Bearers."

47 For a full discussion, see "Why Intensionalists Ought Not Be Fregeans." Note that, on PMT, proper nouns from different languages, such as "Ludwig" and "Louis," are properly taken by PMT not to be translations. The English "white" translates the German "weiss," but the English "Louis" is simply the English name corresponding to the German name "Ludwig." "Jerrold," "Jerold," and "Gerald," in contrast, can be regarded as merely different spellings of the same name. Note that the question of where to draw the line is one belonging to linguistics and that PMT can accommodate any reasonable way in which it is drawn.

48 On PMT, an ordinary American schoolchild who says, "Hitler believed that Germany would win the war" expresses a proposition whose sense mentions "Germany." But also on PMT, Hitler's own belief is a proposition whose sense mentions "Deutschland" instead. So there is a question about PMT's account of how a monolingual speaker of one language communicates the beliefs of speakers of another language: Is PMT committed to claiming that the child is making a false statement? (I wish to thank Scott Soames for raising this question.) The answer is no, since the child's statement can be construed as about Hitler's *de re* belief, and Hitler did believe of Germany that it would win. But even if the child's statement is construed as about Hitler's *de dicto* beliefs, a negative answer is possible. We might say that, even though the child's formulation does not correspond exactly to Hitler's own *de dicto* belief, it comes close enough to count as a correct report. This, however, is not something on which PMT needs to take a stand. PMT is not responsible for the child's being unable to capture exactly Hitler's own *de dicto* belief – PMT certainly does not preclude a report in which "Deutschland" occurs in place of "Germany." The problem, if there is one, lies with the child's ignorance of German.

There can be situations in which the use of "Germany" in place of "Deutschland" is precluded. Suppose we knew that Hitler thought that "Germany" is the name of Italy, and hence did not believe the proposition expressed by "Germany will win the war." Now we have a situation which involves a case which is like Kripke's Pierre case – with Hitler cast in Pierre's role. In certain extensions of this situation, we want to be able to claim that the child who says, "Hitler believed that Germany would win the war" has falsely reported Hitler's *de dicto* belief as the belief that Italy would win. To be able to claim this, just as to be able to claim that Pierre beliefs are consistent, we require a theory of names like PMT.

4

Substitution arguments and the individuation of beliefs

J. A. FODOR

Introduction

The older I get, the more I am inclined to think that there is nothing at all to meaning except denotation; for example, that there is nothing to the meaning of a name except its bearer and nothing to the meaning of a predicate except the property that it expresses.

The popular alternative to the view that there is nothing to meaning except denotation is that meaning is a composite of denotation and *sense*. And, since Wittgenstein (or maybe since Saussure), it's been widely assumed that the sense of an expression is to be understood as somehow emerging from its *use*. Practically everybody who's anybody in modern Anglo-American philosophy has held some or other version of this sense-cum-use doctrine. Still, as I say, I'm increasingly inclined to think that it's a dead end and that there is nothing at all to meaning except denotation.

What I mostly want to do, in this essay, is reconsider a main argument that's supposed to show that there *must* be something more to meaning than denotation. So I don't propose to spend much time reviewing the general considerations that lead me to think that the sense/use story is no good. Roughly, however:

1. Nobody has succeeded in making it clear just *how* the sense of an expression is supposed to emerge from its use; not, at least, if use is taken as something that is nonsemantically and nonintentionally specifiable. (And, if it's not, it's hard to see what the interest of a reduction of sense to use would be.)

At a minimum, a use theory of meaning ought to be a function from uses onto meanings. There are, however, precisely no candidates for the formulation of such a function. Wittgenstein, in the *Investigations*, imagines a "primitive language game" in which one guy is disposed to bring a slab when another guy says (i.e., *utters*) "Slab!" Presumably the fact that utterances of "Slab!" have compliance conditions in this game (and that it's bringing a slab that counts as complying) reduces to the fact that the people playing the game have the dispositions that they do. But how does this reduction go? Why does the fact that one guy brings a slab when the other says "Slab!" constitute "Slab!" meaning *bring me a slab* and not, as it might be, *meet me at the Algonquin* or *two is a prime number*? It is, after all, easy enough to dream up a story in which a guy brings a slab when you say "Slab!" *because* he takes "Slab!" to mean *meet me at the Algonquin*. Imagine, for example, someone whose practice it is to bring you a slab whenever he intends to meet you there. It may be that you could get the Wittgensteinian version of the reduction of sense to use to go through if you threw in a little behaviorism. The which, however, Heaven forfend. (These remarks also apply, mutatis mutandis, to versions of sense/use semantics according to which the sense of an expression is a construct out of its role in a theory, assuming that "role" is construed causally or syntactically – anyhow not inferentially or intentionally or otherwise question-beggingly.)

2. The sense/use theory invites semantic holism via a line of argument that is by now too well known to bother recapitulating in detail. Briefly, there appears to be no atomistic way of individuating uses; hence no atomistic way of individuating senses; hence nowhere to stop short of identifying the units of sense with entire belief systems (or "ways of life" or whatever). When pursued in this direction, however, the sense/use story is not a theory of meaning but the reductio ad absurdum of the possibility of such a theory. On the holistic account of content individuation, it hardly ever turns out that two tokens of a symbol have the same sense. And what's the good of a suicidal semantics?

Whereas, by contrast, a sense-less account of meaning looks to be in better shape in both these respects (assuming that it can be made to satisfy "internal" conditions of adequacy that a semantic theory ought to meet, like assigning the right truth conditions, exhibiting compositional structure, and so forth). Whereas nothing is known about how sense arises from use, there has been some glimmer of progress in attempts to reduce denotation to causation. (See recent work by Dretske, Stampe, Fodor, and others.) And, while the use of a symbol is generally assumed to be at least partly constituted by its intralinguistic relations, denotation is presumably a word/world relation purely.[1] There is thus some hope that an extensional semantics can avoid the holism that plagues use theories. (For more discussion of both these points, see Fodor, 1986.)

So tell me again: Why does there have to be sense as well as denotation? What's wrong with the idea that denotation is all that there is to meaning?

The substitution argument

Here's what's supposed to be wrong: The expressions "Jocasta" and "Oedipus' Mother" are coreferential *and must therefore be synonyms if denotation is all that there is to meaning*. But it's true that Oedipus believed that Jocasta was eligible and it's false that Oedipus believed that Oedipus' Mother was eligible. So the expressions "Jocasta" and "Oedipus' Mother" are not freely substitutable saving truth. So they are not synonyms. So denotation can't be all that there is to meaning.

I'll call this kind of argument a "substitution argument" (and I'll call the implied test for content identity the "substitution test"). I think that substitution arguments are – and have been since Frege – a lot of what's behind the idea that there must be something more to meaning than denotation. But the older I get, the more I wonder whether substitution arguments are any damned good. I therefore propose to have a good look at substitution arguments. Starting now.

On the face of it, substitution *salve veritate* in belief contexts doesn't *look* to be a test for identity of content. What it looks to be is a test for identity of *belief-state*.[2] If "O believes E" is true and "O believes E'" is false, then it must be that believing E and believing E' are different states. In the present case: If believing J to be eligible and believing O's M to be eligible were the same state, then it would be both true and false that O was in it, and that is not allowed. But it's one thing to admit that believing that J is eligible is a different state than believing that O's M is eligible; it would seem to be quite another thing to admit that "J" and "O's M" are nonsynonymous. And it is, decisively, the latter conclusion that we need to be able to draw if we're to infer from the facts about Oedipus that there is more to meaning than denotation.

Recap:

i. What's granted is that if the expression E fails to substitute for the expression E' *salve veritate* in the context "believes that . . . ," then believing that E is a different state from believing that E'.

ii. What's claimed is that if the expression E fails to substitute for the expression E' *salve veritate* in the context "believes that . . . ," then E and E' differ in semantic value.

Required: an argument that gets from what's granted to what's claimed. The older I get, the more I am inclined to doubt that there is one.

I now propose to run through a couple of candidate arguments, neither of which strikes me as very convincing. I then want to tell you a story about the individuation of beliefs that makes it clear why the inference from i to ii shouldn't be expected to go through; and which is, I think, not implausible on independent grounds.

Argument 1

Premise 1: If "believes E" is sometimes true when "believes E'" is false, then E and E' are not freely substitutable *salve veritate*.

Premise 2: Synonyms are freely substitutable *salve veritate*.

Conclusion: E and E' aren't synonyms.

Comment: Premise 1 is common ground; but why should we believe premise 2?

Certainly 2 is false as stated. As everybody and his grandmother points out, substitution of synonyms clearly fails in quotation contexts (like "uttered ' ... ' "); so maybe it fails in belief contexts too? How are we to tell?

I'd prefer to avoid a vulgar squabble over intuitions. For what it's worth, however, it seems to me (as it seemed to Mates) that it is possible for me to doubt (/deny) that everybody who believes that Oedipus is a bachelor believes that Oedipus is an unmarried man even though I don't doubt (/deny) that everybody who believes that Oedipus is a bachelor believes that Oedipus is a bachelor. At a minimum, it's surely possible for it *to seem to me* that [it's possible for me to doubt (/deny) that everybody who believes that Oedipus is a bachelor believes that Oedipus is an unmarried man] even though it doesn't seem to me that [it's possible for me to doubt (/deny) that everybody who believes that Oedipus is a bachelor believes that Oedipus is a bachelor]. For, as a matter of fact, it does seem to me that it seems to me that all of this is so; and I would seem to be in about as good a position as anyone can be to say how things seem to me to be, nicht wahr? So maybe substitution of synonyms *salve veritate* fails in the context "it seems to me that ... ," or in iterations of that context. In which case, the failure of "J" and "O's M" to substitute in such contexts would not show that they aren't synonyms.

In rather similar spirit, it seems to me certain that my daughter, when she was three years old, believed me to be her father. But I really do have my doubts about whether she believed me to be her male parent. Introspection suggests (again, for what it's worth) that the reason I really do doubt this is that I doubt that three-year-olds *have the concept* PARENT, and I'm inclined to hold that you can't believe that someone is your male parent unless you do have the concept PARENT. Merely having the concept FATHER – a concept that's *definable in terms of* PARENT – strikes me as not good enough.

The Mates sort of argument throws doubt on the claim that failures of substitution *salve veritate* in belief contexts are ipso facto arguments for nonsynonymy. Reflection on Kripke's example about Pierre makes this claim seem still more questionable – at least if you're prepared to believe that *translation* is a test for synonymy.[3] For our purposes a stripped-down version of the example will do. Pierre is a French-English bilingual who has come across tokens of the type "Londres" in French texts and tokens of the type "London" in English texts. He understands that "London" and "Londres" both refer to cities, but he doesn't realize that they both refer to the same city; for simplicity, we can assume that he takes it that they don't. So the intuition seems to be that "Pierre believes that London is pretty" is true and "Pierre believes that Londres is pretty" is false. (It is an argument for this intuition that if you say to him: "Pierre, do you believe that London is pretty?" he says, "But no!", whereas if you say to him "Pierre, do you believe that Londres is pretty?" he says, "But yes!") However, "London" translates "Londres" if anything translates anything. So, if translations are ipso facto synonyms, it would seem that there's at least one case where you can't infer difference of meaning from failure of substitution.[4] But that was the very form of inference that we required to get from "O believed ...J..." and "O didn't believe...O's Mom..." to "'J' and 'O's Mom' mean different things." Why is sauce for Pierre's goose not sauce for Oedipus' gander? Since there are cases where the substitution test fails when the translation test is satisfied, the right conclusion would seem to be that if translation tests for sense, substitution doesn't.

But, as I say, all this relies a lot on intuitions, over which I do not wish to squabble. All I ask for at this stage is a Scotch verdict. It turns out that, given a story about the individuation of quotations, together with a story about how embedded formulas function in contexts like "uttered'..."'" we can see how substitution of synonyms could fail in quotation contexts. So maybe there could be a story about the individuation of beliefs that, together with a story about how embedded formulas function in contexts like "believes that...," would show us how substitution of synonyms could fail in belief contexts too. We'll return to this presently.

Argument 2

Premise 1: Distinct intentional states must differ either in their *mode* (e.g., in the way that believing that P differs from desiring that P) or in their *content* (e.g., in the way that believing that P differs from believing that Q).[5]

Premise 2: Believing that J is eligible is an intentional state distinct from believing that O's M is eligible (the failure of the substitution test shows this; see above).

These states do not differ in mode (they're both belief states).

So they differ in contents (they have different propositional objects).

So "J is eligible" and "O's M is eligible" are nonsynonymous (they express different propositions).

So "J" and "O's M" are nonsynonymous (by the principle that if nonsynonymous formulas differ only in that one has constituent C where the other has constituent C', then C and C' are nonsynonymous. I propose to grant this for the sake of argument).

So denotation can't be all that there is to meaning.

Comment: Excellent, except that why should we believe premise 1? Specifically, why shouldn't there be cases where beliefs that are tokens of different state types nevertheless have the same propositional object?

I now propose to tell you a story about belief individuation, and about how embedded formulas function in belief attributions. The relevant peculiarity of this story is that it permits distinct belief-states to have the same contents (the same propositional objects). The point of telling you this story is that since such cases are allowed, the proposition that J is eligible might turn out to be identical to the proposition that O's M is eligible *even though* believing the one proposition is a different state from believing the other. But if these propositions might be the same, then we have, so far, no reason to doubt that 'J' and 'O's M' are synonyms. Which is to say that, at least so far as the facts about Oedipus are concerned, we have no reason to doubt that denotation is all that there is to meaning.

Let's start with belief individuation, leaving the issues about belief attribution till later.

The standard story about believing is that it's a two-place relation, viz., a relation between a person and a proposition. My story about believing is that it's a four-place relation, viz., a relation between a person, a proposition, a vehicle, and a functional (causal) role. According to my story, if all you know is that two of a guy's belief-states differ, then all you can infer is that they differ *either* in content *or* in vehicle *or* in functional role. Since, in particular, you can't infer that they differ in content, argument 2 is invalid if my story about the individuation of belief states is true.

A vehicle is a symbol. A symbol (token) is a spatiotemporal particular that has syntactic and semantic properties and a causal role. Vehicles (like other symbols) are individuated with respect to their syntactic and semantic properties, but *not* with respect to their causal roles. In particular, two vehicle tokens are type distinct if they are syntactically different or if they express different propositions. But type-identical vehicle tokens can differ in their causal roles because the role that a token plays depends not just on which type it's a token of, but also on the rest of the world in which its tokening transpires. (This is true of the causal roles of symbols because it's true of the causal roles of everything. Roughly, your causal role depends on what you are, what the local laws are, and what else there is around.)

I assume, finally, that vehicles can be type distinct but synonymous; distinct vehicles can express the same proposition. So much for the individuation of vehicles.

If you like language of thought stories, then the typical vehicle of believing is a formula of Mentalese. If you don't like language of thought stories, then let it be a formula of anything you please. What's essential to my story is that believing is never an *unmediated* relation between a person and a proposition. In particular, nobody "grasps" a proposition except insofar as he is appropriately related to a token of some vehicle that expresses the proposition. (I think this not only because it strikes me as metaphysically plausible, but also because it is required for a story I like about how graspings of propositions – more specifically, tokenings of attitudes – can eventuate in the behavioral consequences that they do. But I've told that story elsewhere and I don't propose to repeat it here.)

I can now tell you my story about Oedipus, which is that he had two different ways of relating to the proposition that J was eligible (and, mutatis mutandis, to its denial); one way was via tokens of some such vehicle as "J is eligible" and the other way was via tokens of some such vehicle as "O's M is eligible." Since difference of vehicles implies (or, more precisely, *can* imply; see below) correspondingly different mental states, it was possible for Oedipus to have two beliefs with the same content; i.e., two beliefs both of whose object was the proposition that can be expressed as either *Jocasta is eligible* or *Oedipus' Mother is eligible*.

My story about Oedipus is, no doubt, tendentious. It's notoriously possible to hang onto the idea that distinct belief-states imply distinct belief contents by distinguishing between two propositions that extensionalists take to be identical: the proposition that O's M is eligible and the proposition that J is. Since it thus appears that you can tell the story about O either way, O's case doesn't distinguish between my view of belief individuation and the standard view.

But, as we've seen, Pierre is a horse of a different color. In Pierre's case, as in O's, you get the failure of substitution of coextensive expressions ("London"/"Londres"; "J"/"O's M"). But in the Pierre example it's implausible that the explanation of the substitution failure is that the expressions mean different things. "London"/"Londres" is bad news for Frege's strategy of explaining failures of substitution by positing differences of sense. But if it's not difference in sense that explains the substitution failure (as apparently it's not) and if failure of substitution is a test for distinctness of belief-state (as apparently it is), then it must be that distinct belief-states can have the same content; i.e., there must be more to the identity of an attitude than its content and its mode. The vehicle by means of which the content is presented does rather suggest itself since, in Pierre's case, differences in their vehicles seem to be all that's *left* to distinguish his London beliefs from his Londres ones.

A very rough theory of belief individuation might make do with *just* a person, a vehicle, and a content. You get a rather sharper picture if you also allow in a functional role for the vehicle. Loosely speaking, I mean by the functional role of a vehicle the role that it plays in inference; more strictly speaking, I mean its causal role in (certain) mental processes. It seems to me plausible that you can have two beliefs with the same object and the same vehicle, but where the difference between the beliefs comes from differences in the inferential/causal roles that the vehicles play. This happens when, for example, two guys who use the same vehicle to express the same content differ in their background theories; specifically, in the identity statements that they hold true.

Let's suppose – what is plausibly the case – that I know that Janet is my wife. What belief am I expressing when I say "I'm expecting my wife to phone at 3"? It seems to me merely captious to insist that it's the belief that my wife will phone at 3 *and not the belief that Janet will*. On the other hand, what belief is *acquired* by the guy who heard me say what I did but who *doesn't* know about Janet being my wife? Clearly *not* the belief that Janet will phone; clearly only the belief that my wife will. The intuitions get still clearer if you run the example on "Janet" and "Janet D. Fodor"; my believing that Janet will call *is* my believing that Janet D. Fodor will. But if you don't know about Janet being JDF, then your acquiring the one belief isn't your acquiring the other. Or so it seems to me.[6] I admit that this is all the merest intuition mongering;

but if you accept the intuitions, what it looks like we have is: one format ("Janet will call") one proposition (extensionalist principles are assumed to be operative) but two beliefs depending on differences in the background of cognitive commitment.[7]

So much for the belief-state *individuation* according to my revisionist account. What is the story about belief-state *attribution* going to be?

Consider the expression "believes that E" where it is used to attribute to some agent the state of believing that E. How does it go about doing what it is used to do? How, in particular, does the "E" part work?

First off, "E" has somehow to pick out the propositional object of the belief; it has to specify the content of the belief ascribed. I think this works in the following simple and aesthetically satisfying fashion. The proposition that is the object of the belief-state that is *attributed by* using the formula "believes E" is the very same proposition that is *expressed by* using the formula "E." So, for example, the expression "believes that it's raining" is used to attribute a relation to the proposition that it's raining; and this is the very same proposition that the unembedded formula "it's raining" is used to express.

It follows, on my semantic principles, that the function of "believes J is eligible" in "O believes J is eligible" is to attribute to O a belief relation to the proposition that is expressed both by the unembedded formula "J is eligible" and by the unembedded formula "O's M is eligible." It doesn't, of course, follow that believing that O's M is eligible and believing that J is eligible are the same belief-state since, on my metaphysical principles, the identity of a propositional attitude is not determined by specifying a mode and an object.

You must also specify (inter alia) a vehicle; and this is the other thing that the embedded formula in "believes E" can function to do. It does it, to put it roughly, by *displaying* the vehicle. Or to put it slightly less roughly, it does it by displaying a formula that is, to one or another degree, structurally isomorphic to the vehicle. I may, for example, wish to distinguish (see above) between beliefs about one's father and beliefs about one's male parent. I can do so by distinguishing between attributions via the formula "believes ... father ... " and via the formula "believes ... male parent ...." Similarly, mutatis mutandis, I can distinguish between ... O's M ... beliefs and ... J ... beliefs; or between ... Janet ... beliefs and ... my wife ... beliefs. In each case, according to my story about belief individuation, it's the vehicle, not the content, that distinguishes the belief-states. And, in each case, the intended distinction is signaled by a choice among (coextensive but structurally distinct) formulas embedded to the "believes" predicate.

It bears emphasis that a cost of accepting this sort of view is abandoning the principle of strict compositionality of reference: i.e., the principle that its denotation is *all* that a referring expression contributes to fixing the denotation of the referring expressions of which it is a constituent. On the present view, the reason that "the belief that O's M is eligible" picks out a different mental state from the one picked out by "the belief that J is eligible" *despite* the denotational equivalence of "J" and "O's M" is that the denotations of expressions like "the belief that..." are determined by *both* the denotation *and the form* of their constituents.

However, strict composition of reference never was a particularly attractive story about opaque contexts. Classical Fregean semantics preserves it only by endorsing the not wildly plausible view that, although "J" and "O's M" both refer in both opaque and transparent contexts, and although they both refer to the same thing in transparent contexts, they nevertheless refer to *different* things when they occur embedded to verbs like "believes." (Specifically, "O's M" refers to the sense *O's M* and "J" refers to the sense *J*. *O's M* and *J* are *different* senses since "O's M" and "J" are, by assumption, nonsynonymous.) It's arguable that, as between giving up the strict compositionality of reference and giving up what Davidson has called "semantic innocence" (in general, words mean the same in opaque contexts as they do in transparent ones), there doesn't seem to be much to choose. It's not a priori obvious that strict compositionality of reference is worth having if it's going to cost that much.

In fact, the situation is rather worse than this suggests. If referring expressions denote their senses in opaque contexts, and if strict compositionality of reference holds, then belief clauses that differ only in synonyms must corefer; synonymous expressions that denote their senses ipso facto denote the same thing. But then, if translation implies synonymy, it's hard to see how 'Pierre's belief that Londres is pretty' could fail to refer to the same mental state as 'Pierre's belief that London is pretty'. But if they do refer to the same state, how *could* it be that Pierre has one belief and not the other? (Similar arguments could, of course, be constructed from Mates cases.)[8]

It's plausible, given all of this, that a term may contribute not just its referent, but also its vehicle, to fixing the referents of the expressions in which it occurs. How much, then, of the structure of the vehicle is the belief-embedded formula in a belief state attributing expression required to display in order that the attribution should be univocal? In the case of the first of the functions of the embedded formula – viz., specifying the propositional object of the attributed belief – the matter is clear: The embedded formula must express *the very proposition* that the "believes" predicate attributes. I think, however, that it is otherwise with the specification of the vehicle; here everything is slippery and pragmatic. Roughly, what's required is a degree of isomorphism to the vehicle that is appropriate to the purposes at hand; and there isn't any purpose-independent specification of how much isomorphism is enough.

I say: "Baby believes that Santa Claus will come down the chimney." My intention is to specify a belief that is individuated, in part, by reference to a vehicle in which the expression "Santa Claus" occurs essentially. On the other hand, I say: "I believe that Bill Smith will come down the chimney dressed as Santa Claus" and here it's probably *not* essential that "Bill Smith" occur in the vehicle ("he" or "Mary Smith's husband" would perhaps do as well). Similarly, I say: "Some folks believed FDR to be the incarnation of the devil" and practically nothing about the vehicle of the attributed belief matters to the success of the attribution. It doesn't matter, for example, that the folks in question thought of FDR via the formula "the SOB in the White House" or that they thought of the empty set via the vehicle "Old Nick" or "The Arch Fiend" (it does matter, however, that they didn't think of it it via the vehicle "the empty set"). I don't, in short, generally require that my belief attributions be univocal; I am generally satisfied to pick out any of a class of belief states that have their propositional objects and certain features of their vehicles in common. And do not send to know *just how* vehicle independent my belief attributions are required to be, for there is no precise answer. Good enough for the purposes at hand is generally all I have in mind.

There also isn't an answer to the request for a form of embedded expression that is *guaranteed* to specify the vehicle of an attitude uniquely. This is to say that there isn't, in ordinary belief/desire talk, anything that corresponds to the canonical description of a belief or a desire. To put it another way, it's not that there are de dicto attributions and de re attributions; it's rather that there is a continuum along which an embedded expression can be explicit about the vehicle of an attributed belief. If there's a rule in play, it's a rule of conversation: "Kindly so construe my embedded formulas that my belief attributions come out plausible on the assumption that my utilities are rational." If I say that John believes that Cicero was Tully, I *must* be trying to specify John's vehicle; what would be the point of my telling you something that would be true in virtue of John's believing that Cicero is Cicero? On the other hand, if I tell you that the English wanted to seize New

York from the Dutch, I couldn't possibly be wanting to specify *their* vehicle; everybody called the place "New Amsterdam" at the time.

Here's the box score: Beliefs are relations between persons, contents, vehicles, and functional roles. We have a precise semantics for the attribution of beliefs insofar as their identity depends on their contents. We have a less precise, but serviceable, semantics for individuating beliefs insofar as their identity depends on their vehicles: When it matters, and to the extent that it matters, you can indicate the vehicle of a belief by choosing an embedded formula that is more or less structurally isomorphic to it.

There is, however, no parameter of a "believes" formula whose function is to signal the functional role of the vehicle of a belief. Typical cases of belief attribution involve people who share, more or less, the ideology of the believer. When this isn't so, the "believes that E" format breaks down and even a reasonable degree of univocality of attribution may involve telling quite a long story.

Conclusion

I suppose that my polemical strategy must now be embarrassingly clear: Suppose – contrary to what the substitution test assumes – that difference of belief-state does *not* imply difference of belief-content. Then I'm prepared to accept practically anything that practically anyone has ever said about content attribution – even, if you like, that it's pragmatic, holistic, hermeneutic, Ich/Du-istic and so forth. Except that I claim that it's *belief-state* attribution and *not* content attribution that all that stuff is true of, and from truths about the one nothing much of interest follows about the other.

Thus, as we've seen, there are people who say that the substitution test is a test for content identity, and what I say is that they are almost right except that what it tests for is not identity of content but identity of belief-state. In similar spirit, there are such things as functional role semanticists, and they say that functional role makes content. And they are almost right because functional role does make belief-state; it's just that belief state doesn't make content, so content needn't be a functional notion even if belief-state is.

Or, again, there are Kuhnians out there, and they say that differences in cognitive background are sometimes tantamount to content differences. That's OK with me too, except that it's differences in belief-state that differences in cognitive background make and *not* differences in content, so it distinguishes my view from Kuhn's that I'm not committed to the "incommensurability" of radically different theories. The Greeks thought that stars are holes in the sky; I think that they are not. If theoretical background makes content, it's hard to see how the Greeks and I could agree about (e.g.) how many visible stars there are. But differences of theoretical background *don't* make differences of content; all there is to content is denotation.

On the other hand, differences of theory do (can), on my view, make differences of belief-state, so how does it come out of the story I've been telling that what I believe about the cardinality of the visible stars agrees with what the Greeks believed? All that's required for agreement is that the *propositional objects* of the belief-states are the same: If x believes that P and y believes that P, then x and y agree, *whether or not x and y are in the same belief-state*; and what they agree about is true *iff* it's the case that P. Similarly, if x believes that P and y believes that -P, then they disagree regardless of consideration of vehicles and roles; and x is right *iff* P and y is right *iff* -P. This is a reasonable way to assess disputes since what's at issue in a clash of beliefs is, after all, the truth of their propositional objects; and the identity of the propositional object of a belief-state is independent of its vehicle and functional role assuming that vehicle and functional role don't make content.

Also, there are Davidsonians out there, and Davidsonians say that the attribution of content is constrained by conditions of rationality. For example, we have to distinguish between O's believing that *J is not his mother* and his believing that *his mother is not his mother* on pain of uncharitably ascribing to O a belief that is manifestly self-contradictory *and thereby violating the very conditions of intentional ascription*.

Well, maybe Davidsonians are right too. Only, on my view the rationality conditions constrain *belief-state* attribution, not *content* attribution; and, once again, differences of belief-state don't make differences of content. This, surely, is the right end of the stick; it isn't remotely plausible that "principles of charity" constrain intentional attributions per se, however much they may be supposed to constrain attributions of belief-states. In particular, it couldn't conceivably be required that the *propositional objects* of all the attitudes attributed to a guy at a time should be to any extent mutually consistent: There's nothing wrong with hoping that P while fearing that not-P; and believing that P while wishing that not-P practically defines the human condition. If there are rationality constraints on propositional attitude attributions, they apply to relations among the attitudes, not to relations among their propositional objects.[9]

We can put all this in a nutshell: On my view, the most that the standard skeptical arguments about content actually show is that belief individuation is plausibly pragmatic and holistic. But this implies nothing about the individuation of content unless you accept "different beliefs → different propositional objects." Which I don't. What strikes me as especially attractive about this strategy is that it allows me to distinguish between two questions that are practically invariably confused in the philosophical literature: a question about the scientific status of *propositional attitude* psychology and a question about the scientific status of *intentional* psychology. A word about this to close the discussion.

The predictive and explanatory success of commonsense belief-desire psychology strikes me as the second most remarkable fact about the intellectual history of our species. (The first most remarkable fact about the intellectual history of our species is the predictive and explanatory success of commonsense middle-sized-object ontology.) For, here is this delicate and elaborate – and largely inexplicit – psychological theory that we seem, in several respects, to get for free: It is presumably prehistoric in origin; and it is culturally universal; and it is assimilated practically instantaneously and without explicit instruction by every normal child. And, by all reasonable empirical criteria, this theory that we seem to get for free appears to be *true*: Its predictive adequacy is not susceptible to serious doubt, and it has repeatedly proved superior to such rival theories as have sought to replace it (e.g., to behavioristic theories and to pie-in-the-sky neuroscience of the San Diego sort). So impressive are the successes of Grandmother Psychology that the rational strategy for an empirical approach to the mind is surely to co-opt its apparatus for service as explicit science. This has in fact been the strategy of modern intentional realists from Freud to Chomsky, and it seems to me perfectly obvious that it has produced all of the best psychology we've got. It would be barely hyperbolic to claim that it has produced all of the only psychology we've got.

But having said all these reactionary and antirevisionist things, I nevertheless want to distinguish between two versions of intentional realism: one of which is merely conservative, and the other of which is die-hard. The merely conservative view is that the best hope for psychology is the exploitation of intentional categories, just as Granny has always said. The die-hard line, by contrast, is that the intentional categories that we want for science ought to include belief, desire, and the other taxa of commonsense propositional attitudinizing. It's here that I (and, by the way, Freud and Chomsky) finally part company with Granny.

If much of what I've been saying about belief individuation is true, then the identity conditions for belief-states are vague and pragmatic in practice; perhaps they are ineliminably so. On the one hand, there are no guaranteed-univocal descriptors for picking them out. And, on the other, belief-state individuation appears to depend on the individuation of functional roles, and where are we to look for identity criteria for these? But we needn't care if it turns out that believing and desiring are ineliminably infected with vagueness and holism. A conservative intentional realist who is not a die-hard can contemplate with equanimity the abandonment of belief-desire psychology strictly so called, so long as the apparatus of intentional explanation is itself left intact. So, two take-home questions:

1. How much, if any, of the skeptical argumentation about Grand-mother psychology is effective against intentional realism *as opposed to belief/desire realism*?
2. How much, if any, of the predictive/explanatory success of Grand-mother psychology depends on *belief/desire* realism *as opposed to intentional realism*?

It would be a comfort to aging intentional realists like me if the answer to both these questions turned out to be: "None."

Notes

1 Putnam (1983) remarks (plausibly) that "determining the extension of a term always involves determining the extension of other terms" (p. 149). But of course it wouldn't follow that any term's *having* an extension depends on any other term's having one. Epistemic dependence is one thing, metaphysical dependence is quite another.
2 I'm talking in this funny, hyphenated way because it's important to my present purposes to avoid state/object ambiguities. "The belief that P" is notorious for equivocating between the *state of believing* that P and the *proposition* that P. I'm using "belief-state" to indicate the former.
3 It's not very self-evident that translation *is* a test for synonymy: Whereas synonymy is presumably an equivalence relation, "translates" is arguably intransitive, and transla-tions of the same expression need not translate one other. I make this point in light of the tendency of writers like Putnam, Davidson, and Quine to just take it for granted that the constraints (epistemic, metaphysical, whatever) on semantic theories can be just read off from constraints on theories of translation. However, I doubt that these general considerations about translation bear on the moral I want to draw from the Pierre case.
4 I can imagine somebody arguing that this isn't a bona fide failure of substitution on the grounds that since "London" is an English word and "Londres" is a French word, they can't contrast in the (English) frame "Pierre believes ... is pretty" or, mutatis mutandis, in the (French) frame "Pierre croit que ... est jolie." I say pooh to this. "Do you believe that Londres is pretty?" is a question that Pierre perfectly well understands and is perfectly well prepared to answer; the evidence that the form of words "Londres is pretty" expresses a belief that he holds is every bit as good as the evidence that the form of words "London is pretty" expresses a belief that he doesn't.
5 It goes without saying that this claim is made on behalf of state *types*, not state tokens. It will be the individuation of types rather than tokens that's at issue throughout the following discussion except where the contrary is explicit.

78   J. A. FODOR

6 If you're prepared to accept that encapsulated "subdoxastic" states qualify as bona fide belief-states, then they offer further cases where belief-states that are identical in content, vehicle, and format are distinguished by functional roles. For discussion, see Fodor 1986.

7 I'm claiming that you can have difference of functional role (hence belief-state) without difference of vehicle; but does it go the other way around as well? Otherwise, we can do without specifying vehicles in belief individuation; all we need is functional roles.

I'm inclined to think that Mates-type considerations show that there are at least some contexts in which you can slice belief states as thin as you can slice quotations. Since it's hard to imagine a useful criterion for individuation of functional roles that doesn't slice *them* pretty thick, it seems plausible that "vehicle" and "functional role" are, at least in principle, independent parameters in the individuation of beliefs.

8 I'm indebted to Barry Loewer for a discussion that prompted the preceding three paragraphs.

9 Correspondingly, according to the present view, questions of *rationality* are assessed with respect to the vehicle of a belief as well as its content, whereas questions of *truth* are assessed with respect to content alone (see above). It's because the vehicle of his belief that his mother was eligible was, say, "J is eligible" rather than, say, "Mother is eligible" that O's seeking to marry his mother was not irrational in face of his abhorrence of incest. (I've heard it claimed that this won't do because appeals to merely morpho-syntactic differences among vehicles *can't* rationalize differences in behavior; only appeals to differences in the *content* can do that. But the Pierre case looks to be a counterexample.)

References

Fodor, J. *Psychosemantics*. Cambridge, Mass.: MIT Press, 1986.

Putnam H. "Computational Psychology and Interpretation Theory." In *Realism and Reason. Philosophical Papers, Volume 3*. Cambridge: Cambridge University Press, 1983.

5

Meanings just ain't in the head

MICHAEL DEVITT

What makes my image of him into an image of *him*?

Wittgenstein (1953), p. 177

1. Introduction

The descriptive paradigm for theories of reference ruled unchallenged for decades. According to this paradigm, the reference of a term is determined by the descriptions that competent speakers associate with it. Around the end of the 1960s, a radical challenge was mounted, most notably by Saul Kripke and Hilary Putnam. The challenge saw description theories of reference for proper names and natural-kind terms as wrong not merely in details but in fundamentals. It proposed an alternative: the causal paradigm. According to this paradigm, the reference of a term is determined by an appropriate causal chain. With characteristic flair, Putnam coined what might be regarded as the slogan of this challenge: "Meanings just ain't in the head."

Like all new paradigms, the causal paradigm was particularly vulnerable to criticism in its early days. And like all new paradigms it received plenty. Despite this, the causal paradigm slowly but surely gained ground. The re-establishment of the old order clearly called for a more sustained response.

Gareth Evans gave one such response in *The Varieties of Reference* (1982). He makes a significant concession to the causal paradigm: an appropriate causal link to an object is *necessary* for singular reference

Earlier versions of this essay were papers delivered in Brisbane in August 1987 at the Annual Conference of the Australasian Association of Philosophers, and in Cincinnati in April 1988 at the Central Division Convention of the American Philosophical Association. Section 7, and the changes it necessitated elsewhere, are largely the result of a stimulating discussion in Cincinnati. In particular, the section has been heavily influenced by the criticisms of Michael McKinsey (unpublished). The comments of Ray Elugardo were helpful to the discussion of objection (1). Objection (2) was partly prompted by remarks of Michael McDermott in discussing his 1986. Finally, I am indebted to Fiona Cowie, David Lewis, and Ruth Millikan for other suggestions that led to improvements.

in many cases. He would accept Putnam's slogan. However, Evans thinks that the causal link is never *sufficient*. He attempts to reinstate a central tenet of the descriptive paradigm: To think "about an object, one must *know which* object is in question" (p. 65); one must have *"discriminating knowledge"* of the object (p. 89).

Evans hopes for the best of both worlds. John Searle has no interest in such ecumenicalism. His aim in *Intentionality* (1983) is to take us back to the old world. He rejects Putnam's slogan: Meanings *are* in the head. He is dismissive, even contemptuous, of causal theories of reference.

I have criticized Evans's response at length elsewhere (1985). In this essay, I shall criticize Searle's response.

Searle has become well known for his attack on contemporary cognitive science, an attack he launched with his ingenious Chinese-room fantasy (1980a and b; 1981; 1984). We shall see that his rejection of Putnam's slogan is central to that attack.

2. Putnam's slogan

Putnam's slogan concludes a discussion of three now-famous examples in "The Meaning of 'Meaning'" (in Putnam 1975).[1] He is concerned with two assumptions of traditional semantics:

    (I) That knowing the meaning of a term is just a matter of being in a certain psychological state

    (II) That the meaning of a term (in the sense of 'intension') determines its extension (in the sense that sameness of intension entails sameness of extension). (p. 219)

(The extension of a term is, of course, its reference.) Putnam aims to show that "these two assumptions are not jointly satisfied by *any* notion, let alone any notion of meaning" (p. 219).

He establishes first that if the meaning of a term determines its extension then so also must *knowing* its meaning (pp. 221–2). So it follows from assumptions (I) and (II) that a psychological state determines the extension. Putnam's three examples are to show that psychological states do not determine extension.

The first example is about the meaning of 'water' on Earth and Twin Earth (pp. 223–5); the second is about the meaning of 'aluminum' and 'molybdenum' on Earth and Twin Earth (pp. 225–6); the third is about Putnam's use of 'elm' and 'beech' (pp. 226–7). We need only discuss the first. It is so well known that I shall be brief.

We are to consider the use of the word 'water' by Oscar on Earth and by Twin Oscar on Twin Earth in 1750, before the chemical composition of water was known. Twin Earth is exactly like Earth except that the liquid on it with all the superficial properties of water is not H_2O but XYZ. Twin Oscar is an exact duplicate of Oscar. Putnam claims that when Oscar uses 'water' he refers to H_2O, that is, to real water, but when Twin Oscar uses 'water' he refers to XYZ, that is, to what we might call 'Twin water'. Yet Oscar and Twin Oscar are in the same psychological state, for they are duplicates. So their psychological states do not determine the extension of 'water'.

Crucial to understanding this claim is Putnam's stipulation that the psychological states in question are "narrow": that is, they are states according with the assumption of "methodological solipsism." Such a state does not presuppose "the existence of any individual other than the subject to whom that state is ascribed" (p. 220). The idea is that narrow psychological states are entirely supervenient on the intrinsic inner states of the individual; the individual does not have the states in virtue of its relation to anything else, in particular, not in virtue of its relation to environmental causes or effects of the states. Putnam rightly thinks that methodological solipsism is an assumption of the tradition he is criticizing.

The importance of this stipulation to Putnam's claim is clear. It is easy to find "wide" psychological states that can plausibly be thought to determine extension. For example, Oscar's intention in using 'water' is to refer to water, whereas Twin Oscar's is to refer to Twin water. These intentions differ in having different intentional objects. It is plausible to think that such intentions do determine extension. However, they are wide psychological states. Indeed, Putnam is arguing not only that narrow psychological states do not determine extension, but also that they do not determine the intentional objects of thought. Oscar and Twin Oscar have identical narrow states and those states do not determine either intentional object or extension.

Putnam concludes his discussion of the three examples: "Cut the pie any way you like, 'meanings' just ain't in the *head*!" (p. 227).

3. Consequences of the slogan

All the terms treated by Putnam in this discussion are natural-kind terms. However, the discussion has general implications that Putnam brought out in a later book, *Reason, Truth and History* (1981).[2] He raises there the Wittgensteinian questions: "How on earth can one thing represent (or 'stand for', etc.) a different thing?" "How can

thought reach out and 'grasp' what is external?" (p. 2). Putnam emphasizes, with the help of a vivid discussion of brains in vats (pp. 5–17), that
"thought words and mental pictures do not *intrinsically* represent what
they are about" (p. 5). If you were a brain in a vat, you could not think
that you were, for to think that you were you need to be causally linked
to brains and vats in a way that a brain in a vat is not. Even if the
words, "I am a brain in a vat," were to run through your mind, they
would not mean *I am a brain in a vat*.[3] To suppose otherwise is to
suppose that the brain's system of representation has "an *intrinsic*,
built-in, magical connection with what it represents" (p. 5); it is to
believe in "magical theories of reference" (p. 3). There is nothing in my
head that makes my image of him into an image of *him*.

Putnam's discussion helps to bring out something that I am fond of
emphasizing:[4] the essential incompleteness of description theories of
reference. A description theory explains the referential properties
of one category of term by appeal to those of other categories. This
cannot be the whole story. To complete the story, we need an explanation of the referential properties of those other categories. Perhaps
description theories can be used again. But this process cannot go on
forever: There must be some basic terms whose referential properties
are not parasitic on others. Otherwise, language as a whole is cut loose
from the world. The ultimate explanation of reference cannot be by a
description theory.

Consider an example. A description theory might explain the reference of the natural-kind term 'tiger' by appeal to its association with
the description 'large carnivorous quadrupedal feline, tawny yellow in
color with blackish transverse stripes and white belly'. Suppose that the
theory is right. How does it explain the reference of 'tiger'? The answer
is that 'tiger' refers to tigers because the associated description refers to
them. But then in virtue of what does that description refer to tigers?
Its reference cannot be taken for granted. To explain that reference we
need a theory for each of the description's contained terms. Perhaps a
description theory will work for one of them. It will rest on another
description whose reference cannot be taken for granted. So more
theories of reference will be required. In the end, we must look for
something other than a description theory, because *description theories
simply pass the referential buck*. The buck must stop somewhere with a
different sort of theory.

One should not need Putnam's discussion to see that description
theories are incomplete. However, that discussion does drive the point
home dramatically. The explanatory power of description theories comes
from their appeal to the associations of one term with another, for

example, the association of 'tiger' with the above description. These associations are entirely in the heads of speakers and so *could not* be complete explanations of reference. Description theories are not only incomplete, they are looking in the wrong place for the ultimate explanation of reference. For that explanation we must look also to what is outside the head.

What sort of relation between a speaker and the external world *could* determine reference? From a naturalistic viewpoint, there is only one possibility: a causal relation. We have a "transcendental argument" for the causal paradigm!

The idea that psychological states do not determine reference, like many of the best ideas, seems obvious once it is pointed out. *How could* something inside the head determine reference, which is a relation to particular things outside the head? Nothing internal and intrinsic to an object could ever determine such a relation. Consider some examples. (1) Yvonne is playing netball and receives a pass from Raelene. In virtue of what was the pass reception from Raelene in particular? Nothing internal to Yvonne determined that property. It was in virtue of what Raelene did to the ball that Yvonne caught. (2) Norm is Bruce's son. In virtue of what? Nothing internal to Norm determines that he is the son of Bruce in particular. It is because of what Bruce did to Dawn many years ago that Norm has that property. To suppose that these relational properties of Yvonne and Norm are internal is to have magical theories of passing and fathering. Similarly, to suppose that one's thoughts can reach out to particular objects outside the mind is to have magical theories of reference and intentionality.

Putnam does not offer this general argument that meanings cannot be in the head, but it is in the spirit of *Reason, Truth and History*. It turns out to have interesting problems, as do also Twin Earth arguments. (See Section 7 of this essay.)

I have been emphasizing the consequences of Putnam's slogan. It is important to notice some things that are *not* consequences.

First, it is not a consequence that *no* aspect of meaning is in the head. The point of the slogan is simply to deny that meanings are *entirely* in the head. In my view, the meaning of a term is likely to involve many psychological states; so the brain in the vat can have a rich set of proto-thoughts (1989a). The slogan emphasizes that extra-cranial links to reality are also necessary for meaning.

Second, the slogan does not commit one to a theory of "direct reference". The direct-reference theory of names is the view that there is no more meaning or content to a name than its referent. Searle finds the view incomprehensible (1983, p. 220). I sympathize. Yet this curious view has been associated with the causal paradigm by friend and foe alike.[5] My attempts in several publications to break this association seem to have failed.[6] The slogan is quite compatible with the idea that a term has a sense that determines the term's reference. What the slogan denies is that any such sense can be explained solely in terms of what is in the head.

Third, it is not a consequence that any particular description theory of reference is false. One could even adopt the slogan while holding to a description theory of natural-kind terms. Although the Twin Earth discussion shows that this would be a mistake, in my view, it certainly does not show that some other terms are not dependent on associated descriptions for reference; 'pediatrician' is a likely candidate for one that is so dependent.[7] This buck passing does not matter provided the referential buck finally stops with some terms that are explained by a causal theory.

Fourth, accepting the slogan does not involve acceptance of any currently available causal theory of reference. Indeed, all available theories, including my own, seem to me to have severe problems (Devitt and Sterelny 1987, pp. 63–5, 72–9). But these problems are no excuse for giving up the causal paradigm and resorting to magic.

I shall argue that Searle does resort to magic.

4. Searle's response

Chapter 8 of *Intentionality* (1983) is titled, "Are Meanings in the Head?" Searle's answer is an emphatic "Yes."

Searle starts by emphasizing that the question of the relation of language to reality – reference – reduces to the question of the relation of mind to reality – Intentionality (1983, p. 197).[8] He offers an account that is "internalist" in that it is in virtue of "some mental state in the head" (p. 198) that the Intentional, and hence the referential, relation holds: "The internal operations of the brain are causally sufficient for the phenomena"; "if I were a brain in a vat I could have exactly the same mental states I have now" (1980b, p. 452).

Searle describes the view that he rejects as follows:

The speaker's internal Intentional content is insufficient to determine what he is referring to, either in his thoughts or in his utterances. ...we need to introduce (for some? for all? cases) external contextual, non-conceptual, causal relations between the utterances of expressions and the features of the world that the utterance is about. (1983, p. 199)

Searle has described, with characteristic clarity, the view of Putnam that I have been outlining and defending. (The answer to Searle's parenthetical question is that *all* words require external causal relations, either directly, or indirectly via the words they depend on for their reference.)

Searle discusses various reasons that he thinks have led people to reject the internalist view. I shall consider only his discussion of the reasons I have drawn from Putnam. And I shall consider only what I take to be essential to Searle's response.

One way that Putnam draws the moral of his Twin Earth example is as follows: "Words like 'water' have an unnoticed indexical component" (1975, p. 234). We can capture this aspect of Putnam's theory of meaning in the following ostensive definition:

> 'Water' refers to x if and only if x is the same (liquid) as *this* (pointing to water).

So what 'water' refers to as the result of a definition of this sort depends on what the indexical 'this' refers to (pp. 229–34). Searle points out, quite rightly, that the definition substitutes an indexical Intentional content for "the traditional cluster-of-concepts Intentional content" (1983, p. 204). So Putnam's definition will support his slogan only if indexical contents are not in the head.

Searle thinks that indexical contents are in the head. There is something intrinsic and internal to the mental state of someone using the definition that "sets certain conditions which any potential sample has to meet if it is to be part of the extension of 'water'" (p. 206). Searle calls such conditions, "conditions of satisfaction."

Putnam would deny that an indexical Intentional content is internal, as Searle notes (p. 205). Indeed, Putnam thinks that indexicals provide "trivial" counterexamples to the idea that what goes on inside our heads determines meaning and reference (1981, p. 22). Suppose that Oscar and Twin Oscar are in the identical narrow mental state of having the above ostensive definition running through their minds. According to Putnam, their states will nevertheless have different Intentional contents. That difference is explained by things external to the mind: the fact that Oscar's indexical arose from causal interaction with water, whereas Twin Oscar's arose from causal interaction with Twin water. Using Searle's terminology, Putnam's view is that the states have different conditions of satisfaction, and different Intentional contents, determined by external causal relations.

Putnam's mistake, Searle claims, is to assume that because narrow mental states are the same, they cannot determine different conditions of satisfaction and different Intentional contents (pp. 206–7). Searle (1983) thinks that there is something in the head that determines a state's content, even an indexical content. Furthermore he thinks that Oscar and Twin Oscar, having identical mental states, visual experiences, and other experiences, in using the definition, nevertheless have different Intentional contents, *and those contents are internal and intrinsic to the mental states* (p. 22).

This is prima facie mysterious. If the states are internally the same how can they have different internal contents? How can narrow states determine Intentional content? Searle's answer draws heavily on his account of perception in Chapter 2 of *Intentionality*. For, the Intentional content of the indexical 'this,' hence the Intentional content of the ostensive definition, includes the Intentional content of the visual experience that accompanies the definition. So we must consider Searle's account of visual experience.

Searle believes that a visual experience has an intrinsic Intentional content. "Internal to each phenomenon is an Intentional content that determines its conditions of satisfaction" (p. 40). Indeed "the phenomenal properties" of the experience determine its conditions of satisfaction (p. 61). This makes vivid the sense in which the Intentional content is, for Searle, intrinsic and internal to the experience: It is phenomenological, just as the feeling of a sensation is phenomenological.

The content of an experience is always propositional for Searle. "Visual experience is never simply *of* an object but rather it must always be *that* such and such is the case" (p. 40). So the content must be expressed by a sentence. Searle's favorite example is seeing a yellow station wagon. Its content is given by:

> There is a yellow station wagon there and that there is a yellow station wagon there is causing the visual experience. (p. 48)

A crucial feature of this, both for his account of visual experience and for his view that meanings are in the head, is that the content is "self-referential":

The Intentional content of the visual experience requires as part of the conditions of satisfaction that the visual experience be caused by the rest of its conditions of satisfaction, that is, by the state of affairs perceived. (p. 48)

The experience "figures in its own conditions of satisfaction" (p. 49).

So, according to Searle, the visual experience has an Intentional content – a way the world seems phenomenologically – that specifies as a condition of satisfaction that a certain worldly condition caused that very experience. The experience is veridical if there is such a worldly condition that did cause the experience; otherwise, it is illusory. And a particular yellow station wagon is the object of experience if it did, as a matter of fact, cause the experience. Something internal to the experience determines that the car is its Intentional object.

Both Searle and Putnam think that the car's role in causing the experience is important to its being the Intentional object, but they make it important in very different ways. For Putnam the causal role is important because it determines that the car is the Intentional object, thus determining the Intentional content. (The determination may be only partial if previous sightings of the car play a role in determining the content. I shall ignore this complication.) It is "essential" to Searle's account that the causal role have a different importance: The role is *represented* in the Intentional content (p. 48). The content specifies that the object playing that causal role is the Intentional object, thus determining that the car that in fact played that role is the Intentional object. Briefly, Putnam thinks that the car determines the Intentional content; Searle thinks that the Intentional content determines that the car is the Intentional object. More briefly still:

> Putnam: Object determines content.
> Searle: Content determines object.

Putnam and Searle have things the opposite way round.

The distinction between the two views is a little difficult, just as the use/mention distinction in the philosophy of language is. Where Searle thinks that the Intentional content's "mention" of the causal role of the object is determining, Putnam thinks the causal role itself is determining. The distinction is vital because though it may be possible to think that the mention of the causal role of the object is in the head, it should be impossible to think that the causal role itself is.

The distinction needs to be kept firmly in mind in reading Searle because he often writes in ways that blur it. Thus he talks of the presence and features of the object that causes the visual experience "enter[ing] into the Intentional content" (p. 48); he says that "the relationship of causation is part of the content" (p. 124; see also pp. 66, 241); and that various "contextual elements" that Putnam would regard as having a role in determining reference "are part of the Intentional content" (p. 212). Now what are actually parts of the content, according to Searle, are not objects, causation, and contextual elements themselves, but *representations* of them. According to the Putnam view it is the objects, causation, and contextual elements that play the determining role, not the representations of them in Intentional content.

Searle immediately draws a consequence from his discussion of visual experience that is the basis for his later rejection of Putnam's slogan.

Two 'phenomenologically' identical experiences can have different contents because each experience is self-referential. Thus, for example, suppose two

identical twins have type-identical visual experiences while looking at two
different but type-identical station wagons at the same time in type-identical
lighting conditions and surrounding contexts. Still, the conditions of satisfaction
can be different. Twin number one requires a station wagon causing his visual
experience and twin number two requires a station wagon causing his numeri-
cally different visual experience. Same phenomenology; different contents and
therefore different conditions of satisfaction. (p. 50)

We can now return to the ostensive definition of 'water'. A visual
experience accompanies that definition; in particular it accompanies the
use of the indexical 'this'. A straightforward application of the above
account yields the following statement of the content of that experience:

> There is some stuff there and that there is some stuff there is causing this
> visual experience.

This content is contained in the Intentional content of the whole
definition (pp. 207, 225–7). It is because it is so contained that the
identical mental states of Oscar and Twin Oscar can have different
internal Intentional contents. Oscar's Intentional content specifies the
cause of his experience; Twin Oscar specifies the cause of his numeri-
cally different experience. And because of this difference in content, the
states have different Intentional objects: The object of Oscar's is water
because water caused his experience; the object of Twin Oscar's is Twin
water because Twin water caused his experience.

This concludes my account of Searle's response to Putnam's slogan.
In the next section, I shall consider the bearing of that response on two
controversies involving Searle. In the following sections I shall criticize
Searle's response.

5. Applications: proper names; cognitive science

Proper names

Putnam's slogan is linked to causal theories of reference and the
critique of description theories, as I noted in Section 1. Searle was one
of the founders of the modern description, or "cluster," theory of
names in his classic paper, "Proper Names" (1959). Saul Kripke (1972)
and Keith Donnellan (1972) subjected this theory to severe criticisms
and suggested the causal alternative. Searle is not impressed. He
devotes a chapter of *Intentionality* (1983, Chapter 9) to telling us why.

Searle has a number of objections to the causal theory, but the fundamental one arises from the following view of the issue:

Do proper names refer by setting *internal* conditions of satisfaction... or do proper names refer in virtue of some *external* causal relation? (p. 233)

From this perspective, Searle argues that *even where causal theorists are otherwise right* about names,[9] they are wrong in claiming that they have shown description theories to be false. Indeed, what causal theorists are really offering, despite their misleading claims to the contrary, is another version of the description theory. They are offering an internalist view, not a view that makes reference depend on external causal relations.

Searle's line of argument rests entirely on his case against Putnam's slogan. Thus, Searle points out that the causal account of the ostensive introduction of a name makes reference depend on the Intentional content of perception (pp. 234, 240–1). This, we have noted, he thinks to be internal. He has a similar response to the causal theory of how people get their reference with a name from others in communication situations (the theory of "reference borrowing," pp. 244–6), and to some well-known objections to the description theory (pp. 250–5).

In brief, the center of Searle's argument against causal theories of names rests on the case, outlined in the last section, for meanings being in the head.

Cognitive science

Using his famous Chinese-room fantasy, Searle has caused a stir by dismissing contemporary cognitive science in general and the computational theory of the mind in particular (1980a; b). His claim is not just the relatively plausible one that no computer program has come close to capturing Intentionality yet. He claims that it is *impossible* for a program to capture it; the project of finding the right program is "doomed from the start" (1984, p. 39).

His initial case (1980a) can be put briefly: Programs are purely formal and syntactic, whereas Intentional states have content and semantics. This is a good point, but it only counts against a rather naive cognitivism, as the peer commentary on Searle's case showed. Sophisticated cognitivists would claim that the computer running the program has to be linked up to the world before it can have Intentionality; the semantics Searle demands comes from that linkup.[10] Searle, however, rejects even this more sophisticated cognitivism (1980b, pp. 452–4; 1984,

pp. 34–5). The basis of Searle's rejection comes down to his argument
for meanings being in the head. That argument is the core of his case
against anything but rather naive cognitivism.

We must now return to the main issue: Putnam's slogan.

6. Searle's magic

The lines are drawn. What Putnam thinks trivially true, and I think
obviously true, Searle thinks false. My main aim is to argue that Searle's
view of meaning, reference, and Intentionality is magical. That will be
the concern of this section and the next. It seems to me relatively easy
to argue, but I have another aim that is more difficult: to bring out the
dualistic and vitalistic elements in Searle's thinking. These elements
underlie his rejection of Putnam, causal theories of names, and cognitive science. They will be the concern of Section 8, but I will begin this
one with some brief words foreshadowing the later discussion.

The dualistic element is to be found in Searle's attitude to the
Wittgensteinian question: In virtue of what does a mental state have its
particular Intentional content, a content that specifies certain conditions of satisfaction? To dismiss this question is to take it as simply a
brute fact of the world that the mental state does have that content.
This as a sort of dualism. It need not be a dualism about entities, but it
must be at least a dualism about properties – "Dual Aspect" theory. It
supposes that a mental state's property of having a certain content
cannot be explained in more basic physical terms. Searle does *not quite*
dismiss the question, and so he is not straightforwardly dualist. However, he comes close to dismissing it, and his only response to it is an
unsatisfactory appeal to biology, an appeal that amounts to a sort of
vitalism.

The magic is to be found in his view that the property of having a
certain content is internal and intrinsic to the mind. Intentional content
is not only inexplicable, it is in the head.

Dualism and vitalism may be magic enough for most people. However, it is important to see that Searle's rejection of Putnam's slogan
requires a higher level of magic. Consider orgasms. Some "qualia
freaks" will insist that orgasms have phenomenological properties that
cannot be explained physically. That's dualism. But the qualia freak is
not committed, as Searle is, to a mental state having intrinsic properties
that reach out and grasp things that are outside the head. That's real
magic.

We have seen that the disagreement between Putnam and Searle
comes down to one over the Intentional content of visual experience.

According to Searle, the content of Oscar's visual experience specifies that water is the Intentional object. The content specifies this because it is given by

> There is some stuff there and that there is some stuff there is causing this visual experience;

and water is the stuff causing the experience. So, it is because of that content that Oscar's brain reaches out and grasps water.

According to Searle we *give* the Intentional content of a visual experience with a sentence, but what *is* the content? The simple answer would be that it actually is a sentence. Various remarks of Searle's (1983, pp. 12, 40, 49) suggest that this would not be his answer. Nevertheless, it will help our discussion to start by supposing that it is his answer.

On this supposition, as Oscar has his visual experience, a whole lot of words are running through his brain. Now *if we assume* that each bit of this brain writing has the appropriate meaning and hence reference, we can see how the brain reaches out and grasps water. Part of the content of Oscar's experience is a brain word meaning the same as the English word 'stuff' and hence referring to stuff; another part, a word meaning the same as 'cause' and hence referring to causation; and a third part, words meaning the same as 'this visual experience' and hence referring to the visual experience itself. Because of these referential properties, and others, and the way the brain words are put together into a sentence, the sentence picks out water as the Intentional object.

The problem with this explanation lies, of course, in its assumption. By virtue of what do brain words mean *stuff*, *causation*, and *this visual experience*, and hence have the appropriate referential properties? Searle gives no answer. For him these properties of brain words are simply brute facts. Let us waive the problem of how some brain words manage to refer to the visual experience. The experience is in the brain and so this referential relation is at least internal to the brain. In virtue of what does one brain word refer to stuff and another to causality, instances of which are mostly external to the brain? How can something inside the head refer to something outside the head? Searle sees no problem: It just does. That's the real magic.

Consider the brain word that refers to stuff. What relates that bit of the brain referentially to stuff rather than to electricity, kangaroos, Mars, or indeed, to causation or nothing at all? No phenomenological property of the brain can do that. For there can be nothing intrinsic to Oscar's body, hence nothing intrinsic to his brain, that determines this referential relation to something external, anymore than there can be something intrinsic to Yvonne's body that determines her pass-reception relation to Raelene; or than there can be something intrinsic to Norm's body that determines his filial relation to Bruce. The relational properties of something are not internal to it.

I have relied here on my general argument about relational properties: Nothing inside an object is alone sufficient to determine its relation to something outside it. Can we produce also a Twin Earth argument? It is difficult to do so because it is difficult to say what Twin stuff and Twin causation might be. However, here is an attempt with Twin causation.

Suppose, as Searle does, that causation is a non-Humean relation. When Oscar thinks 'cause' here on Earth, he refers to that relation. When Twin Oscar thinks 'cause' on Twin Earth he appears to refer to a relation with all the superficial characteristics of causation. However, on closer inspection it turns out that Twin causation is different from causation: It is Humean; there is nothing more to it than constant conjunction. So although Oscar and Twin Oscar are in the same narrow psychological state in having their visual experiences, their brain word 'cause' has different referents.[11] Nothing in the head is sufficient to determine the reference of 'cause'.[12]

The magic reappears in Searle's account of *Intentional causation*. This is his name for the causal relation that features in explanations "having to do with human mental, states, experiences, and actions" (1983, pp. 117–19). So the relation between Oscar's visual experience and certain stuff is one of Intentional causation.

In cases of Intentional causation, the cause and effect are "*logically related ... regardless of how they are described*" (p. 121; my emphasis). The idea of such logical relations in nature is rather shocking. Searle believes in them because in every case of Intentional causation "there is an Intentional content that is causally related to its conditions of satisfaction" (p. 121). He notes that this "cuts across the distinction between the Intentional content and the natural world" (p. 74). Consider the case of Oscar's visual experience. This experience is causally related to certain stuff. Searle thinks there is also a logical relation between the experience and the stuff because the experience, however described, has an Intentional content that specifies conditions of satisfaction requiring that the stuff, however described, caused that very experience. So the shocking logical relation arises because of the magical power of a mental state to reach out to its own cause.

Searle thinks that part of what has prevented philosophers seeing Intentionality his way is that they have a Humean theory of causation (p. 65). My criticism does not rest on a Humean theory nor indeed on any theory. I can go along with much of Searle's interesting discussion of causation. In particular, I am not committed to denying that "every experience of perceiving or acting is precisely an experience of causa-tion" (pp. 123–4). The part of Searle's view that I do deny is that there is something intrinsic to an experience that makes it represent causa-tion; that it is in virtue of satisfying the internal content of the experience that the causal relation is the particular one referred to.[13]

I have been supposing that not only do we *give* the Intentional content of an experience with a sentence but that it *is* a sentence. However, the evidence suggests that Searle may not suppose this, as I have indicated. The essence of the supposition is that the content is a complex representation: It has parts that have content, and these parts are arranged in a syntactic structure to yield the whole content. This supposition strikes me as the most plausible way to take Searle's notion of content. It has the consequence, for example, that the representation accompanying a person's visual experience when seeing a yellow station wagon has a part in common with that accompanying his experience when seeing a yellow submarine: a representation of yellow. It also has a part that differs: a representation of a station wagon.

Note that it is not essential to the supposition that we call the parts of the representation 'words' nor that we call the reference-determining properties of the parts 'meanings'. Searle objects to applying the term 'meaning' to Intentional states (p. 28), but I take that to be simply a verbal point.

Dropping the supposition is certainly a possibility. There are many examples of simple representations with complex contents, for example, a naval flag that means *there is yellow fever on this ship*. But dropping the supposition is no help to Searle. His account requires that there be *something* in Oscar's brain during his visual experience that is a repre-sentation with the content *there is some stuff there and that there is some stuff there is causing this visual experience*; and because of this content the representation specifies a whole state of affairs including water. My supposition has the small advantage of reducing the problem of explain-ing the content of this representation to that of explaining the contents of its parts. Without the supposition, Searle would be telling us that Oscar's brain state has that complicated content and we can say absolutely nothing about how it does. It cannot be analyzed or ex-plained. It simply reaches out and grasps water, and that's that. In other words, if we drop the supposition, the resort to magic comes earlier.

Indeed, if we are going to drop the supposition, the content of Oscar's experience would be much more appropriately expressed in the following simple way:

> There is some water there.

Searle's more complicated expression suggests that the content specifies water because parts of the content specify stuff, causality, and the visual experience itself. Yet if the supposition is dropped, this is not so and the complicated expression is thoroughly misleading. Once the content is expressed in the simple form, the flaw in Searle's response to Putnam is obvious. It assumes precisely what is in question: that the mental state of thinking 'water' has the intrinsic power to reach out and grasp water (rather than Twin water).

In Section 4, I pointed out that Putnam and Searle have things the opposite way round. Searle's way is exactly the wrong way. It is our interaction with the world that determines that we have mental states that refer to parts of that world and hence have Intentional contents. It is not the internal Intentional contents of mental states that determine that those states refer to parts of the world.

7. Saving Searle?

Two objections to this discussion might seem to be ways of saving Searle.

1. My general argument could be summed up:

> Nothing internal in, and intrinsic to, the body can determine a relation to an object outside the body.

> Intentional content does determine a relation to an object outside the body.

> So, Intentional content is not internal and intrinsic to the body.

The following objection might be made: "Consider the water solubility of salt. Isn't it something internal in, and intrinsic to, salt that determines its relation to something external and hence falsifies the first premise of this argument? Note that salt would have this dispositional property even if there were no water: Having that property does not presuppose the existence of anything other than the salt. So if knowledge of meaning were a disposition, it could satisfy the constraint of methodological solipsism and be in the head, and yet still determine a relation to something external."

First response: The objection is right that water solubility does not presuppose the existence of water. Nevertheless, that solubility is not internal in, and not intrinsic to, salt. For, salt is soluble in water not only by virtue of its own nature but also by virtue of the nature of water. What is intrinsic to the salt is the disposition to dissolve given certain stimuli, whether caused by water or whatever.

Despite this, the objection still has force. Consider the sense in which meanings are in the head according to the tradition Putnam is criticizing. There is supposed to be something in the head that, *given the way the world is*, determines that some part of that world is the Intentional object. In Searle's terminology, what is in the head determines a condition of satisfaction and the Intentional object is whatever, as a matter of worldly fact, satisfies that condition. In characterizing the tradition, Putnam explains his use of 'determines': "Sameness of intension entails sameness of extension" (1975, p. 219). Obviously, it is sameness of intension *in the same world* that is doing the entailing.

In the light of this, taking knowledge of meaning to be a disposition like solubility is indeed a way of avoiding my general argument. Given the way the world is, particularly the way water is, something internal in salt determines that it is soluble in water: Water, as a matter of fact, "satisfies" the internally determined "conditions of satisfaction" of the disposition.

If meanings are dispositions, we need to know what sort of dispositions they are. What is Oscar disposed to *do* as a result of knowing the meaning of a term? What is the meaning analogue of dissolving in water? The natural answer seems to be: *recognizing* the referent. This verificationist path is of course the one taken by many who were part of the tradition, most notably by Carnap and the positivists. It has well-known problems as a theory of meaning.

Perhaps, however, we can avoid verificationism or, at least, avoid falling quickly into a crude version. If the view that meanings are dispositional states answers the general argument, then so also must the view that meanings are functional states. Functional states differ from dispositional ones in being defined by reference to other states as well as to peripheral stimuli and responses. So there may be a complicated story to tell about what Oscar is disposed to do with respect to the referent as a result of knowing the meaning. It is not obvious that this story must be entirely verificationist.

The objection is successful against the general argument, but it is not one that Searle can embrace. He thinks that meaning lies in the phenomenological character of experience. He would reject the dispositional or functional view of meaning on which the objection depends (Section 8).

Second response: Although this objection avoids the general argument, it does not avoid the Twin Earth argument. Nothing intrinsic to salt is sufficient to make it the case that it is soluble in water *rather than in Twin water*, or than in anything else that can supply the appropriate stimuli. No disposition in the head is sufficient to make it the case that 'cause' and 'stuff' refer to causation and stuff rather than anything else tha can supply the appropriate stimuli.

This discussion is interesting for the comparison of the causal-historical theory of reference, favored by Putnam and Kripke, with the causal-dispositional theory of reference favored by Fred Dretske (1981) and other "information-theoretic" semanticists. The examples of Yvonne and Norm are good analogues for reference if the causal-historical theory is right, whereas the example of solubility is a good analogue if the causal-dispositional theory is right. The causal-dispositional theory, with its talk of the reliable correlation of a representation and its referent, is a return to some sort of verificationism.

2. The first objection strikes at only the general argument against meanings being in the head. The next strikes at both this argument and the Twin Earth argument. And it does so using Putnam's very own causal-historical theory of reference. Consider what determines the reference of a basic (nondescriptive) term like 'water' according to that theory. It is determined by two facts:

(i) The nature of the samples demonstrated in ostensive definitions of 'water'
(ii) Which objects share that nature

(ii) "projects" the reference of 'water' from the sample to the full extension. As a result of (ii), the reference of 'water' will vary from possible world to possible world without any change in its meaning; it will refer to whatever water there happens to be in each world. Facts of sort (ii) are obviously not in the head. However, this mind independence is *not* the significant respect in which meanings are not in the head. I have just emphasized that the tradition Putnam is attacking accepts that what is in the head determines reference only relative to the facts about what there is in the world. The significant respect in which meanings are not in the head, according to Putnam, is that nothing in the head is sufficient to determine reference even given those facts. For, to determine that reference, (i) is required, and (i) involves a relation to something outside the head, namely, water.

Now the objection: "Notice that on Putnam's own theory, reference is not determined by what is in the head – in the significant respect – *only because the samples of water mentioned in (i) are not in the head*. It would be crazy to say that they were in the head. However, suppose that we follow Searle in thinking that 'water' is not a basic term but rather a descriptive one dependent for its reference on other terms, which are basic; for example, the terms 'stuff', 'cause', and 'this visual experience'. You have already conceded that the reference of 'this visual experience' may be determined by what is in the head. Why should we not suppose further that the references of 'stuff' and 'cause' are fixed by ostensive definitions relating them to *samples of stuff and causation in the head*? These definitions would supply the facts of type (i) needed for reference, and these facts *would be* in the head. So, despite the general argument and the Twin Earth argument, meanings could be in the head. Of course, the determination of reference also requires facts of type (ii). These facts enable 'cause' to refer to all instances that share the nature of the internal reference-determining samples. These facts, varying from world to world, are certainly mostly outside the head. But that is not significant for the present dispute. Putnam has shown that meaning is not intrinsic to the symbol, but that does not show that it is not intrinsic to the head."

Response: I agree that this objection does circumvent the arguments in this essay. It has problems of its own, however. First the objection requires that the description theory of reference exemplified in its discussion of 'water' is correct and can be generalized to cover all nonbasic terms. This seems very dubious. Second, and more important, the objection depends on it being the case that the basic terms according to this theory of reference – terms like 'stuff' and 'cause' – really do get their reference from internal ostensive definitions. With our inner eye we notice some token mental stuff, and a token of one mental item causing another, and use what we notice in ostensive definitions that fix reference: Reference is to tokens, including very many outside the mind, that share the nature of these mental samples. Perhaps this view is not crazy. The absence of a plausible theory of reference for 'stuff' and 'cause' makes it hard to give a decisive response to it. Nevertheless, the view is a highly implausible return to Cartesianism.

Searle's view of meaning, with its emphasis on phenomenology, does have a Cartesian ring to it (on which more below), but it is nothing like the Cartesianism of this objection. There is no sign that Searle would want to save himself this way.

In sum, objection (1) could save Searle from my general argument at the risk of verificationism, but it could not save him from the Twin Earth argument. Objection (2) could save him from both arguments at the price of a highly implausible Cartesianism. However, Searle would not accept either objection. So I take the conclusions of the preceding section to stand. Searle's theory of Intentionality ascribes to the mind a power that is unique in nature, a magical power. That is my main charge, but I also think that Searle's view has dualistic and vitalist elements. Demonstrating this is not so easy.

8. Searle's dualism and vitalism

Searle acknowledges hardly any need to explain Intentional content. It is in this that I see the dualism.

Searle is well aware, of course, that an explanation of Intentional content is a central part of the causal theories of Putnam and others. He is scornful of such explanations. His objection to them is that they are from "a third-person point of view" whereas the problem is "a first-person internal" one. We need to know "what is it about the experience" that makes one object and not another the Intentional object (1983, p. 63). We need an account of the conditions in which the person "*takes himself* to be seeing," or "*means* to refer to," one thing and not another (p. 64). Cognitive science and the computational theory of the mind cannot be saved by adding the causal theory of reference:

Even if the formal tokens in the program have some causal connection to their alleged referents in the real world, as long as the agent has no way of knowing that, it adds no intentionality whatever to the formal tokens. (1980b, p. 452)

Causal interactions are irrelevant unless they are "represented" in the mind (1984, p. 35).

Searle's objection to the causal theory, hence the core of his case against a sophisticated cognitive science (Section 5), comes down to this. The causal theory appeals to external relations to explain Intentional content and yet *that content is essentially internal and intrinsic.* Searle insists on this view of content time and again. Why? He offers no argument. He insists because when he adopts the first-person perspective and looks into his own mind, he can *just see* that the content is intrinsic. The core of his case is a piece of Cartesian dogma.

And that is not the end of it. Searle can *just see* that Intentional content is not causal at all. It is not to be explained, at least not fully, even by *internal* causal relations. Searle thinks that to give a causal account of mental states, as functionalists do, is to eliminate them (1983, pp. viii–ix, 262–3); it is to deny their essential mentality. Functionalists are not "even close to the truth" (p. 262). For Searle, mentality consists in phenomenological properties that cannot be captured causally. Such a view of bodily sensations is familiar enough from the "qualia freaks." Searle takes it further to cover Intentional states: Even the essence of an Intentional content lies in the way it feels (1981, pp. 417, 420–1). This is the rest of Searle's case against cognitive science. It is just more Cartesian dogma.

We have seen that Searle dismisses attempts to explain Intentional content. He seems not to be struck with the problem. Thus, in contrasting the view that we perceive sense data with his own "naive realism," he has this to say:

What is the relationship between the sense data which we do see and the material object which apparently we do not see? This question does not arise for the naive realist because on his account we do not see sense data at all. (1983, p. 58)

Indeed, that question does not arise, but a very similar one does: What is the relationship between the Intentional content and the material object it represents? This is our question about Intentional content.

To insist on the need to answer this question is not to insist that Intentional properties be *reduced* to the physical in some strong old-fashioned sense; it is not to insist, for example, that they be identified with physical ones. It is to require that they be explained in more basic physical terms. What the requirement amounts to is not perfectly clear to me nor, I suspect, to anyone else. Still, we are all fairly good at recognizing a satisfactory explanation when we see one.

So far, I think, my case that Searle is a dualist is strong. In brief, he thinks that the Intentional contents of mental states are brute phenomenological facts of the world that do not stand in need of explanation. I have, however, ignored one important aspect of his discussion: his appeal to biology.

Searle thinks that

mental phenomena are biologically based: they are both caused by the operations of the brain and realized in the structure of the brain. (p. ix)

So how can he be a dualist? The water gets muddy here. Certainly the view that Intentional content is biologically realized is inconsistent with dualism. However, given what Searle has said, and failed to say, about Intentional content, he does not seem entitled to the view: It is a gratuitous addition. We need some hint, at least, of how an Intentional content *could be* biologically realized.

Suppose someone were to posit a really bizarre mental state – some form of ESP perhaps. Clearly the scientific respectability of this state could not be established simply by claiming that it was realized in the brain. This procedure for avoiding dualism is just too easy.

Consider, for example, Searle's account of the Intentional content behind the utterance "That man is drunk":

((there is a man, x, there, and the fact that x is there is causing *this vis exp*) and x is the man visually experienced at the time of *this utterance* and x is drunk). (p. 227)

How does the brain realize that content in particular? In virtue of what would it be that one and not one about a stoned woman, a sleepy cat, an exploding star, or whatever? Searle has something to say about what goes on in the brain when a person sees something (pp. 266–7; 1980b, p. 452). But that sort of story is beside the point. We need some idea about how these brain activities might relate to Intentional contents. Searle tells us nothing about that.

Searle might object that *nobody* knows much about how the mind is realized in the brain, and yet almost everybody claims that it is. Why should he be any more open to criticism on this score than his opponents? The answer is that Intentional contents – for example, the one above – are not appropriate primitives *at the mental level*. They are not the sorts of thing that are, on the face of them, obviously realizable in the brain. We need to break them down *at the mental level*, relating them to other mental states and to input and output, in order to see that they have a place in a properly scientific worldview. That is the sort of explanation that Searle's opponents attempt and which he scornfully dismisses.

In sum, I think that Searle is not entitled to save himself from dualism simply by claiming that Intentional contents are realized in the brain. That does not constitute a satisfactory explanation in more basic physical terms.

Searle's appeal to biology goes further than that claim. Not only are mental states realized in human brains but they can *only* be realized in such brains, or things *very* like them. He describes his theory of Intentionality as "a kind of biological naturalism" (1983, p. 230). Indeed, he writes often as if mental states were "essentially biological" (1984, pp. 28–30; 1981, pp. 414, 417). For computers to think, they would have to be made of meat. But what is so special about meat? What is special, for Searle, is that brains have the appropriate causal powers, and brains are made of meat. *Perhaps* structures made of some other stuff could have those powers, but Searle seems to doubt it. What he is certain of is that structures made of windmills, water pipes, old beer cans, toilet paper, and paper clips could not have those powers (1980b, pp. 453–4; 1981, pp. 413–15).

Two comments: (1) What are the appropriate causal powers? They are powers to produce Intentionality. Now, of course, everyone who believes in Intentional states will agree that the brain has the power to have them. But whereas Searle's opponents struggle to determine the nature of this power, Searle is content to leave it as a mysterious and unexplained biological phenomenon. (2) Given that Searle says absolutely nothing about the nature of this power it is extraordinary that he is so confident about what cannot have it. I don't think that there is any practical possibility that a system with Intentionality could be built out of old beer cans. I have a half-baked theory of Intentional content that makes me think this. How on earth does *Searle* know since he has no theory at all?

Searle's appeal to biology seems to make Intentionality into a mysterious and inexplicable property of living things. He escapes from dualism into neovitalism.[14]

9. Conclusion

I have found dualistic and vitalist elements in Searle's approach to Intentionality and hence in his criticisms of causal theories of reference and contemporary cognitive science. However, my main point is that Searle's theory of Intentionality ascribes a magical power to the mind, an intrinsic power that is sufficient to relate the mind to particular things external to it. If the mind had this power it would be unique in nature. Searle supplies no reason to suppose that the mind does have this power. Putnam is right: Meanings just ain't in the head.

Notes

1 The parts of this discussion that are most relevant to the slogan first appeared in Putnam 1973.
2 Searle does not refer to this work.
3 Putnam goes on to argue that because you could not *think* that you were a brain in a vat you could not *be* a brain in a vat. I have criticized this conclusion, and other aspects of Putnam's recent antirealism, elsewhere (e.g., 1984, Chapter 11; Devitt and Sterelny 1987, pp. 206–9).
4 1981a, pp. 123–4, 200; Devitt and Sterelny 1987, pp. 51–2, 60, 69–70.
5 Recently, for example, by LePore and Loewer 1986, pp. 600–1.
6 1980, pp. 271–4; 1981a; pp. 152–7; 1984a, pp. 388, 403–5; 1985, pp. 222–3. My most recent attempt is 1989b. I also reject the similar view of natural-kind terms: 1983, pp. 675–7.
7 I think that Putnam (1975, pp. 242–5) goes way too far in his application of causal theories of reference to sociolegal and artifact terms (Devitt and Sterelny 1987, pp. 75–9).
8 I shall follow Searle in using a capital 'I' for this technical notion.
9 Searle's other objections amount to arguing that causal theorists are *not* mostly otherwise right. These arguments seem to me to have no force.
   (1) He thinks that two aspects of the causal theorist's view fail to capture something *essential* about names. First, it is not essential that a name be introduced in an ostensive confrontation with an object: They could all be introduced by descriptions (p. 241). He cites me as if I would disagree (p. 235). I do not. Indeed, I think that some names are *actually* introduced by descriptions (1974, pp. 195–6; 1981a; pp. 40–1; 1981b. 1981a is the work that Searle cites). Second, Searle claims that it is not essential that people borrow their reference from others in communication situations; each person might manage reference on his own. No causal theorist has ever denied

this. In any case, the issue of the essence of names is an unimportant one about the ordinary concept of *name*. What matters to the causal theory is that there be names that it is true of and that the others not be excluded in an ad hoc manner. I think that the causal theory of name introduction – what I call the theory of "grounding" – is true of most names and that there is nothing ad hoc about excluding the others (1981a, Chapter 2). The reference of any name *can* be borrowed, even if those of a few are not in fact borrowed. So I think that the causal theory of reference borrowing applies to all names.

(2) Searle trots out Gareth Evans's old chestnut 'Madagascar' (pp. 237–8), to show that the causal links specified by Kripke and Donnellan are not sufficient to determine reference. But what Kripke and Donnellan were offering was a new paradigm, not a worked-out theory. The interesting question is whether developments within the paradigm can give plausible accounts of cases of mistake and confusion such as those raised by Evans and others. I have argued that such developments can give very plausible ones with the help of the notions of *multiple grounding* and *partial reference*, and of the Gricean distinction between speaker meaning and conventional meaning (1981a, pp. 138–52).

(3) Searle claims that "no causal theorist to date has given a satisfactory answer" to questions about the occurrence of proper names in identity statements, existential statements, and intensional statements (p. 244). He gives no details of his dissatisfaction. I have written a book to answer just those questions (1981a; see also 1989b). His dissatisfaction is striking since his own answer is so ad hoc: A name's contribution to the meaning of those troublesome statements is different from its normal contribution (pp. 258–60).

Searle's discussion is constrained by his assumption that names "obviously lack an explicit Intentional content" (p. 231). This reflects the common, and always unargued, view that content must be descriptive. I think the view should be rejected.

10 On this, see also Putnam 1981, pp. 8–12.

11 I have not claimed that Twin Oscar's 'cause' refers to Twin causation in order to avoid a nice *ad hominem* point made by Michael McKinsey (unpublished) against such a claim: According to the causal theory, Twin Oscar's 'cause' couldn't refer to Twin causation because it has no causal relations to anything. It is enough for my purposes that it fail to refer. Alternatively, perhaps we should adopt a causal/Twin-causal theory of reference, with the consequence that Twin Oscar's term does refer to Twin causation.

12 I owe this paragraph to George Pappas. His inspiration came from Malebranche's idea that God was the only genuine causal power.

13 My remarks here are reminiscent of some of Putnam's in the course of his "model-theoretic argument" against realism, e.g., his suggestion that 'causes' is not "glued to one definite relation with metaphysical glue" (1983, p. 18). I see no reason here for antirealism, however (1984b, pp. 188–91).

14 The description "neovitalism" is due to Stephen Stich.

References

Davidson, Donald, and Gilbert Harman, eds. 1972. *Semantics of Natural Language*. Dordrecht: Reidel.

Devitt, Michael, 1974. "Singular Terms." *Journal of Philosophy* 71, pp. 183–205.

1980. "Brian Loar on Singular Terms." *Philosophical Studies* 37, pp. 271–80.

1981a. *Designation*. New York: Columbia University Press.

1981b. "Donnellan's Distinction." In French, Uehling, and Wettstein, 1981, pp. 511–24.

1983. "Realism and Semantics." Part II of a critical study of French, Uehling, and Wettstein, 1980. *Nous* 17, pp. 669–81.

1984a. "Thoughts and Their Ascription." In French, Uehling, and Wettstein, 1984, pp. 385–420.

1984b. *Realism and Truth*. Oxford: Basil Blackwell (Princeton: Princeton University Press).

1985. Critical Notice of Evans 1982. *Australasian Journal of Philosophy* 63, pp. 216–32.

1989a. "A Narrow Representational Theory of the Mind." In Silvers, 1989, pp. 369–402.

1989b. "Direct Reference." In French, Uehling, and Wettstein, 1989, pp. 206–40.

Devitt, Michael, and Kim Sterelny. 1987. *Language and Reality: An Introduction to the Philosophy of Language*. Oxford: Basil Blackwell (Cambridge, Mass.: MIT Press).

Donnellan, Keith. 1972. "Proper Names and Identifying Descriptions." In Davidson and Harman, 1972, pp. 356–79.

Dretske, Fred. 1981. *Knowledge and the Flow of Information*. Cambridge, Mass: MIT Press.

Evans, Gareth. 1982. *The Varieties of Reference*, Ed. John McDowell. Oxford: Clarendon Press.

French, Peter A., Theodore E. Uehling, Jr., and Howard K. Wettstein, eds. 1980. *Midwest Studies in Philosophy, Volume V: Studies in Epistemology*. Minneapolis: University of Minnesota Press.

1981. *Midwest Studies in Philosophy, Volume VI: The Foundations of Analytic Philosophy*. Minneapolis: University of Minnesota Press.

1984. *Midwest Studies in Philosophy, Volume IX: Causation and Causal Theories*. Minneapolis: University of Minnesota Press.

1986. *Midwest Studies in Philosophy, Volume X: Studies in the Philosophy of Mind*. Minneapolis: University of Minnesota Press.

1989. *Midwest Studies in Philosophy, Volume XIV: Contemporary Perspectives in Philosophy of Language II*. Notre Dame, Ind.: University of Notre Dame Press.

Kripke, Saul A. 1972. "Naming and Necessity." In Davidson and Harman, 1972, pp. 253–355, 763–9.

LePore, Ernest, and Barry Loewer. 1986. "Solipsistic Semantics." In French, Uehling, and Wettstein, 1986, pp. 595–614.

McDermott, Michael. 1986. "Narrow Content." *Australasian Journal of Philosophy* 64, pp. 277–88.

McKinsey, Michael. Unpublished. "Comments on Michael Devitt's 'Meanings Just Ain't in the Head.'" Delivered at the American Philosophical Association Central Division Convention in Cincinnati, 1988.

Putnam, Hilary. 1973. "Meaning and Reference." *Journal of Philosophy* 70, pp. 699–711.

1975. *Mind, Language and Reality: Philosophical Papers, Volume 2*. Cambridge: Cambridge University Press.

1981. *Reason, Truth and History*. Cambridge: Cambridge University Press.

1983. *Realism and Reason: Philosophical Papers, Volume 3*. Cambridge: Cambridge University Press.

Searle, John R. 1959. "Proper Names." *Mind* 67, pp. 166–73.

1980a. "Minds, Brains, and Programs." *Behavioral and Brain Sciences* 3, pp. 417–24.

1980b. "Intrinsic Intentionality." *Behavioral and Brain Sciences* 3, pp. 450–6.

1981. "Analytic Philosophy and Mental Phenomena." In French, Uehling, and Wettstein, 1981, pp. 405–23.

1983. *Intentionality: An Essay in the Philosophy of Mind*. Cambridge: Cambridge University Press.

1984. *Minds, Brains and Science*. Cambridge, Mass.: Harvard University Press.

Silvers, Stuart, ed. 1989. *Representation: Readings in the Philosophy of Mental Representation*. Dordrecht: Kluwer Academic Publishers.

Wittgenstein, Ludwig. 1953. *Philosophical Investigations*, Trans. G. E. M. Anscombe. Oxford: Basil Blackwell.

6

Semantic anorexia
On the notion of "content"
in cognitive science

LOUISE ANTONY

Hilary Putnam, in his 1975 essay "The Meaning of 'Meaning,'" carried philosophers for the first time to the now-legendary planet "Twin Earth," where things are almost but not quite just like home. Through this elegant and ingenious thought experiment, Putnam set the agenda for discussions in the philosophy of language for the last decade, and, no doubt, for decades to come.[1]

Putnam was chiefly concerned with a certain view of semantics, common to a diverse set of thinkers, according to which meanings were both determinative of reference and at the same time fully accessible to any competent speaker. He wanted to show that there were no "meanings" in this sense, at least not for a very large and interesting set of terms in natural language. For natural-kind terms, he argued, nothing *internal* to an individual speaker – no introspectible concept or set of conditions – could serve to determine the terms' extensions. If meanings are supposed to determine extensions, then meanings, Putnam concluded, "ain't in the head."

Putnam argued that the extension of a natural-kind term was fixed by acts of ostension performed in particular environments, so that it was the nomologically relevant features of the objects ostended – their "real essences" – that governed the correct projection of the term, and not some internalized definition. The full story about the meaning of such a term would therefore have to include factors *external* to the speaker, facts about the environment that went well beyond what any speaker, however competent, might reasonably be expected to know.

Putnam allowed that the old notion of meaning could be partially reconstructed in terms of a vector, with the contents of an individual

I want to thank Hilary Putnam for making *Representation and Reality* available to me in manuscript, and to express my deep gratitude for all his support and encouragement over the years. My intellectual debt to him is obvious, and I hope my tremendous admiration for his work is equally evident. I also want to thank David Auerbach and Joseph Levine for their comments on an earlier draft.

speaker's conception as one component, and the extension of the term as another. We could then speak of the meaning or content of a term either in the *narrow* sense, including only the first component, or in the *wide* sense, as including all the determinants of the extension as well. "Narrow content" thereby came to refer to that aspect of the meaning of a natural-language expression that could be specified *individualistically* – without reference to anything outside the speaker's head.

While Putnam's conclusions in "The Meaning of 'Meaning'" bore primarily on issues in semantics, they were soon perceived to have implications for issues in the philosophy of mind. The reason that many of us have become so transfixed by the tales from Twin Earth has to do with a second generational obsession, for which Putnam must again bear a large share of the blame. I refer to the view that the *mind* is actually a kind of *computer* – the view dubbed "functionalism" by its inventor. In a series of provocative papers,[2] Putnam fleshed out the computer metaphor, arguing that mental states should be viewed as abstract, functional states of the brain,[3] defined in terms of input, output, and relations to other states. Functionalism led naturally to *computational psychology*, an empirical theory that treats mental processes as computational processes, pressing the computer analogy even to the extent of positing an internal medium of computation – a "language of thought."

Ironically, while computationalism appeals mainly to liberal-minded materialists looking for a palatable alternative to the identity theory, it is, in one important respect, a very Cartesian theory. Jerry Fodor pointed out in "Methodological Solipsism Considered as a Research Strategy in Psychology"[4] that although computationalism presumes that mental symbols have both syntactic and semantic properties (so that mental symbols can justly be called mental *representations*, or "*MRs*"), a computationalist taxonomy must ignore the semantics and individuate psychological states purely in virtue of their *syntax*. Computational psychology must be, as Fodor puts it (borrowing the term from Putnam),[5] *methodologically solipsistic*. In effect, computational psychology must proceed in its description of the workings of the mind as if the external world did not exist; it must deal exclusively with psychological states *narrowly* construed.

It's the solipsism of computational psychology taken together with the Twin Earth results that's caused the stir. Solipsism would be no problem at all if all one wanted from computational psychology was an internal characterization of psychological processes. But those who took up the cause – including Fodor – saw computationalism as providing the basic framework for an empirical theory that could ultimately give a scientific vindication of belief/desire talk ("folk psychology" as it came to be known). Computationalists of this stripe subscribe to what Fodor has called the "representational theory of mind" (RTM).

It looks like this vindication of folk psychology – what we could call "the RTM ideal" – cannot be realized unless the individuation of psychological states can be shown to square with the individuation conditions implicit in propositional-attitude ascriptions. But since it is mainly through natural-language sentences that we pick out and differentiate mental states, it would seem that the externality of word meanings must also infect our ascriptions of contentful psychological states, imposing a "wide" individuation.[6] If so, then it would seem that the taxonomies of folk and computational psychology are seriously at odds.

In light of all this, it's now widely conceded that the possibility of transforming naive belief/desire talk into a precise scientific psychology rests on the prospects for defending a narrow, or individualistic, construal of attitude ascriptions, and for developing a theory of narrow content.[7]

Never one to leave well enough alone, Putnam argued in "Computational Psychology and Interpretation"[8] that there is no hope for an interpersonal criterion of sameness of narrow content and thus no hope of achieving interpersonal generalizations about the contents of thoughts any more precise than the rough-and-ready generalizations licensed by informal reflection on the linguistic, behavioral, and circumstantial evidence confronting us as "interpreters" of our fellow human beings. Most recently, in *Representation and Reality*,[9] Putnam has elaborated these various considerations into a full-blown attack on RTM, arguing for the irrelevance of computational analyses to ordinary attributions of psychological states, and thus for the failure of RTM's goal of producing a "scientific" vindication of folk psychology.

I would like to add my two cents' worth to the debate about narrow content and computational psychology. I find that the obsession with *narrowness*, evident both in Putnam's attacks on the RTM, and in the responses of many computationalists, has reached the level of pathology. My aim in this essay is to cure this "semantic anorexia": I want to defend RTM and the prospects for realizing the RTM ideal, not by defending the possibility of constructing a theory of narrow content, but rather by disputing Putnam's (widely shared) assumption that narrow contents are necessary for a computationalist construal of the attitudes.

I'll argue that Putnam's criticisms of RTM evince a fundamental misconception about the theory's *purpose*: He mistakenly presumes that RTM is designed to give a psychological answer to a set of *semantic*

questions about natural language. This initial mistake leads to incorrect
views about the semantic properties of mental representations, and
indeed to the view that the contents of MRs must be "narrow"
contents. Once the actual theoretical aims of RTM are clarified (and
clarified vis-à-vis the semantic questions we started with) we'll see, first,
that where content is concerned, "wide" is beautiful, and second, that
content isn't concerned as often as many philosophers think.

In Section 1, I'll describe Putnam's conception of RTM, and explain
how this conception yields the conclusion that mental contents must be
narrow contents. I'll also sketch my alternative conception of the
semantic theory required by RTM. In Section 2, I'll give a detailed
analysis of two of Putnam's most important arguments against the
prospects for realizing the RTM ideal, and show how these arguments
are undercut by a proper understanding of the commitments and goals
of RTM.

1. Meaning and mental contents

It's important to be clear exactly how Putnam views computational
psychology, in order to appreciate the depth of his challenge to RTM.
Putnam is not opposed to a computational approach to human cognitive processes. He still believes, in accordance with his earlier functionalist views, that the mind is a kind of computer, and that its operations
are, *at some level*, correctly describable as symbol manipulations. He
thinks computational psychology may well provide an understanding of
the *syntax* of these mental processes. His skepticism concerns their
semantics. He denies the possibility of providing for the formal objects
characterized by such a psychology a systematic interpretation that
squares with ordinary psychological ascriptions, while respecting the
individualistic constraints of computationalism. In short, he does not
think that the "mental sentences" posited by computational psychology
can turn out to be the "real essences" of the contentful mental states
we routinely ascribe in the course of everyday life.

This is an extraordinarily deep challenge. Putnam wants to take the
"representation" out of "mental representation" – a move that would
decisively undercut the RTM account of the attitudes.[10] RTM presumes
precisely what Putnam denies – that "sentences" in the internal code
have both syntactic *and* semantic properties, and moreover, that it's the
semantic properties of mental sentences that coordinate the causal
mechanisms underlying our rational behavior with the intentional language we routinely use to characterize such behavior. If the RTM ideal
is to be realized, therefore, it's crucial that some notion of content for
mentalese expressions be preserved.

The proper way for RTMers to do this, in my view, is to challenge Putnam's presumptions – absolutely crucial to his attack on representationalist functionalism – about the character of mental contents. Putnam assumes that what RTM requires is a kind of content that corresponds to what he identified in "The Meaning of 'Meaning'" as the psychological component of the meaning vector. Content of this sort would be "narrow" in the sense of being, first of all, *individualistically specifiable* (capable of specification without reference to anything external to the speaker) and, second, *transparent* (or directly introspectible) to the speaker. Each of Putnam's two main arguments against RTM is based on the imputation of one of these two properties.

But mental contents do not need to be either individualistically specifiable or transparent in order to satisfy the needs of RTM. Putnam's presumption that they do is based on a mistaken view of the nature and purpose of representationalism, which leads in turn to a failure to take seriously its central theoretical posit – the language of thought. I contend that mental contents ought to be identified not with the "narrow" contents of expressions in public language (whatever those may be) but, rather, with the "wide" contents (i.e., the extensions) of *expressions in the internal medium of representation*. Such a view of mental contents neutralizes Putnam's attack on the RTM.[11]

Putnam's main error is to treat the RTM as a theory designed to solve a set of problems in the semantics of public language. This error is apparent throughout *Representation and Reality*, and most especially in Chapter 2, where Putnam sets out the essential elements of a view he labels "Aristotelian Mentalism" (I quote):

I. Every word he uses is associated in the mind of the speaker with a certain mental representation.
II. Two words are synonymous (have the same meaning) just in case they are associated with the *same* mental representation by the speakers who use those words.
III. The mental representation determines what the word refers to, if anything.[12]

This view, it should be noted, is primarily a theory of (public) word meanings that makes explanatory appeal to mental representations. Mental contents must, of course, have some systematic relationship to the meanings of sentences, for reasons both intuitive and theoretical. And one way to ensure a systematic relationship between the two is to simply identify them, so that Aristotelian Mentalism does have an initial appeal, regardless of one's other theoretical commitments. But Aristotelian Mentalism does more than just specify, in a neat and intuitive way, the relationship between what I say and what I think. It attempts an answer, in *psychological* terms, to a set of *semantic* questions about public language. Principles (I)–(III) can be regarded as the answers to the following three questions, respectively:

(A) What is it to know the meaning of a word? (The Epistemological Question)

(B) When do two words have the same meaning? (The Individuation Question)

(C) What is, and what determines, the semantic content of a word? (The Ontological/Genetic Question)

These are all questions that philosophers have traditionally looked to a theory of meaning to answer, and Aristotelian Mentalism offers the hope that they can all be answered in one fell swoop, provided that the mind turns out to be structured in the right way.

What would be the "right way"? Putnam tells us: When philosophers had only a vague ontology of "ideas" to work with, Aristotelian Mentalism looked pretty specious; but then along came *functionalism*, and with it, the possibility of giving Aristotelian Mentalism both philosophical legitimacy and empirical credibility. Citing "the increasing tendency to think of the brain as a computer and of our psychological states as the software aspect of the computer," Putnam sees the resurgence of mentalistic semantic theory in what he calls "The Cryptographer Model of the Mind":

> In research based on such an approach ... it is often assumed that the computer has a built-in (and thus "innate") formalized language which it can use as both a medium of representation and a medium of computation ... .
>
> If we identify the computer's *lingua mentis* with Chomsky's "semantic representations" we arrive at a familiar picture: the picture of the mind as a Cryptographer. The mind thinks its thoughts in "Mentalese," codes them in the local natural language, and then transmits them (say, by speaking them out loud) to the hearer. The hearer has a Cryptographer in his head too, of course, who thereupon proceeds to decode the "message". In this picture, natural language, far from being essential to thought, is merely a vehicle for the communication of thought.[13]

The above seems to me to be a reasonably accurate sketch of RTM,[14] though Putnam no doubt intends it as a caricature. What I find objectionable here is not the crudeness of the characterization, but rather the imputation that RTM is primarily an attempt to rehabilitate Aristotelian Mentalism.

RTM is, in the first instance, concerned with characterizing the mental structures and processes that underlie human cognition, with the aim of explaining the phenomenon of intentionality as it is manifested in the domain of thought. Part of the explanatory equipment of RTM is, as Putnam's sketch indicates, an internal system of representation. But the explanatory job of the language of thought (and its constituents, mental representations), is *not*, as the affiliation with Aristotelian Mentalism suggests, to account for the semantic properties of natural-language expressions.

Putnam's misanalysis of the rationale for RTM has two consequences: First, because he insists on treating the RTM as the modern-dress version of a failed approach to questions in the theory of meaning, he makes his target too easy. Putnam's way of construing RTM takes the primary function of mental representations to be the encoding or representation of the *intensions* of expressions in public language.[15] And once MRs have been assigned this function, Putnam can construct for them the same dilemma he set up for meanings in "The Meaning of 'Meaning,'" viz., either they're not "in the head," or they cannot determine extensions. Tying RTM to Aristotelian Mentalism is thus setting RTM up for a fall.

Second, in ignoring the real rationale for RTM, he manages to miss the basic character of mental representation, which is the representation of *objects*. Instead, Putnam assigns to them the function of representing *semantic information*. Although Putnam concludes in "The Meaning of 'Meaning'" and his subsequent work that Aristotelian Mentalism can't work – that "meanings ain't in the head" – he never seems to imagine that what *is* in the head could be anything other than a *meaning*. In identifying an MR with the psychological component of the meaning vector, he treats it as simply an aspect of the meaning of public language expressions, instead of as an expression in an independent representational system, with semantic properties all its own.

In fact, the main problem with Putnam's picture of RTM is that he simply fails to take it seriously enough. If we take the "Cryptographer Model of Mind" at face value, we must assume that the language of thought is *distinct* from any public language, and that the acquisition and use of one's public language involves translation or compilation into this separate representational system. Viewing the language of thought in this way – as an *autonomous* representational system – is crucial to a proper understanding of the role that mental representations actually play within the RTM, and yields a different view from Putnam's of the kind of content they must have. To see the difference, let's return to the three semantic questions I said Aristotelian Mentalism served to answer:

    (A) What is it to know the meaning of a word? (The Epistemological Question)

(B) When do two words have the same meaning? (The Individuation Question)

(C) What is, and what determines, the semantic content of a word? (The Ontological/Genetic Question)

Now first of all, if we take seriously the notion that there is an internal language that uses public language as "merely a vehicle for the communication of thought," then we must appreciate that each of these questions needs to be asked *twice*, once with respect to public language, and once with respect to mentalese. It then becomes quite an open possibility that we'll get different answers to these questions depending on which language we're asking about.

Take (C), for example: There's every reason to think that the account of reference fixation for public expressions must be different from the fixation of reference for private expressions. For one thing, as Putnam himself has noted in a different context,[16] there can be no appeal to *intention* in the explanation of reference fixing for mentalese expressions (as there is in plausible accounts of the reference of public expressions), on pain of circularity. Aristotelian Mentalism, in treating mental representations as nothing more than the posited solutions to the questions with respect to public language, precludes any such complication.

Second, it's worth emphasizing that these questions are *distinct from each other*, a fact obscured by Aristotelian Mentalism's attempt to answer all three at once, with a single psychological hypothesis. Question (A) (with respect to public language), will necessarily have a psychological answer, since it concerns speakers' knowledge, but there is no prima facie reason to expect that (B) or (C) will or can be answered by reference to the contents of speakers' heads. (It is, of course, Putnam himself who has shown this.)

For purposes of illustration, let me rough out an alternative conception of mental representations that respects both kinds of distinctions and treats public and private languages as separate but interrelated representational systems.

Public

Epistemology. Semantic competence consists in the speaker's possession of a formally and extensionally adequate truth theory for public language expressed in mentalese.

Individuation. Expressions are individuated lexically and syntactically. There are coherent but coarse classifications of expressions based on their extensional and syntactic properties (à la Montague). There are also useful, but nonsystematic, classifications based on patterns of speakers' use.

Ontological/Genetic. Semantic values are objects and properties in the world. These values are determined initially by intentions of speakers to refer to particular things or particular kinds of things, and subsequently by a variety of intentional, historical and natural factors (à la Putnam, Kripke, and Burge).

Private

Epistemology. Semantic competence consists in an organism's possession of two specieswide characteristics: (a) the disposition to token primitive mentalese expressions in response to environmental triggers; and (b) the ability to construct complex expressions in accordance with built-in inductive and deductive procedures.

Individuation. Expressions are individuated narrowly, by their functional or causal potentials. Expressions map many-one onto contents (extensions). Mental states are computational relations to mentalese expressions, so that there is a rigorous, coherent, and fine-grained classification of mental states determined by the lexical and syntactic properties of those expressions. There are also useful but nonsystematic classifications of mental states based on presumed relationships between coextensional mentalese and public expressions.

Ontological/Genetic. Semantic values of expressions are drawn from the same domain as the semantic values of public expressions (i.e., mentalese expressions can have as their contents objects external to the speaker). Semantic values of mentalese expressions are determined by their systematic causal relationships to objects and kinds of objects in the environment.

I want to call attention to several important points of difference between this conception of MRs and Putnam's that will have bearing on Putnam's arguments against RTM:

1. Notice that while MRs (and the mental states consisting in computational relations to MRs) are, on this conception, *individuated* narrowly (i.e., without reference to anything outside the speaker's head), their *contents* are not (necessarily) narrowly *specifiable*. (This point will be especially important in addressing the first of Putnam's arguments against the RTM.)

2. Since I expressly stipulate that mentalese expressions can have as their semantic values objects external to the speaker, it follows that the contents of mentalese expressions will not be *transparent* to the speaker; that is, a speaker may not know by introspection whether a given object does or does not fall within the extension of a given mentalese expression. (This point will bear directly on Putnam's second argument against the RTM.)

Now I hardly mean to suggest that the position outlined above is anything like a consensus position among proponents of the RTM. And I'll concede that there may be one or two details that need to be worked out. But all I want to do at the moment is illustrate a conception of mental representations that is adequate for the purposes of RTM, and yet free of the "narrow contents" responsible for RTM's apparent vulnerability to Putnam's arguments.

On this last point, let me emphasize that there is simply no *room* in my account for anything like what Putnam thinks of as "narrow content" – that is, no introspectively available beliefs, images, or ideas associated with a term by the speaker. Narrow content, I claim, is a casualty of the proper separation of the three semantic questions, and of the separation of public language semantics from mentalese semantics. Once these theoretical issues are distinguished, the functions assigned to narrow contents are either picked up by something else (syntactic or lexical form, or wide contents) or else become diffused throughout the theory. Let me give a couple of examples.

1. Narrow contents as the objects of thought. One reason why many philosophers – whether inside or outside the RTM camp – feel that some notion of "narrow content" is indispensable to a functionalist approach to the attitudes stems from what could be called "Frege's Problem." This problem, and the terms in which Frege framed his solution, is an important source (independent of Putnam's Aristotelian Mentalism) for the idea that mental contents must correspond to or be identical with aspects of the meanings of public expressions, and accounts in large part, I believe, for computationalists' allegiance to the idea that mental contents must be narrow. So let me try to show how the scheme outlined above can deal with Frege's Problem *without* narrow contents.

The problem, of course, was this: Frege wanted to know how there could be informative identity statements, since, if extension were all there were to meaning, all identity statements would have the same "cognitive value"[17] or "informational content" as tautologies.[18] The problem, in other words, was that a taxonomy of contents based only on extensions was too coarse-grained for the purpose of characterizing whatever it was that could be expressed or conveyed by means of an expression. Frege's solution was to posit something that mediated between an expression and its referent, something he called the *"sense"* of the expression. Because senses mapped many-one onto referents, a taxonomy based on senses would be sufficiently refined to permit the correct articulation of cognitive values.

Now while few philosophers today would accept all of Frege's theory, many seem to agree that Frege demonstrated that meaning involved *something* other than extension – something potentially more fine-grained – and that this *something* corresponded to the contents of *thoughts*. (Putnam, for example, who is specifically concerned to challenge Frege's notion of sense, doesn't dispute the *existence* of informational content, but only argues for its independence from the extensional element.) That is, there's widespread agreement that whatever serves the function of getting a finer-than-extension grain into meanings, will do double duty as an individuator of the objects of thoughts.

But in all this, Frege's problem has been misdiagnosed. Consider the fact that someone can know or believe that furze grows on the heath without knowing that gorse grows on the heath even though furze *is* gorse. This fact, on its face, shows *nothing* about the meanings of "furze" and "gorse," *nor* anything about the *objects* of thought. What it shows, rather, is something about *mental states*. It tells us simply that the *mental state* of believing that furze grows on the heath must be different from the *mental state* of believing that gorse grows on the heath, since, manifestly, someone can be in the one state without being in the other.

Now of course Frege's solution has the *effect* of enforcing a fine-grained articulation of mental states. But it achieves this effect the same way that Aristotelian Mentalism does – by distinguishing two different meanings for the expressions "furze" and "gorse," associating the two meanings with two different contents (or objects) of thought, and then individuating mental states by reference to these contents. But this is not the only way to do it: We can make the necessary distinctions without appealing to meanings (on the semantic side), or contents (on the psychological side), by appealing instead to the *formal* differences – either lexical or syntactic – among the expressions (whether public or private) themselves.

According to the RTM, psychological states are functional relations to sentences in mentalese, so that it is a sufficient condition for the distinctness of two psychological states that they involve two different mentalese expressions. The mental state of wanting to marry Jocasta, for example, can be distinguished from the mental state of wanting to marry one's mother if we presume that the two states involve distinct mental representations of Jocasta. And since mentalese expressions are, by hypothesis, individuated by functional role, the differences in psychological state entailed by this taxonomy are causally potent: One can act on the basis of wanting to marry Jocasta without thereby acting on the basis of wanting to marry one's mother, whether or not Jocasta happens to be one's mother. The syntactic and lexical properties of mentalese expressions can, in this way, be exploited by a serious RTMer to explain a whole range of phenomena typically classified as *opacity* phenomena.[19]

2. Narrow contents as the objects of semantic knowledge. For the same reasons it's held that meaning must be more than reference, it's sometimes held that *knowing* a meaning must be more than (or something other than) knowing a referent. Thus, it has been argued, knowing the meaning of "furze" can't just consist in knowing the *extension* of "furze," because "furze" has the same extension as "gorse," and yet one can know the meaning of "furze" without knowing the meaning of "gorse." Now, it might be asked, if the semantic value of a term is simply its wide content (as my view claims), won't it turn out that a speaker who knows the meaning of "furze" *automatically* knows the meaning of "gorse," whether she realizes it or not? And isn't that absurd?

The worry here is engendered by Frege's Problem, but is exacerbated by the common conflation of the questions I'm calling the Ontological/Genetic Question and the Epistemological Question. Philosophers from Davidson to Dummett presume that it ought to be a desideratum on a theory of semantic *content* that it provide a characterization of semantic *knowledge* – that it tell us what a speaker knows in knowing her language.[20] If we accept this constraint, then a theory of semantic content that is purely extensional, and which thus assigns the same semantic content to "furze" and "gorse" (as mine does), would fail, since it would seem to predict that knowledge of the meaning of "furze" is the same thing as knowledge of the meaning of "gorse."

Altogether, these considerations could be built into an argument for narrow content: Semantic values must be composed of *both* wide contents *and* narrow contents, so that there's something to account for the possibility of knowing the meaning of "furze" without knowing the meaning of "gorse." But once more, the needed distinctions can be drawn without the expedient of an intervening narrow content.

On my view, to understand a (public) language is to possess an *adequate* mapping (expressed in mentalese) of public language expressions onto expressions in mentalese. The conditions on adequacy must obviously include coextensionality, but need not, I contend, include anything like "sameness of content" where the content in question is nonextensional. All we need to enable us to distinguish knowledge of the meaning of "furze" from knowledge of the meaning of "gorse" is two distinct mentalese *expressions* available for association with each of the two terms in English. The additional constraint on an adequate translation of public language into mentalese is thus a *formality* condition: mentalese must be formally rich enough to permit every lexical distinction in public language to be marked (either syntactically or lexically) in mentalese.

Because we've separated the question of what constitutes semantic knowledge from the question of what constitutes the semantic value of an expression, there is no problem about simply identifying the *meaning* of a term, whether public or private, with the term's extension, that is, with its wide content. What we think of as a difference in *meaning* between "furze" and "gorse" can be accounted for, on the public side, as a case of two distinct lexical items with the same extension, and on the psychological/epistemological side as a case in which two lexically distinct items can be mapped into two lexically distinct, but coextensive, expressions in mentalese. It will then fall out that it's possible to "know the meaning of 'furze' without knowing the meaning of 'gorse'" – that is, to be semantically competent with respect to one term, but not with respect to the other.

This separation of issues, together with the recognition that semantic competence with respect to public language involves possession of a truth theory expressed in a *separate* private language underlines Putnam's error in treating MRs as *aspects* of the meanings of public language expressions. We can see now that there is no reason to think that a speaker's competence with respect to his or her public language involves the *representation* of information rather than simply the *presence* of information (i.e., the presence of symbols that stand for items in the speaker's environment). We don't need to be able to enumerate the properties a horse has in order to possess a concept of "horse" – we simply need to possess a mentalese expression that stands for horses.

The question of what *makes* a particular token "stand for" horses is, of course, a perfectly legitimate and thoroughly pertinent question. But that question is part of the ontological/genetic issue for mentalese, and not one that we can expect to have answered by a theory of semantic knowledge for public languages. It's permissible to take the intentionality of mental representations for granted at the point that one is trying to explain what it is for a speaker to possess or "understand" those representations. (I discuss the interrelation between the theory of content and the theory of semantic knowledge in more detail in the next section, when I discuss the Holism Argument.)

What I've argued is that once we've acknowledged the autonomy of mentalese from public language, and properly distinguished the different theoretical projects we're engaged in when we ask for a "theory of meaning," the need for narrow contents vanishes. We can accomplish everything we want without allowing anything other than expressions and their referents – that the formal differences among mentalese expressions, and the corresponding differences in mental states, provide the means for making any discrimination we need. I've also argued that Putnam's particular arguments against RTM (which are essentially arguments against the possibility of narrow contents) depend on a serious misconception of the nature and theoretical role of mental representations. I turn now to a detailed critique of those arguments.

2. Putnam's arguments against the representational model of mind

Putnam identifies MRs with the psychological component of the "meaning vector," that is, with speakers' introspectible knowledge or beliefs about the referents of their public language terms. It follows from this identification that MRs must be, on Putnam's view, both *individualistically specifiable* and *transparent*. But as I argued in the preceding section, there is no reason for a proponent of RTM to accept the assumption that mental contents must be narrow in this sense. And without this assumption, Putnam's two main arguments against RTM – what I'll call "The Externality Argument" and "The Argument from Holism" – simply don't work.

I. The Externality Argument.[21] This argument appears at first blush to be a straightforward, although surprising, application of the Twin Earth results to psychology. In "The Meaning of 'Meaning,' " Putnam demonstrated that the meanings of natural-kind terms in public language had an *external* component – that nothing internal to the speaker could serve to fix the referents of these terms. Combined with the assumption of methodological solipsism, this point seems to yield the following "fast and dirty" refutation of RTM:

(E1) RTM entails that concepts and beliefs must be individuated *narrowly* (or "individualistically") – without regard to anything outside the speaker.

(E2) "We cannot individuate concepts and beliefs without reference to the *environment*. Meanings aren't 'in the head.' "[22]

(E3) RTM is false.

But in light of arguments in the preceding section, we can see that this argument goes astray in a number of ways.

The main problem is that it confuses the issue of the individuation of mental states (which must be individualistic) with the specification of contents (which need not be). This confusion, as I argued in the preceding section, stems from Putnam's attachment of RTM to Aristotelian Mentalism. Once these two issues are distinguished, we'll see that there is a subtle equivocation between premises (E1) and (E2).

RTM, we've seen, analyzes belief and other propositional attitudes as computational relations to expressions in the language of thought. It is thus mentalese *expressions* that determine the individuation conditions for mental states, and these expressions are individuated *narrowly* – without regard to their semantic properties – in accordance with the strictures of methodological solipsism. Even while it ignores the semantic properties of mentalese expressions for purposes of individuation, however, RTM still insists that these expressions *have* semantic properties – that they are in fact fully interpreted. Now the term "belief" is anyway ambiguous between the mental state of believing, and the object that is believed. The RTM framework compounds the ambiguity: Even on the "object" side, we must distinguish between the uninterpreted mentalese expression (the "narrow" object) and the expression taken together with its interpretation or content (the "wide" object). (There is a corresponding ambiguity for the term "concepts" – between uninterpreted mental symbols, and mental symbols paired with their extensions.)

In light of this, how are we to read the premises in the Externality Argument? For premise (E1) to be true, "concepts and beliefs" must be construed in the narrow sense, i.e., as referring to mental symbols and states, sans interpretations. Rewritten to make this clear, we get the following:

> (E1') RTM entails that mental symbols (and states consisting in computational relations to such symbols) must be individuated narrowly.

But this new premise, (E1'), has nothing to do with (E2). The second premise, if it's meant to follow from the Twin Earth results, must be construed as referring to concepts and beliefs in the wide sense. For there is nothing in the Twin Earth cases to cause pessimism about the prospects for finding a narrow criterion of individuation for the mental *symbols* that, once interpreted, will realize beliefs. Rather, the Twin Earth cases have implications only for the *interpretation* of those mental symbols – they show how differences in environment can affect assignments of content. The argument thus contains a crucial equivocation.

Putnam would hardly be happy with my gloss of his argument, given its talk of interpreted versus uninterpreted mental symbols. He'd insist that he's talking about plain old *beliefs*, period. But the issue is not an artifact of the terminology. The question can be put this way: Are "beliefs" meant to be things whose identity conditions depend on their semantic values, or not? If they are, then they are simply not the things that RTM insists must be narrowly individuable, and whatever identity conditions they do have is irrelevant to the success or failure of RTM.

This brings us to the crux of the matter. While the Twin Earth cases show nothing about how mental states are individuated, they do show something about how the contents of mental states are determined. What Putnam ought to be saying in premise (E2), and what the Twin Earth cases have in fact shown, is not that we need the environment in order to *individuate* concepts and beliefs, or the psychological states associated with them, but rather that we can't tell *what the content of a mental symbol is* without reference to the environment. Even the meanings of expressions in *mentalese* "ain't in the head."

It should be clear from the previous section why the loss of "narrow" or individualistically specifiable contents does not jeopardize the RTM ideal. But just to make sure, let me spell out the consequences of the Twin Earth case as I see them. Take the usual setup, and let "Hermione" and "Twin-Hermione" be the molecularly identical twins on Earth and Twin Earth, respectively. Since Hermione and Twin-Hermione are molecular duplicates, they are functional or computational duplicates as well. In the narrow sense of "belief," then, they share all beliefs.

In the original scenario, we're invited to consider the differences between Hermione's and Twin-Hermione's *utterances* of such sentences as "Water is wet" or "This water sure tastes good after a vigorous game of raquetball." Putnam argued – compellingly, I think – that even though Hermione and Twin-Hermione associate precisely the same images and information with their respective terms "water," the extensions of their terms differ, and differ as a result of the differences in their environments.

Those are the semantic results; to get psychological results, we need to assume something about the relation between meanings of expressions in public languages and the contents of thoughts, but nothing stronger than the following principle:

> (E4) If two sentences differ in meaning, then the beliefs expressed by those sentences differ in content.

This principle is acceptable to RTM (at least to a first approximation),[23] even though RTM rejects the outright identification of meanings and contents entailed by Aristotelian Mentalism's assumption that MRs simply *are* the meanings of items in public language. Indeed, when the difference in meaning between two terms amounts to a difference in *extension*, as is the case in the Twin Earth scenario, then (E4) will be entailed by the constraints on an adequate translation of public language into mentalese, which require sameness of extension. Alternatively, if the "difference in meaning" is supposed to be an *intensional* difference, then RTM can recast the principle in terms of lexical and syntactic differences, in the manner suggested in the previous section.

So I accept principle (E4). I said that I also accepted Putnam's semantic conclusions, and thus accept:

(E5) Hermione's sentence "Water is wet" differs in meaning from Twin-Hermione's sentence "Water is wet."

And (E4) and (E5) immediately entail:

(E6) Hermione's belief that water is wet differs in content from Twin-Hermione's belief that water is wet.

(E6) seems, intuitively, to give the correct result when we extend the original thought experiment in the following way: Suppose that Twin-Hermione is transported to Earth, and together with Hermione, stands gazing at a glass of water, i.e., H_2O.[24] Since they are molecular duplicates, they will both form beliefs that they would be inclined to express by saying "That's water all right." Yet it seems that while Hermione's belief is *true*, Twin-Hermione's is *false*, for Twin-Hermione would be chagrined to discover that the stuff in the glass is not the same kind of stuff as the stuff that on her planet fills the lakes and so forth. Difference in truth-value is arguably the best evidence one could get for difference in content, and so (E6) is confirmed.

But that being so, let's look at what RTM says is going on in this case. If Hermione and Twin-Hermione are molecular duplicates, then RTM must count them as being in the same psychological state, which means that they both stand in the same computational relation to the *same mentalese expression*. So, for some mentalese sentence, say, "(x)(Fx → Gx)", both Hermione and Twin Hermione will be in the state < BELIEVE [(x)(Fx → Gx)] > .

But the issue of whether or not Hermione and Twin Hermione are in the same mental state has no immediate bearing on whether or not their mental states have the same contents. This question must be referred to that part of the overall semantic theory that deals with the ontological/genetic question. On the account of mentalese content that I favor, mental contents are determined by systematic relationships, developed over the evolutionary history of the species, between tokenings of mental symbols and items in the environment. That means that in order to determine whether or not Hermione and Twin-Hermione share beliefs in the wide sense, we would need to look at the environments in which their respective representational systems evolved. And guess what? Because Hermione's species evolved on Earth, the mental symbol "$(x)(Fx \rightarrow Gx)$" in *her* gets interpreted as the claim that water is wet, while the same symbol in Twin-Hermione, whose species evolved on Twin-Earth, gets interpreted as the claim that *XYZ* is wet.[25]

II. The Argument from Holism. This argument, like the Argument from Externality, presumes the need for content-based criteria of individuation for mental states, and hence the need for narrow contents. But while the first argument confused the issues of individuation and content determination, the problems in the second argument have a somewhat different source. Here the difficulty is the tacit assumption that mental contents must be *transparent*, an assumption that reflects the conflation of the ontological question with respect to mentalese with the questions of individuation and semantic knowledge. The main argument[26] goes like this:

(H1) A theory of content for mentalese must be "verificationist."

(H2) On a verificationist semantics, there is no criterion of sameness of content, and no distinction between change in content and change in background information (the "holism premise").

(H3) There can be no theory of content without a criterion of sameness of content, and a distinction between change in content and change in background information.

(H4) There can be no theory of content for mentalese.

Putnam goes on to say that since there can be no adequate formal theory of content for mentalese, the only possible way to interpret mental symbols is a way that's parasitic on the rather fluid and interest-relative "interpretations" or "rational reconstructions" we develop for our own and others' behavior, and thus that "interpreted" mental symbols can hardly serve to explicate ordinary ascriptions of propositional attitudes. The upshot, he argues, is that cognitive or "functionalist" psychology must be kept separate from "interpretation theory"; that the two "deal with quite different projects and that to a large extent success in one of these projects is independent of success in the other."[27]

This argument presents a very serious challenge to RTM: Premise (H3) gives a general condition of adequacy on any theory of content, and premises (H1) and (H2) assert that the specific requirements of a theory of content for mentalese make it impossible for that condition to be satisfied. But while I readily concede the truth of (H2) – the holism premise – I want to argue that it is doubly irrelevant to mentalese semantics: first, because mentalese does *not* require a verificationist semantics, as (H1) asserts, and second, because (H3) should not be imposed as a condition of adequacy on a semantic theory for mentalese.

First the concession. When Putnam speaks of a "verificationist semantics," he seems to have in mind what other philosophers and psychologists have termed "procedural semantics."[28] And clearly, if it's procedural semantics we're talking about, then premise (H2) is true. Procedural semantics identifies the content of a (mentalese) sentence with the procedures the organism invokes in order to "verify" it (i.e., assign it a high subjective probability). Once the meaning of an expression is identified with the means of verifying it, the now-familiar fact that *confirmation* is holistic, clearly entails that *meaning* is holistic as well. And if meaning is holistic, then indeed, there is, as premise (H2) asserts, no clear criterion of synonymy and no principled distinction between change of meaning and change of collateral information.

Now while I intend to argue that there is no reason to accept the conditions laid down in (H3), holism would still be fatal to the RTM, for the following reason. To say that meaning is holistic is essentially to say that the smallest unit of meaning is the entire language. If that were so, then there could be no stable, systematic mapping between public and private language sentences (because these sentences would have no discrete meanings) and thus no hope of realizing the RTM ideal. Thus, mentalese must be shown to have a nonholistic semantics, regardless of the conditions cited in (H2).

If we identify the contents of mentalese expressions with their extensions, as I suggested in Section 1, the particular argument for holism rehearsed above is undercut. So the question we must consider is this: Why think that mentalese needs a verificationist semantics in the first place? What's a verificationist semantics got that an extensional semantics hasn't? Putnam's argument for premise (H1) evinces a confusion of the ontological/genetic and epistemological issues, a confusion that reveals, once more, his tendency to see RTM as an elaboration of Aristotelian Mentalism.

The argument is explicit in "Computational Psychology and Interpretation Theory." Putnam begins by invoking the need for a theory of semantic competence for mentalese, insisting that if we are to take seriously the RTM hypothesis that the brain's medium of computation is a genuine language, then there must be some account given of what it is for the "user" of this internal language to *understand* it. Fair enough, but Putnam goes on to suggest that the account of understanding must constrain the kind of semantics that can be posited for mentalese – that the story we tell about the semantic values of mentalese expressions must somehow jibe with the hypothesized mode of comprehension. And Putnam proposes to coordinate comprehension and content in the following way:

The brain's "understanding" of its own "medium of computation and representation" consists in its possession of a *verificationist semantics* for the medium, i.e., of a computable predicate which can represent acceptability, or warranted assertibility or credibility.

Hence the interpretation of mentalese via rules for assigning degrees of confirmation:

Such rules must be computable; and their "possession" by the mind/brain/machine consists in its being "wired" to follow them or having come to follow them as a result of learning.[29]

Putnam specifically rejects the option I've been advocating, namely, a purely truth-conditional semantics for mentalese, on the grounds that such a semantic theory will yield no account of comprehension. He points out that, on the one hand, a truth-conditional theory, by itself, says nothing about what understanding of mentalese expressions consists in:

If we interpret mentalese as a "system of representation" we do ascribe extensions to predicate-analogs and truth conditions to sentence-analogs. But the "meaning-theory" which represents a particular interpretation of mentalese is not *psychology*. [A meaning theory in Davidson's sense] yields such theorems ... as ... " 'Snow is white' is true in mentalese if and only if snow is white." This contains no psychological vocabulary at all.[30]

But on the other hand, he argues, it's not so easy to *supplement* a truth-conditional semantics with an account of comprehension. The reason we can't simply say that the brain's understanding consists in its "knowing" the relevant T-sentences, is, Putnam says (citing Fodor and Dennett in support):

The notion of *knowing* cannot be a *primitive* notion in sub-personal cognitive psychology.[31]

If, pursuing the possibility, we try to explicate the notion of the brain's "knowing the T-sentences" in terms of the brain's *use* of those sentences, we still are left with the task of explicating "use," and that, Putnam says,

is what a *verificationist* semantics gives (and as far as I can see, what *only* a verificationist semantics gives).

He concludes, therefore, that

verificationist semantics is the natural semantics for functionalist (or "cognitive") psychology. Such a semantics has a notion of "belief" (or "degree of belief") which makes it *cognitive*; at the same time it is a *computable* semantics, which is what makes it functionalist.[32]

So the argument for a verificationist or procedural semantics as a semantic theory for mentalese is that it somehow "fits" a computational account of comprehension. But it's precisely this notion of there being a "natural" semantics for a computational account of comprehension that should be viewed critically: Lurking in the background of this argument is the presumption that a semantic theory for mentalese must provide *at the same time* an answer to both the ontological and the epistemological questions.

Notice that the problem with a truth-conditional semantics for mentalese is supposed to become evident as soon as we ask what *knowing* such a theory could possibly consist in. Now I agree with Putnam that the advocate of RTM will get nowhere by claiming that the brain's "understanding" of mentalese consists in its "knowing," say, an appropriate Davidsonian meaning theory. As Putnam quite rightly points out, the attribution of propositional knowledge to a speaker is, according to RTM, an assertion that the speaker stands in a certain computational relation to a specific sentence of mentalese. Since that sentence must itself be "understood" by the speaker, such an account of semantic competence would quickly become circular.

But while this reasoning is perfectly sound, all that it shows is that we shouldn't try to give a theory of understanding for mentalese in terms of propositional knowledge, specifically, in terms of knowing the theory of reference for mentalese. In that respect, Putnam's argument simply serves to underline two of the points I've been urging all along: (a) that it is a mistake to think of the contents of mentalese expressions as representing information about the referents of public language expressions, and (b) that the project of specifying semantic contents must prima facie be considered separately from the question of what constitutes semantic knowledge.

Oddly enough, Putnam himself argued for just this separation of theoretical tasks in reference to the semantics of *public* languages. In "Reference and Understanding"[33] he argued for a distinction between what he called a "theory of reference" and a "theory of understanding." He even proposed a verificationist theory of comprehension complemented by a truth-conditional theory of reference – the function of which was to explain the organism's success in operating with the verificationistic principles that constituted the organism's understanding.

I'm not endorsing here the picture in "Reference and Understanding" (I don't accept the picture of semantic competence with respect to public language, for one thing), but the fact that Putnam saw this particular division of theoretical tasks as possible in the case of public language makes it all the more surprising that he fails to make the division in the case of internal language. Why not a distinction between a theory of reference and a theory of understanding for mentalese? Why not a use-theoretic account of comprehension coupled with a truth-conditional account of semantic value?

Putnam's reasons for rejecting this option, I believe, stem from the supposed *transparency* of mentalese meanings. Because he assumes that the RTM is motivated by Aristotelian Mentalism (i.e., that it is essentially an attempt to give a psychological solution to a set of semantic problems), he considers that it's part of the *point* of positing a *lingua mentis* that its semantics be fully transparent to its users. Indeed, on the Aristotelian Model, this transparency constitutes the main point of difference between mentalese and public language, where, as his own work shows, the semantic properties of the language can be opaque to even highly competent speakers.

On the AM model, then, mentalese expressions must be essentially *self-interpreting*. The semantic values of internal symbols, unlike those of public language symbols, would need to be determined by what went on inside the speaker's head, by the functional interrelations among the symbols. And that means that a truth-conditional meaning theory would necessarily assign to mentalese expressions the *wrong kinds of things* as semantic values. The argument might run like this: If the semantic values of mentalese expressions are given by a truth-conditional theory (as I propose), then a given mentalese expression – say, "water$_M$" – could have as its semantic value something *external* to the speaker – say, water. But since a symbol that referred to water might behave *internally* no differently than a symbol that referred to *XYZ*, there would be no way that a speaker of "English mentalese" could display her "understanding" of the symbol as a water symbol rather than as an *XYZ* symbol; there would be nothing in the speaker's internal use of the symbol that would *determine* it to be a water symbol rather than an *XYZ* symbol. The speaker thus couldn't properly be said to *know* that she "meant" water rather than *XYZ*, and that, given the assumption that mentalese is fully transparent, would be absurd.

But if we relax the transparency requirement, there is no reason to object to an externalist semantics for mentalese. On the RTM view, semantic competence in mentalese does not require propositional knowledge of any kind, and in particular, does not require the representation of individuating information about the referents of public language expressions. A speaker need not "know that" her mentalese token "water" denotes *water*; it simply must be the case that it does. That is not to say that RTM cannot account for the intuitions that give rise to the transparency condition. Speakers will still be able to introspectively distinguish among the various psychological states that intuition tells us are distinct – but on the RTM view, it will be a formal difference, and not a difference in content, that is being discerned. It will be transparent to the speaker, for example, that thinking of furze is different from thinking of gorse, but only because the distinct mentalese tokens for "furze" and "gorse" engender correspondingly different functional states, and *not* because there is an introspectible difference between the content of one's representation of furze and one's representation of gorse.

Thus, in my view, semantic competence with respect to mentalese, consists in the possession of a representational system, the elements of which represent objects in the world, and the mechanisms of which, operating on these representational elements, enable the organism to function effectively in its environment. But now a different question may arise, concerning the *genesis* of the kind of semantic connections posited by an extensional semantics. A verificationist semantics seems to offer an elegant answer to the genetic question, since the semantic values it assigns to mentalese expressions originate in the internal processing in which the symbols are involved. So, one might ask, if the contents of mentalese expressions are not engendered by their internal functional relationships, then where do these contents come from? In particular, if the semantic values of mentalese expressions can be objects in the external world, then, given the results of the Twin Earth cases, how could the appropriate semantic connections arise?

Even though I've been urging that the question of how the contents of mental symbols are determined must be separated from the question of what those contents are, I must concede that the answer to the second question is constrained by the first to at least this extent: The semantic values of MRs must be such that there can be a naturalistic account of how organisms could come to possess such representations. Moreover, the first question, once distinguished from the ontological question, must be answered.

My answer, as I've indicated, is that a significant subset of mentalese expressions come preinterpreted; that is, mentalese concepts are innate. Putnam himself considers this possibility only to reject it, and this is a position that many philosophers regard as self-refuting. Because it is so widely excoriated, and because I believe that RTM is ultimately committed to it, let me say a few words in defense of concept nativism. I'll focus on Putnam's objections.

In "Computational Psychology and Interpretation Theory," Putnam doesn't really argue against nativism but, rather, registers methodological scruples against nativist appeals: He implies that no theory should have to assume the innateness of mentalese concepts.[34] But in *Representation and Reality*, he argues explicitly against nativist hypotheses. He contends that while evolution provides the only hope for giving a naturalistic account of the presence of innate ideas, it's grossly implausible that evolution could select for the possession of such concepts as "carburetor," "bureaucrat," and "quantum potential."[35]

The best response to Putnam's pessimism would be a richly detailed evolutionary account of the development of representational systems, which I certainly cannot give. But in lieu of that, I can offer the following considerations, which I think ought to mitigate Putnam's concerns:

First, everyone, including Putnam, and even Quine, must acknowledge that a fairly large amount of native cognitive equipment must be assumed in order to explain human beings' theory-making capacities, so that nativism per se is not the issue. The serious disputes concern not the existence of innate ideas but rather the degree to which these ideas are topic specific.[36] The only form of nativism to which I'm here committing RTM is a highly general, all-purpose kind (something in the nature of Quine's "innate quality space" might do), and so ought not to engage empiricist scruples.

Second, no one has a theory of conceptual development that doesn't presume the preexistence of some basic set of concepts, so that a certain degree of nativism seems to be inherent in the best current empirical theories. Recent empirical work reviewing Piagetian models of cognitive development support the conclusion that much of a human being's cognitive architecture, and even a great deal of domain-specific information, is already in place in early childhood, and even in infancy, so that the process of conceptual development is more a process of maturation than of learning.[37]

Third, it should be remembered that on the view I'm defending, MRs do not have to represent *information* about their extensions – it's enough that they represent *their extensions*. It's important to point this out, because I suspect that much of the skepticism about the innateness of concepts is generated by the presumption that possession of a concept means possession of certain information, of quantities and kinds that seem to require experience. Whether or not there's any plausibility to the notion that human beings are born with, for example, detailed and explicitly represented biological theories, my view does not entail the presence of such theories in speculating that the concept of a tiger is innate.

Finally – and this point addresses Putnam's stated concerns most directly – not *every* concept needs to be innate. Putnam ridicules the idea of evolution's selecting for organisms that can discriminate carburetors, and the idea *is* ridiculous, but there could well have been selective pressures favoring organisms with (a) a useful stock of primitive concepts and (b) the combinatorial abilities to generate new, complex concepts out of the old. *Which* concepts are primitive is of course an empirical question, to which a better understanding of human evolution will contribute, but it's not ad hoc to suppose that "carburetor" is not among them.

I've argued that mentalese does not need a verificationist semantics, and that holism, therefore, poses no imminent threat. But that is not to say, of course, that the semantic theory I've defended could satisfy the desiderata laid down in (H3), that it could provide both an interpersonal criterion of synonymy and a clear distinction between semantic and background information. I'll therefore conclude by explaining briefly why I think these conditions are irrelevant to the goals of a semantic theory for mentalese.

Premise (H3) reflects a concern that is properly specific to the semantics of a *public* language, namely, the explanation of *coordinated* linguistic behavior. Speakers seem to be able to communicate, and they seem to do this by using their words in roughly the same ways. How is such coordination possible? What are the conditions under which various linguistic acts can be held to be equivalent? When, in other words, do two expressions "mean the same thing"? This is the question I've called the Individuation Question.

Aristotelian Mentalism tries to answer it by turning the matter inward – hence, Principle II: "Two terms have the same meaning when they are associated with the same mental representation." But it should be obvious by now that this is an improper (as well as ill-fated) appeal to mental representations. Just as it is not the function of MRs to represent extension-determining information, it is not their function to coordinate public linguistic behavior. Questions of synonymy in public language (which may well turn out to be purely pragmatic questions about what we are prepared to accept as "samesaying" for different purposes) must devolve upon the theory of meaning for *public* languages.

Such questions, when they are not settled extensionally, by sameness or difference of referent, must be referred directly to the factors that determine the semantic values of expressions in public language. And these, I'm prepared to believe, are precisely the factors Putnam cites. That is, the semantics of public language will necessarily involve an *idealization* over the use made of expressions by speakers of that language, and will thus include the kinds of facts that Putnam characterizes as aspects of "the social division of labor."

As for the criterion of synonymy for mentalese – who needs one? As I argued in regard to the Argument from Externality, cognitive psychology needs criteria of *individuation* for state types, but these do not need to be – and in fact cannot be – content based. We could construct a criterion of synonymy if we wanted one – the criterion could be sameness of extension (yielding a very coarse-grained individuation of meanings), or it could be sameness of symbol, plus sameness of semantic content (a maximally fine-grained individuation). But what would be the point of either criterion? We have what we need in the way of "an interpersonal criterion of synonymy" in the form of functional characterizations of mentalese expression types. We have no need of a "clear distinction between semantic and background information" because mentalese expressions encode information but do not represent it – our theory of semantic content does not demand that we classify speakers' *beliefs* about referents as either "semantic" or "empirical."

The general point here is that public languages pose at least one set of theoretical problems – problems surrounding the coordination of linguistic behavior – that simply do not arise for mentalese. The fact that public languages are *shared* systems of representation materially alters the way in which component terms are related to the environment, making the semantic connections subject to a host of *intentional* factors that simply cannot operate on the semantics of internal codes. This means that, at least over the long run, public languages have a certain autonomy from mentalese, rendering such views as Aristotelian Mentalism even more deeply misguided.

For example, the fact that public language semantics are, to an extent, determined independently of mentalese semantics, engenders a possibility not allowed for by Principle II – that an individual speaker could *mistranslate* her public language expression; that she could (to take a topical example) map the English word "aluminum" onto the mentalese token that stands for molybdenum, therefore putting herself at odds with the rest of her linguistic community, in thought if not in deed. Such a speaker would thus *speak of* "aluminum" but would be *thinking* all the while of molybdenum. RTM can account for the ambivalence we feel about assigning any single content to the thoughts of individuals who are under some such misapprehension as this: The question of "what she believes" is ambiguous between the questions, What do her words mean? and What is the content of her thought? where these two questions are not necessarily the same. The meaning of her words is given by the theory of content for her *public* language, and the content of her thoughts by the corresponding theory for mentalese. For purposes of evaluating or acting on her *words*, she would be counted as meaning aluminum, but for purposes of explaining any behavior based on her beliefs, we would count her as meaning molybdenum.[38]

I have tried in this essay to diagnose and partially to alleviate the semantic anorexia that afflicts too many proponents of the Representational Theory of Mind. I've argued that RTM has no need, and in fact no place, for "narrow contents," and that all the necessary work can be accomplished either by "wide contents" (extensions) or by formal (lexical or syntactic) properties of mentalese expressions. I've also argued that it's a mistake, born of the Aristotelian Mentalist approach to the relation of language to thought, to view mentalese expressions as devices for representing information about the semantic properties of public language expressions.

Hilary Putnam is currently one of the chief critics of RTM, and if the computational model of mind goes the way of so many other philosophical fashions, it will be largely Putnam's doing. But paradoxically, if the RTM ideal is ever realized, then like it or not, Putnam will have to accept a good deal of the credit for that, too, not merely because he gave us the first clear and compelling articulation of the computational metaphor, and not only because his brilliant insights about the workings of natural language set new terms for discussions of representation generally, but also because his criticisms themselves pose the kinds of questions that are vital to theoretical development, and that a theory can only be improved by answering.

Notes

1 Actually, the "Meaning of 'Meaning'" view was pretty much present in Putnam's 1970 paper "Is Semantics Possible?" The Twin Earth thought experiment was there, too, in embryonic form.
2 "Philosophy and Our Mental Life" (1975d), "Brains and Behavior" (1963), "Minds and Machines" (1960), "Robots: Machines or Artificially Created Life?" (1964), "The Mental Life of Some Machines" (1967a), "The Nature of Mental States" (1967b), all reprinted in Putnam (1975b).

3 I don't mean to suggest that functionalism *entails* materialism, or that Putnam thought
   it did. He himself emphasized that functionalism was perfectly neutral as to the
   metaphysical character of the medium in which the mind was realized. It *could* be
   brains, of course, but it also could be "soul stuff." See Putnam (1967a). Nonetheless,
   I'm going to ignore the possibility of dualistic functionalism for the purposes of this
   essay.
   Also, even if we agree to be materialists, it should be noted that it doesn't follow
   that mental states are *brain* states. They could be states of the whole nervous system,
   or even, as some have suggested, states of the entire body. Nothing I'm going to say
   depends on the truth here, so I'll continue, for simplicity's sake, to assume that mental
   states are functional states of the brain.
4 Fodor (1980a).
5 Putnam introduces the term in Putnam (1975c), pp. 219–20.
6 Tyler Burge developed this point in a series of articles based on Twin Earth-style
   thought experiments: "Individualism and the Mental" (1979), "Other Bodies" (1981),
   and "Two Thought-Experiments Revisited" (1982).
7 Although the consensus is eroding. See van Gulick (1989).
8 See Putnam (1983b).
9 See Putnam (1988).
10 Putnam's view thus has affinities with the views of Stich (1983) and Schiffer (1987).
11 Putnam is hardly alone in his presumption that the contents needed by RTM are
   simply the narrow contents of natural-language expressions. Fodor, for example, keys
   his characterization of the kinds of belief attributions needed for "rational psychology"
   to Putnam's distinction between narrow and wide individuation of psychological states.
   And at the beginning of "Computational Psychology and Interpretation Theory,"
   Putnam refers to a remark by Zenon Pylyshyn to the effect that "cognitive psychology
   is impossible if there is not a well-defined notion of *sameness of content* for mental
   representations," where the content in question is presumed to be narrow. But in
   Putnam's case, the supposition that the contents of mental representations must be
   narrow contents stems from the mistaken assumption that RTM is primarily designed
   to solve a set of problems in the theory of *meaning*.
12 Putnam (1988), Chapter 2, p. 2.
13 Putnam (1988), Chapter 1, pp. 10–11. The reference to "Chomsky's semantic representations" indicates, of course, the time at which this article was written. Chomsky's
   view of semantics has changed considerably since 1982, but Putnam's sketch still
   describes an extant view in the philosophy of mind, viz., Fodor's, and I'm happy to
   defend that one.
14 I'd quibble, perhaps, with the stuff about a "cryptographer," and the references to
   Chomsky require comment.
15 It's quite obvious from the text that Putnam thinks of MRs as mental items that
   record semantic information, rather than as objects that have semantic properties in
   their own right. He refers to "mental representations *or* mental descriptions *or*
   mental pictures" as if these three notions are interchangeable (Putnam, 1988, Chapter
   2, p. 9; my emphasis). He discusses what mental representations "tell us" about the
   referents of expressions in natural language: "In the case of most of us, our mental
   representation doesn't do much beyond telling us that gold is a yellow precious metal"
   (*ibid.*). And he speculates about the kind of information that may or may not be
   "included in" a mental representation: "... my mental representation of an elm
   includes the fact that there *are* characteristics which distinguish it from a beech"
   (Putnam, 1988, Chapter 2, p. 18).
16 In "The Argument from Holism," discussed later in this essay.
17 The term "cognitive value" is taken from Max Black's translation of "Über Sinn und
   Bedeutung." See Frege (1892), p. 56.
18 The evidence Frege marshaled against this being the case was, significantly, epistemological: "*a* = *a* holds *a priori* and, according to Kant, is to be labelled analytic, while

statements of the form $a = b$ often contain very valuable extensions of our knowledge and cannot always be established *a priori*." *Ibid.*

19 Jerry Fodor makes the basic case in "Propositional Attitudes" (1980b). For specific applications of the RTM strategy to problems of opacity, see Levine, "Demonstrating in Mentalese" (1988), and my "Attributions of Intentional Action" (1987).

20 For example, see Davidson (1967), esp. pp. 456–8, Davidson (1974), and Dummett (1976). This view is endorsed by many, including Gareth Evans and John McDowell (1976), "Introduction," LePore and Loewer (1988).

21 My formulation here represents a composite of arguments in Putnam (1983b) and in Putnam (1988), Chapter 5.

22 Putnam (1988), Chapter 5, p. 1.

23 (5) will require some tinkering, on anyone's story – for one thing, something non-circular needs to be said about a sentence's "expressing a belief." RTM can do this, I believe, and I'm not sure that any other realistic psychological theory can. But the present point doesn't depend on the possibility of working out these details.

24 This extension of the original Twin Earth case is identical in all essentials to the cases developed in Burge (1971). Burge agrees with Putnam that an individualistic psychology cannot support an account of the attitudes, but argues that contemporary cognitive psychology is *not* individualistic.

25 Actually, if indicationalism is correct, then it becomes an empirically open question whether anything like the Twin Earth case could arise, i.e., whether MRs with sufficiently similar functional roles to be counted the same mentalese expression could arise in organisms with totally disjoint evolutionary histories. Such a symbol would need to be such that its tokenings would be potentially triggered by either of two completely different and unrelated chemical kinds, one to be found nowhere in the organism's ecological niche. Not impossible, of course, but unlikely on the face of it.

26 The argument appears both in Putnam (1983b) and Putnam (1988), pp. V-15–16. My exposition follows the first presentation more closely.

27 Putnam (1983b), p. 150.

28 "We treat the language as interpreted (in part) *via* a set of rules which assign *degrees of confirmation* ... to the sentence-analogs relative to experiential inputs and relative also to other sentence-analogs" (Putnam, 1983b, p. 142). The qualification "in part" here is puzzling. Taken on its own, it suggests that Putnam is about to advocate some kind of "two-factor" analysis of the semantics of mentalese, with a truth-conditional theory as one part, but in fact, his subsequent argument seems to preclude such an analysis. At any rate, he never tells us what the *other* part is.

29 Putnam (1983b), p. 142.

30 Putnam (1983b), pp. 142–3.

31 *Ibid.*, p. 143.

32 *Ibid.*

33 Putnam (1976).

34 Putnam (1983b), p. 142.

35 Putnam (1988), pp. I-25–6. I actually think the issue of innateness is a red herring in this particular dispute. The issue is what the brain's understanding of mentalese *consists in*, not where that understanding *came from*.

36 Jerrold Katz makes this point in his excellent discussion of rationalism and empiricism, "Innate Ideas" (1966).

37 Chomsky's argument for the existence of domain-specific, innate universals in language is the most famous argument of this form, but see also Gelman (1982) and Keil (1981) for evidence that some highly specific pieces of knowledge are biologically specified.

38 Sarah Patterson convinced me of this last point – that content ascriptions are sensitive to our *purposes* in attributing beliefs and interpreting utterances. See her essay "The Explanatory Role of Belief Ascriptions," forthcoming in *Philosophical Studies*. She argues, against Burge, that our everyday practice of attributing beliefs is

not uniformly individualistic. Patterson is not carrying the heavy baggage I am carrying and makes no appeal to an internal code; nonetheless, I find her arguments friendly to the RTM model.

References

Antony, Louise. 1987. "Attributions of Intentional Action." *Philosophical Studies*, 51, pp. 311–23.

Burge, Tyler. 1979. "Individualism and the Mental." Reprinted in P. French et al. (eds.), *Midwest Studies in Philosophy: Vol. 4. Studies in Epistemology*. Minneapolis, Minn., University of Minnesota Press.

1981. "Other Bodies." In Woodfield (ed.), *Thought and Object*. Oxford, Oxford University Press.

1982. "Two Thought-Experiments Reviewed. " *Notre Dame Journal of Formal Logic*, 23, no. 3, pp. 284–93.

1986. "Individualism and Psychology." *Philosophical Review*, 95, no. 1, pp. 3–45.

Davidson, Donald. 1967. "Truth and Meaning." Reprinted in Jay Rosenberg and Charles Travis (eds.), *Readings in the Philosophy of Language*. Englewood Cliffs, N.J.: Prentice-Hall, 1971.

1974. "Reply to Foster." In Evans and McDowell (1976).

Dummett, Michael. 1976. "What Is a Theory of Meaning? (II)." Reprinted in Evans and McDowell (1976).

Evans, Gareth, and John McDowell, eds. 1976. *Truth and Meaning: Essays in Semantics*. Oxford: Clarendon Press.

Fodor, J. A. 1980a. "Methodological Solipsism Considered as a Research Strategy in Psychology." Reprinted in Fodor (1981).

1980b. "Propositional Attitudes." Reprinted in Fodor (1981).

1981. *RePresentations: Philosophical Essays on the Foundations of Cognitive Science*, Cambridge, Mass.: MIT Press.

Frege, Gottlob. 1892. "On Sense and Reference." In P. T. Geach and M. Black (trans. and eds.), *Translations from the Philosophical Writings of Gottlob Frege*. 2nd ed. Oxford: Blackwell, 1960.

Gelman, Rachel. 1982. "Basic Numerical Abilities." In R. J. Sternberg (ed.), *Advances in the Psychology of Human Intelligence*, vol. 1. Hillsdale, N.J.: Erlbaum.

Katz, Jerrold J. 1966. "Innate Ideas." Reprinted in Stephen Stich (ed), *Innate Ideas*. Berkeley and Los Angeles: University of California Press.

Keil, Frank C. 1981. "Constraints on Knowledge and Cognitive Development." *Psychological Review*, 88, pp. 197–227.

LePore, Ernest, and Barry Loewer. 1988. "You Can Say That Again." Unpublished manuscript. Department of Philosophy, Rutgers University.

Levine, Joseph. 1988. "Demonstrating in Mentalese." *Pacific Philosophical Quarterly*, 69, 222–40.

Patterson, Sarah. In press. "The Explanatory Role of Belief Ascriptions." *Philosophical Studies*.

Putnam, Hilary. 1960. "Minds and Machines." Reprinted in Putnam (1975b).
1963. "Brains and Behavior." Reprinted in Putnam (1975b).
1964. "Robots: Machines or Artificially Created Life?" Reprinted in Putnam (1975b).
1967a. "The Mental Life of Some Machines." Reprinted in Putnam (1975b).
1967b. "The Nature of Mental States." Reprinted in Putnam (1975b).
1970. "Is Semantics Possible?" Reprinted in Putnam (1975b).
1975a. *Mathematics, Matter and Method: Philosophical Papers, Vol. I*. Cambridge: Cambridge University Press.
1975b. *Mind, Language and Reality: Philosophical Papers, Vol. II*. Cambridge: Cambridge University Press.
1975c. "The Meaning of 'Meaning.'" Reprinted in Putnam (1975b).
1975d. "Philosophy and Our Mental Life." Reprinted in Putnam (1975b).
1976. "Reference and Understanding." In *Meaning and the Moral Sciences*. London: Routledge & Kegan Paul.
1983a. *Realism and Reason: Philosophical Papers, Vol. III*. Cambridge University Press, Cambridge, England.
1983b. "Computational psychology and interpretation theory." In Putnam (1983a).
1988. *Representation and Reality*. Cambridge, Mass.: MIT Press. (Page references are to manuscript.)
Schiffer, Stephen. 1987. *Remnants of Meaning*. Cambridge, Mass.: MIT Press.
Stich, Stephen. 1983. *From Folk Psychology to Cognitive Science*. Cambridge, Mass.: MIT Press.
Van Gulick, Robert. 1989. "Metaphysical Arguments for Internalism and Why They Don't Work." In *Rerepresentation: Readings in the Philosophy of Mental Representation*, ed. Stuart Silvers. Philosophical Studies Series 40. Dordrecht: Kluwer Academic Publishers.

7

Can the mind change the world?

NED BLOCK

Hilary Putnam originated the idea that mental states are computational states. At first (Putnam, 1960), his view was that although mental states are not *identical* with computational states (or "logical states," as he then called them), there are useful analogies between them. Later (Putnam, 1967), he argued in favor of the identity on the grounds that it was more plausible to suppose mental states are functional states (as he then called them) than that they are behavioral or physical states. This doctrine – functionalism – has dominated the philosophy of mind for over twenty years. Shortly after proposing functionalism, Putnam rejected it again (1973), and he has maintained this position ever since (Putnam, 1988).

Putnam was my teacher during both my undergraduate and graduate days, and I fear I have absorbed his ambivalence toward functionalism. My teacher has had a habit of changing his mind, but never has he done so within a single essay, and so in this chapter I have surpassed him. My chapter starts out as an argument for functionalism, but it ends up suggesting an argument against it. The issue is whether we can avoid epiphenomenalism, which I here understand as the doctrine that what we think or want has no causal relevance to what we do. I propose functionalism as a way of warding off arguments for epiphenomenalism, but then I argue that functionalism may bring epiphenomenalism in its wake.

The orientation of the chapter is toward the sciences of the mind, and their relation to intentional content, that is, what is shared by the

I am grateful for support to the American Council of Learned Societies and to the National Science Foundation, grant number DIR88 12559. I am also grateful to Jerry Fodor, Paul Horwich, Frank Jackson, Gabriel Segal, and Marianne Talbot for their comments on an earlier draft; to Thomas Nagel, who was the commentator on the paper on which this chapter is based at a conference at Columbia University in December 1988; to Simon Blackburn, who was the commentator on the paper at Oxford in February 1989; to Martin Davies, Dorothy Edgington, and Barry Smith for discussion of the issues while I was at Birkbeck College, University of London; and to the audiences at a number of philosophy colloquia.

belief that grass grows and the desire that grass grows, the *that grass grows* that both states are directed toward. The question at hand is whether the sciences of the mind preclude intentional content from causal relevance to behavior. One argument that the intentional contents of our beliefs, thoughts, and the like have no effects on our behavior could be put this way: The processors in the head are not sensitive to content, so how could content have any effect on the outputs or changes of state of the system of processors? And if content can't affect the operation of this system of processors, how could it play any role in producing behavior? This argument seems formidable whether one thinks of the processors as neural devices reacting to neural inputs or, instead, from the cognitive science point of view, as computational devices processing representations.[1] In this chapter, I confine myself to the problem as it arises in the cognitive science approach that is dominated by the computer model of the mind. I assume a very specific picture of cognitive science and its relation to the commonsense conception of intentional content, namely, the view according to which there is an internal system of representation from whose meanings our intentional contents derive (Fodor, 1975; Pylyshyn, 1984). One of my reasons for couching the discussion in terms of this view is that although those who adopt this view are *motivated* by the aim of showing how our commonsense beliefs about content (including our belief in content's causal efficacy) are vindicated by the computer model of the mind, the problem of the epiphenomenalism of content arises within this view in an extremely simple and straightforward (and poignant) way. The viewpoint assumed throughout the chapter is that of a supporter of the computer model in cognitive science who also would *like* to believe that the contents of our thoughts are indeed causally relevant to what we do.

The problem I have in mind might be put in terms of *The Paradox of the Causal Efficacy of Content*, namely, that the following claims all seem to be true, yet incompatible:

I. The intentional content of a thought (or other intentional state) is causally relevant to its behavioral (and other) effects.

II. Intentional content reduces to meanings of internal representations.

III. Internal processors are sensitive to the "syntactic forms" of internal representations, not their meanings.

The first claim is meant to be part of the commonsense view of the mind. The third is plausibly taken to be a basic claim of the computer model of the mind, and the second is a useful and plausible way of thinking how commonsense psychology meshes with the computer model. This second claim is by far the most controversial, but I won't be questioning it here. My reasons are that I think it is true, that I see no useful purpose to dividing meaning and content in this context, and that I think the best bets for resolving the paradox are to question the third premise and whether the reasoning that leads to the paradox is right.

The reasoning behind the paradox goes something like this: Any Turing machine can be constructed from simple primitive processors such as *and* gates, *or* gates, and the like. (See Minsky, 1967.) Gates are sensitive to the syntactic forms of representations, not their meanings. But if the meaning of a representation cannot influence the behavior of a gate, how could it influence the behavior of a computer – a system of gates? Since intentional content reduces to meanings of internal representations, and since meanings of internal representations cannot influence behavior, content cannot influence behavior either. The reasoning assumes that at least as far as our thinking is concerned, we *are* computers. This idea – which is simply the computer model of the mind (our cognitive mind, that is) – may be wrong, but I will be assuming it to explore where it leads.

My plan for the chapter involves

  I. Explaining each premise
 II. Examining and rejecting a putative solution based on a nomological conception of causal relevance
III. Suggesting a solution based on a functionalist conception of content and meaning and a counterfactual theory of causal relevance
 IV. Discussing a problem with the proposed solution, one that suggests that functionalism actually breeds epiphenomenalism

A subtheme of the chapter is that a nomological theory of causal relevance (a theory that explains causal relevance in terms of the notion of a law of nature) has more of a problem with epiphenomenalism than a counterfactual approach.

1. The premises

The first premise uses the notion of a *causally relevant property*. Some properties of a cause are relevant to the production of an effect, and some are not. Hurricane Eliza broke my window. Eliza's wind speed and geographical path are causally relevant to the breaking, but its name and the location of its records in the United States Weather Bureau are not. According to the first premise, if my belief that the United States is a dangerous place causes me to leave the country, the content of the belief is causally relevant to the behavior; a property that is not causally relevant to the behavior is the last letter of the name of the city in which the belief was formed.

Note that the point is *not* that beliefs, thoughts, desires, and the like (mental states or events that have content) are *causes*, for example, of behavior. (I assume that they are.) Rather, the point is that when mental events have effects, they typically have those effects (rather than different effects) *because* the mental events have the contents that they have, rather than some other contents. Typically, if the beliefs, thoughts, and so forth, had had contents that were appropriately different, they would have had quite different effects. For example, had I believed that everywhere except the United States is a dangerous place, then I wouldn't have left the country.

My metaphysical stance in this chapter is one in which mental events are the causes of behavior, and their contents are properties of those events that may or may not be causally relevant to the events' effects. I shall say that property P of event c is causally relevant to effect e and that c causes e in virtue of P more or less interchangeably. Also, I shall put the claim that content is causally relevant to something by saying that content is causally efficacious, and not epiphenomenal. Of course, my use of 'epiphenomenalism' is importantly different from the traditional one. I'm not raising any possibility of content being a property of a distinct mental substance, events in which are caused by events in the brain even though events in the mental substance never cause anything. And epiphenomenalism in my sense does not entail that content is itself caused by an underlying physical state that also causes behavior. The reason I use this old word ('epiphenomenalism') for this newer problem is that the problem I raise is the modern heir of the old problem.

The second premise – that content reduces to meanings of internal representations (symbols in the head) – is much more tendentious than the first, and is certainly not part of commonsense wisdom about the mind. But it is a straightforward way of making commonsense realism about content compatible with the view that the machinery of the mind is one of computations on internal representations. According to the computer model, the mind (or its cognitive aspect) can be thought of as a system of processors that take representations as inputs, transform them in various ways, and then send them to other processors, as in computers. One can think of the representations in such a system as being in certain computational relations to the whole system. These computational relations are determined by the ways the system would treat the representation given various different states of its component processors. A sample computational relation is that of storing a representation.

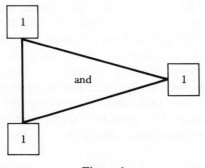

Figure 1

Of course, computers that you can buy don't currently think or remember. But if computers can be programmed to think, or if we are computers, this story can be extended to thinking things. Thus, remembering might consist in the storing of a representation in such a way that it can later be accessed. Remembering that grass grows would be storing a representation that means that grass grows. This is the doctrine of reduction of content to meaning stated in the second premise. More generally, as is argued in Fodor (1975), to have the thought that *p* is to be in a certain computational relation to an internal representation that means that *p*, and likewise for other propositional attitudes. The slogan – and it is only a slogan – is that thinking that grass grows is having 'Grass grows' in the thought box in the head.

Talk of the thought box in the head is (thinly) disguised *functional* talk. The sentences that are in the thought box share a computational situation, a role within the system – in other words, a function within the system. This functional theory of what a thought *is* (and how it differs from a desire) should be firmly distinguished from other functionalisms to be mentioned in this paper, especially the much more controversial idea that the meaning of a representation is itself functional.

The third premise is that internal processors are sensitive to the syntactic form of the internal representations that they process, not their meanings. Consider the *and* gate of Figure 1. What makes it an *and* gate is that it emits a '1' if and only if both inputs are '1's'; all other inputs yield a '0' as output. The *and* gate

   I. Is not sensitive to
  II. Does not react to
 III. Does not detect

whether the '1's' represent truth or the number 1 or nothing at all. Rather, the *and* gate is sensitive to, reacts to, and detects only whether the inputs are both '1's' or not. Thus it is sensitive to the syntax, not the meaning of its inputs, and likewise for the primitive processors postulated by cognitive science accounts of the mind. (The primitive processors of a system are the ones for which there is no explanation *within* cognitive science of how they work; their operation can be explained only in terms of a lower level branch of science, physiology, in the case of human primitive processors, electronics in the case of standard computer primitives.)

Note that the sense of 'syntax' I am using here (somewhat misleadingly) means *form class*. '1' and '0' are different syntactic objects in this sense. It is important to be aware that syntax in this sense of the term is another functional notion. English orthography is also functional, although this may be obscured by the rigidification of function by convention. For %xampl%, you will hav% littl% troubl% figuring out what l%tt%r of th% alphab%t is th% on% to which th% unusual symbol in this s%nt%nc% should b% tr%at%d as functionally %quival%nt.

Consider an input-output system whose input and output registers are bi-stable, and take on values of either 7 volts or 4 volts. Suppose that if both input registers are at 4 volts, then the output is 4 volts, and every other input yields the 7-volt output. Then (1) the system is an *and* gate, (2) the 4-volt value counts as a '1' for this *and* gate, and the 7-volt value counts as a '0'. A differently constructed *and* gate might be one for which 7 volts counts as a '1'. '1' is conventionally assigned to states of computer registers using this type of consideration. The functional roles of the bi-stable states of registers simultaneously determine our identifications of the devices in the system (e.g., as adders and gates) and our identifications of the states of the registers as symbols. So it is having a certain functional role that makes a state satisfy a *syntactic* description, in the sense of syntax used here.

Note that it would be a mistake to say that 4 volts in the first gate mentioned has the same *meaning* as 7-volts in the second gate. We don't know *what* the meanings of the '1's' in either gate are until we see other aspects of their function. These '1's' could be used to mean one, or true, or green; the input-output function does not choose among these and other possibilities. The aspects of function relevant to syntax are different from, though overlapping with, the aspects of function relevant to meaning.

In the next section, I will explain the picture common in cognitive science of sensible or "rational" relations among contents deriving from the correlation between rational relations among contents on the one

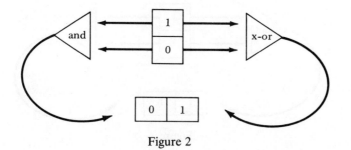

Figure 2

hand, and processing relations among syntactic objects in the brain on the other. This idea will illustrate both the strength and weakness of the cognitive science picture I will be assuming. The strength lies in its potential for a mechanical account of thought and reason, but as we shall see, it does so in a way that relegates syntactic properties to "going proxy" for semantic properties, and that opens it up to the worries about epiphenomenalism discussed here. My aim in the next section is to motivate premise 3 – that internal processors are sensitive to syntax, not meaning – since it will take the heat in my proposed solution.

2. The brain as a syntactic engine driving a semantic engine

The title you just read can be understood by attention to a simple example, a common type of computer adder stripped down so as to handle only one-digit addenda. To understand the example, you need only know the following simple facts about binary notation: 0 and 1 are represented alike in binary and decimal, but the binary translation of decimal '2' is '10'. The adder pictured in Figure 2 will solve the following four problems:

$$0 + 0 = 0$$
$$1 + 0 = 1$$
$$0 + 1 = 1$$
$$1 + 1 = 10$$

The first three equations are true in both binary and decimal, but the last is true only in binary.

Here is how the adder works. The two digits to be added, a '1' and a '0' in this case, are connected both to an *and* gate and an *exclusive-or* gate. The latter gate is a "difference detector," i.e., it outputs a '1' if its inputs are different, and a '0' if they are the same. In the case illustrated in Figure 2, the *exclusive-or* gate sees a difference, and so it

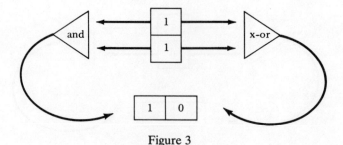

Figure 3

outputs a '1' to the rightmost box of the answer register. The *and* gate outputs a '0', and so the device computes the answer. The *exclusive-or* gate does the "work" in the first three problems, and is needed only for carrying, which comes in only in the last problem as illustrated in Figure 3. Both inputs are '1's', and so the *and* gate outputs a '1' to the leftmost box of the answer register. The other gate makes the rightmost box a '0', and so we have the answer.

Seeing the adder as a syntactic engine driving a semantic engine requires noting two functions: one maps numbers onto other numbers, and the other maps symbols onto other symbols. The latter function is concerned with the numerals as symbols – without attention to their meanings. Here is the symbol function:

'0', '0' → '0'
'0', '1' → '1'
'1', '0' → '1'
'1', '1' → '10'

This symbol function is mirrored by a function that maps the numbers represented by the numerals on the left onto the numbers represented by the numerals on the right. This function will thus map numbers onto numbers. We can speak of this function that maps numbers onto numbers as the *semantic* function, since it is concerned with the meanings of the symbols, not the symbols themselves. (It is important not to confuse the notion of a semantic function in this sense with a function that maps symbols onto what they refer to; I shall discuss this latter function shortly.) Here is the semantic function (in decimal notation – you must choose *some* notation to express any function):

0, 0 → 0
0, 1 → 1
1, 0 → 1
1, 1 → 2

The first function maps symbols onto symbols; the second function maps the numbers referred to by the arguments of the first function onto the numbers referred to by the values of the first function.

The key idea behind the adder is that of a correlation between these two functions. The designer has joined together

I. A meaningful notation (binary notation)
II. Symbolic manipulations in that notation
III. Useful relations among the meanings of the symbols

The symbolic manipulations correspond to useful relations among the meanings of the symbols – namely, the relations of addition. The useful relations among the meanings are captured by the semantic function above, and the corresponding symbolic relations are the ones described in the symbolic function above. It is the *correlation between these two functions* (which establishes a semantic function in the more usual sense of a function from words to their referents) that explains how it is that a device that manipulates symbols manages to add numbers. Now the idea of the brain as a syntactic engine driving a semantic engine is just a generalization of this picture to a wider class of symbolic activities, namely, the symbolic activities of human thought. The idea is that we have symbolic structures in our brains, and that nature has seen to it that there are correlations between causal interactions among these structures and sensible relations among the meanings of the symbolic structures. The primitive processors "know" only the "syntactic" form of the symbols they process (e.g., what strings of 0's and 1's they see), and not what the symbols mean. Nonetheless, these meaning-blind primitive processors control processes that "make sense" – processes of decision, problem solving, and the like. In short, there is a correlation between the meanings of our internal representations and their forms. And this explains how it is that our syntactic engine can drive our semantic engine.[2]

Now the picture just sketched of the brain as a syntactic engine driving a semantic engine reveals how it is that a mechanistic theory of intentionality can invite the charge of epiphenomenalism. It seems that our cognitive processes exploit a *correlation* between the semantic and the syntactic. The syntactic properties of the representations do the causal work, and the semantic properties come along for the ride.

3. The appeal to laws

In this section, I will examine a putative solution, that is, a way of making the cognitive science picture (premises 2 and 3) compatible with the causal relevance of content (to the behavioral and other effects of contentful mental states, of course – I'll be leaving the prepositional phrase out often, just speaking, elliptically, of the causal relevance of content). Actually, I shall start by briefly mentioning a reductionist proposal just to set it to one side. If content properties could be *identified* with, say, neurophysiological properties, then there would be no opening for epiphenomenalism. If content properties are simply identical to neurophysiological properties, then the causal efficacy of the neural would guarantee the causal efficacy of content. Whatever the merits of physiological reductionism, it is not available to the cognitive science point of view assumed here. According to cognitive science, the essence of the mental is computational, and any computational state is "multiply realizable" by physiological or electronic states that are not identical with one another, and so content cannot be identified with any one of them.[3]

Note that in rejecting this putative solution, I am not rejecting a "physicalistic" point of view. If all the nomologically possible things that can have computational properties are physical things, then the computational point of view, embracing this idea, is itself physicalistic. Even if the computational properties that characterize mentality are in this sense *physical*, that does not make them *physiological or electronic* (or syntactic, for that matter), and so physicalism in this sense does not lead to any suggestion that processors in the head can detect content or meaning.

There is another putative solution to which I will devote more attention, one that appeals to a nomological view of causation. The idea is that there are non-strict psychological laws involving content, and that law – even non-strict law – makes for causal relevance. Fodor (1987b, forthcoming) argues that intentional laws provide non-strict intentional sufficient conditions for behavior, and that is what makes content causally relevant to behavior. It will pay us to examine a simple version of this nomist perspective: F is causally relevant to an effect *e* if the instantiation of F is nomologically sufficient for *e* – even if the nomological sufficiency holds only *ceteris paribus*.

The trouble with this simple version of the nomist approach is familiar: there can be correlation without causation – even nomological correlation of F with G without a causal relevance relation between F and G. And nomological correlation can involve nomological sufficiency. Suppose C (for *cause*) is nomologically sufficient for and uncontroversially causally relevant to E (for *effect*). Suppose X is nomologically correlated with C because X and C share a causal source, and so X is not causally relevant to C. Then, X is nomologically sufficient for E

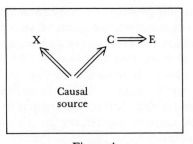

Figure 4

without being causally relevant to E. See Figure 4, which pictures this "fork" case.

Here is an example. Consider a setup in which a metal rod connects a fire to a bomb. So long as the thermal conductivity of the rod is low, not enough heat is transferred from the fire to the bomb to cause an explosion. But if the thermal conductivity of the rod is increased enough (say, by altering its composition), then the heat from the fire will explode the bomb.[4]

Now there is a law – the Wiedemann-Franz Law – linking thermal and electrical conductivity under normal conditions. (The same free electrons carry both charge and heat.) Hence for this setup, rising electrical conductivity, together with other things being equal, is sufficient for an explosion. Hence by the nomist criterion, rising electrical conductivity is causally relevant to the explosion.

I take it that to the extent that we have a pretheoretical grasp on the notion of causal relevance, this consequence of the simple version of the nomist criterion is simply wrong. The electrical conductivity increase does not cause the explosion; certainly it does not cause the explosion *in virtue of being a rise in electrical conductivity*. Rather, the rising electrical conductivity is an inactive concomitant of the causally relevant rising thermal conductivity. It is the rising thermal conductivity that allows more heat to be conducted to the bomb, causing the bomb to explode.

The obvious nomist response would be to reformulate the thesis to avoid these fork cases. The idea would be to formulate what the fork cases have in common that distinguishes them from genuine causal cases, and use this result to produce a definition of causal relevance in terms of "non-fork" nomological sufficiency. I think this is a promising way to go about characterizing causal relevance, but I have two doubts about whether the resulting nomist conception of causal relevance will be one that saves us from epiphenomenalism.

First, recall that the problem of epiphenomenalism arose to begin with because the cognitive science point of view held that nature had produced a correlation between syntax and semantics, only the former being directly causally related to behavior. What reason is there to think that an independently motivated definition of "non-fork" nomological sufficiency would count semantics as any more causally relevant to behavior than rising electrical conductivity is to the explosion in the example considered earlier? Indeed, the correlation between semantics and syntax via a common cause is a good example of a fork.

Second, the issue of the epiphenomenalism of the semantic may simply resurface in a different form in an independently motivated account of causal relevance in terms of nomologicity. Horwich (1987, Chapter 8) frames a definition of causation in terms of the idea of a basic law. A cause is linked to its effects by chains of *direct* nomological determination, and direct nomological determination is determination via basic law. "A direct cause of some effect is an essential part of an antecedent condition whose intrinsic description entails, via basic laws of nature, that the effect will occur" (ibid.). Cause c causes effect e if there is a set of events, $e_1 \ldots e_n$ linked by basic laws, and if $c = e_1$, and $e = e_n$. The account concerns event causation, not the causal relevance of properties. But assuming that it could be supplemented to form an account of causal relevance using the notion of a basic law, we can see that although it shifts the terms of the discussion of epiphenomenalism, it does not solve the problem. Is content epiphenomenal? That depends on whether the laws that determine behavior in terms of content are basic. But one's decisions on whether these laws are basic – and, indeed, what basicness *is* – will be (and should be) conditioned by one's decisions on what is causally relevant to what.

Of course the fact that the nomist conception of causal relevance will not solve this problem all by itself is not a reason to reject the nomist conception.

Fodor (forthcoming) says that if there is a *causal* law that F instantiations cause G instantiations (*ceteris paribus*), then F is causally relevant to the G instantiations that are caused by F instantiations. The appeal to causation in this sufficient condition is harmless for Fodor's purposes, but not for mine. For how are we supposed to know whether the laws that relate content to behavior are *causal* laws? For example, consider the (very low quality) law to the effect that instantiations of wanting G and believing that A is required for G cause instantiations of A, *ceteris paribus*. To know whether the content properties are causally relevant to the action, we must know if the law is causal. But if Fodor's sufficient condition is all we have to work with, the issue of whether the law is causal just *is* the epiphenomenalism issue we are discussing, so no progress has been made.

4. A proposal

We have just been considering an approach to causal relevance in terms of nomologicity, and we have not succeeded in avoiding epiphenomenalism. I know of only one other remotely promising approach to causal relevance, namely, the approach in terms of counterfactuals. In this section, I will first give a version of the argument for epiphenomenalism – the Counterfactual Argument I will call it – in which causal relevance is construed counterfactually. Then I will suggest a functionalist way of avoiding the conclusion.

Suppose we have a computational device (say, an *and* gate) to which a {'1', '0'} pair – representing the numbers 1 and 0 – is input, yielding a '0' output, representing 0. Now the {'1', '0'} input pair would have had just the same effect, viz., the production of '0' as output, even if the '1' and '0' had represented truth and falsity instead of 1 and 0, or even if these symbols had represented black and white, or even if we hadn't been using them to represent anything at all. And what holds for a primitive processor also holds for any system of them. If a syntactic object (say, a string of '0's' and '1's') is input to the whole system, and another string of zeroes and ones is output, the input string would have caused the same output string no matter what it had meant. In common philosophical parlance, the syntax of the representation "screens off" the meaning from having any causal relevance to the output. The conclusion is that since meanings of representations are epiphenomenal, so are the contents of the mental states that they ground.

I want to offer the claim that if the meanings of internal representations are their "functional roles," then the Counterfactual Argument for epiphenomenalism can be vanquished.

The functional role of a representation is its causal role in reasoning, thinking, planning, and in general in the way the representation combines with and interacts with other representations so as to mediate between inputs and outputs. The functional roles of representations arise from the ways processors manipulate their syntactic forms. Some functionalists take inputs to be impingements on the surfaces of the body, others take inputs to be the things in the world that produce these impingements (and likewise for outputs). Thus some functionalists take functional role to be internal, whereas others take it to be partly internal, partly external. My use of the functionalist perspective requires no commitment on this matter. More specifically, nothing I say here should be construed as an endorsement of "narrow content."

A functional role theory of meaning is a theory of what meaning *is* that yields an account of what it is about representations that *gives* them their meanings, not a "semantics" in the sense of a theory of particular constructions in particular languages. Thus, it would not be the job of a functional role theory of meaning to explain why it is that 'The temperature is 70°', and 'The temperature is rising' do not entail '70° is rising'. Theories of the sort that would deal with such questions often address themselves to what meaning is, but they do not yield an account of what gives representations their meanings. Usually, for their purposes any "surrogate" of meaning – anything that acts like meaning in the way that set theoretic entities "act like" numbers – will do. (See Block, 1986, 1987, for more on this distinction.) A functional role theory can be thought of as a "use" theory of meaning, where the uses are at least partly inside the head.

One motivation for such an account can perhaps be seen more clearly if one reflects on a case in which one learns the meanings of words without anything approximating an eliminative definition for them. Consider, for example, the learning of a new scientific theory with its new theoretical terms, e.g., 'force', 'mass', 'momentum', 'energy'. These new terms are not definable in everyday language (or anything like an "observation language"), though they are definable in terms of one another. The student learns these terms by coming to understand how to use them in thought, in experiment and observation, and in solving problems on quizzes. If meaning is functional role, then it is easy to see why learning new terms is acquiring their use. It is a plus for a theory of what meaning is if it also tells us what it is to know and learn meanings.

That is all I will say here to motivate the functional role account.[5] Now on to the Counterfactual Argument.

You will recall that the Counterfactual Argument said that it appeared that a given syntactic object would have caused the same output even if it had meant something quite different from what it actually means or even if it had meant nothing at all, so the syntactic form of a representation screens off its meaning from having any causal relevance.[6]

Suppose, for example, that the sentence 'There is danger coming this way' is in the "belief box" (with its normal meaning), causing one to flee. According to the Counterfactual Argument, the sentence would have caused the fleeing even if it had meant that my long-lost friend approaches, or that Empedocles leaped. But if functional role semantics is correct, then it is not at all guaranteed that 'There is danger coming this way' would have caused fleeing even if it had meant that Empedocles leaped. For if it had had a different meaning, or no meaning at all, its functional role would have been different, and since functional role is causal role, abstractly construed, a difference in functional role typically will include a difference in behavioral effects.

Perhaps the functional role of 'There is danger coming this way' includes an inference to sentences such as 'It would be best not to be here when the danger arrives" (with its normal functional role and hence its normal meaning), and perhaps this inference is part of the causal chain that led to fleeing. Then if the token of 'There is danger coming this way' that was in the belief box had meant that a long-lost friend approaches, the inference would not have taken place, and the fleeing would not have occurred. We would have approach instead of avoidance, and friendly words instead of fear. If the meaning of the sentence in the belief box had been different, its effects would have been different and required different semantic descriptions.

In sum, if meaning is functional role, then it is false that a representation would have had just the effects that it did have if its meaning had been different. Different meaning requires different functional role, and different functional role requires different causes and/or effects. So the Counterfactual Argument is unsound if meaning is functional role.

In terms of the original paradox, the point is that internal processors can be sensitive to *both* syntax and semantics. But how is this possible? Are the meanings of a *gate's* outputs dependent on the meanings of its inputs?

Of course not – and therein lies the fallacy of the original argument. Thinking of internal processors on the model of gates misleads. For a processor that *is a genuine intentional system* the difference between a representation's meaning one as opposed to truth or green, would involve differences in the internal part of the functional role of the representation. Not so for a gate. If we ask whether a representation would have had just the same behavioral effects had it had a different meaning, then for many differences in meaning, the answer will be yes for a genuine intentional system, though not for a simple primitive processor such as a gate. Indeed, the criterion of identity natural for a complex processor allows one to consider whether a given processor would have processed a representation differently had it had a different meaning. But the natural criterion of identity for a gate rules out the possibility of *its* processing differently (while remaining the same gate).

This point is easier to appreciate if we distinguish between autonomous and observer-relative meaning (Searle, 1980; Haugeland, 1980). Observer-relative meanings are inherited meanings, meanings that intentional systems assign (e.g., to linguistic items or states of a machine). Autonomous meanings are meanings of representations or representational states of an intentional system – *for* that system. They get their meanings from their function in the system. The representations of gates have *only* observer-relative meanings. (My representations have autonomous meanings for me, but they can also have a variety of observer-relative meanings for others.) We can decide, if we like, that a '1' that is input to a gate means one, whereas an output '1' means Richard Nixon. We have a free hand. But autonomous meanings are not subject to whim in this way. It is for autonomous meanings that the point I have been making applies. Had an input symbol had a different autonomous meaning (for a genuine intentional system), then it could have had a different functional role and thus different effects. The trick of the argument that originally got us into trouble is to concentrate on the example of a gate in which only observer-relative meaning is relevant, making us forget that we do not have a free hand in this way with autonomous meaning.

Of course the autonomous meanings of my representations could have been different in *certain* ways without any change in the movements of my body. This is what is imagined in the famous "twin earth" examples – referential changes without changes in internal functional roles. But of course twin earth cases are elaborately artificial, and one should not conclude from them that had a representation meant something else, the same behavioral effects would have occurred nonetheless. The misleading effect of the gate example is to trick us into treating *all* hypothetical differences in meanings of representations as if they are twin earth cases. If we compare *and* gates whose '1's' mean one versus truth, we are considering an analog of a twin earth case for gates. But for gates, twin earth cases come cheap. To read this cheapness of twin earth cases back onto genuine intentional systems is in effect to suppose that any old counterfactual situation in which references would be different is a twin earth case, and this is a bad mistake.

When I presented the Paradox of the Causal Efficacy of Content, I mentioned three premises: that intentional content is causally relevant to behavior, that intentional content reduces to meanings of internal representations, and that internal processors are sensitive to syntax, not meaning. Thinking of these as the premises, the argument is unsound because the third premise is false.

But when I spelled the argument out, I said that primitive processors are sensitive to syntax, not meaning. I then argued that the meaning of a representation cannot influence the behavior of a system of processors without influencing any of the particular processors themselves. So if meaning can't influence the behavior of a gate, it can't influence the behavior of a system of gates. This reasoning is mistaken (given the cognitive science assumption that a computer – a system of gates – can be an intentional system – an assumption that I am accepting for the purposes of this discussion) and so understood this way, the original argument is sound but invalid.

5. Internal functional role and external content

Dretske (1988) has argued that the semantic content of a representation is causally relevant to behavior. This section will briefly note that his point has little to do with the problem of epiphenomenalism as I have been discussing it. I think of Dretske's considerations as counting in favor of the idea that the informational values of our representations – what they "indicate" about the world – are causally relevant to the production of the purely "internal" aspect of their functional roles. (In terms of the "two factor" version of functional role semantics [see Block, 1986, and further references there], the external factor is causally relevant to the production of the internal factor.) But – and this is my point – informational value can be causally responsible for our representations' functional roles without being involved in the "triggering" of any actual behavior (in the usual sense of 'behavior').

Consider whatever it is that the frog uses to represent flies – let's call it the frog's fly representer.[7] There is an aspect of the functional role of this representer that is completely internal – mainly a matter of its production by flashes of movement on the frog's retina and its role in controlling the aim of tongue launchings. In addition to its internal functional role, this representer has informational content regarding flies and their locations. The point is that the latter plausibly has been causally relevant to the former. More exactly, the informational value of ancestors of this representer – what they have been indicating about the world – have been involved, or so one might suppose, in the production of the representer's current functional role. Perhaps an ancestor of the frog had an internal state that had some informational content with respect to ancestors of flies or other food on the wing, and influence of this state on tongue launching conferred extra inclusive fitness on the frog ancestors whose fly-information state had the right sort of influence on tongue launchings. We may speculate that evolution recruited a primitive motion detector that provided a modicum of information about winged bugs to guide the prefrog's tongue, thereby improving the prefrog's chances of a meal. As the bugs evolved into (or were replaced by) flies, the detector was turned by evolution to flies.

Then the fact that the frog's fly representer has been carrying information about flies has causally contributed to giving this representation the functional role that it has – being produced by retinal movement flashes and guiding zapping. More generally, the line of thought is that what our representations have been indicating about the world has had an influence – via evolution – on their having the functional roles that they have in our heads.

I do not wish to go into this reasoning in any detail, consider objections to it, or talk about the extrapolation from frogs to people. I want to point out only that even if the reasoning is entirely correct in its own terms, it does not show that the informational content of a representation is part of what is causally relevant to (in the sense of a "triggering" cause) the behavioral output that the representation causes, and so Dretske's proposal is not a solution to the problem being considered in this paper.

Suppose that the frog has a fly-word ('FLY'), the informational content of which has been causally relevant to the establishment of the internal functional role of 'FLY', including the guiding of the frog's tongue zapping behavior. Is this informational content thereby causally relevant to the production of, i.e., involved in the causation of, any particular zapping? This is the epiphenomenalism issue of this paper (applied to this case). The answer is obviously not. X can have causally promoted the pattern of $Y \to Z$ without in any way triggering the current token of Z. For X can have promoted $Y \to Z$ without now causing Y or enabling Y to cause Z. The informational content of 'FLY' does not causally contribute to the appearance of this token of 'FLY' in the frog's head. That is done by the fly that caused it. And once 'FLY' has appeared in the frog, the informational content does not enable or aid 'FLY' in producing a zapping. To dramatize the point, suppose that the current 'FLY' token is a *mis*representation caused, say, by a B-B. This fly token nonetheless indicates flies (a misrepresentation of a fly is still a representation of a fly). The history of correlation of 'FLY' tokens with flies has contributed to the functional role of 'FLY' tokens in the frog, but once that role is set, the past correlation is irrelevant to the process by which the B-B now produces the current 'FLY' token, which in turn produces the zapping that pops the B-B into the frog's gut. We can tell the whole mechanistic story about this causal process without saying anything about how the mechanisms that subserve it arose. And it is this former question that this paper is about: is content part of the causal process by which behavior is produced?

6. Functional properties

The plot so far is: functionalism meets arguments for epiphenomenalism and slays them. It would be nice to stop here, but alas, the story of the victory of functionalism over epiphenomenalism is fiction. I argued that functionalism does defeat the Counterfactual Argument, but you can win a battle and still lose the war. Functionalism loses the war in the end because functional properties are causally inert in certain crucial cases. Or rather, I fear that all this is true. The point of this section is to raise a skeptical doubt. The issues are complex, and I do not have the space to explore them adequately. So my claims must be tentative.

In brief, my point is this. Functional properties are properties that consist in the having of some properties or other (say non-functional properties) that have certain causal relations to one another and to inputs and outputs. In the production of those outputs, it is the non-functional properties that are standardly the causally relevant ones, not the functional properties.

To get at the point, let's consider a slightly more general notion than that of a functional property, the notion of a second-order property, by which I mean a property that consists in the having of some properties or other (say first-order properties) that have certain causal relations to one another. (The greater generality here is just that second-order properties needn't involve inputs and outputs, as with functional properties.) Consider the bullfighter's cape. The myth (which we will accept, ignoring the inconvenient color-blindness of bulls) is that its red color provokes the bull; that is, redness is causally relevant to the bull's anger. The cape also has the second-order property of being provocative, of having some property or other that provokes the bull, of having some property or other that is causally relevant to the bull's anger. But does the *provocativeness* of the cape provoke the bull? Is the provocativeness causally relevant to the bull's anger? It would seem not. The bull is too stupid for that. The provocativeness of the cape might provoke the ASPCA, but not the bull.

Another example: consider dormitivity construed as a second-order property, the possession of some property or other (for example, a first-order chemical property) that is causally relevant to sleep. That is, x is dormitive $= x$ has some property that is causally relevant to sleep (when x is ingested). If a dormitive pill is slipped into your food without your noticing, the property of the pill that is causally relevant to your falling asleep is a (presumably first-order) chemical property, not, it would seem, the dormitivity itself. Different dormitive potions will act via different chemical properties, one in the case of Valium, another in the case of Seconal. But unless you know about the dormitivity of the pill, how could the dormitivity itself be causally relevant to your falling asleep?

Of course if you *do* know about the dormitivity, then it can be causally relevant to your sleep, just as the provocativeness of the cape can affect the ASPCA. In fact, there is a well-known phenomenon in which dormitivity *does* cause sleep, namely, the placebo effect. If a dormitive pill is so labeled, thereby causing knowledge of its dormitivity, this knowledge can cause sleep (though the truth and justification of the knowledge are of course causally irrelevant). So dormitivity can be causally relevant to sleep. (Indeed, there can be a dormitive pill that works without any first-order effect, a pill whose dormitivity requires its own recognition. Suppose I market a sugar pill as a dormitive pill, and it becomes popular and works well. I make a fortune and close my plant. Years later, when all my pills have been used up, one of my customers who had had years of sound sleep as a result of taking my pills finds out that they worked via the placebo effect and sues me. Surely I can point out that he was not cheated – the pills were genuinely dormitive, there was no false advertising.)

My claim is that second-order properties are not *always* causally relevant to the effects in terms of which they are defined.[8] The only cases that I can think of in which second-order properties seem to be causally efficacious are those where an intelligent being recognizes them. That is why I keep mentioning "standard" cases, cases where a second-order property is defined in terms of an effect and that effect is produced without any recognition of the second-order property by an intelligent being. I add to the claim of the first sentence of this paragraph the more tentative claim that in these standard cases, the second-order property is causally inefficacious.

But how can it be that second-order properties are inert in some cases, efficacious in others? Think (temporarily) in terms of a nomist theory of causal relevance. If dormitivity of a pill were nomologically sufficient for the ingester getting cancer (Jerry Fodor keeps trying to convince me that such a thing could happen without recognition of dormitivity by an intelligent being), then (let us suppose) dormitivity would be causally relevant to cancer. But such causal relevance to cancer would not show or even suggest that dormitivity is *nomologically* sufficient for *sleep*. Hence we might have causal relevance to cancer but not to sleep: non-standard causal relevance without standard causal relevance. (More on nomological sufficiency in a moment.)

Second-order properties involve having some properties or other, and though it is often helpful to think of the properties quantified over as first-order, actually they can be any properties at all. There is a general procedure (see Lewis, 1970) for defining a second-order property, given a theory in which the property plays a role so long as the theory allows some sort of a distinction between theoretical and observational terms. (In the case of a psychological theory, the distinction would be cashed as theoretical = mental, and observational = input/output.) If the theoretical terms are 'T_1'...'T_n', we can write the theory as $T(T_1 ... T_n)$, leaving out all mention of the observational entities. Then we can define 'T_1' as follows: x has $T_1 = EF_1 ... EF_n [T(F_1 ... F_n) \& x$ has $F_1]$.

So far, the case I've made for the limited causal inertness of second-order properties is based entirely on examples. But if the counterintuitive consequences of this causal inertness are as bad as I will claim they are, a natural response will be simply to live with rejecting my way of taking such examples. That is, if I am convincing later when I say why the causal inertness of the second-order commits us to a view of the special sciences that is hard to swallow, the reasonable response would be that we should just suppose that dormitivity *is* causally relevant to sleep, and provocativeness does affect the bull. So I will try to get at the principles that underlie our reaction to the examples. I can think of two.

First, let us return to the nomist conception of causal relevance. On that conception, second-order properties are not causally relevant to the effects in terms of which they are defined because they are not nomologically sufficient for those effects. Consider dormitivity and sleep. The relation between the two is more like the relation between being a widow and having had a husband than that between, say, heat and expansion. If a pill is dormitive in the following sense: x is dormitive iff x has some property that causally *guarantees* (this is where this definition differs from the one offered earlier) sleep if x is ingested – and I take the pill, it follows that I sleep. The fact that dormitivity is sufficient for sleep is perfectly intelligible in terms of this logical relation. What reason is there to suppose that there must *also* be a nomological relation between dormitivity and sleep?

Now, I am very much not saying that a logical relation between properties *precludes* a nomological relation. This is as much a fallacy for properties as for Davidsonian token events. Suppose dormitivity is my aunt's favorite property, and sleep is my uncle's, and that my uncle tracks changes in my aunt's favorite property, changing his own so that his is always entailed by hers. Then dormitivity and sleep will be *both* nomologically and logically related. Logically related under one set of descriptions, nomologically under another. My point is not that a logical relation precludes a nomological relation, but rather that the logical relation between dormitivity and sleep tells us perfectly well why dormitivity involves sleep. There would have to be some *special* reason to postulate a nomological relation as well, and since the story about my aunt and uncle wasn't true, I don't see any such special reason. The point that this example is meant to make is that it would be amazing if there was *always* some special reason why a second-order property was nomologically related to the effects in terms of which it is defined.

This consideration is based on the fact that second-order properties are defined in terms of effects. A second argument is based on a different feature of second-order properties, the quantification involved in them.

Supposing that provocativeness provokes the bull would be supposing a strange sort of overdetermination of the bull's anger. Of course overdetermination does sometimes happen. (The placebo effect is an example.) But to suppose that it always happens would be to suppose a bizarre systematic overdetermination. Whenever we have a first-order causal relation we can always define a second-order property on the model of provocativeness, and so every first-order causally relevant property would jointly determine its effect together with a second-order property. Indeed, the procedure iterates (for there is a third-order property that consists in the possession of a second-order property that is causally relevant to the effect), and so whenever there is one causally relevant property there would be an infinity of them. Even if the first-order property is causally sufficient for the effect, there would still be an unending series of other causally relevant properties. And we can define causally sufficient higher-order properties that would also be causally sufficient by the same reasoning.

The relation between second-order properties and the effects mentioned in their definitions is a "fork" relation, a *bit* like the one discussed earlier in the selection on correlation and causation. Both heat and electricity are conducted by free electrons in metals. Rising velocity of free electrons

I. Is responsible for rising thermal conductivity, and thus causally relevant to the explosion
II. Is responsible for the epiphenomenal rising electrical conductivity.

Similarly, there is a first-order chemical property of Seconal that

I. Is causally relevant to sleep
II. "Generates" an epiphenomenal second-order property of possessing some property that is causally relevant to sleep.

In other words, just as the rising velocity of free electrons causes the explosion while engendering an epiphenomenal increase in electrical conductivity, so the chemical property causes the sleep while engendering an epiphenomenal second-order property of dormitivity.

The picture just sketched is attractive, but hardly compelling. The analogy just mentioned is far from perfect. The two engendering relations mentioned in the preceding paragraph are certainly very different, and besides the analogy only holds if I am right about the (limited) epiphenomenality of second-order properties, so it cannot be used to prove that epiphenomenality. (Incidentally, the fact that the chemical property "engenders" dormitivity rather than causing dormitivity illustrates the difference between what I am calling 'epiphenomenalism' and traditional epiphenomenalism.) The overdetermination argument also is far from convincing. We are normally reluctant to accept overdetermination because it is wrong, other things equal, to postulate coincidences. If a man dies by drowning, we cannot suppose that there is always another cause of death as well, say, shooting. But no such coincidence would be involved in the series of higher-and-higher-order causally efficacious properties I mentioned. If accepting such a series of causally efficacious properties is a price that must be paid for avoiding the problems to be mentioned, it can be paid.

In the end, the argument based on nomological theories of causal relevance is the best one. However, we can hardly expect those who favor counterfactual theories of causal relevance to be convinced. *Here, as earlier in the paper, the lesson is that if you want to avoid epiphenomenalism, go for a counterfactual theory of causal relevance, not a nomological theory.* This is, I suppose, the main positive point of the paper, though its significance depends on the fate of the counterfactual approach.

Let me sum up the skeptical thesis. Suppose that a second-order property is instantiated, and the effect in terms of which it is defined occurs; my claim is that the second-order property needn't be causally relevant to the effect. I have mentioned one type of case in which a second-order property can affect the effects in terms of which it is defined (and other things as well), namely, when intelligent recognition of them takes place, as in the placebo effect. Accepting other sorts of second-order effects (e.g., causal relevance of dormitivity to cancer) would not change my claim, since the arguments I gave for the limited epiphenomenality – the nomological argument and the overdetermination argument – were restricted to the causal relevance of a second-order property on the effects in terms of which it is defined, not other effects. The epiphenomenalism I am worried about is not total inertness of content properties, but whether, for example, the content of my

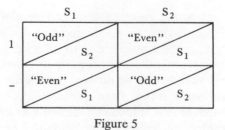

Figure 5

desire for an ice cream cone is causally relevant to my going to the ice cream shop.[9]

At this point, I shall change gears abruptly. Although, as I've said, the case I've made for the (limited) inefficacy of the second-order property is far from conclusive, I think I have said enough for it to be taken seriously. What I now propose to do is simply *assume* that second-order properties are not always causally relevant to the effects in terms of which they are defined, and go on to discuss the consequences of this idea.

The skeptical point of this section depends on the fact that the mechanisms that manipulate genes and the mechanisms that manipulate the internal representations in the brain are not intelligent, and so cannot recognize second-order properties. Hence these are just the kinds of cases in which it would seem that the second-order properties are inefficacious with respect to the effects in terms of which they are defined. Likewise for other special sciences whose properties are plausibly second-order.

By way of an example, consider a simple finite automaton, the one specified by the machine table of Figure 5. What the table requires of any machine that it describes is that it have two states, S_1 and S_2, such that when the machine is in S_1 and sees a '1' it cries 'odd' and goes into S_2; and when the machine is in S_2 and sees a '1', it cries 'even' and goes back into S_1. And when the machine is in S_1/S_2 and sees no input ('–' symbolizes the null input), it cries 'even'/'odd' (respectively), staying in the same state. Thus the machine tells us whether it has seen an odd or even number of '1's' (though not entirely successfully, since it is under the impression that 0 is an even number).

Now suppose we have a machine on the desk in front of us that satisfies Figure 5 (i.e., is described by the table) and is in S_1; it sees a '1', and so it cries 'odd'. Let us ask: is the property of being in state S_1 (of a machine of the type of Figure 5) causally relevant to the production of the cry of 'odd'? If the points made about dormitivity and provocativeness are right, it would seem not. If we think of S_1 as a property, it is the property that consists in having two other properties that are related to one another and to inputs and outputs as specified in Figure 5. These other properties would be mechanical properties in the case of a gears-and-pulleys implementation, electronic properties in a usual computer implementation, and so on. If we are dealing with an electronic implementation, then it is the electronic properties that are causally relevant to the cry of 'odd', not the property of possessing some such implementation property.

The upshot is that *computational properties have no causal relevance to what computers do*, these effects being entirely the product of the implementations of the computational properties. This is indeed a strange conclusion, and if I am right about second-order properties, comparably strange conclusions could be reached about other functional sciences.

Consider the property of being a brown-hair gene. This property is plausibly functionally characterizable in terms of its patterns of inheritance and interaction with other genetic properties in determining actual characteristics, for example, in the fact that brown-hair genes are dominant over blond-hair genes. Such second-order properties are part of the distinctive conceptual apparatus of Mendelian genetics. But there are no genetic mechanisms that detect or are sensitive to the property of being a brown-hair gene. Genetic mechanisms detect biochemical properties, and the property of being a brown-hair gene arises via the processing based on biochemical properties. Similarly, computational properties such as S_1 mentioned above arise via the activity of processors that detect syntactic properties, not computational properties such as S_1. And semantic properties arise via the activity of processors that detect syntactic properties. All these second-order properties are epiphenomenal with respect to the effects in terms of which they are defined, such as brown hair in the case of the brown-hair gene.[10]

In sum, we want to maintain all of the following, but they are inconsistent:

1. Special science properties are causally relevant to the effects those sciences predict and explain.
2. Special science properties are often functional.
3. Functional properties are standardly causally irrelevant to the effects they are defined in terms of.

I have just argued for 3. If I am right, then we have what for many of us is a dilemma: we must either abandon functionalism or accept epiphenomenalism. But am I right about 3? Recall that the case for 3 depended mainly on the nomological approach to causation, and perhaps the way out is to reject that approach. Before accepting that conclusion, however, it would be best to examine another way out.

7. Because

The claim that second-order properties are standardly causally irrelevant to the effects in terms of which they are defined seems to fly in the face of a variety of commonsense and scientific facts, for example, true uses of the following:

> I slept because I took a sleeping pill.
> My muscle tension evaporated because I took a muscle relaxant.
> The vase broke because it was fragile.
> I have blue eyes because I have two blue-eye genes

I shall argue that such facts only seem incompatible with the (standard) causal inefficacy of the second order because of two ambiguities that easily escape notice.

Explanation and causation

One ambiguity is that between explanatory and causal uses of 'because'. It is easy to be unclear about whether a 'because' statement is true in an explanatory or causal sense of 'because'. If the dispositional/functional terms in the sentences listed above are understood to refer to second-order properties, then the sentences are only true on an explanatory, not a causal, reading of 'because' – if the line of thought of the last section is correct.

Audiences who have heard this chapter read as a paper have often objected that although there is a clear distinction between explanation and causation, the distinction between the *causal-explanatory relevance and causal relevance of properties* that I rely on here is a distinction without a difference. Here is the issue: The kind of explanation involved here is causal explanation, which is one of a number of species of explanation. So the kind of explanatory relevance of properties at issue is causal-explanatory relevance. And what is the distinction between causal-explanatory relevance of properties and causal relevance of properties?

Here is a way of seeing that there is a difference and what it is: notice that we can causally explain a case of sleep via appeal to the second-order property of dormitivity. I fell asleep because I took a pill that had the property of having some property or other that causes sleep. This is causal-explanatory because it rules out alternative causal explanations of my falling asleep – for example, that I was grading papers. But second-order properties being (standardly) causally inefficacious, the appeal to dormitivity is not an appeal to a causally relevant property. Dormitivity is causal-explanatorily relevant to sleep without being causally relevant to sleep. Why? The appeal to dormitivity *involves* an appeal to a property that is genuinely causally relevant to the production of sleep, namely, the unnamed property (presumably a first-order chemical property) whose existence is mentioned in the analysis of the second-order property, the one that the dormitivity of the pill consists in the possession of. Dormitivity has causal-explanatory relevance because it involves a causally efficacious property. A causally inefficacious property can nonetheless be causal-explanatory if it "brings in" a causally efficacious property. But the causally relevant property is the first-order one, not the second-order one (assuming that my argument for the standard causal inertness of the second-order was right).

Ambiguity of functional terms

Functional terms are ambiguous. Let's take 'dormitivity' as an example. One construal is the second-order one much discussed here already – dormitivity = *possessing a property that causes sleep*. The other construal, one equally justified in ordinary usage, is *the property that causes sleep*. This is the natural reading of 'dormitive virtue' in the assertion that the dormitive virtue of Seconal is causally responsible for sleep. This latter construal is one in which 'dormitivity' is analyzed as a definite description that picks out the first-order property that is quantified over in the former construal. The two construals are very different in their relation to context. 'Dormitivity', on the former construal, always picks out the same second-order property. But on the latter construal, it picks out different first-order properties in the case of different types of sleeping potions. For the property that causes sleep in the case of Seconal is different from the property that causes sleep in the case of Valium. Similarly, 'the winning number' picks out different numbers in different lotteries (Lewis's example).

To sum up: In the second-order sense, dormitivity is not causally relevant to sleep; in the first-order sense, it is. And the plausibility of the 'because' claims mentioned at the outset of this section can be ascribed to the first-order interpretation.[11]

David Lewis has long advocated a form of functionalism based on Smart's idea of topic neutral analyses of mental terms (Lewis, 1972). Functional terms are defined by Lewis in the latter of the two manners mentioned above – in terms of definite descriptions. Many functional-ists adopt a functional state identity thesis, one that identifies mental states with second-order properties. Lewis, by contrast, says that mental states are *functionally specified* brain states. Many functionalists take pain to be a second-order state, but Lewis takes pain to be the first-order brain state that plays the role characterized by the second-order state. Where some functionalists identify mental states with states that consist in causal roles, Lewis takes mental states to be the entities that have the causal roles. The issue is about how to regiment the language of the mental (and other theoretical languages).

Now some may embrace Lewis's first-order reading of functional terms of the special sciences as a way of having their cake and eating it too. On Lewis's construal, it is correct to say "Dormitivity is causally relevant to sleep," "Content is causally relevant to behavior," and the like.[12] If we accept Lewis's reading, we can preserve the talk that would be appropriate if special science properties were causally efficacious. So it seems that we can avoid epiphenomenalism, and not have to give up functionalism. And there is no need to reject a nomological theory of causal relevance.

Unfortunately, the Lewis solution (as I shall call it) is only cosmetic. To construe the functional terms of a special science in Lewis's manner is to construe them as picking out "lower level" properties, properties of an *implementation* science. 'Believing that grass is green' on the Lewis construal picks out a *physiological* property. (In us, that is; in the case of a hypothetical intelligent computer, it would pick out an electronic property.) And in a certain sense, 'believing that grass is green' does not pick out a *psychological* property; that is, it does not pick out a property that is part of the distinctive conceptual apparatus of psychology. On Lewis's construal, 'brown-hair gene' (a term used by Mendelian geneticists long before the advent of molecular biology) picks out a piece of DNA, the concept of which would have been utterly alien to Mendel. Consider the computational state S_1 of Figure 5. I said it was a computational state, and indeed the computational definition was given in the text. But on Lewis's construal, 'S_1' picks out an electronic state or a mechanical state, or some other implementation state, depending on the way the automaton is constructed. 'S_1' would be defined by Lewis's method as *the (contextually relevant) state that has the role specified in the table of Figure 5*. So 'S_1' does *not* pick out a computational state at all.

Of course, if a "psychological property" is just a property picked out by a psychological term, then 'believing that grass is green' does pick out a psychological property, and likewise 'brown-hair gene' does pick out a Mendelian property and 'S_1' does pick out a computational property. But these construals of "psychological property", etc., are Pickwickian. Psychological properties, on this construal, are not part of the conceptual apparatus of psychology; Mendelian properties are not part of the conceptual apparatus of Mendelian genetics; and computational properties are properties that a computer scientist may know nothing about, properties that are really part of the conceptual apparatus of electronics or mechanics or hydraulics.

My point is this: You do not vindicate the causal efficacy of the properties of a special science by construing its terms as referring to the properties of other sciences, implementation sciences. The Lewis construal does preserve a way of talking that we want. We can speak of the state S_1 being causally relevant to the production of the machine's cry of "Even!" But the cost is that we no longer take S_1 to be a computational state (except in a Pickwickian sense). So a Lewis vindication of the causal efficacy of the computational is certainly Pickwickian. Similarly, since believing that grass is green is a physiological, not a psychological, state, the preservation of talk of the causal efficacy of believing that grass is green is no real vindication of the causal efficacy of the mental.

Construing terms of the special sciences in Lewis's manner does not make the second-order properties I have been talking about any less distinctive of their special sciences. Rather, it merely forces a different way of referring to them. 'Believing that grass grows', construed in Lewis's manner, picks out a physiological state, not a functional state. But 'having the belief that grass grows' picks out the functional state. 'S_1' picks out an electronic or mechanical or some other implementation state, but 'being in S_1' picks out a genuine computational state. Computational states are what are distinctive about the computational sciences, and Lewis's way of talking does not prevent us from referring to them or make them any less distinctive of the computational sciences. The same holds for the functional properties of all the special sciences for which functional properties are part of the distinctive conceptual apparatus. These properties remain distinctive of these special sciences even if we construe terms à la Lewis, and these properties remain causally inert (that is, causally inert with respect to effects in terms of which they are defined).

In sum, moving to the Lewis way of talking does not solve the epiphenomenalism problem, but only provides a way of talking that allows us to avoid facing it. The basic picture provided by the Lewis way of talking is the same as the one I have been trying to avoid: special sciences whose distinctive properties are causally inert but that can be used to pick out causally efficacious properties of lower-level sciences.

This brings me to a second objection to the Lewis solution. Second-order properties in the sense discussed here are properties that consist in the having of properties with such and such relations to one another. As I mentioned earlier, the properties quantified over need not be first-order. In the case of our mental properties construed as second-order properties, the quantified properties are physiological. Physiological properties are biological properties, and biological properties generally are prime candidates for functional analysis. Thus 'believing that grass grows' construed in the Lewis manner, since it picks out a physiological property, *may pick out another functionally individuated property*. Perhaps biological terms themselves pick out first-order properties, but perhaps not. Perhaps only the most fundamental of physical properties are genuinely first-order. In that case, even much of physics would be epiphenomenal! Or perhaps not even the most fundamental physical properties are first-order. (Maybe there isn't any most fundamental level.) Perhaps science is functional "all the way down." (Recall that there is a case made by Lewis himself for functional analysis of all theoretical terms.) This is not a matter that is easily resolved, but without a resolution that rules out the "functional all the way down" option, we cannot rely on construing mental language in Lewis's manner to rescue us from epiphenomenalism.

Construing special science terms in Lewis's manner makes epiphenomenalism easier to stomach, but epiphenomenalism with controlled heartburn is still epiphenomenalism. Perhaps the solution is to reject functionalism, but if functionalism is rejected, we must begin anew to confront the arguments for epiphenomenalism in the computer model all over again. Functionalism at least has the virtue of disposing of epiphenomenalism on a counterfactual understanding of causal relevance. However, if we prefer the nomological approach to causal relevance, I am doubtful that there is any way of avoiding epiphenomenalism.

Notes

1 There are, however, important differences that I don't have the space to go into. Briefly, it is more plausible that content supervenes on the neural level than that content supervenes on the "syntactic" level. (More about the meaning of 'syntactic' here shortly.) An appeal to supervenience of content on lower levels can be used to attempt to avoid the epiphenomenalism argument.

2 The idea described here was, as far as I know, first articulated in Fodor (1975, 1980). See also Dennett (1981) in which the terms 'semantic engine' and 'syntactic engine' first appear, and Newell (1980) and Pylyshyn (1984). I spoke of a correlation between causal interactions among symbolic structures in our brains and sensible relations among the meanings of the symbol structures. This way of speaking can be misleading if it encourages the picture of the neuroscientist opening the brain, just *seeing* the symbols, and then figuring out what they mean. Since syntactic objects (and perhaps meanings as well) are functional entities (though different types of functional entities), identifying either of them in the brain will require considerable appreciation of neurological functioning.

3 This has long been a central dogma of the computational point of view, and has long been challenged by some philosophers. For arguments against the claim stated here, see Kim (1972), Richardson (1979), Enc (1983), and Patricia Churchland (1986). Block (1980a) argues against Kim, Patricia Kitcher (1980, 1982) argues against Richardson, and Blackburn (forthcoming) argues against Enc and Churchland.

4 Alternatively, we could raise the thermal conductivity of the rod by raising its temperature, in which case part of the additional heat that causes the bomb to explode will come from the heat source that raises the temperature of the rod, and part will come from the fire via the increased thermal conductivity of the rod. I take it to be uncontroversial that rising thermal conductivity of the rod is causally relevant to the explosion. Further, this case fits the nomist model. For in this setup, rising thermal conductivity, *ceteris paribus*, is sufficient for an explosion, (and the *ceteris paribus* condition is satisfied).

5 See Block (1986, 1987) for other reasons for taking functional role theories seriously. See Fodor (1987a), Chapter 3, and Schiffer (1987), Chapter 2, for opposing arguments.

6 LePore and Loewer (1987) give an objection (in effect) to Sosa's (1984) version of the Counterfactual Argument. Putting the matter in my terms, they agree that if a syntactic object with a certain meaning produces an output, the syntactic object would have caused the same output even if it had had a different meaning. But they add that meanings are lawfully related to behavior in some circumstances, so in such circumstances, the meaning would have caused the same output even if it had been carried by a different syntactic object. If the first counterfactual shows that syntactic forms screen off meanings from causal relevance, then the second shows the converse, that meanings screen off syntactic forms from causal relevance. But if both are true, both the syntactic form and the meaning of a representation are epiphenomenal, and since that is absurd, the obvious conclusion is that something is wrong with the form of the Counterfactual Argument. According to LePore and Loewer, semantics and syntax are *symmetrically* related to the production of behavior; if one is epiphenomenal, so is the other, so the Counterfactual Argument cannot use the causal relevance of syntax as a club against the causal relevance of semantics.

This issue deserves much more detailed treatment, but I can only summarize briefly. The LePore and Loewer argument fails to take into account the distinction between a particular event token, and *some* token of that type. Suppose I have a syntactic object in my head, Sally, with certain syntactic and semantic properties that produces behavior, Bruce. As I mentioned in the last paragraph, LePore and Loewer and I agree that Sally would have caused Bruce even if it had had a different meaning or no meaning at all. But can we make the *symmetrical claim* that Sally would have caused Bruce even if it had had a different syntactic identity or no syntactic identity at all? Certainly not! If Sally had had a different syntactic identity or no syntactic identity at all, then it simply would not be the syntactic object I originally picked out as 'Sally'. Had the original meaning been "carried" by a syntactic object not identical to Sally, we may suppose that the result would have been a Bruce-*like* behavior. But this Bruce-like behavior would not be identical to Bruce – given that events are individuated causally, as all good Davidsonians (such as LePore and Loewer) believe. Bruce's identity requires being caused by Sally. LePore and Loewer may feel that the way out is to talk not about the production of Bruce, but rather of Bruce-like events – types, not tokens. (There is some hint of this in their paper.) But the screening argument only works with tokens. What makes us want to say that the syntactic screens off the semantic is that the very same bit of behavior would have been produced even if the syntactic event that produced it had had a different meaning. (See Enc [1986] for a dissection of another fallacy that falls afoul of the type/token distinction together with causal individuation.) LePore and Loewer are right that there is a *nomological symmetry* between syntax and semantics. That is, there are circumstances in which both the semantic and syntactic properties of an event are nomologically sufficient for a certain type of behavior. But what is at issue here is counterfactual symmetry rather than a nomological symmetry, and this they have not argued for.

7 Note that it is no part of the "Language of Thought" view to insist that the frog has a language of thought. The argument for a language of thought in humans depends on the productivity and systematicity of human thought, and this argument will not apply to creatures whose thought is not at least as productive and systematic. See the epilogue of Fodor (1987a).

8 My point differs from the usual skepticism about the causal efficacy of dispositional properties in this respect, and also in that it is about a category of properties – second-order properties – of which dispositional properties are only a special case.

9 After writing this chapter, I read Jackson and Pettit (1988), which claimed that second-order properties are inefficacious before I did. However, Jackson and Pettit say that second-order properties are inert, not just with respect to the effects in terms of which they are defined, but all effects. They don't give any of the arguments used here, though Jackson tells me (in correspondence) that the overdetermination argument is essentially consonant with their way of looking at things. They go further, committing themselves, I think, to the claim that all "multiply realizable" properties are causally inert. Thus if an increase in temperature of a gas inside a sealed glass container results in the glass shattering, they take the fact that there are many configurations of molecules that could realize this process to show that the increase in temperature did not cause the shattering, but rather the cause was the specific molecular interactions. They do not note that the same point applies to the molecular interactions, which are themselves multiply realizable in terms of interactions among electrons, protons, neutrons, etc. And of course, some of these particles are perhaps realizable in different ways by still smaller particles. The upshot of their position would be that the only genuine causality inheres at the level of basic physics. But what if there is no such level? This is a real physical possibility. (See Dehmelt, 1989, 1990.) *Their position dictates that we do not now know for sure whether there are any causally efficacious properties at all.* Jackson tells me that they are prepared to locate all genuine causality at the basic physics level, so long as one distinguishes between two types of causal relevance: the notion used here and the notion of causal relevance that corresponds to their idea of a causal programming explanation. The idea of causal programming can be illustrated by their example of an explanation of why trees grow faster in Melbourne than in Canberra: Why? Because there are more frosts in Canberra. There being more frosts in Canberra causally programs there being faster growth in Melbourne. They hold that second-order properties (and other multiply realizable properties) can be causally relevant to something in this causal programming sense, but not in the sense appropriate only to basic physics.

10 For the purposes of this example, I am ignoring the issue of whether there is anything at the molecular level that corresponds very well to the gene. See Philip Kitcher (1982).

11 See Block (1980a) for a more detailed discussion of the difference between the first- and second-order interpretations.

12 Block (1986), pp. 668–9, takes this way out, as does Jackson and Pettit (1988).

Bibliography

Block, Ned, 1980a. *Readings in Philosophy of Psychology, Vol.* 1. Cambridge, Mass.: Harvard University Press.

  1980b. "What Is Functionalism?" In Block (1980).

  1986. "Advertisement for a Semantics for Psychology." In P. A. French et al., eds., *Midwest Studies in Philosophy,* Vol. X. Minneapolis: University of Minnesota Press, 615–78.

  1987. "Functional Role and Truth Conditions," *Proceedings of the Aristotelian Society,* supplementary volume, 61, 157–81.

Churchland, P. S., 1986. *Neurophilosophy.* Cambridge, Mass.: MIT Press.

Dehmelt, Hans, 1989. "Triton,... electron,... cosmon,...: An infinite regression?" *Proceedings of the National Academy of Sciences,* 86, 8618.

  1990. "Experiments on the structure of an individual elementary particle," *Science,* 247, 539–45.

Dennett, Daniel, 1981. "Three Kinds of Intentional Psychology." In R. Healy, ed., *Reduction, Time and Reality.* Cambridge: Cambridge University Press.

Dretske, Fred, 1988. *Explaining Behavior: Reasons in a World of Causes.* Cambridge, Mass.: MIT Press.

Enc, Berent, 1983. "In Defence of the Identity Theory," *Journal of Philosophy,* 80, 279–98.

  1986, "Essentialism with Individual Essences: Causation, Kinds, Supervenience, and Restricted Identities." In P. A. French et al., eds., *Midwest Studies in Philosophy.* Vol. XI. Minneapolis: University of Minnesota Press, 403–26.

Fodor, Jerry, 1975. *The Language of Thought.* Cambridge, Mass.: Harvard University Press.

  1980. "Methodological Solipsism Considered as a Research Strategy in Cognitive Psychology," *Behavioral and Brain Sciences,* 3, 417–24.

  1987a. *Psychosemantics.* Cambridge, Mass.: MIT Press.

  1987b. "Making Mind Matter More." This is Fodor's reply to Lepore and Loewer (1987). The abstract appeared in *Journal of Philosophy,* 84, 642.

  In press. "Making Mind Matter More," *Philosophical Topics.*

Haugeland, John, 1980. "Programs, Causal Powers, and Intentionality," *Behavioral and Brain Sciences,* 3, 432–3.

  1981. *Mind Design.* Cambridge, Mass.: MIT Press.

Horwich, Paul, 1987. *Asymmetries in Time.* Cambridge, Mass.: MIT Press.

Jackson, Frank, and Philip Pettit, 1988. "Functionalism and Broad Content." *Mind,* 97, 387, 381–400.

Kim, Jaegwon, 1972. "Phenomenal Properties, Psychophysical Laws, and the Identity Theory," *Monist,* 56, 177–92. Partially reprinted in Block (1980).

  1984. "Epiphenomenal and Supervenient Causation." In P. A. French et al., eds., *Midwest Studies in Philosophy.* Vol. IX. Minneapolis: University of Minnesota Press; 257–70.

Kitcher, Patricia, 1980. "How to Reduce a Functional Psychology," *Philosophy of Science*, 47, 134–40.

    1982. "Genes, Reduction and Functional Psychology," *Philosophy of Science*, 49, 633–6.

Kitcher, Philip, 1982. "Genes," *British Journal for the Philosophy of Science*, 33, 337–59.

LePore, E., and B. Loewer, 1987. "Mind Matters," *Journal of Philosophy*, 84, 630–41.

Lewis, David, 1970. "How to Define Theoretical Terms," *Journal of Philosophy*, 67, 427–46.

    1972. "Psychophysical and Theoretical Identifications," *Australasian Journal of Philosophy*, 50, 249–58. Reprinted in Block (1980).

Minsky, Marvin, 1967. *Computation*. Englewood Cliffs, N.J.: Prentice-Hall.

Newell, Alan, 1980. "Physical Symbol Systems," *Cognitive Science*, 4, 135–83.

Putnam, Hilary, 1960. "Minds and Machines." In S. Hook, ed., *Dimensions of Mind*. New York: New York University Press.

    1967. "Psychological Predicates." In W. H. Capitan and D. D. Merrill, eds., *Art, Mind, and Religion*. Pittsburgh: University of Pittsburgh Press. Retitled "The Nature of Mental States" in Putnam's collected papers. Reprinted in Block (1980).

    1973, 1975. "Philosophy and Our Mental Life." *Mind, Language and Reality: Philosophical Papers*, Vol. 2. Cambridge: Cambridge University Press. Reprinted in Block (1980), and in somewhat different form, in Haugeland (1981). Originally published in *Cognition*, 2 (1973), with a section on IQ that has been omitted from all of the reprinted versions.

    1988. *Representation and Reality*. Cambridge, Mass.: MIT Press.

Pylyshyn, Zenon, 1984. *Computation and Cognition: Issues in the Foundations of Cognitive Science*. Cambridge, Mass.: MIT Press.

Richardson, Robert, 1979. "Functionalism and Reductionism," *Philosophy of Science*, 46, 533/558.

Schiffer, Stephen, 1987. *Remnants of Meaning*. Cambridge, Mass.: MIT Press.

Searle, John, 1980. "Searle's Reply to Critics of 'Minds, Brains and Programs'," *Behavioral and Brain Sciences*, 3, 450–7.

Sosa, Ernest, 1984. "Mind-Body Interaction and Supervenient Causation." In P. A. French et al., eds., *Midwest Studies in Philosophy*. Vol. IX. Minneapolis: University of Minnesota Press, 271–82.

8

Realism, conventionality, and "realism about"

RICHARD BOYD

0. Realism and conventionality

0.0. Realism

Scientific realists hold (against social constructivism) that the characteristic product of successful scientific research involves knowledge of
causal structures whose existence and properties are independent of the
adoption of the theories and conceptual frameworks that describe
them, and (against empiricism) that this remains true even when the
causal structures in question would have to be unobservable. In general,
the case for scientific realism depends on the observation that many
apparently central features of scientific concepts and practices seem to
involve reference to such theory-independent and unobservable structures; the concepts appear to be theoretically defined and the practices
to be theory-dependent (Boyd 1972, 1973, 1979, 1982, 1983, 1985a, b, c,
1988a, 1989, 1990; Hacking 1984; Glymour 1984; McMullin 1984;
Putnam 1972, 1975a, b; for a general account of arguments for realism
that appeal to this observation, see Boyd 1983, 1988, 1990).

0.1. Anti-realism and conventionalism

A variety of anti-realist responses to arguments for realism from the
theory-dependence of scientific practice are possible, but one characteristic and pervasive anti-realist strategy has been to acknowledge that
various scientific concepts and practices implicate theoretical knowledge but to provide an interpretation of scientific language and
concepts according to which the relevant knowledge is grounded in
linguistic convention or social construction rather than knowledge of
theory-independent unobservable phenomena.

Thus, for example, according to the operationalism and phenom-
enalism of Carnap 1928, theoretical claims apparently referring to
unobservables are knowable because they are translatable into the
physical-thing language, and ultimately into the sense-datum language.
Crucially, the rules of translation, which certainly look as though they
embody claims about the observable effects of unobservable phenomena and about the sensory effects of medium-sized physical objects, are
to be rationally reconstructed as truths by convention. The culmination
of this tendency within logical empiricism is surely the position of
Carnap 1950, according to which the methodological role of *un*reduced
theoretical laws is acknowledged but according to which those laws
themselves are to be understood as reflections of linguistic conventions
establishing the relevant scientific languages.

Quite similar treatments of the theoretical commitments that govern
scientific research were of course advanced by philosophers in the
constructivist tradition (see, e.g., Hanson 1958; Kuhn 1960); indeed, the
treatment of the semantics of theoretical terms in Kuhn 1960 owes so
much to the tradition embodied in Carnap 1950 that it is an interesting
question how to tell late Carnap from Kuhn. (For an answer see Boyd
1989, 1990.) Thus the strategy of treating certain methodologically
significant theoretical doctrines as reflections of linguistic convention
has been a central component of anti-realist philosophical arguments
within each of the important anti-realist traditions in the philosophy of
science.

0.2. Realism and conventionalism

The dialectical situation established by the conventionalist argumenta-
tive strategy within anti-realist philosophy of science led to the establishment within the realist tradition of a strong anti-conventionalist
outlook, bolstered by supporting realist conceptions of the semantics of
scientific terms. One consequence is that, almost always, philosophers
in the realist tradition diagnose a much lower level of linguistic or social
conventionality in a given body of scientific discourse than do their
empiricist or constructivist colleagues; indeed, one of the most significant recent contributions of scientific realism to philosophy generally
has been the articulation of the naturalistic conceptions of natural kinds
and of reference that underwrite the realist suspicion of appeals to
conventionality (Putnam 1972, 1975a, b; Kripke 1971, 1972; Boyd 1979,
1982). As we shall see, however, this deep antipathy to conventionalism

also poses problems for scientific realism; these problems are the subject of the present essay.

1. Realism and "realism about"

1.0. Realism and what there isn't

In an influential passage Putnam (1975c, p. 290), following Boyd 1971, presents a realist conception of science as embodying the principle that "terms in a mature scientific theory typically refer; Laws of a mature scientific theory are typically approximately true." Surely scientific realism, if it is to be thought of as a systematic conception of science, must be committed to something like this principle. There are, however, some terms in some mature sciences that pretty unproblematically don't refer. There was (and there is) no ether, so the term "ether" in the theory of electromagnetic radiation didn't refer. Arguably, "caloric" didn't either, nor did "phlogiston." Perhaps *most* of the terms in Ptolemaic astronomy failed to refer to features of the natural world, however apt they may have been for the calculation of the relative position of the earth and various other bodies. Scientific realism must account for occasional cases of *reference failure* – and perhaps for some wholesale failures of reference, unless a non-question-begging defense of the non-maturity of Ptolemaic astronomy is available.

There are other things there aren't (or perhaps aren't) for which realists must account. As Putnam (1972, 1975a, b) emphasized, it is an intended consequence of contemporary realist conceptions of kinds, properties and other natural categories that they usually possess natural, real, or "essential" – as opposed to conventional or "nominal" – definitions (see also Kripke 1971, 1972; Boyd 1979, 1988a, 1989, 1990). Of course it is unproblematical that some aspects of the definitions of scientifically important categories are arbitrary or conventional (the sign of the charge of the electron, the unit of measurement for mass, ...). What is interesting is that there are, at least arguably, cases of *unexpected conventionality of definition* – cases in which we find nominal definitions where realists would ordinarily expect to find real ones. For example, there certainly are species *and* higher taxa, but some systematists (cladists) insist that although species are "real," higher taxa aren't "real." By this they mean that the definitions of higher taxa are largely conventional. Although the reasons cladists make explicit for this surprising conclusion are usually laced with simplistic positivist principles that no sophisticated empiricist could accept, their position can best be understood as ultimately and plausibly grounded in a particular theoretical conception of the mechanisms of macroevolution. (For a defense of this nonpositivist "rational reconstruction," see Guyot 1987.) They are thus the sorts of reasons a scientific realist must prima facie take seriously. Among the paradigm cases of apparent natural kinds, then, are some that a realist might have to admit are nominal rather than natural.

Once the possibility of unexpected conventionality of definition is acknowledged, it can be seen that there is the closely related possibility of *unexpected conventionality of laws or generalizations*: cases in which the truth (or approximate truth) of laws or empirical generalizations turns out to depend in unexpected ways on conventions in scientific practice – either conventional definitions of particular terms or broader conventions of methodological and linguistic practice. I am inclined to think that examples of this sort are commonplace, but it's hard to find one that's altogether uncontroversial. Here is a plausible example: IQ test scores in typical populations exhibit a normal distribution. Plainly this is an empirical generalization; it is conceivable that it should turn out to be significantly wrong about the results of some methodologically appropriate IQ testing. It has, moreover, been cited as providing evidence bearing on an important scientific question: the question of the genetic contribution to intelligence differences. According to Lewontin 1976, Jensen 1968 reasons that, since a normal distribution is characteristic of certain sorts of polygenetically determined traits, the normal distribution of IQ scores provides some evidence that intelligence is such a trait.

In response one might quite plausibly suggest that the normality of the distribution of IQ scores is an artifact of conventions of test design and test standardization. While normality of distribution is not, strictly, part of a nominal definition of IQ (so that the normality of actually obtained measurements is an empirical fact), normality may well obtain largely because of conventions and practices in psychometrics rather than because of any underlying structure (genetic or otherwise) in the relevant experimental subjects. If this is right, then here is unexpected conventionality in a law or empirical generalization, one that renders the generalization evidentially irrelevant with respect to the question of the genetics of intelligence differences.

1.1. *"Realism about" and the integrity of scientific realism*

When the issue is raised of whether some apparently referring expression in some scientific theory really referred, or of whether some theoretical expression has a real rather than a nominal definition, it is common (if, as I shall argue, misleading) to describe the issue as the issue of "realism about x," where x is the relevant expression. Thus the question of the existence of the ether is the question of "realism about the ether" and the question of whether or not higher taxa have non-conventional definitions is the question of "realism about higher taxa." Presumably questions about the absence or presence of unexpected conventionality in laws or generalizations would receive a similar formulation: Jensen and Lewontin differ, I suppose, regarding "realism about the normality of IQ score distributions."

This terminology encourages and, more important, reflects a certain fragmented conception of scientific realism, one according to which realism is deeply topic specific. One may be a realist about some sorts of alleged natural phenomena (or natural definitions or laws or generalizations) and an anti-realist about others, picking and choosing as one's philosophical inclinations dictate. Such a conception weakens the case for scientific realism in several respects. First, part of the attraction of scientific realism is that it appears to offer a distinctive and coherent conception of scientific knowledge – one which, for example, preserves a certain commonsense (or perhaps common science) conception of the way in which scientists exploit causal interactions with natural phenomena in order to obtain new knowledge. If instead there is no coherent overall realist picture but instead a piecemeal amalgamation of realist and anti-realist conceptions of various components of scientific theorizing, the philosophical attractiveness of realist positions is significantly reduced.

The absence of a coherent overall realist position weakens the case for "realism about" any particular set of alleged entities or definitions in another way. The philosopher with realist inclinations will, presumably, be a "realist about" those (alleged) entities or definitions or laws with respect to which defending a realist position is easiest, and an "anti-realist" about those regarding which the defense of realism is most difficult. If there is no coherent realist conception of scientific knowledge to rationalize or underwrite this picking and choosing, there will be the reasonable suspicion that the realist is only apparently winning even the easy battles: that eventually these too will provide victories for the systematic anti-realist (or, perhaps, will prove to be cases the systematically anti-realist empiricist or constructivist need not contest).

This latter difficulty is compounded by another consideration. It is reasonable to argue that the history of recent philosophy of science is a history of concessions by anti-realist philosophers to scientific realism (I develop this theme in Boyd 1988a and 1989). Thus, for example, the development of theories of the semantics of scientific language seems to be driven almost entirely by the necessity to accommodate the apparent growth of knowledge about unobservable (and/or naturalistically defined) entities. Surely it is a significant part of the prima facie case for realism that such concessions have been characteristic of the development of the opposing positions. Of course if realism is the fragmented position suggested by the "realism about" terminology then this case is undermined. Not only is there no coherent realist position to which concessions have been made, but each case of reference failure, or of unexpected conventionality of a definition or of a law or generalization, will count as a failure of "realism about," and its acknowledgment will count as a concession to systematic anti-realism.

1.2. Toward unfragmented realism

Several considerations suggest that the situation may not be so bad for systematic realism as the "realism about" terminology suggests. In the first place, it seems plain that there are some kinds of conventionality actually present in scientific practice whose recognition poses no threat to scientific realism, supposing there to be such a philosophical position. No one worries about "realism about the choice of units of length" or about "realism about the (exact) number of levels in the Linnean hierarchy." If we had an adequate understanding of why explicit and near-explicit conventional features of scientific language and practice pose no special problems for the integrity of scientific realism, we might expect to see that actual cases of unexpected conventionality pose no problems either.

That this should be so is suggested by the fact that scientific realism – presuming that there is such a coherent and systematic position – seems to predict the occurrence of unexpectedly conventional features of scientific theories. Recall that, on contemporary realist and naturalistic accounts of definition, the establishment of natural definitions for scientific terms arises under circumstances in which there are reasons (typically "theoretical reasons") to believe that certain sorts of similarity and difference in (often unobservable) properties are causally relevant to the behavior of systems under study. Terms are introduced and natural definitions proposed in order to "map" these presumed similarities and differences. Central to the realist's conception of definition is the understanding that particular definitional proposals may be, and often are, mistaken and that naturalistic definitions may thus be revised in the light of the growth of theoretical knowledge. It is precisely this conception of scientific definitions as a posteriori that underwrites the realist's response to incommensurability claims of constructivist philosophers of science like Kuhn (1970) (see Putnam 1975a).

If particular definitional proposals often reflect mistaken theoretical commitments, so too might broader definitional projects. Suppose that researchers justifiably believe that certain sorts of similarity and difference are causally important but that they are mistaken, not with respect to individual definitions but with respect to all or most of their conceptions of the sorts of similarity and difference that matter causally. Suppose that they introduce (apparently) appropriate terminology and establish tentative definitions that govern the use of that terminology. When (and if) their fundamental error is discovered, it is plausible that the terminology in question should be understood as possessing wholly or largely nominal definitions (Putnam 1975a). If the terminology has been central in the development of the relevant literature, it may be appropriate to retain it, acknowledging its largely arbitrary conventional character. Retrospectively it will be seen that the terminology in question exhibited unexpected conventionality.

Nothing in the scenario just sketched appears incompatible with a systematic realist conception of the growth of scientific knowledge. Indeed, some such scenario should be expected on a realist conception of inquiry about a sufficiently complex world. The scenario just sketched is precisely what, according to (an appropriate interpretation of) cladism, has happened with respect to taxonomic terminology above the species level. It hardly seems that a realist should find this possibility difficult to accommodate; no concession to anti-realism seems involved. Instead, it would appear that it is precisely because we have a workable realist conception of how definitions of scientific terms ordinarily work that we can understand what, according to cladists, is peculiar about higher taxa.

Nevertheless, it seems obvious that there are certain alleged cases of reference failure or of unexpected conventionality that a realist could not acknowledge without making a genuine concession to systematic anti-realism. In order to assess the prospects for non-fragmented realism we need to ascertain whether historical and scientific facts and sound philosophical arguments ever dictate acknowledgment of such cases. Of course, there is a prior question; namely, how much conventionality (and how much reference failure) can a systematic scientific realist consistently acknowledge? It is with this question that we shall be primarily concerned in the rest of this essay.

2. Realism and the limits of conventionality

2.0. Toward unfragmented realism: dialectics and philosophical packages

In Part 2 I'll try to formulate and defend a workable answer to the question of what a realist must be a "realist about." I'll focus primarily on the question of the sorts of conventionality in science that a systematic realist can acknowledge, and I'll indicate how the answer to that question generalizes naturally to the corresponding question about reference failure.

Elsewhere (Boyd 1988a, 1990) I address the general question of how a particular component of a realist treatment of scientific knowledge is to be assessed with regard to the question of its appropriateness vis-à-vis competing anti-realist conceptions. I argue that, in general, such components are properly assessed not in isolation but in terms of the extent to which they contribute to cogency of (one or more versions of) a broader realist "philosophical package" that presents a systematic treatment of epistemological, semantic, and metaphysical issues and incorporates relevant findings from the various special sciences that are the objects of philosophical investigation and from such disciplines as the history and sociology of science, psychology, and social theory. The cogency of such packages is itself to be assessed dialectically in terms of their relation to the best available anti-realist philosophical packages of similar scope.

Thus, for example, a proposal by a realist to treat a particular feature of scientific theorizing as largely conventional (or to treat a particular theoretical term as non-referring) is to be assessed in terms of the contribution that proposal makes (or fails to make) to the cogency of available realist philosophical packages vis-à-vis anti-realist alternatives. If a proposal of the sort at issue contributes to their cogency (or, perhaps, makes no difference to their cogency), then no concession to systematic anti-realism is involved in being "anti-realist" about the relevant phenomenon. If, on the other hand, the adoption of the proposal weakens available realist philosophical packages relative to (some of) their anti-realist competitors then a concession has been made and the "anti-realist" expression is not misleading.

What I propose to argue in the rest of Part 2 is that developments in the philosophy of science have proceeded (I think advanced) to a point at which, in consequence of the resulting dialectical situation vis-à-vis realism and systematic anti-realism, we can identify with some precision a constraint on realist philosophical packages that provides a clear answer to the question of what a realist must be a "realist about."

2.1. *Recent philosophy of science: two fixed points*

As I indicated in Section 0.0, arguments for realism and against empiricism in the philosophy of science have almost always proceeded from the observation that some aspect or other of scientific theorizing or practice is dependent on "theoretical" considerations in a way that would be surprising if knowledge of "unobservables" were impossible. Arguments for realism grounded in this sort of observation have taken many different forms. Thus, for example, it was often held that various methodologically central scientific practices are unintelligible if the concepts they employ are interpreted according to a verifiability criterion of meaningfulness or that they refute some other empiricist proposal regarding the semantics of scientific terms (see, e.g., Feigl 1956; Hempel 1965: Putnam 1975d; Quine 1961b). Various empiricist proposals for eliminating reference to unobservables were held to be incompatible with the logic of the quantificational structure of scientific theories (Quine 1961a), and it was held that any but a realist understanding of scientific theories would render the predictive success of some of them an inexplicable "miracle" (Putnam 1978).

Against these and other realist arguments, it was for some time common for empiricists in the philosophy of science to deny that – on a proper understanding – scientific practices and concepts are so theory-dependent as they at first appear. Examples of empiricist responses embodying such denials were the defense of operationalism and related eliminativist analyses of theoretical terms in science, and the articulation of an alleged sharp distinction between the "context of theory invention" (where theoretical considerations could play an epistemically harmless role) and the "context of confirmation" (which was to be free of theoretical commitments). The classic example (and the most durable) was the contemporary version of the Humean conception of causation and the associated deductive-nomological account of explanation, which, if successful, eliminate reference to unobservable causal powers of underlying mechanisms from the methodologically crucial notions of causation and explanation.

The developments within recent philosophy of science that, I shall argue, permit us to say with some certainty what a realist must be a "realist about" concern the variety of pro-realist philosophical arguments and the available anti-realist responses. In the first place, there has emerged a near consensus affirming *the ineliminability of theoretical commitments* from the rational methodological and linguistic practices of science. The anti-realist responses rehearsed above do not work, or at any rate they do not work well enough to eliminate wholesale theoretical commitments from the most clearly rational practices of even the most unproblematically scientific work.

In describing this position as near consensus I mean, of course, to indicate that it is widely accepted by those anti-realists to whom it might seem troubling, as well as by realists and constructivists for whom it is grist for their respective philosophical mills. Thus, for example, van Fraassen (1980) and Fine (1984) join the later person-stages of Putnam (1979, 1981) in acknowledging the ineliminable theory-dependence of scientific method while, of course, dissenting from a realist explanation for its rationality. Theoretical commitments may be understood realistically (Boyd 1982, 1983; McMullin 1984), according to "internal realism" (Putnam 1979, 1981; Fine 1984), as the social construction of reality (Kuhn 1970), or as a matter of rational acceptance without belief (van Fraassen 1980). They cannot be made to go away. Moreover, and this is important in what follows, not only is there near consensus about the ineliminability of theoretical considerations in science, there is very substantial descriptive, if not philosophical, agreement (due, I believe, largely to the persuasiveness of Kuhn 1970) about how such considerations influence theory choice, experimental design, assessment of evidence, improvements in instrumentation and so forth, for both actual cases and a significant range of philosophically relevant counterfactual cases.

The second important development in recent philosophy of science has been the recognition of the centrality of a class of "abductive" arguments for realism: arguments that exhibit a realist understanding of scientific theories as part of the best naturalistic explanation for the success of various features of scientific methods (Putnam 1975c; Boyd 1973, 1979, 1982, 1983, 1985a–c; for important critiques see especially Fine 1984; Laudan 1981; van Fraassen 1980). According to these arguments the *instrumental* reliability of scientific methods – their reliability as a guide to (approximate) truth about *observables* – is parasitic upon their reliability with respect to (approximate) truth about unobservables.

The arguments in question rely on the observation just discussed that the methods of science are profoundly theory dependent. If they are successful, what they show – about all of the central methodological practices of science – is that their reliability even with respect to observational knowledge is not explicable, nor is their application in seeking such knowledge justifiable, except on the assumption that they typically operate against a background of approximate theoretical knowledge and are reliable in the production of new theoretical knowledge. The methods of science work because they employ available approximate theoretical knowledge to establish an appropriate "fit" between the actual (and often unobservable) causal structures of the relevant phenomena and the methods and practices by which scientists gain additional knowledge (both observational and theoretical) about those phenomena. The selective skepticism of empiricist philosophy of science – accepting scientific knowledge of observables while denying it with respect to unobservables – is thus shown to be untenable, and realism to be the only alternative to extreme skepticism. Once the centrality of these arguments is understood and once it is recognized that the doctrine of the ineliminability of theoretical commitments on which they depend is near consensus, we are in a position to identify the crucial dialectical constraints on realist philosophical packages and assess their implications for the question of "realism about."

2.2. The central core of scientific realism

We are concerned to distinguish those cases of denying "realism about" some phenomena or other that are harmless to, or required by, a systematically developed realist philosophical package from those cases whose incorporation in a realist philosophical package would be genuine concessions to systematic anti-realism. In the light of the developments in the literature just rehearsed, I propose that we can identify two philosophical doctrines that define the essential central core of any realist philosophical package. The systematic realist, I suggest, is compelled to accept "realism about" in just those cases in which "realism about" is a necessary component in any defensible philosophical package that treats the relevant scientific cases and that incorporates the two central core realist doctrines.

The central arguments for realism are the abductive arguments for realism as a component in the best explanation for the instrumental reliability of various (uncontroversially) theory-dependent methods. It will be central to any realist philosophical package, then, that the relevant realist explanations are, almost always, the correct ones. The first central core component of scientific realism is the doctrine of the *epistemic centrality of theoretical knowledge*: When reliable methodological practices that contribute to the criteria for theory choice, experimental design, assessment of evidence, judgments of projectability, and the like in successful scientific research are theory-dependent in the now familiar ways, their reliability is (almost always) explained by the approximate truth (as accounts of the causal structure of the relevant phenomena) of the background theories on which they depend, and their application is (almost always) justified by the approximate knowledge thus embodied in those theories. The epistemic centrality doctrine differs from the almost uncontroversial doctrine of the ineliminability of theoretical commitments in that it entails that the success of theory-dependent methodological practices is explained by background theoretical knowledge, and thus that knowledge of unobservables is possible.

The astute reader will have observed that what has been said thus far about the dialectical situation of realism in the current literature does not obviously apply more to realist than to constructivist conceptions of scientific knowledge. The ineliminability of theoretical commitments is every bit as central to constructivist philosophy of science as to realist philosophy of science; indeed, it may be largely through the efforts of philosophers and historians influenced by constructivism that it has emerged as almost uncontroversial. Likewise, although the term "abductive" seems much too naturalistic, the central abductive arguments for scientific realism against empiricism would seem equally available to the constructivist; indeed, Kuhn's (1970) arguments that the world scientists study must be one in which the most fundamental laws in the relevant paradigm are true has much in common with abductive arguments for realism. In consequence, the doctrine of the epistemic centrality of theoretical knowledge may be as central to constructivist as to realist philosophical packages. We thus have yet to see upon what principle we can distinguish viable realist philosophical packages from those whose rejection of various instances of "realism about" represents an untenable concession to constructivist anti-realism.

The answer is ultimately provided, I believe, by a recognition that the realist denies, while the constructivist affirms, that the adoption of theories, paradigms, research interests, conceptual frameworks, or perspectives in some way constitutes, or contributes to the constitution of, the causal powers of and the causal relations between the objects scientists study in the context of those theories, frameworks, and so forth. Of course, the realist does not deny that the adoption of theories, frameworks, and so forth is a causal phenomenon and hence will contribute *causally* to the establishment of, for example, those causal factors that are explanatory in the history, philosophy, and sociology of science. (Thus in particular the adoption of a theory in such a discipline could contribute causally to the causal powers and relations that are the subject matter of the theory itself.) What the realist denies is that there is some further sort of contribution (logical, conceptual, socially constructive, or the like) that the adoption of theories, conceptual frameworks, and so forth makes to the establishment of causal powers and relations. Realists affirm, and constructivists deny, the *no noncausal contribution doctrine*, which holds that the adoption of theories, frameworks, paradigms, projects, intellectual or practical interests, and so forth, makes no non-causal contribution to the causal structure of the world scientists study. This is the second central core doctrine of scientific realism, the one whose successful incorporation into a philosophical package in the philosophy of science assures us that it makes no crucial concessions to constructivist anti-realism. (In the immediately preceding discussion I borrow heavily from material appearing in Boyd 1989b.) It remains to see how the identification of these two central core realist doctrines permits a solution to the problem of "realism about."

2.3. What must a realist be a "realist about"?
I: How much conventionality can a realist accept?

Even those, like social constructivists, who adopt a deeply conventionalist conception of scientific theories ordinarily do not hold that the content of theories is entirely conventional: at least in the empirical sciences conventionality affects some features of theories and not others. If we are to investigate the acceptable levels of conventionality in realist philosophical packages, we need some terminology to reflect this fact. Let us say that the choice between one or another of two theories or descriptive schemes (henceforth: conceptions) is *arbitrary from a realist perspective* (henceforth: arbitrary; but recall that this abbreviated terminology might be unacceptable to the constructivist: world-constituting theories will hardly seem arbitrary) just in case the correctness of such a choice would depend on facts about linguistic conventions or about the particular history of language use within the scientific community rather than on a difference in how well the conceptions reflect causal structures that are themselves independent of such choices. Our question then is this: Under what circumstances may the systematic realist acknowledge that the choice between two conceptions is arbitrary, and under what conditions must she not, on pain of having made a concession to systematic anti-realism?

We have identified the two central core doctrines of scientific realism. Let us restate the second of these using the terminology just introduced: If the choice between two conceptions is arbitrary (in

particular, if it is conventional), then they reflect the causal structure of
the world exactly equally well (or badly). (Note that this is a distinctly
anti-constructivist claim, as required; it might be acceptable to an
empiricist.)

Consider now how this principle interacts with the other central core
realist principle: the doctrine of the epistemic centrality of theoretical
knowledge. According to the latter, methods dictated by theoretical
conceptions are reliable because, and to the extent that, the background theories they depend on provide a relevantly accurate account
of causal structures; it is the "fit" of theory-dependent methods to the
actual causal structure of the world that explains their reliability. Two
theories between which the choice is arbitrary reflect the relevant
causal structure exactly equally well. What should we then say about
the case in which the arbitrariness of the choice is not recognized –
about the case in which scientists mistakenly take two such theories to
reflect different or competing conceptions of causal structure?

Well, where there are features of the two theories that *appear* (by the
best prevailing standards) to be reflections of competing or different
conceptions of causal structures but are in fact a matter of arbitrary
choice between the theories, scientists will warrantedly take those
features to be methodologically significant – to be relevant to methodological judgments about, e.g., the assessment of the import of experimental evidence or about the explanatory power of other theoretical
proposals. They will see the two theories as underwriting different or
competing methodological standards. What the realist must hold, in the
light of the doctrine of the epistemic centrality of theoretical knowledge, is that in such cases the scientists in question are (non-culpably)
mistaken. *The methodological judgments that are peculiar to one rather
than another of two theories between which the choice is arbitrary will be
reliable, if at all, only accidentally*: Two such theories are *epistemically
equipotent* – exactly equally reliable as guides to the identification of
reliable methods. This equipotency doctrine is an important corollary to
the two central core doctrines of scientific realism.

Here's another: When it is concluded about two theories that the
choice between them is, by realist standards, arbitrary, it must be held
that all prior methodological judgments that reflected commitment to
one as opposed to the other must have been (if at all) only accidentally
reliable, and it must be held that subsequent methodological applications of the theories (if they are still, or come to be, well confirmed)
must reflect the arbitrariness of the choice between them by being
insensitive to which is chosen.

We are now, I think, in a position to answer the question of how much conventionality a scientific realist can acknowledge. Notice that we are not asking how much conventionality a scientific realist should ideally acknowledge – how much conventionality would be acknowledged in the best possible realist philosophical package. We're asking what sorts of conventionality, if acknowledged, would be significant concessions to systematic anti-realism (and thus support the implicatures of the "realism about" idiom) and what sorts would not. Let us consider what constraints respect for the central core realist doctrines puts on the assembling of a realist philosophical package.

In the first place, the doctrine of the epistemic centrality of theoretical knowledge commits the realist prima facie to holding, about every background theoretical principle that contributes to the instrumental success of theory-dependent methods in a successful science, that it so contributes because it is relevantly approximately true. Moreover, except for background theoretical claims appearing in the earliest stages in the construction of a successful research program, the realist will need to present the relevant background theoretical claims as *themselves* a reflection of approximate knowledge, and will thus prima facie need to explain the reliability of the theory-dependent methods by which those claims were obtained by appealing to the approximate truth of the background theories that determined *those* methods, and so forth. Prima facie the realist must accept the approximate truth of all those background theoretical principles that are thus directly or indirectly implicated in the methods by which instrumental knowledge is obtained in well-developed successful sciences. (For a treatment of the issue of the earliest stages in successful research traditions, see Boyd 1982, 1988a, 1990.)

What the equipotency principles (and the no non-causal contribution doctrine that underwrites them) tell us is that, in the relevant realist explanations of the success of methods, respects of (approximate) truth that are merely conventional (or otherwise arbitrary) don't count. The realist must hold that the distinction between theories between which the choice is arbitrary is irrelevant to questions of justification and method. Thus the realist can successfully incorporate the claim that such a choice is arbitrary into a successful realist philosophical package only when, in the light of the equipotency principles, that claim does not compromise her commitments arising from the doctrine of the epistemic centrality of theoretical knowledge.

What I propose is that this is the only fundamental constraint on realist attributions of conventionality. Realist acknowledgments of conventionality that don't conflict, given the actual conduct of science and in the light of the equipotency principles, with the doctrine of the epistemic centrality of theoretical knowledge may be mistakes, but they preserve the central doctrines on which the defense of realism against empiricism and constructivism depend. They should not be viewed as concessions to anti-realism.

What does this mean in practice? Where features of theoretical claims are central to the methodological judgments directly or indirectly implicated in the methods by which apparent instrumental knowledge is obtained in an established science, the burden of proof is strongly on the realist who claims that those features are conventional or otherwise arbitrary. That burden can be discharged *only* (as in the case of the cladist assessment of higher taxa, if, and to the extent that, it succeeds) by a *scientific* critique of the scientific community's assent to the relevant features of the theoretical claims in question – one that results in a rebuttal to the causal claim that the methods associated with those features are systematically reliable. With respect to features of theoretical claims that are not so implicated in the establishment of instrumental knowledge, the realist can affirm conventionality without thus being "anti-realist" in any interesting sense and certainly without making concessions to systematic anti-realism.

What must a realist be a "realist about"? Insofar as the issue of conventionality is concerned: Only about what is implicated in instrumentally reliable methodology.

2.4. What must a realist be a "realist about"? II: How much reference failure can a realist accept?

Let us turn now to the question of how much reference failure the systematic scientific realist can acknowledge. Here the answer is considerably easier than in the case of the question of conventionality since concessions to constructivist anti-realism will not ordinarily be at issue. I propose that, as before, we take the realist to be *required* to be a "realist about" when such "realism about" is required in order to permit the articulation of a defensible philosophical package incorporating the two central core doctrines. The no non-causal contribution doctrine will not ordinarily be at issue, so our concern will be only with the doctrine of the epistemic centrality of theoretical knowledge. As before, where features of theoretical claims are central to the methodological judgments directly or indirectly implicated in the methods by which apparent instrumental knowledge is obtained in an established science, the realist must prima facie portray those features as approximate reflections of actual causal structures. Again as before, the realist can justifiably avoid this obligation with respect to a particular feature of the relevant theoretical claims only if, and to the extent that, she can offer a justifiable *scientific* critique of those features and of the methodological judgments in which they are implicated.

Perhaps the most common way for a body of theory to provide approximate truth about causal relations is for all of its constituent terms to refer to real phenomena, about which the relevant theoretical principles say things that are approximately true. But this is by no means the only way. Some terms in a body of approximately true theories may partially denote (Field 1973). Some terms may fail to enter into any reference-like relation whatsoever; their introduction may represent deeply mistaken theoretical commitment. Even in such cases, statements embodying those terms may reflect important approximations to the truth; consider, for example, a deeply Platonist early nineteenth century biological work that discourses about "specific forms" but which uses that terminology to present some significant information about the differences between various species of birds.

Hence the realist, in portraying methodologically central theories as relevantly approximately true, need not treat all of their constituent terms as (even partially) referring. What she must do is to portray them as being approximately true in respects suitable to explain the reliability of the methods they underwrite. The standards for assessing realist explanations of the reliability of particular methods are just those of ordinary science. (See Boyd 1989b, especially sections 3.3 and 3.4.) Thus the realist must treat a theoretical term as referring (or partially denoting) only when such a treatment is required, by ordinary scientific standards, in order to causally explain the instrumental reliability of some particular scientific methods.

What must a realist be a "realist about"? With respect to the issue of reference failure, as with respect to the issue of conventionality: Only about what is implicated in instrumentally reliable methodology.

3. Applications

3.0. Interest-dependence of kinds

Scientific language, according to realists, must be employed to "cut the world at its joints" where the appeal to joints is an appeal to the notion

RICHARD BOYD

of causally significant similarity and difference. What we have just seen is that the realist may be faithful to this naturalistic conception of the semantics of scientific language while still acknowledging even inexplicit and unexpected conventionality in the definitions of scientific terms. In particular, where the no non-causal contribution doctrine is honored no concession to constructivist anti-realism or related conceptions is involved in the acknowledgment of conventionality.

Sometimes it is held that realist treatments of natural definitions must make a fatal concession to constructivism on a related point. It is an interesting but uncontroversial fact that the location of the "joints" at which the world must be cut must be thought of as depending on the particular sort of natural phenomena under study: Respects of similarity and difference may be causally significant with respect to one sort of phenomenon and insignificant with respect to another. Sometimes this point is put by saying that natural kinds (or the naturalness of natural kinds, or the reality of natural kinds) are interest-dependent: Which sorting procedure is appropriately natural will depend on the interests of the investigating parties. Some philosophers appear to hold that these phenomena of interest-dependence by themselves constitute a refutation of the realist's conception that scientists study a largely mind-independent reality and that they thus favor some sort of social constructivist conception.

The considerations rehearsed in the preceding section suggest that the "interest-dependence" of natural kinds just discussed is unproblematically compatible with realism. To describe either the definitions of natural kinds, magnitudes, and the like or their "reality" as "interest-dependent" is potentially misleading. It is fruitful to talk about possible intellectual or practical projects – sets of questions and problems together with some specification of the form of the anticipated answers or solutions. According to the realist conception, for the problems and questions set by a project to be answered and solved the terms in which the solutions and answers are formulated would have to be defined a posteriori in terms of the relevant sorts of (similarities and differences in) causal powers. That this is so does not, according to the realist, depend at all on whether the project in question is one in which humans (or others) are actually interested or engaged. Neither the causal powers (differences, similarities) of the possible objects of study, nor the appropriateness of methods for studying them, depend non-causally on actual study or actual interest or on any other candidate for "social construction." Or, at any rate, nothing in the unproblematical "interest-dependence" of natural kinds suggests otherwise. There is no reason to suppose that the no non-causal contribution doctrine would have to be abandoned in a coherent philosophical package that acknowledged the "interest-dependence" of scientific definitions.

3.1. Ontological pluralism

Once we have seen that the interest-dependence of natural definitions does not threaten systematic realism we are in a position to employ the resources of Part 2 to examine a related issue about the philosophical plausibility of realism. Some philosophers (see, e.g., Putnam 1983b) have suggested that realism is committed to the highly implausible view that there is a single true theory – in a sense of that notion which implies that there is a single true way of "cutting the world at its joints" and thus a single true conceptual scheme. I have argued elsewhere (Boyd, 1989a) that insofar as this conclusion rests on the (correct!) assumption that the contemporary realist should be a materialist (as it does in Putnam 1983b) it rests as well on a reductionist conception of materialism that the realist can, and indeed must, reject. We have just seen that another line of argument to the same conclusion is mistaken: It would be inappropriate to hold that the realist must deny the plurality of conceptual schemes that arises from the interest-dependence of natural definitions.

One final reason for thinking that realism is in trouble with respect to the question of the plurality of conceptual schemes is the following: Suppose that realists are right in this: that the dictates of a particular scientific project require that scientists use a conceptual scheme that "fits" the world in some special way suitable to the project in question. Still it seems plausible that there may be a large, perhaps infinite, number of different ways of "carving up the world" that would equally satisfy the demands of any particular scientific project. Even the realist will have to acknowledge that the choice between these alternative conceptions is arbitrary or conventional; she must therefore abandon realism about natural kinds and other scientific categories, thereby defeating the broader realist project.

We saw in Section 2.3 that the realist must be a "realist about" only those features of scientific theories that are central to reliable methodology. Thus the realist can quite coherently accept the pluralistic conception of scientific categories even within a single scientific discipline. There are "hairy" issues in analytical metaphysics raised by the pluralistic proposal we are considering, but this is clear: without abandoning anything central to coherent scientific realism the realist could acknowledge that for every particular scientific program there is an infinite plurality of appropriate conceptual schemes that fit the causal structure of the world equally well and between which the choice is arbitrary.

3.2. "Realism about," one more time

Scientific realism is apparently not the fragmented position which the "realism about" terminology would suggest. Why not? The answer suggested by the discussion in Part 2 is that two factors are responsible. First, an identifiable naturalistic account of methodology, independently identifiable as central to the case for scientific realism, affords us a standard by which to assess the acceptability from a realist point of view of acknowledgments of conventionality or reference failures in scientific theorizing. In the light of that standard, being a non-realist, on scientific grounds, about the ether, for example, or about higher taxa is no concession to anti-realism. Second, the naturalistic account of methodology and the arguments for realism it underwrites are applicable across the range of the natural sciences. We are thus not faced with the serious prospect of there being "realism about physics" but not, for example, "realism about chemistry" or "realism about biology." The wide applicability of the naturalistic account of methodology and the associated arguments for realism arises because of deep methodological similarities between the natural sciences, and because in each there is the history of unproblematical instrumental reliability of methods on which the crucial argument for realism depends.

I propose a reform in the use of the expression "realism about." By "realism about" a subject area I propose to mean the doctrine that the characteristic intellectual achievement in that area involves the acceptance of statements that are, when understood literally, approximately true of a reality that is largely logically independent of the theories, conceptual schemes, research interests and so forth, that one adopts. If we accept the largely uncontroversial doctrine that contemporary scientific theories are often literally about putative unobservable phenomena, then realism in this sense about the natural sciences is just scientific realism. Let us ask, in the sense of this reformed definition, What must the (scientific) realist be a realist about? The answer suggested by our discussion of the integrity of scientific realism is: About those subject areas that (1) unproblematically share a common methodology with the natural sciences, and (2) unproblematically exhibit a level of instrumental reliability of method appropriate to the abductive argument for realism. For subject areas that fail to meet these two conditions, there may be deep considerations favoring realism but, prima facie, there is no reason why scientific realists are obliged to take these considerations much more seriously than other philosophers must.

I think that the considerations just rehearsed explain several features of the current dialectical situation with respect to "realisms about" (in the reformed sense). They explain, for example, why it seems possible cogently to accept realism about the natural sciences while denying it about at least some of the social sciences, where both the methodological similarities to the natural sciences and the level of instrumental success are controversial. They explain, as well, why scientific realists find it harder to deny realism about "cognitive science" than about other social sciences whose methods and records of instrumental success less closely resemble those of the natural sciences, and why the temptation to realism about mathematics is often greater when one focuses on mathematical theories in their scientific application than when one focuses on their more "pure" development. It likewise explains why scientific realists rarely feel compelled to be moral realists.

In saying that prima facie scientific realists need be realists only about those subject areas satisfying the two conditions above I mean to discuss the *current* dialectical situation of scientific realism vis-à-vis realism of other sorts. If certain naturalistic and anti-foundationalist features of much recent scientific realist philosophy come to be seen as central to scientific realism, as I think they should be, then scientific realists might be obliged to assess realism about other subject areas in a more favorable light than (scientific) anti-realists. In particular, it is plausible that acceptance of certain naturalistic and anti-foundationalist principles that are arguably central to scientific realism greatly enhance the plausibility of moral realism (Boyd 1988a; see also Brink 1984, 1989; Sturgeon 1984a, b). But even when those principles are accepted, moral realism emerges as a controversial empirical hypothesis about the history of moral discourse, one a scientific realist could reject on empirical grounds without compromise.

3.3. Methodological spectra

Arbitrariness or conventionality of theories comes in respects and degrees, and it has been fruitful here to specify the extent to which a theory is conventional by considering the range of alternatives to it with respect to which choice would be arbitrary or conventional. This "measure" of arbitrariness does not, by itself, answer all of the questions that might be put by asking, How arbitrary is this theory? It does not indicate what the methodological import is of the theory's respects of arbitrariness or non-arbitrariness. The epistemological equipotency doctrines discussed earlier suggest a way of assessing that import. By the *methodological spectrum* of a theory let us mean the class of methodological judgments that (given prevailing background theories) it properly underwrites. If the equipotency doctrines are right then two theories between which the choice is arbitrary by realist standards will, if properly understood, have the same methodological spectrum. In consequence, the claim that a theory is unexpectedly arbitrary in particular respects entails that its methodological spectrum is narrower than prevailing methods would suggest; competing claims regarding respects of arbitrariness will thus entail different conceptions of a theory's methodological spectrum.

I think that it will prove important to applied philosophy of science to make explicit the connection between claims about arbitrariness and claims about methodological spectra. It will help, I believe, in formulating the methodology appropriate for assessing arbitrariness claims as they arise in actual scientific practice. For example, I have referred to cladist claims that higher taxa are unexpectedly arbitrary, and I have indicated that the theoretical reasons that appear to underwrite those claims are worthy of serious consideration. It seems to me, however, that it would help cladists and others to formulate those claims more perspicuously (and, I believe, more modestly) if the consequences of the equipotency doctrines were acknowledged.

Cladists often claim that the only non-arbitrary constraint on higher taxa is that they be monophyletic (that they consist of all the species that are the descendants of some particular species) and that their definitions should conform to the formal structure of the Linnean hierarchy. Should they claim this level of arbitrariness? Well, the theoretical claims that appear to underwrite cladism are claims about macroevolution (Guyot 1987). The literature on macroevolution is centrally concerned with the explanation of facts about the pace and tempo of evolution, and with the explanation of apparent evolutionary trends. Cladism apparently rests on a critique of standard macroevolutionary explanations that emphasize the role of natural selection, and upon the defense of a class of alternative explanations that places much less emphasis on selection.

One feature of the literature on macroevolution is that in assessing evidence about pace and tempo of evolution and about possible evolutionary trends evolutionary biologists routinely employ statistics defined in terms of higher taxa – comparing, for example, the rate of emergence of new classes or orders at different intervals in evolutionary history. It is a consequence of the equipotency doctrines that, if higher taxa are as arbitrary as the strongest cladist claims suggest, then these statistics are methodologically irrelevant. It is by no means clear that the case for cladism can survive so deep a methodological critique of the current literature. There are special reasons for cladists to formulate and defend their claims about the arbitrariness of higher taxa with much greater care, and the equipotency doctrines indicate just where the greatest care is needed.

This conclusion is, I hope, plausible on scientific grounds independently of any special philosophical reflections. This is so because many instances of the equipotency doctrines are uncontroversial methodological principles in everyday successful science. For the realist, of course, all of its instances are acceptable. The constructivist must somehow pick and choose. Whether that constructivist picking and choosing can be suitably justified is a topic for another essay (Boyd 1988b).

References

Boyd, R. 1971. "Realism and Scientific Epistemology." Unpublished manuscript.
   1972. "Determinism, Laws and Predictability in Principle." *Philosophy of Science*, 39: 431–50.
   1973. "Realism, Underdetermination and a Causal Theory of Evidence." *Nous*, 7: 1–12.
   1979. "Metaphor and Theory Change." In A. Ortony (ed.), *Metaphor and Thought*. Cambridge: Cambridge University Press.
   1980. "Materialism without Reductionism: What Physicalism Does Not Entail." In N. Block (ed.), *Readings In Philosophy of Psychology*. Vol. 1. Cambridge, Mass.: Harvard University Press.
   1982. "Scientific Realism and Naturalistic Epistemology." In P. D. Asquith and R. N. Giere (eds.), *PSA 1980. Volume Two*. East Lansing, Mich.: Philosophy of Science Association.
   1983. "On the Current Status of the Issue of Scientific Realism." *Erkenntnis*, 19: 45–90.
   1985a. "Lex Orendi est Lex Credendi." In P. Churchland and C. Hooker (eds.), *Images of Science: Scientific Realism Versus Constructive Empiricism*. Chicago: University of Chicago Press.
   1985b. "Observations, Explanatory Power, and Simplicity." In P. Achinstein and O. Hannaway (eds.), *Observation, Experiment, and Hypothesis In Modern Physical Science*. Cambridge, Mass.: MIT Press.
   1985c. "The Logician's Dilemma." *Erkenntnis*, 22: 197–252.
   1987. *Realism and the Moral Sciences*. Unpublished manuscript.
   1988a. "How to Be a Moral Realist." In G. Sayre McCord (ed.), *Moral Realism*. Ithaca, N. Y.: Cornell University Press.
   1988b. "Constructivism, Realism, and Philosophical Method." Unpublished notes.

1989. "What Realism Implies and What It Does Not." *Dialectica*, 43: 5–29.
1990. "Realism, Approximate Truth, and Philosophical Method." In Wade Savage (ed.), *Scientific Theories*. Minnesota Studies in the Philosophy of Science, vol. 14. Minneapolis: University of Minnesota Press.

Brink, D. 1984. "Moral Realism and the Skeptical Arguments from Disagreement and Queerness." *Australasian Journal of Philosophy*, 62: 111–25.
1989. *Moral Realism and the Foundations of Ethics*. Cambridge: Cambridge University Press.

Carnap, R. 1928. *Der logische Aufbau der Welt*. Berlin: WeltKreis-Verlag.
1934. *The Unity of Science*. Trans. M. Black. London: Kegan Paul.
1950. "Empiricism, Semantics, and Ontology." *Revue internationale de philosophie*. 4th year.

Feigl, H. 1956. "Some Major Issues and Developments in the Philosophy of Science of Logical Empiricism." In H. Feigl and M. Scriven (eds.), *Minnesota Studies in the Philosophy of Science*, Vol. 1. Minneapolis: University of Minnesota Press.

Field, H. 1973. "Theory Change and the Indeterminacy of Reference." *Journal of Philosophy*, 70: 462–81.

Fine, A. 1984. "The Natural Ontological Attitude." In J. Leplin (ed.), *Scientific Realism*. Berkeley: University of California Press.

Goodman, N. 1973. *Fact Fiction and Forecast*. 3rd ed. Indianapolis and New York: Bobbs-Merrill.

Hanson, N. R. 1958. *Patterns of Discovery*. Cambridge: Cambridge University Press.

Hempel, C. 1958. "The Theoretician's Dilemma." In H. Feigl, M. Scriven, and G. Maxwell (eds.), *Concepts, Theories and the Mind-Body Problem*. Minneapolis: University of Minnesota Press.
1965. "Conceptions of Cognitive Significance." In Hempel, *Aspects of Scientific Explanation and Other Essays in the Philosophy of Science*. New York: Free Press.

Jensen, A. 1968. "How Much Can We Boost I.Q. and Scholastic Achievement?" *Harvard Educational Review*, 39:1–123.

Kripke, S. A. 1971. "Identity and Necessity." In M. K. Munitz (ed.), *Identity and Individuation*. New York: New York University Press.
1972. "Naming and Necessity." In D. Davidson and G. Harman (eds.), *The Semantics of Natural Language*. Dordrecht: Reidel.

Kuhn, T. 1970. *The Structure of Scientific Revolutions*. 2nd ed. Chicago: University of Chicago Press.

Laudan, L. 1981. "A Confutation of Convergent Realism." *Philosophy of Science*, 48: 218–49.

Lewontin, R. 1976. "Race and Intelligence." In N. Bolck and G. Dworkin (eds.), *The I.Q. Controversy*. New York: Pantheon.

McMullin, E. 1984. "A Case for Scientific Realism." In J. Leplin (ed.), *Scientific Realism*. Berkeley: University of California Press.

Putnam, H. 1962. "The Analytic and the Synthetic." In H. Feigl and G. Maxwell (eds.), *Minnesota Studies in the Philosophy of Science*, Vol. 3. Minneapolis: University of Minnesota Press.

  1972. "Explanation and Reference." In G. Pearce and P. Maynard (eds.), *Conceptual Change*. Dordrecht: Reidel.

  1975a. "The meaning of 'Meaning'." In Putnam, *Mind, Language and Reality*. Cambridge: Cambridge University Press.

  1975b. "Language and Reality." In Putnam, *Mind, Language and Reality*. Cambridge: Cambridge University Press.

  1975c. "Language and Reality." In H. Putnam, *Mind, Language and Reality*. Cambridge: Cambridge University Press.

  1975d. "What Theories Are Not." In Putnam, *Mathematics, Matter and Method*. Cambridge: Cambridge University Press.

  1979. *Meaning and the Moral Sciences*. London: Routledge & Kegan Paul.

  1981. *Reason, Truth and History*. Cambridge: Cambridge University Press.

  1983. "Vagueness and Alternative Logic." In H. Putnam, *Realism and Reason*. Cambridge: Cambridge University Press.

Quine, W. V. O. 1961a. "On What There Is." In Quine, *From a Logical Point of View*. Cambridge, Mass.: Harvard University Press.

  1961b. "Two Dogmas of Empiricism." Quine, *From a Logical Point of View*. Cambridge: Harvard University Press.

  1969a. "Natural Kinds." In Quine, *Ontological Relativity and Other Essays*. New York: Columbia University Press.

  1969b. "Epistemology Naturalized." In Quine, *Ontological Relativity and Other Essays*. New York: Columbia University Press.

Sturgeon, N. 1984a. "Moral Explanations." In D. Copp and D. Zimmerman (eds.), *Morality, Reason and Truth*. Totowa, N. J.: Rowman & Allanheld.

  1984b. "Review of P. Foot, *Moral Relativism* and *Virtues and Vices*." Journal of Philosophy, 81: 326–33.

van Fraassen, B. 1980. *The Scientific Image*. Oxford: Oxford University Press.

9

Invidious contrasts within theories

LAWRENCE SKLAR

1

The classical positivist understanding of the nature of theories provided a clear basis for contrasting the role within theories of two kinds of concepts. The radical difference in epistemological status between terms that purported to refer to entities and features of the world open to direct observability and those that instead purported to refer to entities and features whose existence and nature could be known to us only by inference, when combined with familiar doctrines about the way in which terms in language acquired their ability to refer to the contents of the world, led to the famous doctrine that real ontology presupposed by a theory was exhausted by the ontology required by its observational consequences, the remaining putative reference of the "theoretical" vocabulary being explained away as fictive or instrumental. Observational terms of a true theory referred to the substance of the world. Nonobservational terms served merely as place-holders in a holistic network designed to mediate inferences between observational assertions, but did not have the semantic role of genuinely referring to entities or features in the world. Similarly, observational sentences, those containing only observational terms, were genuinely true or false; the other sentences, those containing non-observational terms, were not genuine statements at all. Since their terms failed of genuine reference, not because of error but because of their semantic role, the sentences containing these terms failed of being true or false at all.

The natural corollary to this contrasting treatment of the semantics of the observational and non-observational terms was the doctrine of conventionalism and its use to undercut at least a component of traditional skepticism. If the non-observational component of a theory consisted of assertions that were neither true nor false but only components of a complex syntactical whole that functioned as a unit to ground inferences from observational to non-observational facts, then the exis-

tence of alternative theories all equally compatible with the same total
sets of observational data, one of the standard grounds for traditional
skepticism about the possibility of rationalizing our body of scientific
beliefs, no longer had the destructive consequences for rationality in
science it appeared to have. Since the alternative theories grounded
exactly the same intra-observational inferences, the non-observational
portions of the theories were instrumentalistically equivalent to one
another. Appearances of contradiction grounded on contradictions between the theories totally isolable at the non-observable level were just
that, appearances. Since the assertions were only pseudo-assertions
anyway, and since the non-observational components of the theories as
a whole performed the same inferential task among the observable
consequences of the theory, the theories were, really, one and the same
theory and no choice of which one to believe need be made. So the
combined rigid epistemological distinction and semantic doctrine, in
various differing forms, was made to do the job of eliminating at least
some room for skeptical doubt.

But, of course, the possibility of rigidly partitioning the terms of a
theory into observational and non-observational, and at the object level
making such a rigid partitioning of the entities and feature referred to
by the theory, has come in for much criticism. Inability to find a strict
"observational language," theory-ladenness of terms at all levels of a
theory, the relativity of 'observable' to context and purpose, as well as
the dreadful apparent anti-realistic consequences of the positivist model
of theories, all have led to skepticism that any such hard-and-fast,
theory- and context-independent, characterization of the strictly observable can be made. And, it is usually claimed, the weaker and more
relative kinds of observable/non-observable distinction which can take
the place of the old positivist distinction cannot support the burden of
semantic distinctness at the linguistic level or metaphysical distinctness
at the object level that grounded positivistic instrumentalisms and
fictionalism.

The reaction to skepticism about the existence of a "pure observational basis" can go in different directions. One reaction is to argue that
the posits of theory must be construed just as realistically as the entities
and features of observation, and to take the demise of the positivistic
model as an argument for theoretical realism. But then reflection on
the fact that if facts are "soft (theory dependent) all the way down" to
the observational level, the relativity of the epistemic warrant to our
theoretical presuppositions is also "soft all the way down," and reflection on the conventionalist arguments about the theoretical level in the

positivists and already present in earlier idealist views about our world-pictures, may lead us, instead of pushing realism outward from the observable to the unobservable, to push some version of anti-realism or conventionalism inward. Hence the familiar suggestion that the demise of the rigid observable/non-observable distinction leads not to "realism" but to "internal realism," and the recognition that the views about scientific theories to which one is led resemble more the doctrines of the pragmatists than those acceptable to any "metaphysical realist."

But whichever way one is inclined to move on this issue, a line of agreement seems clear. This is the claim that all of the terms and assertions of our scientific theory are fundamentally on a par as far as considerations of epistemology, semantics, and metaphysics go. To believe a theory is to believe its posits about what there is in the world. Good scientists and philosophers ought to adopt the "natural ontological attitude," accepting as the real whatever we need to talk about within the theories we posit to find our way about the world. As far as reference goes, 'red patch here now,' 'table,' and 'quark' are all on a par. To be sure we may have greater or lesser confidence in a theory, and hence greater or lesser confidence in its ontological posits. But doubts about the genuine reference of a term in a theory are legitimate only insofar as they are scientific doubts. And ontological questions, insofar as they are genuine questions at all, are to be settled only by the typical means of scientific decision making where we do our best to fit theory to the ever changing data of observation.

The extreme version of this attitude is that which refuses even to make a distinction between the putative ontology of our scientific theories and the "ontology" of apparent reference of our evaluative discourse. Linguistically, it is said, a declarative sentence is a declarative sentence, and all such are genuine candidates for having full-fledged truth values. The apparent reference of all apparent referring terms within such sentences is to be taken at its face grammatical value. If reference to goodness and beauty helps us get on in the world when we attribute or deny the former to states of society or the latter to works of art, then our "natural ontological attitude" is one that must encompass goodness and beauty as putative components of the world. Once again, of course, we might be wrong in attributing any given feature in any given situation. But what is denied is the old positivist claim that the apparent ontological commitment of the apparent assertions ought not to be taken straightforwardly at all, that is, the old positivist claim that such moral and aesthetic "assertions" aren't really assertions at all and that the apparent referring terms in them are, when properly understood, seen to play a completely different semantic role from that of genuine referring expressions.

2

Let us put the extreme doctrine to the side, letting others worry about the intelligibility and plausibility of "moral realism" or "aesthetic realism." Let us stick to the context of what all would take to be natural science. Is it obviously true that within the context of scientific theories we ought to treat all the putative referring apparatus on a par? Or are there, still, general methodological grounds for making the distinction between the portion of the apparently referring apparatus that ought to have its semantic role taken straightforwardly and the portion that ought to be construed as not genuinely referential but only giving that appearance? This is not the issue of how to construe theories in general, realistically, or in some more pragmatic way, for the issue remains even if the question of parity for all of the putatively referential apparatus is accepted. Rather this is the preliminary question as to whether the familiar dismissal of the positivist bifurcation of the apparatus into two parts, the genuinely and the only apparently referential, is to be accepted by all as a clearly established preliminary point about the place of terms in theories.

What I want to do here is not in any way even to begin to approach a resolution of this question but, rather, simply to outline a few considerations about theories that have repeatedly led those who think about them to resurrect, in one form or another, the positivist claim. What are some of the general features that distinguish terms in theories into terms of different kinds and that have been proposed as being distinguishing features, sorting out the genuine from the spuriously referential terms? I think that what one discovers is a number of different grounds for denying genuine reference to a term (and, once again, not because one is rejecting the theory in which it appears as a false theory). The grounds overlap and in their vagueness can't always be completely discriminated from one another. But as an indication of some "first intuitions" about terms they do provide some categories of grounds for suspicion of genuine referentiality worth noting.

3

A distinction based on epistemic accessibility

A general claim underlying much of the case for denying genuine reference to some terms of scientific theory is that there is at least a portion of truth to the old positivist claim about the distinction between observables and unobservables. Many of the arguments against that doctrine rest on attempts to make us doubt that any term has the virtues ascribed by the positivist doctrine to true observable terms. But the skepticism about genuine reference for some scientific terms rests not so much on any claim to the effect that some terms are observation terms, as on the claim that many terms could *not* be such. It is the insistence that many of the entities and features putatively referred to in scientific discourse could never enter into the domain considered as the directly observable that leads to some of the skepticism, conventionalism, and accompanying semantic doctrine of absence of genuine reference for the vocabulary attempting reference to these entities and features.

There are, of course, plenty of arguments to the effect that any item of science is "in principle" observable. But the familiar arguments from the implasticity of perception, and other arguments grounded on various intuitions, do lead many to still believe that, come what may, there are things talked about in our theories that will remain, forever, at best inferred and never observed. We might imagine, they say, talking about observing atoms, but will we ever say that we observe the strangeness of strange particles, except in the derivative sense of observing some remote causal consequence of a particle having strangeness?

But even if there are in-principle unobservables, how can we have an invidious contrast between the genuinely referring and the only putatively referring, if we can't put forward any examples of the latter category? Here resort will be made to the line familiar since C. I. Lewis. Even if the "given" is not catchable in our language, infected as it is "all the way down" with theoretical presupposition, we must posit that elusive realm to make coherent sense of epistemology at all. How the positing of observables as ideals not truly catchable in language can lead to a coherent doctrine of "mere apparent" reference for the normal terms of science as opposed to those that (if they existed) would have genuine reference isn't very clear. But it is still the case that insofar as we can be assured that the entity or feature apparently referred to by a term is in the genuine realm of the forever unobservable, then for those entities and features we can be assured that the old problems of skepticism and theoretical under-determination will arise. And so for them ought we not to resist the too easy dismissal of the one doctrine that plausibly avoids those skeptical consequences? The doctrine, which by denying genuine reference to the terms and genuine truth-value to the sentences in which they appear obviates the need for an epistemically grounded rule for deciding which of the empirically indistinguishable alternatives really is true, is one many would like to hold on to. By positing as at least an ideal the "limit point" of genuine observables and assertions dealing only with them, perhaps this denial of genuine reference and truth at the upper level of theory can be prevented from becoming full-fledged pragmatism or "internalism" of some other sort.

There are those, of course, who while maintaining something like this epistemic view, deny its semantic consequences. To be sure, they say, there are the in-principle unobservable components of scientific theory. To be sure the old skeptical doubts about ever having good reason to take such theories as genuinely true have their ineluctable force. But the way out of the dilemma is not to downgrade the semantic value of the components of theory putatively dealing with the unobservable. Rather one ought to take the assertions dealing with the unobservable at their semantic face value but reinterpret the aim of science not as producing the truth, but as producing a theory "adequate" to its purposes of "saving the phenomena." Here one will go about trying to disassociate "scientific acceptance" of a theory from genuinely believing the theory to be true. But I think such an approach will ultimately founder on many rocks, not the least of which will be that of trying to make a coherent picture within it of our epistemic attitudes that comes down to anything more than skepticism accompanied by blasé indifference to its consequences. In any case, the old positivist claim that the reach of genuine semantic value (and with it genuine reference and truth) is, because of the way in which meaning accrues to language, bounded by the limits of genuine epistemic access to truth, one that is very persuasive. Once we have placed part of the domain of our theory forever outside the limits of epistemic determinability, the tendency to view the language outside those limits as devoid of its apparent semantic value will be hard to resist.

Insofar as we remain at least partially persuaded that some elements posited by our theories will remain forever and in principle outside of what we can call the genuinely observable, then, we will remain at least open to the claim that not all of the language of science ought to be taken at face value. And if this is so we remain open to the suggestion that there might be limits to the domain of scientific vocabulary that ought to be taken as genuinely referential. And this will be so even if when challenged to present the virtuous terms of genuine reference with which the only apparently referential terms are to be invidiously contrasted, we abashedly admit that, perhaps, we cannot actually display them but only posit them as an ideal.

A distinction based on semantic projectability

Not all of those who would make a distinction between the genuinely referring terms and those non-referring in a "depth" analysis of their semantics would draw the line as that between terms referring to observables and those putatively referring to non-observables. Usually those putting the line somewhere else are those who wish to extend the realm of genuine reference into at least some regions of the unobservable. Dismayed with the wholesale irrealism with respect to the realm of being knowable only by inference and not by observation, but persuaded by some of the positivist argument, they wish to argue that some, but only some, of the terms putatively referring to the unobservable, have genuine referential status. The others are to be treated as the instrumentalist or fictionalist would treat them, as not genuinely referring at all, but instead playing their place-holder role in the theoretical inferential network.

One way in which this distinction between the genuinely and the spuriously referring at the level of unobservables has been drawn is by distinguishing between those putative referring terms that can get meaning at the level of the observational and "project" it into the nonobservable, and those terms at the unobservable level that cannot have referential meaning accrue to them in this way. The idea is a recurrent one (discussed by H. Putnam, for example, in his "What Theories Are Not").[1] Terms dealing with shape, for example, can have meaning given them by ostensive association with observable shapes. We can then understand what we are talking about when we talk of shapes "too small to see," by taking 'square', for example, at the unobservable level to "mean the same thing" when talking about unobservable squares as it did in the context of talking about observable objects.

The claim would be, then, that insofar as a term can accrue meaning by being associated with observable elements of the world, it should be construed as genuinely referential even when it does its referring job in contexts where the entity or feature referred to is beyond observability. And, the claim goes on, theories ought to be construed realistically at the unobservable level only when they posit entities or features of the kind we understand from our experience of the observable. The other putative reference they make is to be taken only instrumentalistically.

Naturally this line is fraught with difficulty. To what degree is it legitimate to "project" referential ability in this way? Isn't this just the old misunderstanding which stood in the way of grasping the fundamental truth that it is in use that meaning is accrued, and that insofar as the term used in the theory to denote unobservables differs in its place in our epistemic structure from its use to refer to observables, its meaning differs as well? If we allow for "projection of meaning by semantic analogy," assuming that we understand the meaning of new whole assertions insofar as we grasp their grammar and grasp the reference of their terms from other contexts, won't we be trapped into just the misunderstanding of "meaning by analogy" that Wittgenstein warned us of when we thought we could grasp the mental reference to others "from our own case"?

Yet most of us do think we know what 'pain' means for the other because we know what it means for us from its ostensive association with our own immediately available experience. And a distinction framed on this basis has much intuitive appeal. Surely some of the reason why we tend to think of molecules as "real" but of "strangeness" as not a genuine property of elementary particles at all but as just a way of assigning numbers to particles that keeps track of various allowed and disallowed particle transformations, is that we talk of molecules as "tiny little objects too small to see" and attribute to them (in at least our more classical and less quantum mechanical moments) familiar features of the macroscopic ball-and-stick models we make of their structures.

A distinction of this sort also underlies, I think, much of the appeal of doctrines like that of N. Campbell that "explanation is the reduction of the unfamiliar to the familiar."[2] Isn't part of the reason the billiard-ball model of molecules seems "explanatory" to us in a way in which attribution of strangeness does not grounded on the intuition that the molecular model, by attributing to the unobservable world features we understand from their place in the observable, tells us about the "reality" of the unobservable whereas attribution of strangeness tells us nothing about it at all? The claim that reference is genuine only insofar as the putative referring term has its referential meaning accrued to it by its employment in at least some contexts where it is ostensively associable with the observable is not one that ought to be dismissed without further thought.

A distinction based on richness of theoretical structure

If we accept the existence of in-principle unobservables, then we must also, it would seem, accept the conclusion that our knowledge of what they are like can only be grounded on inference, since direct observational determination of the truths about them is, by definition, out of the question. But what can such inference be like? There are, of course, lots of posited answers to that question. Here what I want to note is that a doctrine about the structure of legitimate inference to the truth of a claim about unobservables may be accompanied by a doctrine about the legitimacy of taking the putative referential structure of the assertion straightforwardly as well. There are lines about epistemic inference to unobservables that will discriminate among the assertions at the unobservable level, positing different places for them in the overall epistemic-inferential scheme. Such a differentiating approach to epistemic grounding may be accompanied by a view that the apparently referential apparatus of the assertions is to be viewed differentially as well.

Consider, for example, the claim that inference to unobservable structure is justified only when positing unobservable entities and features leads to a "unification" of the phenomena. Here the major goal of theory is taken to be the assimilation of the accounts governing a diverse range of phenomena into a single unified theory doing justice to the previous disconnected body of truths about experience. The extreme unificationist argues that only when a genuine unification of phenomena is accomplished by positing unobservable structure is that posit justified. For it is the ability of the positing of novel ontology, even if unobservable, to unify the phenomena that constitutes the only legitimate ground for so expanding our view as to the contents of the world. Without a unifying role an ontological posit is otiose and ought, by a general principle of the desirability of the simplest theory that does justice to the facts, to be eliminated from our posits about what there is in the world.

So one arrives at a position that argues that the apparently referential apparatus of an assertion at the level of unobservables ought to be read straightforwardly as genuinely referential only if the assertion plays a unifying role in the theory in question. Since unification is obtained, presumably, only when the assertion in question is placed in a rich enough network of assertion in the theory so that a multiplicity of inferences into differing realms of phenomena are mediated by postulating the assertion, it is this richness of place that differentiates the assertions whose referential apparatus is to be taken seriously from other assertions containing spurious, only apparently, referring expressions.

An example will make this clearer. In order to explain the presence of inertial forces, Newton posited absolute space as the reference frame relative to which accelerations were genuine ("absolute") accelerations. Neo-Newtonians posit only the inertial reference frames as sufficient for this purpose, rather than the full Newtonian absolute place. Relationists typically argue that the positing of these is not to be taken seriously from an ontological point of view. After all, all the facts about the relative motion of objects and the relative inertial forces experienced can be accommodated without positing such a mysterious realm of pure spacetime structure.

M. Friedman, on the other hand, has argued that while the relationist case holds up when only mechanical phenomena are taken to be in the realm of the phenomena to be understood, as soon as electromagnetic phenomena are introduced the relationist case fails.[3] The inertial reference frames are both those in which no inertial forces are felt by objects when they are at rest in these frames, and the reference frames relative to which the familiar laws of electromagnetism hold (and relative to which, for example, light has its standard velocity isotropically). If it were only as a means of keeping track of the fact that some objects feel inertial forces and others do not, and of the relative motions and relative felt forces, positing inertial frames as a structure of spacetime could be eliminated as a serious ontological posit. But once the phenomena of mechanics and electromagnetism are unified by the positing of the inertial structures, they must be taken seriously as part of the posited stuff of the world.

Naturally this view is fraught with problems. How much unification is enough for taking the putative ontology seriously? After all any assertion of general form will at least serve to "unify" particular instances of a phenomenon, even if they are the same kind. And we will have deep questions as to *why* we ought to take unifying power as the mark of the referentially serious. But there is no question that a common intuition lies behind this doctrine. The richer the theoretical structure into which a referential linguistic element enters and the more complex a role it plays in a diversity of theoretical inferences, the more inclined we are to think of the referential apparatus as genuinely picking out some feature of the world and not merely serving as a place-holding index term masquerading as a referring device.

A distinction based on metaphysical presuppositions

For some, the distinction between the genuine and the spurious referring terms in theories is based not on considerations of epistemology or semantic projectability, but, rather, on the kind of entity or feature putatively referred to. For them, some sorts of putative objects and features could not be the genuine referents of the terms that purport to denote them, since entities of the kind in question must be taken as spurious because of their very nature.

The distinction is drawn on differing grounds, depending on one's metaphysical presuppositions. For some, entities of a spatio-temporal sort, either concreta (material objects) and their features in spacetime or even spacetime itself and its features, are legitimate objects of reference. But the platonic denizens outside of the realm of the spatio-temporal cannot be seriously countenanced as real by them. For others it is concreta and their features that are real. Any reference to spatio-temporal objects themselves or features of them must be viewed with ontological suspicion. For the former group, any reference to sets, numbers, and the like in our theoretical account must be viewed as phony reference, with a non-referential place-holding role found to take the place of a referential role for the terms purporting to refer to them. For the latter group, the spacetime relationists, it is reference to spacetime itself and its features that must be explained away by a denial of genuine reference to such things as "the inertial frames," or "the local curvature of spacetime," and by finding the alternative place-holding role for the spurious referring terms.

There are, of course, many attempts to demonstrate the absence of a need to take the dubious terms as genuinely referential by showing that some alternative to our standard theory can be found that is equally adequate to the explanatory tasks of the original theory, and which has eliminated from it the objectional referring terms. Thus we have putative nominalistic surrogates for platonistic physics and putative relationistic surrogates for the theories that refer to spacetime and its features. Depending on one's demands on the necessary components of an adequate scientific theory (for example, must it be finitely or at least recursively axiomatizable?), one is faced with a task of greater or lesser difficulty in actually producing such a purified surrogate.

But it is important to note that such a program of "eliminating" the allegedly spurious terms is not an essential component of a view that maintains that a hard-and-fast distinction between the genuinely referential and the only apparently referential can be drawn. A "fictionalist" line that simply leaves the original theory alone, with its non-referring terms in place in the inferential structure that takes us from assertion to assertion where the ends of the inference are assertions devoid of any of the non-referring expressions, is perfectly coherent. It might be that for a theory to do the work we want it to do and to have the structural requirements we demand of it we will require the introduction of terms that while apparently referential can't really refer because of the metaphysical unacceptability of their putative referents. But that doesn't automatically force us, unless we buy into the pragmatist line, to take all apparent reference at face value.

The program of separating the referential sheep from the pseudo-referential goats within theories by means of metaphysical considerations regarding the putative referents of the terms is frequently associated with views about the legitimacy of ontological posits for explanatory purposes. Nominalists often insist that it is simply a misunderstanding of what it is to explain the phenomena to think that any explanation could be given that genuinely required the positing of platonistic entities, which being outside the realm of spacetime are outside the realm of causality as well. And relationists have frequently maintained that anything pretending to be an explanation that relies on positing the existence of pure spacetime entities and their features must be unsatisfactory. It is notoriously difficult to turn such intuitions into a genuine theory of what is and is not legitimate *qua* explanation, but the intuitions are familiar and recurrent.

A distinction based on the place of putative ontology in our general scientific ontology

Closely related to the metaphysically grounded doubts about the seriousness of reference of some theoretical terms just discussed, but slightly different from it in its premises, are the approaches that cast cross-theoretical doubt on the referential status of a group of terms because the entities and features required to exist for the terms to have reference are too anomalous from the point of view of our generally pervasive scientific ontology. Like the cases above, the doubts about referentiality rest on the objectionable nature of the entities and features allegedly referred to. But here it isn't quite the broad metaphysical character of those alleged entities that makes them dubious as objects of reference but, rather, the fact that to posit them would introduce elements into the world that are hard to fit into what we presuppose to be an overall complete scheme of scientific description of the world.

The obvious example of such a doubt about a whole class of allegedly referring terms genuinely referring is the doubts many have expressed about the legitimacy of taking mentalistic language of theories as seriously referential. Without specific objections of the usual empirical-scientific sort being laid against particular mentalistic posits, one gets global objections to the interpretation of mentalistic language being taken as genuinely referential on the basis of, again quite global and general, arguments to the effect that our overall science forces us to the broad ontological assertion that being is exhausted by the physical.

This kind of sorting of terms into the genuinely referential and the spuriously misleading only apparently referential is like the distinction based on metaphysical presuppositions, in that it is the kind of entity allegedly referred to that shows us in advance that the reference can't be genuine, but a little unlike the earlier distinction in that it is frequently claimed that the dubiousness of the ontology to the allegedly spuriously referential terms rests not on some more-or-less a priori consideration, but rather on a very general conclusion of the accumulated scientific knowledge of the world.

But the broadness of the position, its generality, and its systematic distinction of terms into kinds antecedent of considerations of particular observational facts and attempts at theoretical explanations of them also distinguishes approaches of this kind from the more familiar scientific rejections of some limited portion of the ontology of previously existing theories. Claims to the effect that mentalistic theories could not be correct if interpreted as genuinely referential, based on broad considerations of physicalism, are not just like such straightforward bits of scientific eliminationism as the denial of the existence of phlogiston or caloric. And the physicalistic rejection of referential mentalistic theories is also often accompanied by the familiar line that the mentalistic theories can still be retained as instrumentalistically reconstrued.

A distinction based on special considerations of the structure of a particular theory

In at least one case of great importance, a doctrine of the distinction between the truly referring terms and mere place-holding impostors of them, but which insists on an important role in the theory for the mere place-holders, is grounded not on general epistemic, semantic, or metaphysical considerations but, rather, on puzzling features of the specific theory in question and difficulties in understanding what it is telling us about the world. The theory that provides the arena in which this line of thinking is proposed is, of course, quantum mechanics.

Here the difficulties encountered in understanding the place of the wave-function (or one of its surrogates) in the theory led at least some of those trying to understand how the theory fit into our general theoretical structure for describing the world to distinguish between the classical variables used to describe the outcome of "measurements" from the quantum variables used to correlate values of these measurement outcomes in the probabilistic sense. In a manner highly reminiscent of the older positivist assertion that only the terms referring to observables designated genuine constituents of the world, some of these interpretations of quantum mechanics were explicitly instrumentalist about the wave-function, positing no real referential status for it and trying to understand its role as mere intermediary between the real phenomena of the world, outcomes of measurements, designated in the theory by the retained classical observables.

Of course the interpretation differs from classical positivism in important ways. Most crucial is the Bohrian claim that while a strict line must always be drawn between classical reality and quantum mechanical instrument, this line can be drawn at different "levels" even when one physical process is under consideration. Whether that doctrine can be made coherent, or whether, instead, it collapses to a more traditional positivism (as the "idealist" interpreters of quantum mechanics would have it, reserving the classical quantities for those "in the mind" of the observing subject) is a long story.

It is also true, of course, that many other interpretations of quantum theory try to avoid such a dichotomization of the terms of the theory. Many "realist" interpretations (ranging from those that take measurement to be the interaction of the test system with a large but still completely quantum measuring apparatus, to many-worlds interpretations) will take the wave-function as the genuine referring describer of a quantum reality.

But even if one argues that Bohr has been misled by traditional positivism in his attempt to offer a coherent interpretation of quantum theory, it remains true that it is the very special nature of this theory in its standard formal presentation, especially with its mysterious "collapse of the wave-packet" upon measurement taken as a process outside the realm of ordinary dynamical descriptions, which leads Bohr and others to posit a splitting of the vocabulary into the genuinely referential and the mere place-holding syntactical intermediary classes. Here a special feature of the theory and its accompanying interpretive problems rather than general philosophical considerations has led, once again, to a denial that all of the terms of the theory are on a par vis-à-vis referentially.

4

The approach to the semantics of theories that takes all putatively referring expressions as being on a par with one another, taking an expression to have genuine reference as being guaranteed by the acceptance of the theory and the surface syntactical referring nature of the term, has many attractions to it. If we accept a theory as correctly describing the world, then if it seems to talk of some kinds of entities and features, why not affirm that we are committed to the existence of those entities and features? In deciding on our ontological commitments, what else is there, really, to go on than the *form* of the assertions we accept? Add to this the notorious difficulty of making genuinely clear and coherent any of the philosophically motivated proposals for drawing invidious distinctions among the putatively referring terms, and the notoriously disturbing consequences for scientific realism of presupposing that such distinctions can genuinely be drawn.

Isn't the proposal to eschew such philosophically grounded distinctions between genuine and spurious referrers also consistent with the motto that science is all we have to go on in deciding on what there is in the world? What grounds for affirming or denying the existence of an entity or feature could we possibly expect other than our acceptance or rejection of the appropriate scientific theories that take the posits of those entities, as revealed by their surface modes of reference, as part of their description of the world? Why shouldn't we forgo the search for such dubious philosophical principles for critiquing apparent reference and adopt, instead, the "natural ontological attitude"?

But this stance neglects the crucial fact that the scientific theories presented to us by the scientific community, especially where fundamental physical theories are concerned, have been developed by a methodological process that includes just such philosophically motivated critiques of apparent reference as a part. The theories we have, in the surface form in which we have them, are, at least in part, the result of applying to the empirical data of science inferential processes grounded on just the sort of epistemological, semantic, and metaphysical presuppositions noted above as grounding critical attacks on apparent reference as only apparent.

Reflections on the reasoning behind the denial of simultaneity for events at a distance that grounds the special theory of relativity, the denial of the legitimacy of the postulation of global inertial reference frames and gravitational fields that grounds the general theory of relativity, and the process of deletion and abstraction that grounds attempts to reformulate quantum theory first in the algebraic and then in the propositional logical mode, all show that within science itself there is an ongoing process of first criticizing the surface referential apparatus of theories, and then attempting to reformulate the theories in novel ways that contain fewer of the allegedly non-referential components masquerading as referential components in the novel theory than were present in the theory replaced. If this is so, to adopt the attitude that we ought to accept as real that which science tells us is real, as revealed by the surface structure of best accepted scientific theories, is just to refuse to do explicit philosophical critique on our own, relying instead on the scientific community to do it for us in applying its conscious or unconscious methodology, resting on explicit or implicit philosophical presuppositions.

If philosophy ought to be viewed as really nothing but "science continued," then it ought to be realized the science is itself, at least in its more foundationally theoretical portions, continuous with philosophy. From this perspective the attempt to utilize presuppositions of epistemology, semantics, and metaphysics to delineate between that portion of the grammatically referential portion of scientific discourse that ought to be construed as genuinely referential and that portion that ought first to be reconstrued in some other instrumental or place-holding way, and then eliminated if possible from a reformulated theory to avoid its deceptive appearance misleading us as to what there really is in the world, is a part of ongoing science.

The presuppositions behind this critical program are of great intuitive appeal. They are, indeed, hard to make clear and precise and hard to defend once the full light of philosophical attention has been paid to them. But that is all the more reason why one ought to explore carefully the assumptions behind these philosophical-methodological critiques of apparent reference to understand further to what degree the program can be made coherent and viable in the light of the familiar objections to them.

One thing at least is clear: It is a mistake to think that one can avoid all of the problems that arise as soon as one begins to think in terms of invidious contrasts among apparently referential terms based on epistemological, semantic, and metaphysical presuppositions by simply asserting that the proper ontological attitude is to believe in all and only those things referred to in our best available scientific theories. For which theories those will be will itself be the outcome, rightly or wrongly, of just such critical distinctions among apparent referrers on the part of the scientific community that generates the theories for the philosophers to base their "natural" ontology upon.

Notes

1 H. Putnam, "What Theories Are Not," in E. Nagel, P. Suppes, and A. Tarski (eds.), *Logic, Methodology, and Philosophy of Science* (Stanford, Calif.: Stanford University Press, 1962), pp. 240–51.
2 N. Campbell, *Foundations of Science* (New York: Dover, 1957), Chapter 5.
3 M. Friedman, *Foundations of Space-Time Theories* (Princeton, N. J.: Princeton University Press, 1983), Chapter 6, secs. 3, 4.

10

Mathematics and modality

HARTRY FIELD

It is a pleasure to write an essay in a volume for Hilary Putnam. I well remember the enormous impact that the first Putnam paper I read ("Minds and Machines") had on me when I came across it as an undergraduate in the spring of 1966. The impact was due not only to the specific content of that paper but also to the manner in which it approached philosophical questions, which was very unlike anything I had seen before; and over the years I have continued to regard Hilary's way of doing philosophy as a model. In more specific ways too, Hilary's work has been of enormous influence on my own: my views on such subjects as scientific realism, scientific methodology, philosophy of mind, and philosophy of mathematics probably owe more to him than to anyone else; despite much doctrinal disagreement, I usually find that Hilary more than just about anyone else raises the right questions and correctly locates their philosophical importance.

The present essay is excerpted from a longer one[1] that is on a subject to which Hilary has devoted a great deal of attention, namely, realism and platonism in the philosophy of mathematics. One of the things argued in this excerpt is that there are serious difficulties with the idea that modality serves as a general surrogate for ontology in the philosophy of mathematics. This is in opposition to the central theme of Hilary's work in the philosophy of mathematics from the time of "Mathematics Without Foundation" (Putnam 1967b); but my view of the role that modality does play in the philosophy of mathematics has considerable affinities to the views expressed in his earlier essay "The Thesis That Mathematics Is Logic" (Putnam 1967a).[2]

I

I advocate a form of anti-platonist view about mathematics – one in which modality plays a role, though a rather limited role; and where the modality involved is a modality of the least controversial kind. What my anti-platonism involves is a disbelief in mathematics. Or at least, it involves a disbelief in mathematics if mathematics is taken at face value; coupled with a lack of commitment to (and lack of much interest in) the program of finding a non-face-value interpretation of mathematics on which the mathematics becomes more believable.

Some terminology: I take platonism to be the doctrine that there are mathematical entities and that they are in no way mind-dependent or language-dependent. And it is platonism that I primarily want to deny. That denial is compatible with a sort of idealist view about mathematics: the view that mathematical entities exist but are mind-dependent or language-dependent. But I would like to ignore such idealist views here: the alternative to platonism that I am interested in is the denial that there are any mathematical entities. Since mathematics, taken at face value, postulates the existence of mathematical entities (numbers, functions, sets, and so forth), this means that an anti-platonist of the sort I want to be cannot literally believe mathematical theories (at least when taken at face value).

Why be an anti-platonist? There are several reasons; I will mention only one, probably the most well known. That reason is that mathematical entities as the platonist conceives them exist outside of space-time and bear no causal relations to us or anything we can observe; and there just don't seem to be any mechanisms that could explain how the existence of and properties of such entities could be known.

The problem can be put without use of the term of art 'knows', and also without talk of truth (though talk of disquotational truth enables us to give a more snappy formulation of it).[3] The platonist believes that his or her own belief states about mathematics, and the belief states of platonist mathematicians, are to a large extent true – disquotationally true. This means that those belief states are highly correlated with the mathematical facts: more precisely (and put without talk of truth or facts), that for most mathematical sentences that you substitute for 'p', the following holds:

(1) If mathematicians accept 'p' then p.

Indeed, if various restrictions on the type of mathematical sentence substituted for 'p' are imposed, the converse schema also holds for the most part: there are certain types of mathematical facts that most mathematicians know. Now, the fact that these schemata hold for the most part is surely a fact that requires explanation: we need an explanation of how it can have come about that mathematicians' belief states and utterances so well reflect the mathematical facts. But because of the lack of causal connection or spatio-temporal connection between us and the aphysical realm of mathematical entities, there don't seem to be any mechanisms that could explain how their belief states or utterances can have come to correctly reflect the facts about that realm.

It seems to me that this raises a serious epistemological problem for believing in mathematical entities. For if a platonist were to grant that it is impossible in principle to give a satisfactory explanation of the fact that (1) generally holds, he would be left with two unpalatable alternatives: (a) he could deny that it is a fact that (1) generally holds, or (b) he could say that it is simply a brute fact that needs no explanation. But to maintain a class of beliefs while holding the meta-belief that most of those beliefs are false seems plainly unsatisfactory, so we must certainly reject (a). And (b) seems pretty dubious too: there is nothing wrong with supposing that some facts *about mathematical entities* are just brute facts, but to accept that facts *about the relation between mathematical entities and human beings* are brute and inexplicable is another matter entirely. I conclude that unless a platonist can make it plausible that it is in principle possible to provide an explanation of the assumed fact that (1) generally holds, then platonism has a serious problem.

The problem I have been raising is of course a reformulation of the problem made famous in Benacerraf 1973. Benacerraf formulated the problem in such a way that it depended on a causal theory of knowledge. The present formulation does not depend on *any* theory of knowledge in the sense in which the causal theory is a theory of knowledge: that is, it does not depend on any assumption about necessary and sufficient conditions for knowledge. Instead, it depends on the idea that we shouldn't continue claiming to know (or justifiably believe, or whatever) facts about a certain domain if we believe it impossible in principle to explain the reliability of our beliefs about that domain.

In a recent book, David Lewis (1986) has adopted a similar formulation of the Benacerraf problem; but he holds that it does not pose a genuine problem in the mathematical case, because all facts about the realm of mathematical entities hold necessarily. More fully, Lewis's idea is that we do need – and do have, at least in outline – an explanation of the reliable correlation between the facts about electrons and our 'electron' beliefs (i.e., the beliefs we would express using the word 'electron'). Or as he puts it, we need and have an account (in this case a causal account) of the way in which 'electron' beliefs counterfactually depend on the existence and nature of electrons. But it is only because the existence and nature of electrons is contingent that it makes sense to ask for an explanation of the counterfactual dependence of 'electron' beliefs on the existence and nature of electrons. In

Lewis's words,

Nothing can depend counterfactually on non-contingent matters. For instance nothing can depend counterfactually on what mathematical objects there are .... Nothing sensible can be said about how our opinions would be different if there were no number seventeen. (p. 111)

Consequently, since mathematics consists entirely of necessary truths, there can be no sensible problem of explaining why it is that our mathematical beliefs are a reliable indicator of the mathematical facts.

I think, though, that there are at least four reasons why this fails to undercut the epistemological challenge.

Point One: The premise that all facts about the mathematical realm hold necessarily is false. Let's grant that all facts *purely* about the mathematical realm hold necessarily; that still leaves facts about the mathematical and non-mathematical realms jointly, like such facts (or purported facts) as

(A) $2 =$ the number of planets closer than the Earth to the sun;

(B) For some natural number n there is a function that maps the natural numbers less than n onto the set of all particles of matter;

(C) Surrounding each point of physical space-time there is an open region for which there is a 1-1 differentiable mapping of that region onto an open subset of R^4 (the space of quadruples of real numbers);

(D) There is a differentiable function Ψ from points of space to real numbers such that the gradient of Ψ gives the gravitational force on any object per unit mass of that object.

These facts are, by almost anyone's standards, contingent. But they are partly about the mathematical realm (they involve reference to mathematical entities), so even if what Lewis says about the explanation of the correlation between the *pure* mathematical facts and our belief states is correct, the problem of explaining the correlation between these "mixed mathematical facts" and our belief states remains.

There is an obvious strategy for solving the problem of explaining the reliability of our "mixed" mathematical beliefs, on the supposition that Lewis is right about the purely mathematical beliefs. The strategy is to divide the mixed mathematical beliefs into two components, a purely mathematical component and a purely non-mathematical component; where the purely mathematical component is a piece of pure mathematics unmixed by physical theory of any sort, and the purely non-mathematical part involves no reference to mathematical entities.[4] The strategy is easy to illustrate, and to carry out, in example (A): (A) can be "divided into" the purely non-mathematical claim

A(i) $\exists x \exists y (Px \ \& \ Py \ \& \ x \neq y \ \& \ \forall z(Pz \supset z = x \lor z = y))$,

(where '*Px*' abbreviates '*x* is a planet closer than the Earth to the Sun')
and the purely mathematical claim

A(ii) [2 = the number of *u* such that *Pu*] if and only if
$[\exists x \exists y (Px \ \& \ Py \ \& \ x \neq y \ \& \ \forall z (Pz \supset z = x \lor z = y))].$[5]

Because (A) is a consequence of A(i) and A(ii), there can be no
problem about the reliability of our belief in (A) unless there is a
problem about the reliability of our belief in A(i) or A(ii). But A(i) is a
purely non-mathematical belief, and explaining the reliability of such
beliefs is presumably non-problematic in principle; and A(ii) is a purely
mathematical belief, and we are assuming for the moment that Lewis's
argument works for beliefs of that sort. So "mixed" statements like (A)
present no more of an epistemological problem than do purely mathematical statements; and the same holds for any other "mixed" statement that can be decomposed into purely mathematical and purely
non-mathematical components.

Unfortunately, however, the task of splitting mixed statements into
purely mathematical and purely non-mathematical components is a
highly non-trivial one: it is done easily in case (A), but it isn't at all clear
how to do it in cases (B)–(D) (at least without introducing some
controversial devices). Indeed, as I will argue later on, *the task of
splitting all such assertions into two components is PRECISELY THE
SAME as the task of showing that mathematics is dispensable in the
empirical sciences*; that is, the task of showing that in any application of
a mixed assertion like (B) or (C) or (D), a purely non-mathematical
assertion could take its place. Certainly, then, no one doubtful of the
possibility of carrying out the nominalist program of showing the
dispensability of all reference to mathematical entities in science could
consistently advocate the strategy just outlined for solving the problem
of explaining our reliable access to the "realm of mathematical facts"
(even if we grant Lewis's claims about the triviality of the problem of
explaining our reliable access to the *purely* mathematical facts).

Point Two: Even with regard to the purely mathematical facts,
Lewis's response *at least by itself* is too easy. To explain what I mean,
let's ask in what sense mathematical facts (assuming for the moment
that there are such) *are* necessary. They are not logically necessary, nor
do they reduce to logically necessary truths by definition. They are of
course *mathematically* necessary in the sense that they follow from basic
laws of mathematics. Similarly, the existence of electrons is presumably
physically necessary; that is, it follows from basic physical laws. But
Lewis does not think the epistemological problem of explaining how our
'electron' beliefs can reliably indicate the existence of electrons is really
a pseudo-problem, just because the existence of electrons is physically

necessary; so why should the fact that the existence of numbers is mathematically necessary show that the corresponding epistemological problem about numbers is a pseudo-problem?

One might try to answer this by saying that mathematical necessity is *absolute* necessity or *metaphysical* necessity, while physical necessity is necessity only of a restricted sort. But it is hard to see how to give any content to this that is of any help. In the first place, it is worth noting that there are perfectly good senses in which mathematical necessity is *not* unrestricted necessity: for instance, it is not logical necessity. What then is the content of the distinction between "absolute" or "metaphysical" necessity and necessities of lesser sorts, and what are the grounds for saying that mathematical necessity is of the former sort but that physical necessity is not? One could just *stipulate* that the term "absolute necessity" is to cover mathematical necessity but not physical necessity. But then the question becomes: what are the grounds for thinking that it is absolute necessity so defined, rather than, say, logical necessity or physical necessity, that is epistemologically relevant? Alternatively, one could try to somehow build it into the definition of "absolute necessity" that the epistemological problem can't arise for absolutely necessary truths; but then the question is, why suppose that mathematical claims unlike claims of basic physics are "absolutely necessary" in this sense? Clearly the introduction of talk of "absolute necessity" is of no help: on either of the two conventions for using this phrase, we need an argument that the epistemological problem doesn't arise for claims that are mathematically necessary, in other words, those that follow from the accepted mathematical axioms. In particular, we need an argument that the epistemological problem does not arise for the mathematical axioms themselves. Unless an answer to this is given, one suspects that the claim that mathematical necessity is "absolute necessity" simply amounts to the decision not to take the problem of explaining the reliability of our mathematical beliefs seriously; if so, it cannot be used to justify that decision.

The point I am making can be reinforced by noting how easy it is to invoke "metaphysical necessity" to defend metaphysical beliefs against epistemological challenge. If a believer in God is embarrassed by an inability to explain the fact (that is, what he or she takes to be a fact) that his or her belief in God and beliefs about God are fairly reliable, the solution is simple: declare the problem a pseudo-problem on the grounds that God is a necessary being and has all his properties necessarily. If a believer in possible worlds as Lewis conceives them – that is, possible worlds more or less like the real world but bearing no spatio-temporal relations to the real world – is embarrassed by the inability to explain the reliability that, he supposes, our beliefs about these otherworldly entities possess, the solution is again simple: declare the problem a pseudo-problem, on the analogous grounds. Lewis himself, of course, employs this tactic in the possible-worlds case (though not in the theological case). Indeed, the quotation above comes from a part of his book where he is trying to defend possible worlds as he conceives them against a Benacerrafian epistemological challenge. I suspect that many readers will feel that the application of the tactic to the possible-worlds case (possible worlds construed as Lewis construed them, not simply as mathematical entities), and to the theological case, is a cheat; but that in application to the mathematical case the tactic is reasonable. Maybe so, but if so some justification is needed for this choice of in which cases to regard the tactic as legitimate and in which cases not to do so. I myself incline to the more evenhanded view that the tactic is unreasonable in all three cases.

In the longer essay from which this is taken, I give a diagnosis of the common view that there is a sense of necessity that is akin to logical necessity in a way in which physical necessity is not, in which mathematics is, if true, necessary. If this diagnosis is correct, I think it further undermines the idea that the problem of explaining the reliability of our beliefs about the mathematical realm, given the assumption that there is such a realm, is a pseudo-problem.[6] That's the end of Point Two.

On Points Three and Four, I'll be briefer. Point Three is that Lewis is assuming a controversial connection between counterfactuals and necessity, and that even those who think that there is some sort of "absolute necessity" to mathematics may find countermathematical conditionals perfectly intelligible in certain contexts. It is doubtless true that nothing sensible can be said about how things would be different if there were no number 17; that is largely because the antecedent of this counterfactual gives us no hints as to what alternative mathematics is to be regarded true in the counterfactual situation in question.[7] If one changes the example to "Nothing sensible can be said about how things would be different if the axiom of choice were false," this seems wrong (assuming platonism – see note 7): if the axiom of choice were false, the cardinals wouldn't be linearly ordered, the Banach-Tarski theorem would fail, and so forth.

But what should a platonist say about what *the opinions of mathematicians* would be like if the axiom of choice failed? That is a hard question, not because it seems unintelligible, but because it poses a dilemma. There is a strong case to be made for saying that if the axiom were false, mathematicians' opinions would be just as they are now:

after all, sets don't causally interact with us, and so forth, so what could make their opinions different? But if we are platonists, we will *want* to say that if the axiom were false, then mathematicians would believe it false; that's what we seem to need to say if our present opinion that the axiom is true is to have epistemological value. The epistemological problem, if put in terms of counterfactuals, is to figure out how to say what we (in our platonist moods) want to say, rather than what we seem forced to say by the causal inertness, mind independence (etc.) of the mathematical objects.

My fourth and final point is this: there was no obvious reason to put the challenge of explaining the reliability of our mathematical beliefs in modal or counterfactual terms in the first place. Indeed, the phenomenon that our beliefs about electrons are reliable is not *simply* that our 'electron' beliefs counterfactually depend on the facts about electrons: it is that our beliefs depend on the facts about electrons *in such a way that* the correlation of our believing the sentence 'p' and its being the case that p would be maintained given a variation in the facts about electrons. It is *this type of* counterfactual dependence that needs explaining, not counterfactual dependence by itself. But now, if the intelligibility of talk of counterfactual dependence is challenged in the mathematical case, it can easily be dropped without much loss to the problem: there is still the problem of explaining the *actual* correlation between our believing 'p' and its being the case that p. That, in fact, is the way I put the problem at the beginning of this essay.

I have in a very sketchy way tried to make plausible that if one postulates mathematical entities one is going to have a serious problem explaining the correlation between our mathematical beliefs and the facts about those entities; and I have tried to argue that *to the extent that providing such an explanation appears impossible*, believers in a mathematical realm face a genuine epistemological problem. Note that this way of putting the worry about mathematical realism does not involve the claim that there can be no good reason to believe in mathematical entities. That claim would be quite wrong, I think: there can be strong reasons to believe in mathematical entities, having to do with the apparent indispensability of mathematical entities to important theories outside mathematics; I believe that these reasons can ultimately be rebutted, but it isn't entirely clear how best to rebut some of them. The point, rather, is that however good the reasons *for* believing in mathematical entities, still the difficulty in explaining the reliability of those beliefs remains, and it raises a serious epistemological puzzle for those not happy with taking a perception of the realm of mathematical entities as primitive. That epistemological puzzle is reason against believing in mathematical entities, which has to be weighed against the reasons in favor of mathematical entities. Actually it isn't a simple case of weighing: we have a case of competing arguments; for a satisfactory view to be achieved, we must find a way of disarming one of the competing lines of argument. I do not declare it misguided to try to show that it is possible to explain the reliability of our access to a purported realm of mathematical facts;[8] or to try to show (as Lewis does at least in the case of pure mathematical facts) that the lack of such an explanation should not be upsetting.[9] But I know of no way to do either of these things at all convincingly, and my bet is that the anti-platonist program of undercutting the reasons for literally believing mathematics is more promising.

II

There are two central aspects to my version of anti-platonism:

1. I conjecture that you don't need mathematical entities in formulating physical theories or in formulating anything else that it is important to believe strictly.

(This conjecture is by no means fully established, but I think I've shown elsewhere that it isn't as obviously false as people used to think. To put it more positively, I think that the program of trying to establish it is a fairly promising one.)

2. Given 1, you can explain the legitimacy of using mathematics without assuming the mathematics true: the explanation involves the fact that mathematics has a feature called *conservativeness*, according to which if A and the members of Γ are nominalistic assertions (i.e., don't involve commitment to mathematical entities) then A doesn't follow from Γ *plus mathematics* unless it follows from Γ *alone*.

It might be thought that to believe that mathematics is conservative is to violate 1. More fully, the argument is that the notion of "following from" employed in the definition of conservativeness needs to be explicated either in terms of proofs or (better) in terms of models, and proofs and models are mathematical entities that we then must believe in if we are to believe that mathematics is conservative. My response is that "following from" is a modal notion, explicable in terms of a primitive modal operator "it is logically possible that" or (better) "it is logically consistent that"; model theory and proof theory are simply dispensable devices for aiding us in finding out about the properties of this primitive operator. I have elaborated this claim elsewhere (Field 1989, Introduction and Essay 3), and will not repeat the elaboration here.

The question I want to discuss in the remainder of this essay is this: in the past, when I have argued that (in accord with claim 1) we can develop physical theory without reference to mathematical entities, I have implicitly assumed that the needed development of physical theories also should make no use of modal notions. But since I am now allowing the use of a modal notion, logical possibility, in connection with claims of consistency and conservativeness and the like, the question arises as to whether I shouldn't allow it in connection with physical theory as well. That is, the question arises whether I mightn't have achieved a mathematics-free physics more easily – and whether I mightn't have fewer difficulties in extending the program of developing a mathematics-free physics to more complicated physical theories than the ones I considered – if I were to have allowed the use of modality in the development of physics.

It might initially be thought obvious that a notion of possibility could be invoked to avoid the postulation of mathematical entities in physics, and indeed it might be thought that it is totally trivial to turn a platonistic physics into a nominalistic physics if an operator of possibility is regarded as nominalistically acceptable. For it might be thought that if S is the mathematical theory we use in developing our platonistic physics, then $\Diamond AX_S$ could just replace S in the application of the mathematics within science. (AX_S is the conjunction of the axioms of S; I put aside problems about how to treat theories that aren't finitely axiomatized.) But this is incorrect: it fails to take into account the fact that insofar as mathematics is needed at all in science, what is needed isn't just *pure* mathematical statements, but *mixed* statements that speak of mathematical entities and physical entities in the same breath. It is these mixed statements that an anti-platonist must find a means to handle.

But they can't be handled by prefixing them with the modal operator '$\Diamond$': for though prefixing them with '$\Diamond$' would have the desirable effect of replacing the requirement that there *actually are* entities satisfying the mathematical theory by the weaker requirement that there *might be* such entities, it would equally have the undesirable effect of replacing the requirement that the physical world *actually* be such as to satisfy the scientific law by the weaker requirement that the physical world *might* be such as to satisfy the law. This would of course totally remove all of the physical content of the law. The problem then is that it is not at all obvious that there is any way to "modalize away" the mathematical content of the physical law (i.e., the commitment to mathematical entities) without at the same time "modalizing away" the physical content.

There *would* be a way to modalize away the mathematical content of a mixed statement (such as a platonistically stated physical law) without modalizing away the physical content, if we could show that the mixed statement can be represented as a conjunction of a purely mathematical component M and a purely physical component N (purely physical in that it makes no reference to mathematical entities). If such a separation could be achieved, it would allow us to reformulate the mixed statement modally as N & $\Diamond M$. It isn't hard to see, though, that the program of separating the mixed statements of science into purely mathematical and purely physical conjuncts is precisely the program of showing that mathematics is dispensable in science. (I announced this fact earlier without proof, in connection with David Lewis's attempt to undermine the epistemological objection to mathematical platonism. Here is the proof.) Suppose that M is purely mathematical and N is purely non-mathematical; then the conservativeness of mathematics implies that the conjunction of M and N has no more purely physical consequences than N alone has; this means that if we could separate a physical law or theory into a purely mathematical conjunct and a purely physical conjunct, the purely mathematical conjunct would be dispensable without any loss of physical content to the theory. If modalizing away the mathematical content of mixed statements without modalizing away the physical content requires this sort of separation, then the introduction of modal operators, necessary though it is for dealing with metalogic, can serve no role in answering the argument that we ought to believe mathematical theories because they are indispensable to science.

III

The foregoing makes it hard to see how the introduction of a logical possibility operator *by itself* (or a mathematical or metaphysical possibility operator by itself, on any natural understanding of what that might involve) could ever be of any help in showing how to reformulate empirical applications of mathematics in such a way as to avoid commitment to mathematical entities. But perhaps we could do better if we used some other sort of possibility operator, or used a logical possibility operator in conjunction with other special logical apparatus (such as an "actuality operator" or sophisticated variants of it). I shall now discuss one modified conception of possibility, in order to see if it can be used to avoid the problem just discussed for the purely logical possibility operator; what I have to say can be extended to the (slightly more flexible) approach involving the fancy actuality-type operators.

I think that the concept of possibility that gives the idea of modalizing away the existential commitments of mathematics the best chance of working is the concept "is a possible extension of the actual world." We are to understand a "possible extension of the world" as a possible world that contains all actual objects, and that is such that for any formula in which all quantifiers are restricted to actual objects, an n-tuple of actual objects satisfies the formula in that world if and only if it satisfies it in the actual world. Restriction of quantifiers to actual objects is to be accomplished by a special predicate 'Actual'; this applies to all and only the actual objects, even when it is in the scope of a modal operator.

The idea of invoking this apparatus in connection with the applications of mathematics is that if we want to formulate some theory S of mathematical physics in such a way as not to entail the existence of mathematical entities, we do it by saying

$$S^* \quad \Diamond_e[S \ \& \ \forall x(\text{if not Math}(x), \text{ then Actual}(x))];$$

where 'Math' is a predicate that is satisfied by just those things that are mathematical objects. ('$\Diamond_e$' is to be read "there is a possible extension of the world in which." Intuitively, S^* says that S would hold in at least one possible world that is just like ours except in containing some extra entities *all of which are mathematical*.) This avoids commitment to mathematical entities, since all quantifiers over mathematical entities are within the scope of a possibility operator and since there is no use of the actuality predicate to "undo the possibility." But it is not hard to see that any non-modal consequence of S in which there are no singular terms for mathematical objects and in which all variables are restricted to physical objects is a consequence of S^*. I have heard it said that S^* or close variants of it show that Putnam's program of "mathematics as modal logic" has no difficulty in handling the application of mathematics to the physical world.

But does it? Does this show that we now have a way to "modalize away" the commitment to mathematical entities in science? There are two reasons to doubt this. The first (which I'll call the technical reason) is that it turns out to be possible to use this result to modalize away the commitment to mathematical entities in science *only on the assumption that an important part of the program of the non-modal nominalist can be carried out*. And the second reason (the "philosophical reason") is that the method of eliminating commitment to mathematical entities is

suspiciously powerful: an analogous method would enable one to eliminate commitment to nearly all unobservables from scientific theories. I
will take up these two points in reverse order.

The point to be argued first, then, is that the above method of
eliminating mathematical entities is, in a sense, "too easy": it licenses
the easy elimination of far too much. (As we will see, the elimination of
mathematical entities by this method is actually rather problematic –
that is the substance of the technical objection that I am now deferring
– but the method *does* license the easy elimination of commitment to
subatomic particles, to viruses, and to most other unobservables.) Suppose that T is a consistent theory that postulates subatomic particles,
and that we want to find a theory that avoids commitment to such
particles but meets all uncontroversial conditions of adequacy just as
well as does T. In particular, we will want it to be as observationally
adequate as T. To simplify the discussion slightly, we can suppose that
'subatomic particle' is a primitive predicate of T. Then in complete
analogy to S^*, we can formulate a modal theory T^* as follows:

$$\Diamond_e [T \ \& \ \forall x (\text{if } x \text{ is not a subatomic particle then Actual}(x))].$$

Then we have (THEOREM 1) that T^* does not imply 'There are
subatomic particles'; but (THEOREM 2) that it licenses precisely the
same inferences among O-sentences that T licenses, where now an
O-sentence is a non-modal sentence that doesn't talk about subatomic
particles. The proof of these theorems is identical with the proof of the
corresponding claims for S^*.

It is probably obvious how this result could be applied by a modalist
to eliminate subatomic particles in a way that is *technically* unproblem-
atic (even if philosophically quite dubious). But it is worth spelling this
out explicitly: this will help in connection with my later claim that the
analogous modal elimination of mathematical entities is technically (as
well as philosophically) problematic. What we need to argue, then, is
that T^* not only avoids commitment to subatomic particles (which
seems incontestable in light of Theorem 1) but also that it meets all
uncontroversial conditions of adequacy just as well as does T. In
particular, we will need to argue that it is as observationally adequate as
T. The argument for this is clear enough: presumably, anything that
could be regarded as an "observation report" for T will be equivalent
(modulo T) to a sentence free of reference to subatomic particles and
in which quantifiers are restricted to exclude such particles (i.e., to an
O-sentence). If so, then Theorem 2 gives us that T^* is as observationally adequate as is T: any inference among observation reports licensed
by T can be put as an inference among O-sentences, and when it is so
put it is licensed by T^*; conversely, any inference among observation

reports expressed as O-sentences that is licensed by T^* is licensed by T.

As I remarked, I am not claiming that this vindicates anti-realism about subatomic particles; I think it is reasonable to believe T. Indeed, I suspect that there can be no reason to believe T^* that isn't *based on* reason to believe T: so that there is really no significant epistemological gap between T^* and T. (One way to try to defend this – not the only possible way – would be to try to argue that T^* is not explanatory in the way that T is; if this is right, then since the only reason to believe either theory is presumably that it explains our observations, then it is only T that could be directly supported, and T^* would derive its believability from T. I think that this is a plausible line to take, although arguing that T^* isn't explanatory in the same way as is T is somewhat tricky.) In any case, I take it that for one reason or another most philosophers would agree that the replacement of T by T^* isn't of much philosophical value. If this is so, it is hard to see why the completely analogous replacement in the mathematical case should be assumed to have any philosophical value. (For instance, it's hard to see why, if T^* is less explanatory than T, then S^* shouldn't be less explanatory than S.)

I now turn to the technical objection: I claim that the cheap anti-realism about subatomic particles, which is at least technically possible, cannot be carried over to mathematics, at least not so cheaply. Of course, we still have Theorems 1 and 2 in the mathematical case. But the argument for elimination in the case of subatomic particles did not consist solely in the appeal to these theorems; rather, it appealed to these theorems together with a supplementary argument that in the case of subatomic particle theory, the class of O-sentences in the language of T is comprehensive enough to enable us to formulate our observations. (More generally, the requirement is that in going from T to the O-sentences that follow from T, one can't lose the ability to formulate what even the would-be denier of subatomic particles would want to recognize as facts.) But when we shift to a physical theory committed to mathematical entities and the use of the predicate 'is a mathematical entity' in defining the starring operation, the class of O-sentences (sentences with no singular terms for mathematical entities, and in which quantifiers are explicitly restricted by the formula 'is not a mathematical entity') will not normally be comprehensive enough to formulate all of the observational facts (let alone all of the facts that the nominalist would want to recognize).

To illustrate this, suppose that S is a theory of gravitation, expressed in the usual platonist fashion. In the language of S one might express one's observations in the following way: "The distance in meters between *b* and *c* is between 13.7 and 13.8"; "the mass in kilograms of *b* is less than 17.4"; and so forth. These are not O-sentences; reference to real numbers is involved in their formulation. I maintain that in the language typically used to formulate physics, this use of sentences that are not O-sentences to express one's observations[10] is essential: the language does not contain O-sentences capable of doing the job. If this is right, then Theorems 1 and 2 are not by themselves of much use in the mathematical case: when applied to typical theories of mathematical physics, they yield theories S^* that don't enable us to make the inferences about distances and masses and so forth that platonist mathematical physics allows us to make.

There is, of course, a way around this problem: apply Theorems 1 and 2 not to a typical platonist formulation of physics but to a modified formulation S_{mod}, which contains some new predicates, chosen so that all the claims about distance, mass, velocity, acceleration, and so forth that we want to preserve are expressible in terms of O-sentences. The O-sentences in question prima facie require a very large number of infinite families of primitive predicates; a very small sample of such families might include

(i) the distance between *x* and *y* is *r* times the distance between *z* and *w*;
(ii) the velocity of *x* with respect to *y* is *r* times the velocity of *z* with respect to *w*;
(iii) the velocity of *x* with respect to *y* multiplied by the temporal difference between *z* and *w* is *r* times the spatial distance between *u* and *v*

(where '*r*' is to be replaced by a specific rational number; which rational number you plug in is what distinguishes one member of each infinite family from the next). But I will assume that our modal nominalist would not be content to employ a large number of infinite families of primitive predicates; rather, he will want to find a fairly small finite stock of predicates to employ as the primitives of S_{mod}, and he will want to express his observations (and other claims he regards as factual) in terms of O-sentences involving this finite vocabulary.

But it is far from immediately obvious how this is to be done; in fact, the task of finding such a stock of primitive predicates and defining the members of the various infinite families in terms of them was the main technical task I set myself in Field 1980. To a large extent I solved the problem: I showed there how *in the case of classical field theories in flat space-time*, and *assuming a realist attitude toward space-time points*, one *can* define from a small number of primitive predicates all of the claims about distance, mass, velocity, acceleration, and so forth (including how these quantities interrelate) that are needed in physics and that a nominalist would want to preserve. We can use this result, then, to solve what I've called "the technical problem" for the modal starring method, in the case of flat space-time field theories: we apply the "starring" operator not to S, but to a theory S_{mod} that employs a space-time ontology and the specially chosen set of primitive predicates used in my book, and we express the needed observational claims in terms of O-sentences involving these special primitives in the manner done in that book.

It is noteworthy, though, that this solution to the technical problem relies both on the technical work and on some of the controversial philosophical assumptions necessary to complete the *non-modal* nominalist's program (the program of my book), leading one to wonder what the value is in introducing the special modal apparatus ('$\Diamond_e$' and 'Actual'). The solution relies on the technical work; for in cases where the non-modal nominalist's program has not yet been carried out (e.g., for theories in curved space-time), it is not obvious how to express in terms of O-sentences our observations (much less other claims about the physical world that a nominalist would want to preserve, e.g., claims about the current distribution of mass in space). The solution also relies on some of the controversial philosophical assumptions; just as the non-modal nominalist has to assume a realist (substantivalist) view of space-time in order that his definitions of various concepts in terms of O-sentences be adequate, so too must the modal nominalist. For instance, the modal nominalist must presuppose substantivalism if he adopts as his spatial primitives betweenness and congruence, and expresses his claim "the distance from x to y is 1.5 times the distance from z to w" in the usual manner (viz., as "there are u_1 and u_2 and v such that u_1 is between x and y, u_2 is between u_1 and y, v is between z and w, and xu_1 congruent to u_1u_2 and to u_2y and to zv and to vw"). That definition requires points of space. (For instance, it works only on the assumption that midway between any two points of matter there is *something*, even if there is no matter there.) Of course, the modal nominalist could take "the distance from x to y is 1.5 times the distance from z to w" as one of his primitive predicates; but the point is that this sort of problem arises for the definition of virtually all quantitative predicates in non-numerical terms. If our modal nominalist is to avoid having to take each member of a huge number of infinite families of quantitative predicates as primitive, I think there is no alternative to adopting an ontology of space-time points. In general, then, the promise that modality might help make it easier or more attractive to carry out an elimination of commitment to mathematical entities in the sciences appears to have vanished.

It might be contended that the problem I have been discussing arises from not taking the use of modality far enough: for, it might be said, there is nothing to stop us from formulating even our observations modally. For instance, why not just formulate the observation that the distance from a to b is approximately 1.5 times the distance from c to d by saying

OBS $\diamondsuit_e$[(i) there are real numbers r_1 and r_2 such that r_1 is the distance from a to b, r_2 is the distance from c to d, and r_1 is approximately the product of 1.5 and r_2;
             (ii) standard mathematics holds;
and   (iii) $\forall x$(if not Math(x), then Act(x)).

There are at least two very serious problems with this suggestion. The first is that Theorem 2 no longer applies: since our observation sentences are not O-sentences as previously defined, we have no reason to think that S^* licenses the same inferences among observation sentences as does the platonist theory S. If the suggestion is to be of any interest, then, it must be accompanied by an extension of Theorem 2 to a much more general class of sentences than O-sentences. (In fact, no such extension is possible, for the conclusion is false; this follows from the next paragraph.)

The second problem is that even putting the deductive connections among our observations aside, the suggested modal formulation of our observations is grossly deficient. Indeed, the displayed sentence OBS that attempted to state modally the distance relations between a, b, c, and d in fact is true *whatever* the distance relations between a, b, c, and d. Why? First, the real numbers postulated in the extended world in clause (i) are not asserted in clause (iii) to be actual; consequently, the numerical distance relation that holds in the extended world between r_1, a, and b and between r_2, c, and d is not being asserted to hold between them in the actual world. (Indeed, if there are no numbers in the actual world, as the modal nominalist holds, then these relations *can't* hold there since one of their terms is absent.) Second, there is no clause in OBS that forces the distance function in the extended world to be connected in any specific way in that world with those primitive relations among physical objects that *are* required (by the semantics of $\diamondsuit_e$) to be the same in the actual and extended worlds. Consequently the existence of a distance function with specific properties in the extended world imposes no constraints on the spatial relations in the actual world.

Can we fix up OBS so as to be immune to this problem? It is not easy to do so, short of introducing the means for a non-modal and non-platonistic formulation of the observation. For the most obvious way to fix up OBS would be to add inside the brackets a fourth conjunct that says enough about the relation between the numerical distance function and some primitive physical predicates so as to determine an explicit non-modal definition of distance relations like (i) in terms of these primitive predicates. We see again that if we solve the non-modal anti-platonist's problems, we solve the modal anti-platonist's too – but only by making the appeal to modality otiose.

Perhaps, though, there is another way to improve on OBS, one that uses a still more powerful modal apparatus, such as a full actuality operator in conjunction with a quantifier over relations. This would enable us to add a different kind of fourth clause to OBS, not requiring new predicates in the language:

OBS$^+$ $\Diamond_e[$(i) there are real numbers r_1 and r_2 such that r_1 is the distance from a to b, r_2 is the distance from c to d, and r_1 is approximately the product of 1.5 and r_2;
(ii) standard mathematics holds;
(iii) $\forall x$(if not Math(x), then Act(x)).

and   (iv) $\forall R \forall x_1 \ldots \forall x_4$(if Act$(x_1)$ and...and Act(x_4) then $[R(x_1,\ldots,x_4)$ if and only if actually $R(x_1,\ldots,x_4)])].$[11]

In (iv), R ranges over 4-place relations. (We should really add a clause similar to (iv) for relations of all other finite adicity, but for sake of readability I will stick to adicity 4.) In effect what we're doing here is introducing a more powerful operator $\Diamond_e^+$, where $\Diamond_e^+A$ means that A holds in some enlargement of the actual world in which *all* relations among actual entities are preserved, not just those relations expressible in atomic predicates in the original language; and we are replacing $\Diamond_e$ by $\Diamond_e^+$ in OBS.[12]

Is OBS$^+$ any better than OBS? Basically the answer is no; but to say why, one has to distinguish between different readings that could be given to the relation quantifier in the new actuality clause (iv).

(1) If we understand the relation quantifier in OBS$^+$ as ranging over *all* relations, or even all relations definable in platonist physics, then OBS$^+$ is of no use whatever to the modal nominalist, for it does not avoid the commitment to mathematical objects. For clause (i) of OBS$^+$ expresses a platonist spatial relation between a, b, c, and d: the relation R_i of there being numbers r_1 and r_2 such that $r_1 = $ dist(a, b) and $r_2 = $ dist(c, d) and $r_1 = 1.5 \times r_2$. If the relation quantifier in (iv) ranges over *all* relations, even platonistic ones, then part of the content of (iv) (given that a–d are actual, by (iii)) is that a, b, c, and d stand in R_i in the actual world if and only if they stand in it in the extended world. Consequently, clause (iv) allows us to export the commitment to numbers in (i) from the extended world back to the actual world. We

have succeeded in making OBS$^+$ constrain the actual spatial relations among a, b, c, and d; but we have done so only at the cost of making it as committed to mathematical entities as the platonist formulation of the observation statement from which we started.

(2) Clearly, then, if OBS$^+$ is to serve our purposes we must restrict the relation quantifier in (iv) to *non-platonistic* relations among physical objects – that is, to relations among physical objects that "do not in any way involve" mathematical objects. A natural way to interpret the restriction to "relations that don't in any way involve" mathematical objects is as a restriction to relations definable in the vocabulary of physical theory without reference to or quantification over mathematical entities. But it is easy to see that if this is how we interpret it, then OBS$^+$ becomes equivalent to OBS. In other words, on this construal of the relation quantifier, OBS$^+$ is not committed to mathematical entities, which is good; but it also does nothing to constrain the spatial relations among objects. (In the longer version of this essay, I argue that there is nothing to be gained by construing the relation quantifiers impredicatively.) It seems as if one cannot properly constrain the spatial relations among objects without introducing mathematical entities – at least, we can't do this unless we can solve the problems of the *non-modal* anti-platonist.

There are further moves that one could make in trying to find a modal formulation of our observations that avoids the demonstrable extensional adequacy of the attempt just considered, but I see little reason to pursue this. After all, the problem of demonstrable extensional adequacy that we have been discussing in the last few paragraphs was only one of the two serious technical problems that arose for the idea of construing our observations modally. The other problem, that there is no reason to expect Theorem 2 to extend to this enlarged class of observation sentences, would still arise in full force.

It should also be noted that the use of the more powerful modal operator $\Diamond_e^+$ instead of $\Diamond_e$ could be of no use independent of construing our observations modally. That is, there is no hope of solving our earlier problems by going back to the idea of using O-sentences that expressed observations non-modally (so that we get Theorem 2), and just using $\Diamond_e^+$ instead of $\Diamond_e$ in the formulation of our modal physical theory S^*. For the technical problem with S^* was that it did not enable us to express our observations as O-sentences, and the introduction of the more powerful modality can obviously do nothing to solve that.

It is worth reiterating that even if the modal nominalist could find a way around the sort of technical difficulty I have been discussing (and even if his way around it did not simply piggyback on the work of the *non*-modal nominalist), it is not clear that much would have been gained. All that such a technical success would show is that there is a way to avoid the special technical difficulties that seemed to beset the modal elimination of mathematical entities and that don't arise for the modal elimination of subatomic particles and viruses. In other words, the solution to the technical problem would only show that we can have a modal elimination of mathematical entities that is every bit as good as the modal elimination of subatomic particles and viruses. Almost everyone would agree, I think, that that conclusion should be of little solace to the nominalist. If modality is to be useful in eliminating the commitment to mathematical entities in science, it must be employed in some less trivial way. I doubt that there is a way, both workable and non-trivial, to modalize away the mathematical content of empirical science without at the same time modalizing away its empirical content (unless of course one relies on a non-modal nominalization); in any case, if there is such a way, it would have to be very different from any I have been able to find.

Notes

1 The title essay of my book *Realism, Mathematics and Modality* (Oxford: Basil Blackwell, 1989). An earlier version of "Realism, Mathematics and Modality" was published in *Philosophical Topics*, and I thank both Blackwell's and *Philosophical Topics* for allowing me to use material again here.

2 On some of the affinities and differences between my views and his views in that early paper, see the preface of Field 1980; and Field 1989, pp. 82–3 and 113–15. For further comparisons between my views and his present views, particularly on the objectivity of mathematics, see Section 8 of "Realism, Mathematics and Modality," in Field 1989.

3 The view that there can be no conceivable epistemological case against platonism that doesn't rely on a heavy-duty notion of truth is curiously widespread. See, for instance, Tait 1986.

4 Observe that I do not say that the purely mathematical part involves no reference to non-mathematical entities. That would be too strong: it would rule out such purely mathematical theories as set theory with urelements. The important feature of the purely mathematical, for the purposes of the argument in the text, is that it can be regarded with some plausibility as "necessarily true."

5 More precisely, the purely mathematical belief A(ii) is such that modulo A(ii), (A) is equivalent to the purely non-mathematical belief A(i). That is what I really mean by my slightly inaccurate talk of "dividing": it is not essential to suppose (as the "dividing" talk suggests) that the content of A(ii) is part of the content of (A).

6 In this discussion I have avoided taking a stand on whether even logical necessity should be viewed as "absolute" necessity. One view, to which I am attracted, is to reject the whole notion of "absolute" necessity as unintelligible. Another view, also with some attractions, regards the notion as intelligible but regards the only things that are absolutely necessary as logic and matters of definition; in particular (as Hume and Kant held) there can be no "absolutely necessary" entities, and so mathematics (taken at face value) cannot be absolutely necessary since it implies the existence of mathematical entities of various sorts.

Whichever of these two views one prefers, the fact that mathematics involves existential commitment in a way that logic doesn't makes for a sharp distinction between mathematical necessity and logical necessity. The view that these two sorts of necessity are closely akin cries out for explanation. The only candidate I know of for explaining this is the one I offer in my "hygienic explanation of mathematical necessity" in Section 3 of the essay from which this is excerpted.

7 Actually, a fictionalist can explain the unintelligibility of the counterfactual in a different manner: there is no number 17, so the question is like asking how things would be different if there were no Santa Claus. But let us assume platonism for the moment, since we are discussing an epistemological problem for the platonist.

8 For an attempt to do this, see Maddy 1980.

9 For another attempt to dismiss the sort of epistemological problems involving mathematics that I have been considering, see Wright 1983. I have argued against this attempt in Field 1989, Essay 5.

10 It isn't really required for my point that we regard claims about distance and mass as strictly "observational": what is important is that they are claims that almost anyone, however nominalistically inclined, will want to find a way to preserve.

11 The Act predicate is, of course, definable in terms of the actually operator, as 'actually $\exists y(y = x)$'.

12 We would do slightly better in defining $\Diamond_e^+$ (or formulating OBS$^+$) to use, not the standard actuality operator, but Harold Hodes's "backspace operator" (Hodes 1984). But which we use will not affect the points to follow.

References

Benacerraf, Paul. 1973. "Mathematical Truth." *Journal of Philosophy*, 19: 661–79.

Field, Hartry. 1980. *Science Without Numbers*: *A Defense of Nominalism*. Oxford: Blackwell, and Princeton: Princeton University Press.

1989. *Realism, Mathematics and Modality*. Oxford: Blackwell.

Hodes, Harold. 1984. "On Modal Logics Which Enrich First Order S5." *Journal of Philosophical Logic*, 13: 423–54.

Lewis, David. 1986. *On the Plurality of Worlds*. Oxford: Blackwell.

Maddy, Penelope. 1980. "Perception and Mathematical Intuition." *Philosophical Review*, 89: 163–96.

Putnam, Hilary. 1967a. "The Thesis That Mathematics Is Logic." In Ralph Schoenman (ed.), *Bertrand Russell*: *Philosopher of the Century*. London: Allen & Unwin, pp. 273–303.

1967b. "Mathematics Without Foundations." *Journal of Philosophy*, 64: 5–22.

Tait, William. 1986. "Truth and Proof: The Platonism of Mathematics." *Synthese*, 69: 341–70.

Wright, Crispin. 1983. *Frege's Conception of Numbers as Objects*. Aberdeen: Aberdeen University Press.

11

Ontological commitment
Thick and thin

HAROLD HODES

Mathematical discourse is filled with existential assertions, assertions of the form "There is a number (or function, or set, or space or structure or whatever) such that... ." Some philosophers find such statements puzzling, or even unbelievable. This response is both healthy and misguided: misguided because some such statements are true, and not merely in some non-literal way; healthy because it indicates sensitivity to differences between the basis of the truth or falsity of such statements and that of existential statements living in other corners of our languages. The answers to questions like "Are there numbers?" and "Do sets exist?" are, trivially, "Yes." To not see these answers as trivialities bespeaks a misunderstanding of mathematical discourse. But to go on and say that there is a *realm* of mathematical objects is to engage in obscurantist hyperbole. Mathematical objects are second-rate; they are not among "the furniture of the universe." For a philosophically adequate understanding of mathematics, we must distinguish between what I'll call thick and thin ontological commitment.[1] And if ontological commitment is our subject, where should we begin but with Quine?

1

Quine's doctrine on this matter is, as he himself insists, a truism: ontological commitment is expressed by existential quantification. A chunk of discourse is ontologically committed to whatever it (or rather the assertive statements it contains or implies) says that there is.

When I inquire into the ontological commitments of a given doctrine or body of theory, I am merely asking what, according to that theory, there is. [15, p. 203]

What is being said in a chunk of discourse might not be evident at a glance. Regimentation into formal languages can make this more evident. Regimentation clarifies logical aspects of syntactic, including quantificational, structure. Thus it can help us assess what I'll call the thin commitments of the chunk of discourse, a matter of *what is said to be*.

In his own characterizations of ontological commitment, Quine studiously avoids use of expressions like 'says that', or even 'implies that'. For example:

A theory is committed to those and only those entities to which the bound variables of the theory must be capable of referring in order that the affirmations made in the theory be true. [14, pp. 13–14]

The entities to which a discourse commits us are the entities over which our variables of quantification have to range in order that the statements affirmed in that theory be true. [15, p. 205]

The question of *what there would have to be in order for certain statements to be true* is a question of what I'll call thick ontological commitment. To answer it we must assess the alethic underpinnings for the statements in question: the semantic properties of their basic constituents and the recursive "process" that determines their truth-conditions. These underpinnings are a matter of semantic[2] form.

Two tangential points deserve mention. To specify what is said is, at best, to give the sentences used (assuming that the language in which they were used is understood and known to be the language in which they were used). At worst, it's to give a paraphrase or translation of the sentences used. Thus such a specification can be tainted with intensionality. Perhaps this is why Quine has tended to avoid the "what is said to be" formulation. But it is important to realize that Quine's preferred explications of his phrase 'ontological commitment'[3] also involves intensional idioms. As Quine himself teaches, 'must' and 'have to' are also intensional, as is the subjunctive "in order to" formulation of thick commitment given above.[4] Suffice it to say that thin commitments are tied to logical syntax; so when we assess thin commitments, tightness of paraphrase is an important virtue.

Second, the sort of regimentation that Quine would have us use when assessing ontological commitments is regimentation into a first-order language. But this is unnecessarily restrictive. Some discourse is most naturally construed as involving higher-order quantification, though its order need not be syntactically explicit. Of course the syntax of mathematical discourse is virtually always first-order. Numbers, sets, and the like are values of first-order variables, that is, are objects (in Frege's sense of 'object'). So our initial focus will be on the commitments carried by first-order quantification, commitments to objects.[5]

In the cases most central to our languages, there is no difference between what is said to be and what there would have to be for what is said to be true. Semantic and logical form, and with them thick and thin ontological commitments, come apart only in peripheral sorts of discourse.

Consider singular terms. Singular termhood is a logico-syntactic matter. To classify an expression as a singular term is to assign it a certain role within a recursive description of the totality of sentences and valid inferences in a language. Although the second sort of description concerns what Quine called "the interanimation of sentences," it is as syntactic a project as that of characterizing sentencehood. In the cases most central to learning and mature use of language, all closed singular terms do the same sort of semantic work: designating objects.[6]

This fact greases the slide from logico-syntactic role to semantic role for all closed singular terms. Crispin Wright, for example, takes it as self-evident that

what we say metalinguistically by "'a' has a reference' is just the object-language, '$(\exists x)x = a$' ... [16, p. 83]

To make this slide when discussing a species of mathematical discourse is to adopt what I call "the Mathematical-Object theory" of that discourse. Frege's famous slogan "Numbers are objects" expressed his adherence to the Mathematical-Object theory of finite arithmetic. Frege took the semantic job of numerals and closed singular terms of the form 'the number of Fs' to be designation. Correspondingly, he took the semantic job of arithmetic predicates to be applying or failing to apply to (tuples of) objects; and he took phrases like "for all natural numbers" to express quantification over objects of a special sort. He also accepted the analogous theory about set-theoretic discourse.

In this essay I'll present an alternative to the Mathematical-Object theory, to be called the Alternative theory.[7] I contend that some closed singular terms, including those that are properly mathematical, do a sort of semantic work that is not designation. Nor are mathematical predicates built for applying or failing to apply to (tuples of) objects. Rather the linguistic apparatus of a branch of mathematics is a package built to allow certain higher-order statements to be encoded "down" into a more familiar and tractable first-order form. When a singular term, represent it by 'a', is part of such a package, 'a exists' is still correctly parsed as '$(\exists x)x = \mathbf{a}$'; but it will not entail, let alone be or express, the metalinguistic statement "'a' designates something' or "'a' has a reference'. When a predicate, say a one-place predicate represented by 'P', is part of such a package, 'There is a P' is still to be parsed as '$(\exists x)Px$'; but it will not entail that 'P' applies to something. I'll introduce the Alternative theory obliquely, mixing some model-theory with philosophical claims about what this model-theory models.

2

Models, in the logician's sense, are sets.[8] Let S be a set of "uninterpreted" non-logical expressions; for our purposes each member is a predicate- or individual-constant (or, if you wish, a function-constant). A model $\mathscr{A}$ for S may then be taken to be an ordered pair, construed set-theoretically, whose left-component is a non-empty set $|\mathscr{A}|$ (the model's universe) and whose right-component is a function on S assigning each predicate-constant to a subset of an appropriate cartesian power of $|\mathscr{A}|$, and each individual-constant to a member of $|\mathscr{A}|$. (If S contains function-constants, it assigns to each function-constant a function from an appropriate cartesian power of $|\mathscr{A}|$ into $|\mathscr{A}|$.) All functions may be taken to be sets of ordered pairs. In keeping with usual notation, $\zeta^{\mathscr{A}}$ is the value the model assigns to any $\zeta \in S$.

Tarski first introduced models, in "On the Concept of Logical Consequence" (1935), to give a set-theoretic definition of logical consequence. They are appropriate for that project because they model in the engineering sense (that is, they mirror, reflect, represent) the relationship between possible sense-bearing languages and reality that would underlie the distribution of truth-values among the statements in such languages.[9] A model itself does not assign senses to the vocabulary items, or even grant them references. Genuine reference arises only with sense; it is a facet of the life words take on within a sense-bearing language.[10] Models are interesting sets because they model, in a set-theoretic way, the basic alethic underpinnings of possible sense-bearing languages (or fragments thereof), their basic semantic facts (whose specification would serve as base-clauses in a definition of truth). The elements of a model's universe represent objects (perhaps all objects, perhaps only special ones); its assignment of individual-constants to elements of its universe represents designation, each individual-constant and its value playing the parts of designator and designatum respectively; its assignment of sets to predicate-constants represents the "falling under" relation between (tuples of) objects and predicates of level-one.

Tarski showed how to set-theoretically define a binary relation, usually expressed by '$\models$', between models and sentences in their languages. Why is this relation of any interest? Taking a model $\mathscr{A}$ to represent the basic alethic underpinnings for a sense-bearing language, bearing the converse of this relation to $\mathscr{A}$ then represents being true for statements in that language. Truth-in-a-model is a model of truth.[11]

Although it's not essential to the project at hand, let's slightly modify the usual notion of modelhood. Sense-bearing languages can contain empty designators, a phenomenon that was idealized away by the notion of modelhood just introduced. To remedy this we broaden our notation of modelhood by weakening the requirements on naming-functions for models; we now say merely that a model $\mathscr{A}$ may assign an individual-constant in S to any element of $|\mathscr{A}|$; we'll allow that it also may fail to assign such a constant to anything. (Similarly function-constants may be assigned to partial functions defined on subsets of appropriate cartesian powers of $|\mathscr{A}|$.) In the special case in which $\mathscr{A}$ assigns something to each individual-constant in S, call $\mathscr{A}$ total.[12]

Once we have non-total as well as total models, there are several relations that might reasonably be called "truth-in-a-model." Since our final model-theoretic semantics will be three-valued, we will adopt a three-valued approach from the start. This is not essential at this stage; but it has the advantage of making truth and falsity symmetric truth-values. There are several kinds of three-valued semantics. I prefer the so-called strong Kleene semantics with the "strong" semantics for '$=$'.

Fix an infinite set of variables. Let $L = L(S)$ be the uninterpreted language based on S, determined as follows. The terms of L are the variables and individual-constants from S, and whatever is generated from these using function-constants in S. The formulae of L are constructed as usual using the logical lexicon '$\supset$', '$\perp$', '$\exists$' and '$=$'. Let $\mathscr{A}$ be a model for the vocabulary set S.

To handle quantifiers with minimal clutter, expand L to $L_{\mathscr{A}}$ by introducing for each $a \in |\mathscr{A}|$ an individual-constant $\mathbf{a}$ and letting $\mathbf{a}^{\mathscr{A}} = a$. We then define $\tau^{\mathscr{A}}$ for all closed terms τ in the usual way. Since $\mathscr{A}$ may be non-total, the assignment of τ to $\tau^{\mathscr{A}}$ in $|\mathscr{A}|$ may be non-total; "$\tau^{\mathscr{A}}\downarrow$" means that $\tau^{\mathscr{A}}$ is defined; i.e., for some a, $\tau^{\mathscr{A}} = a$; "$\tau^{\mathscr{A}}\uparrow$" means that $\tau^{\mathscr{A}}$ is undefined. We define the relations $\models$ ("makes true") and $\dashv$ ("makes false"), between $\mathscr{A}$ and sentences of $L_{\mathscr{A}}$, by a simultaneous recursion. Suppose γ is an n-place predicate-constant and the τ's are closed terms; let:

$$\mathcal{A} \models \gamma(\tau_0, \ldots, \tau_{n-1}) \quad \text{iff} \quad \tau_i^{\mathcal{A}}{\downarrow} \quad \text{for all } i < n \quad \text{and}$$

$$\langle \tau_0^{\mathcal{A}}, \ldots, \tau_{n-1}^{\mathcal{A}} \rangle \in \gamma^{\mathcal{A}};$$

$$\mathcal{A} \dashv \gamma(\tau_0, \ldots, \tau_{n-1}) \quad \text{iff} \quad \tau_i^{\mathcal{A}}{\downarrow} \quad \text{for all } i < n \quad \text{and}$$

$$\langle \tau_0^{\mathcal{A}}, \ldots, \tau_{n-1}^{\mathcal{A}} \rangle \notin \gamma^{\mathcal{A}};$$

$$\mathcal{A} \models \tau_0 = \tau_1 \quad \text{iff} \quad \tau_0^{\mathcal{A}}{\downarrow} \quad \text{and} \quad \tau_0^{\mathcal{A}} = \tau_1^{\mathcal{A}};$$

$$\mathcal{A} \dashv \tau_0 = \tau_1 \quad \text{iff either } \tau_0^{\mathcal{A}}{\downarrow}, \tau_1^{\mathcal{A}}{\downarrow} \quad \text{and} \quad \tau_0^{\mathcal{A}} \neq \tau_1^{\mathcal{A}},$$

$$\text{or } \tau_0^{\mathcal{A}}{\downarrow} \quad \text{and} \quad \tau_1^{\mathcal{A}}{\uparrow}, \text{ or } \tau_0^{\mathcal{A}}{\uparrow} \quad \text{and}$$

$$\tau_1^{\mathcal{A}}{\downarrow};$$

$$\mathcal{A} \dashv \bot .$$

For any sentences φ, ψ, and $(\exists \nu)\theta$ of $L_{\mathcal{A}}$, let:

$$\mathcal{A} \models (\varphi \supset \psi) \quad \text{iff either } \mathcal{A} \dashv \varphi \text{ or } \mathcal{A} \models \psi;$$
$$\mathcal{A} \dashv (\varphi \supset \psi) \quad \text{iff } \mathcal{A} \models \varphi \text{ and } \mathcal{A} \dashv \psi;$$
$$\mathcal{A} \models (\exists \nu)\theta \quad \text{iff for some } a \in \mathcal{U} \; \mathcal{A} \models \text{Sub}(\mathbf{a}, \nu, \theta);$$
$$\mathcal{A} \dashv (\exists \nu)\theta \quad \text{iff for each } a \in \mathcal{U} \; \mathcal{A} \dashv \text{Sub}(\mathbf{a}, \nu, \theta).[13]$$

For a sentence φ based on S we adopt these definitions:

φ is valid iff for all models $\mathcal{A}$ for S, $\mathcal{A} \models \varphi$;

φ is bivalent iff for all models $\mathcal{A}$ for S either

$$\mathcal{A} \models \varphi \quad \text{or} \quad \mathcal{A} \dashv \varphi.[14]$$

Let $\mathcal{A} | \varphi$ iff $\mathcal{A} \not\models \varphi$ and $\mathcal{A} \not\dashv \varphi$; i.e., iff φ is neither true nor false in $\mathcal{A}$. Our definition allows for this, e.g., if φ is $\gamma(\tau)$ or $\tau = \sigma$ and $\tau^{\mathcal{A}}{\uparrow}$ and $\sigma^{\mathcal{A}}{\uparrow}$.[15] Introduce '$\neg$', '$\&$', '$\vee$', '$\equiv$', and '$\forall$' by the familiar abbreviations. Let $E(\tau)$ for a term τ abbreviate $(\exists \nu)\nu = \tau$, where ν may be any variable distinct from τ; read it as "τ exists." We then have:

$$\mathcal{A} \models E(\tau) \quad \text{iff } \tau^{\mathcal{A}}{\downarrow}; \quad \mathcal{A} \dashv E(\tau) \quad \text{iff } \tau^{\mathcal{A}}{\uparrow}.$$

Imagine a sense-bearing language (or fragment thereof) $\mathcal{L}$ containing no vocabulary enabling the speakers to speak about mathematical objects (or any other potentially problematic abstract objects like possibilities or the like). Suppose its alethic underpinnings can be adequately represented by models of the sort introduced above: its closed singular terms are all built for designation, its predicates for applying and not applying to (tuples of) objects, and its only resources for the construction of sentences are truth-functional connectives and first-order universal and existential quantification. We now consider three ways in which $\mathscr{L}$ could be enriched with mathematical vocabulary, and two ways of modeling such enrichments: one in keeping with the Mathematical-Object theory, the other in keeping with the Alternative theory.

3

Case 1: $\mathscr{L}$ is enriched to $\mathscr{L}^p$ to allow talk "about" ordered pairs. We'll model this enrichment with the uninterpreted language L^p formed from L by adding the expressions '**p**' and '**OP**', governed by the following new clauses into the definitions of termhood and formulahood, respectively:

> for any terms τ and σ, $\mathbf{p}(\tau, \sigma)$ is a term;
> for any term τ, $\mathbf{OP}(\tau)$ is a formula.

Given a model $\mathscr{A}$ for S, let ρ be a pairer for $\mathscr{A}$ iff ρ is a function from $|\mathscr{A}|^2$ one-one into $|\mathscr{A}|$. Assuming the Axiom of Choice, $\mathscr{A}$ has a pairer iff card($|\mathscr{A}|$) is either one or infinite. For any term τ we define $\tau^{\mathscr{A},\rho}$ by relativizing the corresponding definition in §2 to ρ and adding:

$$\mathbf{p}(\tau, \sigma)^{\mathscr{A},\rho} = \rho(\tau^{\mathscr{A},\rho}, \sigma^{\mathscr{A},\rho});$$
$$\mathbf{p}(\tau, \sigma)^{\mathscr{A},\rho}\uparrow \quad \text{iff either } \tau^{\mathscr{A},\rho}\uparrow \quad \text{or} \quad \sigma^{\mathscr{A},\rho}\uparrow.$$

For sentences φ of $L_{\mathscr{A}}$ we define $\mathscr{A},\rho \overset{p}{\models} \varphi$ and $\mathscr{A},\rho \overset{p}{\dashv} \varphi$ by relativizing the corresponding definition in §2 to ρ and adding the clause:

$$\mathscr{A},\rho \overset{p}{\models} \mathbf{OP}(\tau) \quad \text{iff } \tau^{\mathscr{A},\rho}\downarrow \text{ and } \tau^{\mathscr{A},\rho} \in \text{rng}(\rho);$$
$$\mathscr{A},\rho \overset{p}{\dashv} \mathbf{OP}(\tau) \quad \text{iff } \tau^{\mathscr{A},\rho}\downarrow \text{ and } \tau^{\mathscr{A},\rho} \notin \text{rng}(\rho).$$

Case 2: $\mathscr{L}$ is enriched to $\mathscr{L}^\#$ to allow talk "about" the natural numbers, with number-terms, and predicates for numberhood and order on the numbers. We'll model this enrichment with the uninterpreted language $L^\#$, formed from L by adding '#' (a variable-binding term-forming operator on formulae), 'N' and '$\leq$' (syntactically like one- and two-place predicates, respectively). A representor π for a model $\mathscr{A}$ is a one-one function from the finite cardinality quantifiers on $\mathscr{A}$ into $|\mathscr{A}|$; $\overset{\#}{\models}$ and $\overset{\#}{\dashv}$ relate pairs $\langle \mathscr{A}, \pi \rangle$ to sentences of $L^\#_{\mathscr{A}}$. Details are given in [11], so are omitted here.

Case 3: $\mathscr{L}$ is enriched to $\mathscr{L}^{\hat{}}$ with talk "about" sets. Let's suppose that $\mathscr{L}$'s speakers adopt the "limitation of size" conception, first articulated by Cantor and implicit in standard ZF-like set-theories: there are absolutely infinitely many objects, indeed, absolutely infinitely many sets; no sets are absolutely infinite; that is, no set has as many members as there are objects, though of course there are infinite (i.e., relatively infinite) sets.

We enrich L with the new symbols 'Set', '$\in$', and '$\hat{\ }$' to form $L^{\hat{\ }}$. Termhood and formulahood are now defined by a simultaneous induction, with these new clauses:

> For any formula φ and variable ν, $\hat{\nu}\varphi$ is a term;
> For any term τ, $\mathbf{Set}(\tau)$ is a formula;
> For any terms τ and σ, $\tau \in \sigma$ is a formula.

For any set x, let $\operatorname{card}(x)$ be the cardinality of x. Given a model $\mathscr{A}$ for S, let $\kappa = \operatorname{card}(|\mathscr{A}|)$. Let an extensor for $\mathscr{A}$ be a one-one function from $\operatorname{Power}^{K}(|\mathscr{A}|) = \{A \subseteq |\mathscr{A}| : \operatorname{card}(\mathscr{A}) < \kappa\}$ into $|\mathscr{A}|$. Assuming the Axiom of Choice, $\mathscr{A}$ has an extensor iff $|\mathscr{A}|$ is infinite.

Given an extensor e for $\mathscr{A}$, we simultaneously define a partial function from closed terms into $|\mathscr{A}|$ and two relations $\models$ and $\dashv$, writing $\tau^{\mathscr{A},e}$, $\mathscr{A}, e \models \varphi$ and $\mathscr{A}, e \dashv \varphi$ where τ is a term and φ is a sentence of $L_{\mathscr{A}}^{\hat{\ }}$, by relativizing to e the clauses used in the previous section, and adding these clauses:

$\hat{\nu}\varphi^{\mathscr{A},e} = e(A)$ if $A = \{a : \mathscr{A}, e \models \operatorname{Sub}(\mathbf{a}, \nu, \varphi)\} \in \operatorname{dom}(e)$;

$\hat{\nu}\varphi^{\mathscr{A},e}\uparrow$ if there is no such A;

$\mathscr{A}, e \models \mathbf{Set}(\tau)$ iff $\tau^{\mathscr{A},e}\downarrow$ and $\tau^{\mathscr{A},e} \in \operatorname{rng}(e)$;

$\mathscr{A}, e \dashv \mathbf{Set}(\tau)$ iff $\tau^{\mathscr{A},e}\downarrow$ and $t^{\mathscr{A},e} \notin \operatorname{rng}(e)$;

$\mathscr{A}, e \models \tau \in \sigma$ iff $\tau^{\mathscr{A},e}\downarrow$, $\sigma^{\mathscr{A},e}\downarrow$,   and for some A

         $e(A) = \sigma^{\mathscr{A},e}$ and $\tau^{\mathscr{A},e} \in A$;

$\mathscr{A}, e \dashv \tau \in \sigma$ iff $\tau^{\mathscr{A},e}\downarrow$, $\sigma^{\mathscr{A},e}\downarrow$,   and there is no A

         with $e(A) = \sigma^{\mathscr{A},e}$ and $\tau^{\mathscr{A},e} \in A$.

From now on we restrict our attention to infinite models.

4

According to the Mathematical-Object theory, in each of these three cases, the speakers of $\mathscr{L}$ have acquired access to objects of a peculiarly mathematical kind. They have acquired a term-forming operator to construct singular terms designating such objects, and a one-place predicate to apply to all and only such objects. In the second and third cases they have also acquired a two-place predicate that stands for an important relation involving such objects.

To understand the importance of these relations, we must recognize the connection between certain higher-order entities and certain objects. Each natural number n corresponds to a cardinality-quantifier, represented by expressions of the form 'there are exactly n many xs'; each set s corresponds to the level-one Fregean concept represented by predicates of the form 'belongs to s'. Furthermore these correspondences are, in some mysterious way, intrinsic to the numbers and sets. In other words, the Mathematical-Object theory claims that there is a "standard representor" assigning each cardinality-quantifier to its corresponding number, and a "standard extensor" assigning to each level-one Fregean concept fortunate enough to have an extension that extension.[16] The first case almost fits this mold: the Mathematical-Object theory holds that any two objects given in a definite order correspond intrinsically to an ordered pair, as determined by the "standard pairer."

Thus, according to the Mathematical-Object theory, models for S are no longer adequate to represent the alethic underpinnings for $\mathscr{L}^P$, $\mathscr{L}^\#$, or $\mathscr{L}^{\hat{}}$. Consider $\mathscr{L}^{\hat{}}$. By itself a model for S doesn't represent anything about the work done by locutions for set-abstraction, sethood, and membership. These additions require a new notion of modelhood; For example, in case 3 we need pairs of the form $\langle \mathscr{A}, e \rangle$ where $\mathscr{A}$ is a model of the old sort appropriate to L, and e is an extensor for $\mathscr{A}$; e is needed to represent the standard extensor. Relative to a choice of $\mathscr{A}$ and e, the assignment of a term τ to $\tau^{\mathscr{A},e}$ represents designation; the truth of an interpreted sentence parsed by φ is represented by $\mathscr{A}, e \models \varphi$, and its falsehood by $\mathscr{A}, e \dashv \varphi$. Since the models of the new sort, pairs $\langle \mathscr{A}, e \rangle$, tell us what to do with '$\hat{}$', '**Set**', and '$\in$', these expressions should be classified as non-logical vocabulary.

Because this theory takes terms like 'the empty set' to be genuine and successful designators, it suggests that sentences like 'The empty set is blue' or 'The empty set = Julius Ceasar' have definite truth-values.[17] This is mirrored by the modeling under case 3: if φ is '$\mathbf{B}(\hat{x}(x \neq x))$' or '$\hat{x}(x \neq x) = \tau$', where '$\mathbf{B}$' $\in S$ is a one-place predicate-constant and $\tau^{\mathscr{A}}\!\downarrow$, either $\mathscr{A}, e \models \varphi$ or $\mathscr{A}, e \dashv \varphi$.

According to the Alternative theory in none of these cases have the speakers stumbled across peculiarly mathematical objects. Nor have they constructed or otherwise manufactured objects that somehow hadn't existed before. Instead they have developed ways of extending (or in case 1, of simplifying) the expressive resources of $\mathscr{L}$. So in all cases a model for S by itself, without supplementation by a pairer, representor, or extensor, can still model the alethic underpinnings of $\mathscr{L}^p$, $\mathscr{L}^\#$, and $\mathscr{L}^{\hat{}}$.

Here is how that modeling works for $\mathscr{L}^{\hat{}}$. For any infinite model $\mathscr{A}$, any sentence φ and term τ of $L^{\hat{}}_{\mathscr{A}}$, let:

$$\mathscr{A} \models \varphi \text{ iff for every extensor } e \text{ for } \mathscr{A}, \mathscr{A}, e \models \varphi;$$

$$\mathscr{A} \dashv \varphi \text{ iff for every extensor } e \text{ for } \mathscr{A}, \mathscr{A}, e \dashv \varphi;$$

$$\tau^{\mathscr{A}} = a \text{ iff for every extensor } e \text{ for } \mathscr{A}, \tau^{\mathscr{A}, e} = a;$$

$$\tau^{\mathscr{A}}\!\uparrow \qquad \text{iff there is no such } a.$$

As just defined, $\models$ and $\dashv$ extend the corresponding relations defined in §2: if φ is a sentence of L, then $\mathscr{A} \models \varphi$ holds in the sense of §2 iff $\mathscr{A} \models \varphi$ holds as defined above; similarly for $\dashv$, and for the assignment of τ to $\tau^{\mathscr{A}}$. Definitions of validity and bivalance carry over from §2, with one significant change: the quantifier over models is restricted to infinite models. Let $\mathrm{Biv}(L^{\hat{}})$ be the set of bivalent sentences of $L^{\hat{}}$. An the following logical notion now merits attention:

φ is logically truth-valueless iff

for all infinite models $\mathscr{A}$ for S, $\mathscr{A} | \varphi$.

Analogous definitions apply to φ and τ in $L^p_{\mathscr{A}}$ and $L^\#_{\mathscr{A}}$.

According to the Alternative theory, relative to a choice of a model $\mathscr{A}$, $\models$ and $\dashv$ model being true and being false in $\mathscr{L}^{\hat{}}$, and the assignment of terms τ to $\tau^{\mathscr{A}}$ models designation in $\mathscr{L}^{\hat{}}$. There is no "standard" extensor that needs to be represented in a model-theoretic semantics adequate to model the underpinnings of set-theoretic discourse.

Thus 'The empty set', for example, is not a designator, and 'The empty set = Julius Ceasar' has no truth-value. Correspondingly, '$\hat{x}(x \neq x)$'$^{\mathscr{A}}$ is undefined for every model $\mathscr{A}$, and '$\hat{x}(x \neq x) = a$' is logically truth-valueless. And a sentence like 'The empty set is blue' need not have a truth-value; '$\mathbf{B}(\hat{x}(x \neq x))$' is not bivalent; indeed it will be true iff '$(\forall x)\mathbf{B}(x)$' is true, and it will be false iff '$(\exists x)\mathbf{B}(x)$' is false. Furthermore the semantic job of words expressing sethood and membership is not to apply or fail to apply to (tuples of) objects: so a sentence like 'Julius Ceasar is a set' has no truth-value; correspondingly, '$\mathbf{Set(a)}$' is logically truth-valueless.

Such sentences are peculiar in that they employ mathematical vocabulary, but clearly lack mathematical content. The Alternative theory characterizes the semantic basis of their peculiarity. Nonetheless 'The empty set exists' and 'There are sets' are true, even logically true;

correspondingly, '$E(\hat{x}(x \neq x))$' and '$(\exists x)\mathrm{Set}(x)$' are valid. It should be emphasized that these sentences do not rely on any peculiarly mathematical construal of 'exists' or its synonyms; our semantics handles occurrences of '$\exists$' uniformly through $L^{\hat{}}$.

Thus $\mathscr{L}^{\hat{}}$ carries commitment to the existence of sets. But it is a thin commitment, for the truth of 'There are sets' is not based on the applicability of 'is a set' to some objects. Similarly for $\mathscr{L}^p$ and ordered pairs, and $\mathscr{L}^{\#}$ and natural numbers.

On this view, the assignment of term τ to $\tau^{\mathscr{A},e}$, and the relations $\models$ and $=\!\!|$ relative to a pair $\langle \mathscr{A}, e \rangle$ are supervaluations, doing no representational work; there are no facts about $\mathscr{L}^{\hat{}}$ for them to model. They are, in Kaplan's phrase,[18] artifacts of the model-theory, mere stepping-stones to the definition of $\models$, $=\!\!|$, and $\tau^{\mathscr{A}}$. The semantic roles of abstraction terms, and of expressions for sethood and membership, are modeled by the role of $\hat{}$-terms, '**Set**', and '$\in$' in the latter definitions. A model $\mathscr{A}$ itself tells us nothing about that role. Thus for the Alternative theory '$\hat{}$', '**Set**', and '$\in$' are logical constants. Similar remarks apply to L^p and $L^{\#}$.

The virtues of the Alternative theory are particularly clear when we consider ontological reduction. Suppose that the enriched language from case 1 is now further enriched by set-theoretic talk. (The discussion to follow easily carries over to case 2.) As is well known, the mathematical work done by ordered pairs can be done as well by certain sets, e.g., by Wiener-Kuratowski pairs. For the Mathematical-Object theorist, either (1) some such "reduction" of ordered pairs to sets is right, or (2) none are right: ordered pairs are *sui generis*, and in particular, are not sets.

Option (1) is indefensible.[19] According to option (2), in replacing the *sui generis* notion of ordered-pairhood by a set-theoretic one, we choose to ignore a portion of mathematical reality. It's universally agreed that this loss is of no mathematical interest. If the point of mathematics is to describe mathematical reality, why should mathematicians glibly ignore a part of this reality? For the Mathematical-Object theorist, this aspect of mathematical practice should seem unreasonable.

The Alternative theory avoids this uncomfortable dilemma: It sees "no fact of the matter" to ontological reduction.[20] Enrich L^p to $L^{p,\hat{}}$ in the obvious way. Given a model $\mathscr{A}$, a pairer $\wp$, and an extensor e for $\mathscr{A}$, define $\tau^{\mathscr{A},\wp,e}$, $\overset{p\hat{}}{\models}$, and $\overset{p\hat{}}{=\!\!|}$ in the obvious way. To model truth, falsity, and designation in $L^{p,\hat{}}$ define $\tau^{\mathscr{A}}$, $\mathscr{A} \models \varphi$, and $\mathscr{A} =\!\!| \varphi$ according to the pattern set for L^p and $L^{\hat{}}$, but now universally quantifying over both pairers and extensors. Equations of the form '$\mathbf{p}(\tau, \sigma) =$

$\{\{\tau\}, \{\tau, \sigma\}\}$' (in primitive notation the right-hand side would be written out using '$\hat{\ }$') are logically truth-valueless, as is '$(\exists x)(\mathbf{Set}(x) \& \mathbf{OP}(x))$'. Indeed, it is precisely the sentences that intuitively do have mathematical content that come out bivalent. Unlike its rival, the Alternative theory offers a semantic basis for the obvious lack of mathematical content to the choice between different set-theoretic definitions of ordered pairs.

5

According to the Mathematical-Object theory, the point of enriching $\mathscr{L}$ in cases 2 and 3 is straightforward: to allow the speakers of $\mathscr{L}$ to talk about mathematical objects, real things that, for one reason or another, might merit talking about. The Alternative theory sees a different point: a way of encoding statements in higher-order languages into a first-order syntax, making them both notationally and conceptually more tractable.

We'll now look at such a language, a dyadic second-order language that corresponds exactly to Biv($\hat{L}$).[21] Form L' from L by introducing a single variable 'X' of type $(0, 0)$, letting $X(\tau, \sigma)$ be a formula for any terms τ and σ, and letting '$\exists$' bind 'X' as usual. Relative to a model $\mathscr{A}$, define $\models$ and $=\!\!|$ by letting 'X' range over Power($|\mathscr{A}| \times |\mathscr{A}|$). If e is an extensor for $\mathscr{A}$, let

$$e' = \{\langle a, b \rangle : \text{for some } A \in \text{dom}(e), a \in A \text{ and } e(A) = b\}.$$

It's easy to write down a formula Ext(X) in which 'X' is the only free variable such that for any model $\mathscr{A}$ and $E \subseteq |\mathscr{A}| \times |\mathscr{A}|$,

$$\mathscr{A} \models \text{Ext}(\mathbf{E}) \text{ iff } E = e' \text{ for some extensor } e \text{ for } \mathscr{A}.$$

We may then syntactically specify a translation s from sentences of $\hat{L}$ to formulae of L' in which 'X' is the only free variable so that for any infinite model $\mathscr{A}$:

$$\text{for } \varphi \in \text{Sent } (\hat{L}) \quad \mathscr{A} \models \varphi \text{ iff } \mathscr{A} \models (\forall X)(\text{Ext}(X) \supset s(\varphi)).$$

So for $\varphi \in \text{Biv}(\hat{L})$, $\mathscr{A} =\!\!| \varphi$ iff $\mathscr{A} =\!\!| (\forall X)(\text{Ext}(X) \supset s(\varphi))$.[22] The logic of $\hat{L}$ is a fragment of second-order logic.

For $\varphi \in \text{Biv}(\hat{L})$, $(\forall X)(\text{Ext}(X) \supset s(\varphi))$ represents φ's semantic form, since its syntax makes plain, more perspicuously than does φ itself, the role of basic semantic facts in fixing φ's truth-value. Why this asymmetry between φ and this sentence?

Let a language (sense-bearing or model-theoretic) be semantically uniform iff for each of its logico-syntactic lexical categories all items of that category have semantic jobs of the same sort. L' is semantically uniform. $\hat{L}$ is not. Some singular terms are in $\hat{L}$ to designate; but

$\hat{}$-terms are built to encode Fregean concepts. Some predicates are in $L^{\hat{}}$ to apply, or fail to apply, to (tuples of) objects; but '**Set**' and '$\in$' do quite different work. Correspondingly, $\mathscr{L}^{\hat{}}$ is not semantically uniform; it runs more risk of philosophic misconstrual than would an enrichment of $\mathscr{L}$ whose logical-syntax were modeled by L'. This danger is the price of $\mathscr{L}^{\hat{}}$'s practical advantages. Thick ontological commitment is determined by semantic form. When limning the ultimate furniture of reality, we do best to speak, or at least think, in terms of a semantically uniform language. L' is better than $L^{\hat{}}$; and in L' there is no talk of sets.

On the other hand, φ wears its logical form on its surface: $(\forall X)(\mathrm{Ext}(X) \supset s(\varphi))$ does not represent φ's logical form. A sentence's logical form is a matter of its potential roles in inferences. Some of the structure of $(\forall X)(\mathrm{Ext}(X) \supset s(\varphi))$, e.g. the initial universal quantifications and the conditional structure of what follows it, is irrelevant to the inferential practice of the speakers of $\mathscr{L}^{\hat{}}$. The practice does not involve speakers making reference to particular extensors, and so doesn't involve their instancing such an initial quantification, or applying modus ponens to statements of the form $\mathrm{Ext}(\mathbf{E}) \supset \mathrm{Sub}(\mathbf{E}, X, s(\varphi))$. (For statements parsed as $(\forall x)(\mathrm{Set}(x) \supset \psi)$, inferential practice would include instancing of the initial quantifier and applying modus ponens to the result.) Parsing is a matter of making logico-syntactic (i.e., logical) form perspicuous. Thin ontological commitments are to be determined merely from logico-syntactic form, which need not coincide with semantic form.

Points analogous to these apply to $L^{\#}$. Unlike $L^{\hat{}}$ and $L^{\#}$, the bivalent fragment of L^p does not extend the expressive power of L (though it might yield greater expressive convenience).[23] But if L is first enriched to a monadic second-order language L^1 by introducing infinitely many type-1 variables, and then L^1 is enriched by $L^{1,p}$, the latter is in effect a dyadic (and thus a full) second-order language; so $L^{1,p}$ does extend the expressive power of L^1.

6

Let a sentence of L^p, $L^{\#}$, or $L^{\hat{}}$ be pure if S is empty. By a symmetry argument, all pure sentences are bivalent. Many familiar mathematical principles may be expressed as pure validities in these languages.

For example, consider the Basic Fact about ordered pairs:

$$(\forall x)(\forall y)(\forall u)(\forall v)(\mathbf{p}(x, y) = \mathbf{p}(u, v) \supset (x = u \,\&\, y = v)).$$

This Basic Fact seems to express "all there is to ordered pairing." The Mathematical-Object theorist can't agree: for example, '⟨France, England⟩ = Julius Ceasar' is not decided by the Basic Fact. But the

Alternative theory offers a precise statement of this thesis, one that is a theorem.[24]

No principles expressible in $L^\#$ or $L\hat{}$ are complete for the natural numbers or for sets as the Basic Fact is for ordered pairs. This is because the expressive powers of these languages are greater than that of any first-order language. As the other side of this coin, some of their pure bivalent sentences are neither valid nor have valid negations: the cardinality of a model can determine truth-value. Note that the axioms of extensionality, of pairs, the axioms of separation, and the existence of the null-set are all expressible by valid sentences in $L\hat{}$.[25]

Does the Alternative theory deserve the label 'Logicism'? This issue is made delicate by our need to restrict attention to infinite models. Although 'logical' is a vague label, few are willing to regard 'There are infinitely many objects' as a logical truth. And unless we do so, the Alternative theory is only logicist "modulo actual infinity."

An initially promising way to avoid assuming that there are infinitely many objects is to go modal, assuming only a "possible infinity."[26] Unfortunately, if we allow quantification over mathematical objects within the scope of the modal operator, it will have to be a special sort of quantifier. For more detail, see [11]. This rather weakens the appeal of going modal.

7

Confusion of the semantic notion of real truth with the set-theoretic notion of truth-in-a-model has contributed to some confusion about the role of set-theory in a definition or theory of real truth. Although this matter is tangential to this essay, the apparatus introduced here will, in §8, reconnect with our main thread. Impatient readers may skip both sections.

Sets do play a small but essential role in a definition of truth for a quantificational language: such a definition will use the notion of satisfaction, and so presuppose the existence of variable-assignments, which are functions, which (for our purposes) are sets.

In this section we'll model the relation between a sense-bearing first-order language and a metalanguage for it by the relation between uninterpreted languages L and M^*. Working in appropriate models for M^*, we'll consider a definition of truth for sentences of L that models a definition of real truth for statements of a first-order object-language.

Suppose that $1P$ and $2P$ are sets of one- and two-place predicate-constants, respectively, and IC is a finite set of individual-constants; let $S = 1P \cup 2P \cup IC$, $L = L(S)$. Let S_0 be the set of quote-names for all

elements of S, for the logical constants ' $\perp$ ', ' $\supset$ ', ' $\exists$ ', ' $=$ ', for '(' and
')', and for all variables. These quote-names are individual-constants;
let δ' be δ's quote-name for $\delta \in S$. Let S_1 be:

$$S_0 \cup \{' * ', \text{'1P'}, \text{'2P'}, \text{'IC'}, \text{'Var'}, \text{'Fm1'}, \text{'FV'}, \text{'Sent'}\},$$

where ' $*$ ' is a two-place function-constant introduced to represent
concatenation, **'FV'** is a two-place predicate-constant, and the rest are
one-place predicate-constants. Suppose $\mathscr{A}$ is a model for S' with
$S_1 \subseteq S'$; under the following conditions we may think of $\mathscr{A}$ as contain-
ing L: all $\mathscr{A}$-values of members of S_0 are distinct; $\text{'1P'}^{\mathscr{A}} = \{\gamma'^{\mathscr{A}} : \gamma \in$
$1P\}$; analogously for $\text{'2P'}^{\mathscr{A}}$ and $\text{'IC'}^{\mathscr{A}}$; $\text{'Var'}^{\mathscr{A}} = \text{'}\nu\text{'}^{\mathscr{A}} : \nu$ is a variable$\}$;
$\text{'Fm1'}^{\mathscr{A}}$ is the set of "formulae" generated appropriately from S_0 using
' $*$ ' $^{\mathscr{A}}$; $\text{'Sent'}^{\mathscr{A}}$ is the corresponding set of "sentences"; ' $*$ ' $^{\mathscr{A}}$ is cycle-free
on the closure of S_0 under it; $\text{'FV'}^{\mathscr{A}} = \{\langle a, b \rangle : a \in \text{'Var'}^{\mathscr{A}}, b \in \text{'Fm1'}^{\mathscr{A}},$
and "a occurs free in b"$\}$. Under these conditions we'll say that $\mathscr{A}$ is
syntactically adequate for L.

Let $S_2 = S_1 \cup \{\text{'Unv'}, \text{'1Ap'}, \text{'2Ap'}, \text{'Des'}\}$, where '1Ap' and **Des** are
two-place predicate-constants and '2Ap' is a three-place predicate-
constant. First, let's confine our attention to total models. Let a model
$\mathscr{A}$ for S_2 be adequate iff: it is syntactically adequate, and the following
"basic semantic axioms" are true in $\mathscr{A}$:

$(\exists x)\text{Unv}(x)$;
$(\forall x)(\forall y)(\text{1Ap}(x, y) \supset [\text{1P}(x) \& \text{Unv}(y)])$;
$(\forall x)(\forall y)(\forall z)(\text{2Ap}(x, y, z) \supset [\text{2P}(x) \& \text{Unv}(y) \& \text{Unv}(z)])$;
$(\forall x)(\forall y)(\text{Des}(x, y) \supset [\text{IC}(x) \& \text{Unv}(y)])$;
$(\forall x)(\forall y)(\forall y')([\text{Des}(x, y) \& \text{Des}(x, y')] \supset y = y')$;
"Totality": $(\forall x)(\text{IC}(x) \supset (\exists y)\text{Des}(x, y))$.

Such a model determines a total model $\mathscr{B}$ for L with $|\mathscr{B}| = \text{'Unv'}^{\mathscr{A}}$ and
such that for any $\gamma \in S$:

if $\gamma \in 1P$ then $\gamma^{\mathscr{B}} = \{a : \langle \gamma', a \rangle \in \text{'1Ap'}^{\mathscr{A}}\}$;
if $\gamma \in 2P$ then $\gamma^{\mathscr{B}} = \{\langle a, b \rangle : \langle \gamma', a, b \rangle \in \text{'2Ap'}^{\mathscr{A}}\}$;
if $\gamma \in IC$ then $\gamma^{\mathscr{B}}$ is the unique a such that
$\langle \gamma', a \rangle \in \text{'Des'}^{\mathscr{A}}$.

Letting $M = L(S_2)$, M expresses (relative to $\mathscr{A}$) the basic semantic
facts about L (relative to $\mathscr{B}$).[27] Relative to $\mathscr{A}$ we want to define truth
for sentences of L (relative to $\mathscr{B}$). The inductive definition of satisfaction will have to be represented by axioms involving the new expression
'Sat'; but some set-theoretic machinery is also needed.

Form M^* by adding 'Sat' to the logical lexicon of $\hat{M}$, with 'Sat' behaving syntactically as a two-place predicate-constant. Since we want our theory to apply in any adequate model, even a countable one, and since our sets will conform to the limitation-of-size conception, we must permit all sets to be finite; in particular we must allow variable-assignments that are finite. Relative to $\mathscr{A}$, let a variable-assignment be simply a function into 'Unv'$^{\mathscr{A}}$ such that all members of its domain are variables. Thus the empty set is a variable-assignment. Let Asgmt(x) be the formula of M^* saying "x is a variable-assignment." Let Vrnt(x, z, w, x') be the formula saying "x' is the variant of x assigning z to w."

Given an infinite model $\mathscr{A}$, let e be an extensor for $\mathscr{A}$ and $\jmath \subseteq |\mathscr{A}| \times |\mathscr{A}|$. We now define $\tau^{\mathscr{A}, e, \jmath}$ for terms τ of M^*, and $\mathscr{A}, e, \jmath \models \varphi$ and $\mathscr{A}, e, \jmath \dashv \varphi$ as usual, taking $\jmath$ as the extension of 'Sat'. Let $\jmath = \mathrm{Sat}^{\mathscr{A}, e}$ iff the appropriate axioms governing 'Sat' come out true in the sense of $\models$ relative to $\langle \mathscr{A}, e \rangle$. First we'll need a bookkeeping axiom:

$(\forall x)(\forall y)(\mathbf{Sat}(x, y) \supset$

$\qquad [\mathrm{Asgmt}(x) \,\&\, \mathbf{Fm1}(y) \,\&\, (\forall u)(\mathbf{FV}(u, y) \supset u \in \mathrm{dom}(x))]).$

Then we need formulations of the familiar clauses from the recursive definition of satisfaction, e.g.:

$(\forall x)(\forall p)(\forall y)([\mathrm{Asgmt}(x) \,\&\, \mathbf{1P}(p) \,\&\, \mathbf{Var}(y) \,\&\, y \in \mathrm{dom}(x)]$

$\qquad \supset [\mathbf{Sat}(x, p * y) \equiv \mathbf{1Ap}(p, x(y))]);$

$(\forall x)(\forall p)(\forall i)(\forall z)([\mathrm{Asgmt}(x) \,\&\, \mathbf{1P}(p) \,\&\, \mathbf{IC}(i) \,\&\, \mathbf{Des}(i, z)]$

$\qquad \supset [\mathbf{Sat}(x, p * i) \equiv \mathbf{1A}(p, z)]);$

$(\forall x)(\forall y)(\forall z)([\mathrm{Asgmt}(x) \,\&\, \mathbf{Var}(y) \,\&\, \mathbf{Fm1}(z)] \supset$

$\qquad [\mathbf{Sat}(x, \text{'}('* \text{'}\exists\text{'} * y * \text{'})\text{'} * z) \equiv$

$\qquad (\exists v)(\exists x')(\mathbf{Unv}(v) \,\&\, \mathrm{Vrnt}(x', x, y, v) \,\&\, \mathbf{Sat}(x', z))]).$

From these samples, the reader should be able to figure out what the remaining axioms should be. Relative to $\mathscr{A}, e$ these axioms implicitly define $\mathrm{Sat}^{\mathscr{A}, e}$.

As usual, we let:

$\mathscr{A} \models \varphi$ iff for every extensor e for $\mathscr{A}$: $\mathscr{A}, e, \mathrm{Sat}^{\mathscr{A}, e} \models \varphi$;

$\mathscr{A} \dashv \varphi$ iff for every extensor e for $\mathscr{A}$: $\mathscr{A}, e, \mathrm{Sat}^{\mathscr{A}, e} \dashv \varphi$.

We may now define truth for sentences of L. For any adequate $\mathscr{A}$, fix $\mathscr{B}$ as above; for any $\psi \in \text{Sent}(L)$, let $a \in \text{'Sent'}^{\mathscr{A}}$ "be" ψ; then:

$$\mathscr{B} \models \psi \text{ iff } \mathscr{A} \models \textbf{Sat}(\hat{x}(x \neq x), \mathbf{a}).$$

We abbreviate '$\text{Sat}(\hat{x}(x \neq x), z)$' as '$\text{True}(z)$'. (By our bookkeeping axiom, '$\text{True}(z)$' entails '$\textbf{Sent}(z)$'.)

To accommodate non-total models and represent a three-valued semantics, we must drop the "totality" axiom used in the definition of adequacy. We also change M^*, supplementing '$\textbf{Sat}$' with '$\textbf{Frus}$' to represent frustration (= anti-satisfaction), and introducing appropriate axioms to implicitly define $\text{Frus}^{\mathscr{A}, \,\epsilon}$. We may then define '$\text{False}(z)$' in terms of '$\textbf{Frus}$'. Details are left to the reader.

Notice that $\mathscr{A}$ only represents basic semantic facts of designation and application. '$\textbf{Sat}$' and '$\textbf{Frus}$', like '$\textbf{Set}$' and '$\in$', are used "supervaluationally"; their semantic roles are not that of an ordinary two-place predicate constant. But since their semantic roles are tied to those of the members of S_2, which are not logical constants, we can't consider them full-blooded logical constants; at best they are hybrids of the logical and the non-logical. On the other hand, '$\textbf{1Ap}$', '$\textbf{2Ap}$', and '$\textbf{Des}$' are ordinary predicate-constants. If we wanted to make heavier use of mathematical machinery, we could avoid using distinct predicate-constants to handle application for predicate-constants in S of different "adicity": we could use a single two-place predicate-constant '$\textbf{Ap}$' to handle all predicate-constants in S, taking a two-place predicate-constant as applying to ordered pairs, etc. '$\textbf{Ap}$' would be a logical expression. Building in ordered pairs "at the ground floor" encourages the illusion that basic semantic facts involve mathematical objects, and that basic semantic relations have the logical status of mathematical relations; thus it is best avoided. Of course we could also have built in mathematical objects "at the basement," construed syntactic objects (e.g., formulae), as tuples or as sets.

8

According to the Alternative theory, the semantics for mathematical notions differs significantly from that for less arcane notions. Our model-theoretic semantics for $L\hat{}$, for example, is intended to model the alethic underpinnings of talk "about" sets, to show how set-theoretic statements get truth-values even though 'set' does not stand for a genuine kind, ' $\in$ ' doesn't stand for a genuine relation, and set-terms do not designate.

It is tempting to formulate this Alternative theory as the claim "Sets are not objects." The spirit may be right; but taken literally, this claim is trivially false; 'x is an object' may be parsed as '$x = x$' (or even as '$\neg \perp$ ').[28] Clearly '$(\forall x)(\textbf{Set}(x) \supset x = x)$' is valid.

This is why the Alternative theory is a theory about the semantics of mathematical discourse: it cannot be "pulled down," using Carnap's phrases, from the formal to the material mode. But it may appear that the Alternative theory is undercut by similar reasons: once it has been conceded that, for example, the empty set is an object, why not say that 'the empty set' designates the empty set? Since it is set, why not say that 'set' applies to it?

In fact, this can be said; but in so saying the notions of designation and application are being stretched. 'Julius Caesar' robustly designates, and 'Roman' robustly applies to, a famous general; but to say that 'the empty set' designates and 'set' applies to a famous set is to use 'designates' and 'applies to' in a non-robust disquotational way.[29] To clarify the difference, we consider how to define truth for sentences of $L^{\wedge}$.

First we expand S_0 and add to the notion of syntactic adequacy of a model $\mathscr{A}$ to handle the syntax of $L^{\wedge}$. In particular, we'll need a one-place predicate-constant '$\textbf{Trm}$' to apply to exactly the $^{\wedge}$-terms of $L^{\wedge}$, and the right-domain of '$\textbf{FV}$'$^{\mathscr{A}}$ will include $^{\wedge}$-terms. But we would not have to expand the $\mathscr{A}$-values of '$\textbf{1Ap}$', '$\textbf{2Ap}$', and '$\textbf{Des}$' so as to make $\mathscr{A}$ represent applicative facts about '$\textbf{Set}$' and ' $\in$ ', for there are no such facts! Form M^+ from M^* by adding the two-place predicate-constant '$\textbf{1Ap}^+$' and the three-place predicate-constant '$\textbf{2Ap}^+$' and '$\textbf{Des}^+$'. Given $\mathscr{A}, e$, let $1\text{Ap}^{+\mathscr{A}, e}$ be implicitly defined by this axiom:

$$(\forall x)(\forall y)(\textbf{1AP}^+(x, y) \supset [\textbf{1P}(x) \vee x = \text{'Set'}];$$
$$\text{for each } \gamma \in 1P: (\forall y)(\textbf{1Ap}^+(\gamma', y) \equiv \textbf{1Ap}(\gamma', y));$$
$$(\forall y)(\textbf{1Ap}^+(\text{'Set'}, y) \equiv \textbf{Set}(y)).$$

Analogous axioms, using ' $\in$ ' rather than '$\textbf{Set}$', implicitly define $2\text{Ap}^{+\mathscr{A}, e}$. '$\textbf{1Ap}^+$' and '$\textbf{2Ap}^+$' "stretch" '$\textbf{1AP}$' and '$\textbf{2Ap}$'. Unlike the latter two, they do not play the semantic role of ordinary predicate-constants; they are partly non-logical like '$\textbf{1Ap}$' and '$\textbf{2Ap}$', and partly logical like '$\textbf{Set}$' and ' $\in$ '. Notice that, for example, '$(\forall y)(\textbf{1Ap}^+(\text{'Set'}, y) \equiv \textbf{Set}(y))$' comes out valid with respect to adequate models.

Let e be a '$\textbf{Unv}$'-extensor for $\mathscr{A}$ iff e is an extensor for $\mathscr{A}$ and for every $A \subseteq$ '$\textbf{Unv}$'$^{\mathscr{A}}$, if $A \in \text{dom}(e)$ then $e(A) \in$ '$\textbf{Unv}$'$^{\mathscr{A}}$. For e a '$\textbf{Unv}$'-extensor for $\mathscr{A}$, we implicitly define $\text{Sat}^{\mathscr{A}, e}$, $\text{Frus}^{\mathscr{A}, e}$, and $\text{Des}^{+\mathscr{A}, e}$

with axioms, including these bookkeeping axioms:

$$(\forall x)(\forall y)(\forall z)\big(\mathbf{Des}^+(x,y,z) \supset \big[\mathrm{Asgmt}(x) \,\&\, (\hat{\ }\text{-}\mathbf{Trm}(y) \vee \mathbf{IC}(y))$$
$$\&(\forall v)(\mathbf{FV}(v,y) \supset v \in \mathrm{dom}(x))\big]\big);$$
$$(\forall x)(\forall y)(\forall z)(\forall z')\big([\mathbf{Des}^+(x,y,z) \,\&\, \mathbf{Des}^+(x,y,z')] \supset z = z'\big);$$
$$(\forall x)(\forall y)(\forall z)\big([\mathrm{Asgmt}(x) \,\&\, \mathbf{IC}(y)] \supset$$
$$[\mathbf{Des}^+(x,y,z) \equiv \mathbf{Des}(y,z)]\big).$$

We'll also need the following axiom:

$$(\forall x)(\forall y)(\forall z)(\forall u)\big([\mathrm{Asgmt}(x) \,\&\, \mathbf{Fml}(y) \,\&\, \mathbf{Var}(z)$$
$$\&(\forall v)(\mathbf{FV}(v,y) \supset v \in \mathrm{dom}(x))] \supset$$
$$\big[\mathbf{Des}^+(x, {}^{\check{\ }}\!\ast z \ast y, u) \equiv (\forall w)(w \in u \equiv [\mathbf{Unv}(w)$$
$$\&(\exists x')(\mathrm{Vrnt}(x', x, z, w) \,\&\, \mathbf{Sat}(x', y))])]\big).$$

Otherwise the definition of truth for sentences of $L^{\hat{\ }}$ within M^+ runs as it did for L; details are left to the reader. Unlike '**Des**', '**Des**$^+$' does not play the semantic role of an ordinary three-place predicate; like '**1Ap**$^+$', '**2Ap**$^+$', '**Sat**', and '**Frus**', it is a hybrid of the logical and the non-logical.

We define $\mathscr{A} \models \varphi$ and $\mathscr{A} \dashv \varphi$ for φ a sentence of $M^+_{\mathscr{A}}$ as before. There is a slight twist to the definition of truth for sentences of $L^{\hat{\ }}$. Let '$\mathrm{True}(z)$' abbreviate:

$$(\forall y)((\forall u)[u \in y \supset \mathbf{Unv}(u)] \supset \mathbf{Unv}(y)) \supset \mathbf{Sat}(\hat{x}(x \neq x), z).$$

We define '$\mathrm{False}(z)$' analogously. The antecedent of these conditionals has the effect of "restricting our attention" to '**Unv**'-extensors as we unpack $\mathscr{A} \models \mathrm{True}(\mathbf{a})$ and $\mathscr{A} \dashv \mathrm{False}(\mathbf{a})$.

The moral: we can define truth in a set-theoretic language in terms of partially non-robust notions of designation and application, without compromising the Alternative theory. Of course, this definition uses the meta-language's set-theoretic apparatus more heavily than did the definition of truth for sentences of a non-set-theoretic language: we don't only need variable-assignments; we also need to use '**Set**' and '$\in$' in the disquotational semantic axioms governing '**Set**', and '$\in$', and '$\hat{\ }$'.

To think in terms of the disquotational semantics for mathematical discourse is to adopt a certain picture of that discourse: the Mathematical-Object picture. We picture truth for such discourse as structurally analogous to truth for robustly referential discourse. For mathematical purposes, this picture is fine. Indeed, that picture is overwhelmingly natural, given the logical syntax of our mathematical discourse. As the applications of model-theory to algebra show, it has mathematical value; models can represent non-robust semantic "facts" as well as robust ones. The Mathematical-Object theory transforms this picture into a theory of the alethic underpinnings of mathematical discourse. A natural error; but an error nonetheless.

9

According to our Alternative theory, mathematical theories are first-order encoding of higher-order logics. The ontological commitments to mathematical objects that the Mathematical-Object theory takes to be thick, the Alternative theory takes to be merely thin. Unlike thin commitments, thick commitments are preserved by encoding (indeed, by any sort of paraphrase that preserves semantic form). So the alternative theory saddles mathematical discourse with whatever thick commitments are carried by the higher-order quantification in the encoded logic. Why should we be more comfortable with, for example, second-order quantification than with quantification that purports to be over mathematical objects?

First of all, second-order quantification is found even in central areas of linguistic practice. For example, Dummett offers 'There is something that Plato was and Socrates was not'. The second-order nature of its initial quantifier-phrase is made especially clear by its instancings. Suppose a speaker uses this sentence assertively, and then backs up her assertion with 'For example, a dramatist', shorthand for 'For example, Plato was a dramatist and Socrates was not'; here the syntactic role of 'a dramatist' is certainly predicative. The first assertion carries at least a thin commitment to the existence of something that Plato was and Socrates wasn't. I can see no reason to deny that this commitment is also thick, that for this statement logical and semantic form coincide.[30] Of course, the syntax of natural languages forces us to complete the phrase 'is an example of the things to which that assertion is committed' with a noun-phrase such as 'being a dramatist' or a variant of Frege's preferred form 'the concept *dramatist*'. But these are not designators; indeed, they strike me as ersatz singular terms, as English make-do for constructions whose logical form involves variable binding.[31]

Second-order quantification can be rather subtle. Some plural noun-phrase constructions involve second-order quantification, e.g. the Geach-Kaplan example 'Some critics admire only one another'. But even for these statements, logical and semantic form appear to coincide. Suffice then to say: since central parts of our linguistic practice already saddle us with whatever thick commitments second-order quantification carries, exchanging an additional thick commitment to problematic mathematical objects for those of second-order quantification is a good deal.

George Boolos has argued that second-order quantification need carry no ontological commitments, I take it not even thin commitments, beyond those carried by first-order quantification.[32] If this is right, the advantage in exchanging thick commitment to mathematical objects for second-order quantification is clear. But suppose we accept Frege's doctrine that second-order quantification carried commitment to unsaturated entities, Fregean concepts and relations. Is thick commitment to such entities better than thick commitment to mathematical objects?

I think so. There are psychological and sociological facts about our linguistic practice, some historical in form, some structural in form, that constitute a supervenience base for facts about the application and non-application of predicates to objects. There seems to be no such base for purported facts about designation of mathematical objects.[33] Furthermore, as Furth claims, facts about the application and non-application of predicates are really all there is to facts about reference for predicates.[34] Even when thick, commitments to Fregean concepts and relations are light. But commitments to mathematical objects are heavy, too heavy, I contend, to be borne by a reasonable theory of reference.[35]

Are mathematical objects fictions? At least in part the answer depends on the extent of analogy between mathematical and meta-fictional statements. Quite unlike mathematical discourse, the telling of tales, performance of plays, and so forth largely consist of pretended assertion, whereas mathematical discourse involves genuine assertion. But meta-fictional discourse is different: attributions of fictional content (e.g., 'Hamlet was Danish', or even 'Hamlet existed'), construed as if prefixed with 'According to Shakespeare's *Hamlet*', can have truth-values; some singular terms in them (e.g., 'Hamlet' in the above example) contribute to determining that truth-value, but do so without designating anything.

The semantic form of such attributions of fictional content starts off with the "According to ... ' prefix, though in actual speech it's usually omitted. One might press on with the analogy as follows: the semantic form of statements that appear to be about mathematical objects should also start off with a prefix whose force is "Construe the following within the mathematical-object picture," and whose semantic role is simply to indicate that what follows is to be evaluated in the supervaluational way modeled in §4. But this would be both unnecessary and misleading.

The distinctively fictional vocabulary of fiction has an attenuated life in our assertive practices outside of attributions of fictional content;

'Hamlet existed' can be asserted under a construal that lacks an operator like 'According to *Hamlet*'; and there would be a point to such assertions, for example, to make the (false) claim that *Hamlet* was based on Danish history. But our actual mathematical vocabulary has absolutely no life outside of the mathematical-object picture; so occurrence of such vocabulary in a statement is a sufficient cue that it is to be construed within that picture, that is, as the Alternative theory would have it. An operator explicitly indicating this is unnecessary.

But more importantly: 'According to *Hamlet*' shows that the statement with which it starts is about *Hamlet*. What could be to mathematical statements as Shakespeare's play is to statements construed as starting with 'According to *Hamlet*'? As far as I can see, nothing. Mathematical discourse itself may be the only remotely plausible answer, and such reflexivity strikes me as still quite implausible. In short, the analogy between mathematical statements and attributions of fictional content remains rather limited.

I can imagine that some philosophers will react to the Alternative theory by impatiently asking for the bottom line: "Are there really numbers, sets, and so forth?" In his testimony before the McCarthy committee, Dalton Trumbo responded to a well-known question by saying, "Many questions can be answered 'yes' or 'no' only by a moron or a slave." Presumably he thought that the question he had been asked, whether he was or had ever been a member of the Communist Party, was such a question. I doubt that he took membership in such a party to involve borderline cases. More likely, his point was this: even though there is a correct "Yes or No" answer, such an answer can easily give a wrong impression and by itself is unilluminating.

Perhaps Trumbo was wrong on this matter. But if the question had been "Are there really sets?" or "Does the number 3 really exist?" his response would have been right on target.

These questions are formulated within a language representable by $L^\wedge$ and $L^\#$. Understood straightforwardly, their answers are straightforwardly, indeed trivially, "Yes." But these commitments are thin. Mathematics does not require the Mathematical-Objective picture. In a semantically uniform language for mathematics, of a sort representable by, for example, L', there would be no talk of mathematical objects. One might clumsily express this by saying that sets and numbers are unreal, not part of the furniture of the universe. Perhaps the point of the 'really' in these questions is to try to bend them into addressing this issue. But this strains our language; use of the words 'set' or 'number' pushes us into the Mathematical-Object picture. Once this picture is seen right, even the ontologically scrupulous philosopher should be comfortable with it.[36]

Notes

1 Chihara's distinction between ontological and mythological platonism from [4] may be a gesture toward this distinction.

2 I am excluding from the scope of semantics matters not relevant to truth-conditions of statements, even matters that are relevant to understanding.

3 In the original version of "On What There Is," Quine uses 'ontological presupposition'; later, e.g., in *Word and Object*, he prefers 'ontic commitment'.

4 This point in made in [5] and [3].

5 One further point. In general we state commitments by specifying kinds, e.g., numbers, electrons, cabbages, kings. But if there is only one thing of that kind, we may say that the commitment is to that thing. (A looser use of 'ontological commitment' has some currency, according to which a piece of discourse is committed to each thing in the range of its variables.)

6 Of course for some singular terms designating is their semantic job, though they fail to do their job: They are empty. And a singular term containing free variables, e.g., 'the capital of x', is not a designator at all (though its semantic role is parasitic on the roles of its instances). Frege would say that it stands for a function; but such standing-for is *not* what I'm calling designation, because functions of this sort are not objects. I use 'designates' to mean reference at level-zero, the sort that only holds between closed singular terms and objects.

7 In [9] I called the Alternative theory 'Coding-Fictionalism'. The root 'fiction' seemed to encourage misunderstanding; hence the change.

8 I ignore the more general topos-theoretic notion of modelhood.

9 To bear sense is (schematically summing Wittgenstein and Putnam) to have a use in a niche. Natural languages are sense-bearing; sometimes formal languages bear sense, especially among contemporary mathematicians. Sense-bearing languages are often called 'interpreted'. This usage encourages conflation of understanding and interpreting; to interpret is to try to re-express in more understandable words.

10 Of course *a specification* of a model could give sense to a previously non-sense-bearing language. Also, given any model $\mathscr{A}$ there could be a population such that, for example, $\alpha^{\mathscr{A}}$ was the designatum in their language of α for every individual-constant α in the vocabulary of $\mathscr{A}$'s a model, and so forth. Then the language of that model would be used, and so sense-bearing; the model itself would be an especially "lifelike" representation of its alethic underpinnings.

11 A statement is true or false only as a statement in a sense-bearing language. Truth is a genuine semantic property; truth-in-a-model is a set-theoretic ersatz-semantic relation. A definition of truth-in-a-model models a definition of truth, though this modeling can be confusing. Here's why. For a sense-bearing quantificational language, truth must be defined in terms of satisfaction (or the like). Truth-in-a-model can be defined in terms of satisfaction in a model, making the relation between these definitions clear. But other definitions are notationally simpler, and so are often preferred (e.g., in this essay); philosophically, they are best conceived as shorthand for a definition in terms of satisfaction in a model.

12 Non-total models could be made more partial: we could have allowed them to assign predicate-constants partial extensions. Our models are, in the terminology of [10], extension-wise total.

13 Here Sub(a, ν, θ) is the result of substituting **a** for all occurrences of ν free in θ.

14 For more on the logic determined by this model-theoretic semantics, see [10].

15 ' = ' is not handled as a two-place predicate-constant with extension $\{\langle a, a \rangle : a \in |\mathscr{A}|\}$. Motivation: given that 'Venus' designates something and 'Vulcan' doesn't, an equation like 'Vulcan = Venus' seems false, not merely truth-valueless.

16 Russell's paradox showed that not every Fregean concept of level one can be fortunate enough to have an extension. When restricted to sets, it becomes Cantor's Theorem: in effect, that no $\mathscr{A}$ has an extensor with domain Power($|\mathscr{A}|$).

17 Proponents of the Mathematical-Object theory usually think that such sentences are false. But on what basis? Do they describe brute facts, knowable only by pure intuition? Their falsity is not required by mathematics. That alone should render suspect any theory requiring them to have a truth-value. Of course some have claimed that a predicate like 'blue' is partial, only applying, or genuinely failing to apply, within the appropriate "category." Are these categorial constraints brute facts? How do we find out about them? Unlike the Mathematical-Object theory, the Alternative theory gives some basis for so-called intuitions about category-errors.

18 See [13]. Kaplan's actual phrase is 'artifact of the model'; but a model-theoretic semantics is itself a model, as explained in note 11.

19 See the discussion of sets and the natural numbers in [1].

20 Although plainly incompatible with the Mathematical-Object theory, this view has found proponents.

21 [11] presents the fifth-order language $L^{0,4}(exactly)$ and a translation t from its sentences into Biv($L^{\#}$), such that for every $\varphi \in$ Sent($L^{0,4}(exactly)$) and any infinite model $\mathscr{A}$:

$$\mathscr{A} \models \varphi \text{ iff } \mathscr{A} \models t(\varphi); \quad \mathscr{A} \not\models \varphi \text{ iff } \mathscr{A} =| t(\varphi).$$

In [12] I introduce the ω-order language L^{ω} under what I there called the weak higher-order semantics, with a translation t from its sentences into Biv($L\hat{\ }$) that meets an analog for Sent(L^{ω}) of the above condition. The sentences in the images of these translations can be regarded as formulations of their inverse-values within a first-order syntax. For each of these translations it is an open question whether they are onto Biv($L^{\#}$) and Biv($L\hat{\ }$) up to equivalence; I conjecture that in both cases this is not the case.

22 Form L'_u from L_u of [10] as above. With L'_u in place of L', there is a translation t for which we could replace Biv($L\hat{\ }$) by Sent($L\hat{\ }$) in this result.

23 This follows by a three-valued interpolation lemma.

24 Let a sentence φ of L^p be truth-valueless relative to a set of sentences Δ iff for any infinite model $\mathscr{A}$, if $\mathscr{A} \models \Delta$ then $\mathscr{A}|\varphi$. This is the theorem: for any $\neg$-complete set Δ of sentences of L and φ as above, either φ is truth-valueless relative to Δ or $\Delta \cup$ {the basic fact} decides φ in first-order logic. In particular, if φ is pure then either φ is logically truth-valueless or the basic fact decides φ.

25 Where C is a class of models, let φ be valid with respect to C iff φ is true in all members of C. The union axiom and the axioms of replacement are valid with respect to models of regular cardinality; the axiom of infinity is valid with respect to models of uncountable cardinality; the power-set axiom is valid with respect to models of strong-limit cardinality. So, except for the axiom of regularity, all axioms of ZF are valid with respect to models of inaccessible cardinality. This suggests that the status of these axioms is not as straightforward as that of those axioms that are valid simpliciter. Acceptance of these less self-evident axioms is, I suggest, an expression of a view about the size of the universe. (The power-set, infinity, and replacement axioms were never as self-evident as extensionality, pairs, and even separation.) The axiom of Regularity (and perhaps even Union?) derives its appeal from the iterative conception of sethood. From the Alternative view, that conception is unnecessarily restrictive. Regularity is a restrictive axiom. In many contexts we could live without it, faking its effect by restricting quantification over sets to well-founded sets. See [12] for more discussion.

26 For each natural number n, let φ_n say "There are at least n objects." To assume actual infinity is to assume $\{\varphi_1, \varphi_2, \ldots\}$. To assume potential infinity (against an S5 background) is to assume $\{\Diamond\varphi_1, \Diamond\varphi_2, \ldots\}$.

27 If S is finite and we replace S_1 by $S_0 \cup S$, then '$1\mathbf{Ap}(x, y)$' could be replaced by a conjunction:

$$(x = \text{'}\mathbf{P}\text{'} \& \ \mathbf{P}(y)) \lor (x = \text{'}\mathbf{Q}\text{'} \& \ \mathbf{Q}(y)) \lor \ldots$$

and similarly for '$2\mathbf{Ap}(x, y, z)$'.

28 Objecthood is implicit in 'x''s syntactic status as a type-0 variable. This is why in the *Tractatus* Wittgenstein calls objecthood a formal property.

29 This distinction brings out what some might call the "transcendental realism" implicit in the Alternative theory.

30 This example is from [6, p. 219]. One might argue that this sentence is logically equivalent to 'Socrates $\neq$ Plato', and so its commitments are those of the latter as well. This presupposes a fixed and broad range for the second-order quantifier (including at least being Socrates or being Plato); but the contexts in which this sentence would most comfortably be used severely restrict the range of that quantifier. Indeed, the truth of a statement made with Dummett's sentence would be sensitive to that feature of context; 'Socrates $\neq$ Plato' shows no such sensitivity. That difference alone indicates enough non-equivalence to defeat this move.

31 Fregean reference for predicates is a relation of type $(?, 1)$; so in a perspicuous notation we might express the referential work of the predicate 'is a horse' by: (Stands-for x) ('is a horse', x is a horse). (There is a question mark in the preceding because the type of level-one predicates is a matter of controversy; in [8] Geach may be read as arguing that they are not objects; in the *Tractatus* Wittgenstein appears to agree.) Similarly, we might say: (Witnesses x) (the Dummett sentence, x is a dramatist). I agree with Frege's assessment of the so-called paradox of the concept *horse*: that it is not a serious problem for the Fregean doctrine of reference for incomplete expressions.

32 See [2]. Boolos would take the Geach-Kaplan example to carry commitment only to the existence of some critics. As an assessment of thin commitment, this requires that thin commitments be preserved by only very tight paraphrase. 'There is something that some critics are, only critics are, and all who are admire only others who are' is a paraphrase of the Geach-Kaplan example; but I'd guess that Boolos would think that it carried different thin commitments. Suppose that the Mutual Admiration Society (MAS) is a club of critics who admire only one another. One might back up a statement made with the last sentence by going on to say 'For example, a member of the MAS'. This suggests that being a member of the MAS is in the range of the initial second-order quantifier. If the above paraphrase does preserve thin commitments, then even the Geach-Kaplan sentence could carry commitment to being a member of the MAS (and would if all critics who admire only one another are members of the MAS, and the MAS has exactly two members, each admiring the other).

33 See [9].

34 See [7], a remarkable paper that has been remarkably ignored.

35 Given the Furthean (Pickwickian?) view of what reference to Fregean concepts and relations amounts to, the disagreement expressed in [2] between Boolos and myself may be merely verbal.

36 The sort of approach here applied to mathematical discourse can, modulo vagueness about identity conditions, also be applied to talk "about" fact-like entities (states-of-affairs) including possible worlds, and "about" some meaning-like entities. A rather different approach applies to talk "about" Peircean types. Although the view presented here is undoubtedly at odds with his own, Hilary Putnam, through his writing and teaching, had an enormous influence on the thinking that led to this essay.

References

[1] P. Benacerraf, "What Numbers Could Not Be," *Philosophical Review*, 1965.

[2] G. Boolos, "Nominalistic Platonism," *Philosophical Review*, 1985.

[3] R. Cartwright, "Ontology and the Theory of Meaning," *Philosophy of Science*, 1954.

[4] C. Chihara, *Ontology and the Vicious-Circle Principle*. Ithaca, N.Y.: Cornell University Press, 1973.

[5] N. Chomsky and I. Sheffler, "What Is Said to Be," *Proceedings of the Aristotelian Society*, 1958.

[6] M. Dummett, *Frege: The Philosophy of Language*. London: Duckworth, 1973.

[7] M. Furth, "Two Types of Denotation," in N. Rescher (ed.), *Studies in Logical Theory*. APQ Monograph no. 2. Oxford: Basil Blackwell, 1968.

[8] P. Geach, "Names and Identity," in S. Guttenplan (ed.), *Mind and Language*. Oxford: Clarendon Press, 1975.

[9] H. Hodes, "Logicism and the Ontological Commitments of Arithmetic," *Journal of Philosophy*, 1984.

[10] H. Hodes, "Three-valued logic," *Annals of Pure and Applied Logic*, vol. 43 (1989).

[11] H. Hodes, "Where Do the Natural Numbers Come From?" *Synthese* (1990).

[12] H. Hodes, "Where Do Sets Come From?" *The Journal of Symbolic Logic* (in press).

[13] D. Kaplan, "How to Russell a Frege-Church," in *Journal of Philosophy*, 1975.

[14] W. V. O. Quine, *From a Logical Point of View*. Cambridge, Mass.: Harvard University Press, 1961.

[15] W. V. O. Quine, *Ways of Paradox*. Cambridge, Mass.: Harvard University Press, 1976.

[16] C. Wright, *Frege's Conception of Numbers as Objects*. Aberdeen: Aberdeen University Press, 1983.

12

The standard of equality
of numbers

GEORGE BOOLOS

One of the strangest pieces of argumentation in the history of logic is found in Richard Dedekind's *Was sind und was sollen die Zahlen?*, where, in the proof of that monograph's theorem 66, Dedekind attempts to demonstrate the existence of infinite systems. Dedekind defines a system S as *infinite* if, as we would now put it, there are a one-one function ϕ from S to S and an element of S not in the range of ϕ. Since it is now known that set theory without the axiom of choice does not imply that a set that is infinite in the usual sense is infinite in Dedekind's sense (although it does imply the converse), it is now common to prefix "Dedekind" when speaking of infinity in this stronger sense. The sets with which we shall be concerned are Dedekind infinite if they are infinite at all, however, and I shall therefore omit "Dedekind" before "infinite."

Theorem 66 of *Was sind* reads, "There are infinite systems"; the proof of it Dedekind offered runs:

Proof.[1] The world of my thoughts, i.e., the totality S of all things that can be objects of my thought, is infinite. For if s denotes an element of S, then the thought s', that s can be an object of my thought, is itself an element of S. If s' is regarded as the image $\phi(s)$ of the element s, then the mapping ϕ on S determined thereby has the property that its image S' is a part of S; and indeed S' is a proper part of S, because there are elements in S (e.g., my own ego [mein eigenes Ich]), which are different from every such thought s' and are therefore not contained in S'. Finally, it is clear that if a, b are different elements of S, then their images a', b' are also different, so that the mapping ϕ is distinct (similar). Consequently, S is infinite, q.e.d.

It is tempting to think that Dedekind isn't in as deep a hole as his mentioning so wildly nonmathematical an item as his own ego might suggest and to suppose that he has merely chosen a bad example. Wouldn't the sentence *Berlin ist in Deutschland* and the operation of

I am grateful to Ellery Eells, Dan Leary, Thomas Ricketts, and Gabriel Segal for helpful comments. Research for this essay was carried out under grant no. SES-8808755 from the National Science Foundation.

prefixing *Niemand glaubt dass* have been just as good as Dedekind's own ego and the operation that takes any object *s* in the world of Dedekind's thoughts to that funny thought about *s*? Instead of the things that can be objects of his thought (whatever these might be) couldn't he have cited (say) the set of German sentences, i.e., sentence-types, as an example of an infinite set? And had he cited that set, wouldn't he have given an obviously correct proof of theorem 66 by giving an obviously correct example of an infinite set?

It is significant that nowhere in the remainder of *Was sind und was sollen die Zahlen*? does Dedekind appeal to theorem 66 in the proof of any other theorem. Why, one might wonder, did not Dedekind simply omit the theorem and its proof, the incongruity of whose argumentation and subject matter Dedekind himself could not have failed to find glaring?

Recall that the aim of *Was sind*, according to Dedekind, was to lay the foundations of that part of logic that deals with the theory of numbers – thus the theory of numbers is a part of logic – and that his answer to the title question of his monograph was that numbers are "free creations of the human mind." Some of what that saying means emerges in section 73, where he writes:

If in observing a simply infinite system *N*, ordered by a mapping φ, the special character of the elements is completely disregarded, only their distinguishability is held fixed, and account is taken of only those relations to one another in which they are placed by the mapping φ that orders them, then these elements are called *natural numbers* or *ordinal numbers* or also simply *numbers*, and the basis element 1 is called the basis-number of the number series *N*. With regard to this freeing of the elements from all other content (abstraction), one can justifiably call the numbers a free creation of the human mind. The relations or laws which are derived just from the conditions $\alpha, \beta, \gamma, \delta^2$ in 71 [these are Dedekind's versions of what have come to be known as the "Peano Postulates"] and therefore are always the same in all simply ordered infinite systems, however the names accidentally given to the individual elements may be pronounced, form the first object of the *Science of Numbers* or *Arithmetic*.

Thus, arithmetic is about certain objects, the numbers, abstracted from simply (we now say "countably") infinite systems, systems satisfying the "Peano" conditions $\alpha, \beta, \gamma, \delta$ under some appropriate choice of base element and successor operation. Since they have been abstracted from systems satisfying $\alpha, \beta, \gamma, \delta$, the numbers too satisfy these conditions. Logic, Dedekind would appear to be claiming, suffices for the derivation of all, or at any rate all familiar, arithmetical facts from the mere assumption that the numbers, together with 1 and successor, are objects that satisfy the "Peano" conditions. (Dedekind proves that the existence of simply infinite systems follows from that of infinite systems.)

The trouble with trying to prove theorem 66 by mentioning the set of sentences of German is that Dedekind would probably have regarded a sentence (or any other abstract object) as as much a free creation out of ink-tracks or other physical objects as a number is a free creation out of objects. Dedekind did not cite the most obvious infinite system, the system of the natural numbers themselves, in the proof of theorem 66. It would thus appear that he thought that a satisfactory proof of it must mention some infinite set of non-abstract items, out of which the natural numbers could have been freely created, and that he was therefore not at liberty to cite a set of sentences or abstract objects of any other sort as an example of an infinite set.

Dedekind's proof, however, is fallacious if thoughts are taken to be actual physical occurrences. Ignoring worries about opacity, we may grant that if u is a thought that s can be an object of my thought, and likewise for v and t, then $u = v$ if and only if $s = t$. It does not follow, and it is indefensible to assume, that for every object s, or at least for every object s that is an object of my thought, *there is* such a thing as the thought that s can be an object of my thought. There just aren't all those thoughts around. (As Frege, commenting on theorem 66, put it, "Now presumably we shall not hurt Dedekind's feelings if we assume that he has not thought infinitely many thoughts.")[3] Dedekind makes this unwarranted assumption in the proof by using the definite article and speaking of "*the* thought that s can be an object of my thought." Of course, without some guarantee that all those thoughts exist, the proof fails: Dedekind hasn't defined a function on the (whole) world of his thoughts. The present king of France strikes again.

Thus Dedekind is in trouble that we do not appear to be in. We, but not he, can use the set of sentences of German as an example of an infinite set. The difficulty for us in doing so will shortly emerge.

Dedekind's notion of free creation[4] raises too many problems for us to find it satisfactory: One somewhat less obvious difficulty it poses is a "third man" difficulty, that of saying why we don't get different systems when we abstract *twice* from a system satisfying conditions $\alpha, \beta, \gamma, \delta$. Or *do* we get different, but isomorphic, systems? Or can we abstract only *once*? Best not to take him too seriously here.

The view can be made more appealing and more plausible if we forget about abstraction and free creation, and take Dedekind to be saying that statements about the natural numbers can be regarded as logically true statements about *all* systems satisfying conditions $\alpha, \beta, \gamma, \delta$. Charles Parsons, in an illuminating study, "The Structuralist View of Mathematics,"[5] has called this the eliminative reading of *Was sind*. Perhaps we might take Dedekind to be claiming that an arithmetical statement, expressed by a sentence S is in the notation, say, of second-order logic, in which all number quantifiers are relativized to the predicate letter N, 1 denotes one, and s denotes successor, has the logical form: $\forall N, s, 1(\alpha, \beta, \gamma, \delta(N, s, 1) \rightarrow S)$. (Addition and multiplication, etc., can be handled by familiar techniques due to Dedekind.) Thus the monadic predicate letter N, the monadic function sign s, and the constant 1 turn into a second-order monadic predicate variable, a second-order monadic function variable, and a (peculiarly shaped) first-order variable, which are then universally quantified upon. To complete the interpretation of the resulting sentence, we might want to add that the first-order variables range over *all* the things there are.

For any such arithmetical sentence S, let $D(S)$ be the second-order sentence $\forall N, s, 1(\alpha, \beta, \gamma, \delta(N, s, 1) \rightarrow S)$. $D(S)$, it will be observed, contains no non-logical constants at all. We now want to inquire into the relation between S and $D(S)$.

Suppose that S is true, i.e., true when interpreted over the natural numbers, together with successor and one and that N', s', and $1'$ satisfy $\alpha, \beta, \gamma, \delta(N, s, 1)$. Then since the natural numbers together with successor and one also satisfy $\alpha, \beta, \gamma, \delta(N, s, 1)$, by a valid second-order argument given by Dedekind, N', s', and $1'$ are isomorphic to the natural numbers, successor, and one and therefore satisfy S. Thus $D(S)$ is a logical truth. Conversely, suppose that $D(S)$ is a logical truth. Let (*) N', s', and $1'$ satisfy $\alpha, \beta, \gamma, \delta(N, s, 1)$. They therefore also satisfy S. Since the natural numbers, successor, and one also satisfy $\alpha, \beta, \gamma, \delta(N, s, 1)$, they are isomorphic to N', s', and $1'$, and therefore also satisfy S; that is, S is true. Thus, it would appear, we have shown that S is true if and only if $D(S)$ is a logical truth. Does not this argument show that arithmetical truths are logical truths disguised only by the omission of an antecedent condition and a few symbols of logic?

Of course – on the assumption (*), true, by our lights, that *there are* N', s', and $1'$ together satisfying $\alpha, \beta, \gamma, \delta(N, s, 1)$: We used this assumption when we argued that if $D(S)$ is a logical truth, then S is true.[6] We have had to make a true assumption, but one that we have as yet found no reason to regard as logically true, in order to show that we can effectively associate with each sentence of arithmetic, a sentence in the vocabulary of logic in such a way that with each truth and no falsehood of arithmetic there is associated a logical truth. To succeed this far in reducing arithmetic to logic we have had to make an assumption not yet certified as logically true: There are infinite systems.

Is that a difficulty? It might seem not. We make a non-logical assumption to reduce arithmetic to logic. We then throw away the ladder. But ladder or no, we have reduced arithmetic to logic, haven't we?

Parsons has pointed out a difficulty in supposing that we have.[7] He notes that if there are no infinite systems, then $D(S)$ is true, for every arithmetical sentence S "... both A and $\neg A$ have true canonical forms, which amounts to the inconsistency of arithmetic."

Parsons's observation leads us to the heart of the matter. Logicism is not adequately characterized as the view that arithmetic is reducible to logic if all that is meant thereby is that there is an effective mapping of statements of arithmetic to statements of logic that assigns logical truths to all and only the truths of arithmetic. Nor is it vindicated merely by exhibiting such a mapping E. For E to vindicate logicism, it must show that arithmetic is "reducible to" logic, "really" logic, logic "in disguise," "a part of" logic. Then at least, for any arithmetical sentence S, $E(S)$ must give the content of S, must state, in the language of logic, how matters must be if and only if S is true.[8] But then E must do for falsity what it does for truth and also assign logical falsehoods to the falsehoods of arithmetic; otherwise there will be certain truths S of arithmetic such that $E(S)$ is compatible with $E(\neg S)$, and no mapping that thus violates negation can be regarded as giving the content of statements of arithmetic in logical terms and hence as reducing arithmetic to logic.

For arithmetical sentences, like all others, come in triples: For any two arithmetical sentences there is a third, their conjunction, that, however matters may be, holds when matters are that way if and only if both sentences hold when matters are that way. A mapping E under which $E(S \& S')$ is not equivalent in this sense to the conjunction of $E(S)$ and $E(S')$ cannot be thought to give the content of all three of S, S' and $(S \& S')$ and cannot therefore count as a reduction of arithmetic to logic.

Similarly for negation: If for some arithmetical sentence S, $E(\neg S)$ is not equivalent to the negation of $E(S)$, then E does not give the content of both S and $\neg S$, and therefore does not show arithmetic reducible to logic. In advance of any possible reduction to logic certain arithmetical statements immediately (logically) imply certain others, and certain arithmetical statements are immediately incompatible with certain others. A reduction of arithmetic to logic, although it may reveal previously unrecognized implications or incompatibilities among the statements of arithmetic, cannot disclose that these immediate implications and incompatabilities actually fail to obtain.

For a mapping E to vindicate logicism, then, E must at the very least respect the truth-functional operators on closed formulae. Since $E(S)$

will always be logically true if S is true, E will respect negation if and only if $E(S)$ is always logically false for false S. It is clear that Dedekind's mapping D respects conjunction.

But D does not respect negation. $\neg \forall N, s, 1(\alpha, \beta, \gamma, \delta(N, s, 1) \to S)$ is not logically equivalent to $\forall N, s, 1(\alpha, \beta, \gamma, \delta(N, s, 1) \to \neg S)$. The latter follows logically from the former, as Dedekind showed. But the former follows from the latter in general only under the assumption that infinite systems exist. Indeed, if S is, say, $1 = 1$, then the former is equivalent to $\perp$, the latter to "there are no infinite systems," and the conditional with antecedent the latter and consequent the former is then equivalent to "there are infinite systems."

If S is the statement "there are infinite systems," a truth, but presumably not a logical truth, then $D(S)$ is a logical truth, as desired; but $D(\neg S)$ is equivalent to $\neg S$, and therefore not a logical falsehood.

A third example: The mapping D assigns to "$\neg 17 \times 14 = 228$" a sentence that is (absent logically guaranteed infinite systems) consistent with what it assigns to "$17 \times 14 = 228$." D cannot therefore count as reducing arithmetic to logic in any reasonable sense of the phrase.

All would be well, of course, if, as a matter of logic, there were infinite systems, if theorem 66 had been established as securely as, and in the manner of, theorems 65 and 67. But no purely logical ground has been given for thinking theorem 66 true. That, and not the non-mathematical character of the objects it mentions, is the real problem with Dedekind's proof of theorem 66.

We ought to mention that there can be no effective mapping of sentences of arithmetic to sentences of logic under which truths of arithmetic are mapped to logical truths and falsehoods to logical falsehoods: Otherwise arithmetic would be decidable, since the truth-value of any statement could be ascertained by calculating the truth-value of its image under the mapping in any one-element model. Nor is there a mapping of sentences of arithmetic to sentences of *first*-order logic under which the truths of arithmetic and only those are mapped to logical truths. Otherwise it would be possible to decide effectively whether an arithmetical sentence S is true or false: Effectively enumerate all first-order logical truths; then the image of S under the mapping appears in the enumeration if and only if that of $\neg S$ does not, and S is true if and only if its image appears.

Infinity is cheap. As Dedekind showed, a domain S will be infinite if there are a one-one function ϕ from S to S and an object in S not in the range of ϕ. Indeed, it's often easier than one may suspect to show a domain infinite. For example, in conjunction with the trivial truth "$\exists x \exists y \ x \neq y$," the ordered pair axiom, commonly thought to be innocuous, is an axiom of infinity. Any domain in which both hold is infinite, for if $a \neq b$, then the function that assigns to each object x in the domain the ordered pair $\langle a, x \rangle$ will be one-one and omit $\langle b, b \rangle$ from its range.

It is well known that very weak systems of set theory guarantee that there are infinitely many objects: the conjunction of the null set and unit set axioms supply an object and a one-one function meeting Dedekind's criterion. It is thus not difficult to provide a theory committed to there being infinitely many objects. The difficulty (insuperable, I will urge) is to find a logically true theory with this commitment.

We have seen that in order to be able to claim that the function that assigns $\forall N, s, 1(\alpha, \beta, \gamma, \delta(N, s, 1) \rightarrow S)$ to any sentence S of arithmetic shows that "arithmetic is a part of logic," Dedekind needs a proof from logical truths that there are infinitely many objects. No satisfactory way has yet presented itself.

I want to consider the suggestion that a principle I call Hume's principle can be used to help Dedekind out. As we shall see, Dedekind would probably not like the suggestion. And in the end, I shall argue, we can't accept it, either.

"We are possest of a precise standard," wrote Hume, "by which we can judge of the equality and proportion of numbers; and according as they correspond or not to that standard, we determine their relations, without any possibility of error. When two numbers are so combin'd as that the one has always an unite answering to every unit of the other, we pronounce them equal; and 'tis for want of such a standard of equality in extension, that geometry can scarce be esteem'd a perfect and infallible science."[9] Reflecting on Frege's idea that statements about numbers are assertions about what he called concepts, we may formalize Hume's dictum as a second-order formula. Let "$\#F$" abbreviate "the number of objects falling under the concept F" and "$F \approx G$" express the existence of a one-one correspondence between the objects falling under F and those falling under G.[10] Then Hume's principle may be written: $\forall F \forall G(\#F = \#G \leftrightarrow F \approx G)$.

Frege attempts to prove Hume's principle in section 73 of his *Foundations of Arithmetic*. The difficulty with the proof he gives there is that it appeals to the theory of concepts and objects, whose inconsistency Russell pointed out in his first letter to Frege. After having derived Hume's principle from this inconsistent theory, Frege derives the axioms of arithmetic from Hume's principle.

More exactly, in the *Foundations of Arithmetic* Frege gives definitions of *zero*, *succeeds* ("*follows directly after*"), and *finite* (*natural*) *number*, and shows, easily enough, that zero is a finite number, that anything that succeeds any finite number is a finite number, that zero succeeds nothing and that if m, m', n, and n' are finite numbers, n succeeds m, and n' succeeds m', then $m = m'$ iff $n = n'$. It is by no means evident, however, that every finite number is succeeded by something, and it was a matter of considerable difficulty for Frege to prove it. The central argument of the *Foundations of Arithmetic* is a fairly complete sketch of a proof that every finite number is succeeded by a finite number; in proving this and the other facts about the numbers, Frege makes use only of Hume's principle and the system of logic set forth in his *Begriffsschrift*. The intricacy of his reasoning is astonishing and repays careful attention. See the appendix for a reconstruction. I do not know whether Frege realized that Hume's principle plus the logic of the *Begriffsschrift* was all he used or needed. Perhaps not; *he* would have had no reason to value the observation. In any event, it is a pity that the derivability of arithmetic from Hume's principle isn't known as *Frege's theorem*.

Frege thus succeeds where Dedekind has failed. He has demonstrated the existence of an infinite system. With hard work, he has proved the analogue of what Dedekind simply assumes to be the case for the system of objects x of his thought, that for each x, *there is* a y to which x bears the appropriate relation.

Do not be deceived by the absence of the sort of wallpaper found in the *Begriffsschrift* into thinking that the *Foundations* is not fundamentally a mathematical work.[11] In a letter of September 1882, Carl Stumpf suggested to Frege that it might be "appropriate to explain your line of thought first in ordinary language and then – perhaps separately on another occasion or in the very same book – in conceptual notation. I should think that this would make for a more favorable reception of *both* accounts."[12] Frege apparently took Stumpf's suggestion, which was that his *mathematical* ideas be first published in ordinary language. At the heart of the *Foundations* there lies a *proof*.

Frege outlines a demonstration in the *Foundations* that arithmetic, i.e., the basic axioms of the second-order arithmetic of zero and successor (from which that of full second-order arithmetic, of addition and multiplication, can be derived, as in *Was sind*; Frege seems never to have been interested in deriving the axioms of addition and multiplication), can be derived from Hume's principle. Second-order arithmetic is consistent, presumably; Frege derives Hume's principle from an inconsistent theory of concepts. Nevertheless, an inconsistent theory may, indeed must, have consistent consequences, and it turns out that in the same sense in which second-order arithmetic may be derived from Hume's principle in the system of logic of the *Begriffsschrift*, Hume's principle may be derived back from second-order arithmetic. (Deriving axioms from theorems has been called "reverse mathematics" by Harvey Friedman.) Hume's principle and second-order arithmetic, which is sometimes called "analysis," are thus equiconsistent, and very effectively so: A proof of an inconsistency from either could easily be turned into a proof of an inconsistency from the other.

In analysis, there are two sorts of variables, one sort ranging over the natural numbers, the other over sets of natural numbers. The axioms are the usual ones: the Peano axioms, together with the usual axioms for addition and multiplication (which, as Dedekind showed, are dispensable), and a comprehension scheme: For any formula of the language of analysis, there is a set of all and only the numbers satisfying the formula.

The *Foundations* of course shows that if analysis is inconsistent, so is Hume's principle. How may the converse be shown? Let α be a set of natural numbers. Call the natural number n the *grumber* belonging to α if either α has infinitely many members and $n = 0$ or α has $n - 1$ members. The grumber of U.S. senators is 101, the grumber of roots of the equation "$x - 5 = 0$" is 2, and the grumber of even numbers is zero, which is also the grumber of numbers divisible by four. It is then a *theorem* of analysis that the grumber belonging to α = the grumber belonging to β if and only if the members of α and those of β are in one-one correspondence. Any derivation in second-order logic of a contradiction from Hume's principle could thus be turned into a derivation in analysis of a contradiction from the theorem of analysis about grumbers just cited. Thus if analysis is consistent, so is the result of adjoining Hume's principle to second-order logic.

Some trick like the introduction of grumbers is necessary because "the natural number belonging to" is not defined for all sets of natural numbers, indeed not defined for any set containing infinitely many natural numbers. There is no natural number that is the number of members of the set of evens; but the grumber zero belongs to this set.

Frege, then, gave an intricate and mathematically interesting derivation of arithmetic from a simple, consistent, and trivial-seeming principle. Since the principle is as weak as any from which arithmetic can be derived, Frege's derivation was "best possible."

Dedekind, of course, might well have objected to our suggestion that Hume's principle be used to obtain an infinite system on the ground that the arithmetical notion *the number belonging to* that figures in the principle is undefined, and that arithmetic is therefore not shown to be entirely a part of logic. A weak reply can be made: There is a principle, discussed farther on, that deals only with objects and concepts, which licenses a definition of number, from which Hume's principle can be derived. The principle is that for every concept F there is a unique object x such that for all concepts G, G is in x if and only if F and G are equinumerous. Unlike Hume's, this principle does not explicitly mention numbers. The number belonging to F may of course be defined to be the unique x such that for all G, etc.

Even if the objection that the expression "is in" is not a logical "constant" is waived, this principle cannot be held to be a logical principle for a reason we shall consider at length: It commits us to the existence of too many objects. Here we should note that a truth's being couched in purely logical terms is not sufficient for it to count as truth *of* logic, a logical truth, a truth that is true solely in virtue of logic. A distinction must be drawn between truths of logic and truths expressed in the language of logic. I suspect that failure to draw this distinction was largely responsible for there ever being any thought at all that the axiom of infinity might actually count as a logical truth.

According to Hume's principle, for any concepts F and G, there are certain *objects*, namely, the number x belonging to F and the number y belonging to G, such that x is identical to y if and only if F and G are equinumerous. It is the objecthood of numbers that explains why Hume's principle, despite appearances, cannot be considered to be a truth of logic, a definition,[13] an immediate consequence of a definition, analytic, quasi analytic, or anything of that sort.

The reason that it may appear so is that it can easily be confused with a principle that has a considerably greater claim to the status of truth of logic. Assume that some version of the theory of types, including axioms of comprehension and extensionality, counts as logic. Then matters are as the theory of types has it: There are individuals, sets of individuals, classes of sets of individuals, etc. (The words "set" and "class" are used here just to keep the types straight: We've got classes of sets of individuals.) According to a comprehension axiom, for any set, there will be a class containing all and only the sets that are equinumerous with that set; by extensionality, there will be at most one such class. We may call classes containing all and only the sets that are equinumerous with any one set *Russellnumbers*, and say that the Russellnumber of a set is the Russellnumber that contains the set. The proposition that Russellnumbers are identical if and only if the sets they are Russellnumbers of are equinumerous is then a theorem of (this version of) the theory of types.

Russellnumbers are classes of sets of individuals. One of the (ineffable?) doctrines of the usual formulation of the theory of types is that the types are disjoint. No set is a class or individual, and no class is an individual. Russellnumbers are not individuals.

The disadvantage of this way of defining numbers, of course, is that arithmetic cannot be derived in the theory of types without postulating that there are infinitely many individuals. With honest toil, however, Frege succeeds in proving from Hume's principle the infinity of the natural numbers.

Observe that although the theory of objects and concepts that is sketched in the *Foundations* is almost certainly inconsistent, there is a consistent fragment of it that is all Frege needs, or uses, to derive arithmetic. According to this fragment, there are objects (or individuals), first-level concepts, under which objects may or may not fall, and second-level concepts, under which first-level concepts may or may not fall. So far, matters look pretty much as they do on the theory of types, if one substitutes "object," "first-level concept," and "second-level concept" for "individual," "set," and "class." Crucially, though, Frege does not analogously define the numbers as those second-level concepts under which fall all and only those first-level concepts that are equinumerous with some one concept. Call such second-level concepts *numerical*. Instead, he introduces a new primitive relation between objects and concepts ("is the extension of") and then defines a number to be an object that is the extension of some numerical concept. (Numerical concepts, to repeat, are second-level.) Thus Frege assumes that for every first-level concept F there is a unique object that is the extension of the second-level concept under which fall all and only those first-level concepts that are equinumerous with F.

The introduction of second-level concepts is not necessary. All that Frege need do is introduce a primitive predicate "is in" for a relation between first-level concepts and objects and assume that for any first-level concept F there is exactly one object x such that for any first-level concept G, G is in x if and only if F and G are equinumerous. Frege may then define the number "belonging to" F as that object x.

Notice the additional step Frege has taken. Unlike Russell, Frege has assumed there is a way of associating objects with numerical concepts so that different objects are associated with different numerical concepts. (Assume that coextensive concepts are identified.) This cannot be done, if there are only finitely many objects; if there are (say) eighteen objects, then there will be nineteen numerical concepts. It is a weighty assumption of Frege's, to put it slightly differently, that the first-level concepts can be mapped into objects in such a way that concepts are mapped onto the same object only if they are equinumerous, and *it is a lucky break that the assumption is even consistent*.

The well-known comparison that Frege draws in sections 64–9 of the *Foundations* between "the direction of line *l*" and "the number belonging to concept *F*" is therefore seriously misleading. We do not suspect that lines are made up of directions, that directions are some of the ingredients of lines. Had Frege appended to the direction principle, "The direction of line l is equal to the direction of line k if and only if l and k are parallel," the claim that directions are points, we would never have regarded the principle as anything like a definition, and would perhaps have wondered whether there are enough points to go around. (In fact, there are: There are continuously many points and continuously many directions.) The principle that directions of lines are identical just in case the lines are parallel looks, and is, trivial only because we suppose that directions are one or more types up from, or at any rate are all distinct from, the things of which lines are made.

The principle that numbers belonging to concepts are identical if and only if the concepts are equinumerous, then, should count as a logical truth only if it is supposed that numbers do not do to concepts or sets the corresponding sort of thing, namely, fall under, or be elements of, them. On the theory of types, matters so fall out. But Frege's proof from Hume's principle that every number has a successor cannot be carried out in the theory of types: the proof cannot succeed unless it is supposed that numbers are objects.

For how does Frege show that the number 0 is not identical with the number 1? Frege defines 0 as the number belonging to the concept *not identical with itself*. He then defines 1 as the number belonging to the concept *identical with* 0. Since no object falls under the former concept, and the object 0 falls under the latter, the two concepts are, by logic, not equinumerous, and hence their numbers 0 and 1 are, by Hume's principle, not identical. Notice that for this argument to work it is crucial that 0 be supposed to be an object that falls under the concept *identical with* 0. 2 arises in like manner: Now that 0 and 1 have been defined and shown different, form the concept *identical with* 0 *or* 1, take its number, call it 2, and observe that the new concept is coextensive with neither of these concepts *because the distinct objects* 0 *and* 1 *fall under it*. Conclude by Hume that 2 is distinct from both 0 and 1.

Frege proves that if n is a finite number, then it is succeeded by the number belonging to *being less than or equal to* n; the proof works because n is an object that can be proved not to fall under *being less than* n.

Thus it is only to one who supposes that numbers are not objects that Hume's principle looks analytic or obvious. Frege's proof that every number has a successor depends vitally on the contrary supposition that numbers are indeed objects.

A sentence is a logical truth only if it is true no matter what objects it speaks of and no matter to which of them its predicates or other non-logical words apply. (The vagueness of the consequent, including that as to which words count as logical, is matched by that of the antecedent.) A sentence is not a logical truth if it is false when interpreted over a domain containing infinitely many things, and it is not a logical truth if, like Hume's principle, it is false when only finitely many things belong to the domain.

It is clear that an account of logical truth that attempts to distinguish Hume's principle as a logical truth will have the hard task of explaining why Hume's principle is a logical truth even though two other similar-looking principles are not. These are the principle about extensions embodied in Frege's rule V and a principle about relation numbers that is strikingly analogous to Hume's principle. They read: Extensions of concepts are identical if and only if those concepts are coextensive; and: Relation numbers of relations are identical if and only if those relations are isomorphic. Russell showed the former inconsistent; Harold Hodes has astutely observed that the latter leads to the Burali-Forti paradox.[14]

It will not do to say: Hume's principle, unlike the other two, and like the principle by which we take ourselves to introduce the two truth-values, is a logical truth because it is consistent.

For say that the concepts F and G *differ evenly* if the number of objects falling under F but not G or under G but not F is even (and finite). The relation between concepts expressed by "F and G differ evenly" is an equivalence relation (exercise), and can of course be defined in purely logical (second-order) vocabulary. Now introduce the term "the parity of" for a function from concepts to objects and consider the parity principle: The parity of F is identical with that of G if and only if F and G differ evenly.

The parity principle is evidently consistent. Let X be any finite domain containing the numbers 0 and 1. Let the parity of a subset of X be 0 if it contains an even number of objects and 1 otherwise. Then with "parity" so defined, the parity principle is true in the domain X, and is therefore consistent.

However, the parity principle is true in no infinite domain. Here's a sketch of the proof.

Let X be an infinite set. Then if Y, Z are subsets of X, Y evenly differs from Z iff for some disjoint finite subsets A, B of X such that $A \cup B$ is even, $Y = (Z \cup A) - B$. Since X is infinite, $|\{(A, B): A$ and B are disjoint subsets of X and $|A \cup B|$ is even$\}| = |X|$, and for each subset Z of X, $|\{Y : Y$ evenly differs from $Z\}| = |X|$.

Suppose now that $f:PX \rightarrow X$ and for all Y, Z, if $fY = fZ$, Y evenly differs from Z. Then for each x in X, $|\{Y : fY = x\}| \leq |X|$, and $|PX| \leq |X| \times |X| = |X|$, contradiction.[15]

Consistent principles of the form: The object associated in some manner with the concept F is identical with that associated in the same manner with G if and only if F and G bear a certain equivalence relation to one another, may therefore be inconsistent with each other. Hume's principle is inconsistent with the parity principle. Which is the logical truth?[16]

Indeed, not only do we have no reason for regarding Hume's principle as a truth of logic, it is doubtful whether it is a truth at all. As the existence of a number, 0, belonging to the concept *non-self-identical* is a consequence of Hume's principle, it also follows that there is a number belonging to the concept *self-identical*, a number that is the number of things that there are. Hume's principle is no less dubious than any of its consequences, one of which is the claim, uncertain at best, that there is such a number.

Crispin Wright claims that "there is a programme for the foundations of number theory recoverable from *Grundlagen*."[17] He calls the program "number-theoretic logicism" and characterizes it as the view that "it is possible, using the concepts of higher-order logic with identity to explain a genuinely sortal concept of cardinal number; and hence to deduce appropriate statements of the fundamental truths of number-theory, in particular the Peano Axioms, in an appropriate system of higher-order logic with identity to which a statement of that explanation has been added as an axiom."[18] He adds that he thinks that it would "serve Frege's purpose against the Kantian thesis of the *synthetic a priori* character of number-theoretic truths. For the fundamental truths of number theory would be revealed as consequences of an explanation: a statement whose role is to fix the character of a certain concept."[19]

Wright regards Hume's principle as a statement whose role is to fix the character of a certain concept. We need not read any contemporary theories of the a priori into the debate between Frege and Kant. But Frege can be thought to have carried the day against Kant only if it has been shown that Hume's principle is *analytic*, or a truth of logic. This has not been done. Nor has the view Wright describes been shown to deserve the name "(number-theoretic) logicism." It's logicism only if it's claimed that Hume's principle is a principle of logic. Wright quite properly refrains from calling it one.

We have noted that Dedekind would not have been happy with the suggestion that the existence of infinite systems be derived from Hume's principle. Nor, presumably, would Frege have rested content with it as the foundation of arithmetic. Hume's principle may yield a great deal of information about the natural numbers, but it doesn't tell us how they may be viewed as logical objects, nor even which objects they are. Nor, as Frege noted in section 66 of the *Foundations*, does it enable us to eliminate the phrase "the number belonging to" from all contexts in which it occurs, in particular not from those of the form "x = the number belonging to F."

Well. Neither Frege nor Dedekind showed arithmetic to be part of logic. Nor did Russell. Nor did Zermelo or von Neumann. Nor did the author of *Tractatus* 6.02 or his follower Church. They merely shed light on it.

Appendix: Arithmetic in the *Foundations*

Hume's Principle: $\#F = \#G \leftrightarrow F \approx G$.

Def. $0 = \#[x : x \neq x]$. (*Foundations*, 74)

1. $\#F = 0 \leftrightarrow \forall x \neg Fx$. (75)

Proof. Since $0 = \#[x : x \neq x]$, $\#F = 0$ iff $F \approx [x : x \neq x]$. Since $\forall x \neg x \neq x$, $F \approx [x : x \neq x]$ iff $\forall x \neg Fx$.

Def. mPn iff $\exists F \exists y (Fy \wedge \#F = n \wedge \#[x : Fx \wedge x \neq y] = m)$. (76)

2. mPn and $m'Pn' \to (m = m' \leftrightarrow n = n')$. (78.5)

Proof. Suppose mPn and $m'Pn'$. Let F, y, F', y' be as in the definition of P. Suppose $m = m'$. Then $\#[x : Fx \wedge x \neq y] = \#[x : F'x \wedge x \neq y']$, whence $[x : F'x \wedge x \neq y'] \approx [x : F'x \wedge x \neq y']$ via some ϕ. Since Fy and $F'y'$, $F \approx F'$ via $\phi \cup \{< y, y' >\}$ and then $n = \#F = \#F' = n'$. Conversely, suppose $n = n'$. Then since $\#F = \#F'$, $F \approx F'$ via some ψ. For some unique x, $x\psi y'$; for some unique x', $y\psi x'$. Let

$$\phi = ((\psi - \{< x, y' > , < y, x' >\}) \cup \{< x, x' >\}) - \{< y, y' >\}.$$

Then $[x : Fx \wedge x \neq y] \approx [x : F'x \wedge x \neq y']$ via ϕ and $m = m'$. (Since x and x' might be identical with y and y', it is necessary to include "$-\{< y, y' >\}$" in the definition of ϕ.)

3. $\neg mP0$. (78.6?)

Proof. Otherwise for some y, Fy and $\#F = 0$, contra 1.

Def. xR^*y iff $\forall F(\forall a \forall b([(a = x \vee Fa) \wedge aRb] \to Fb) \to Fy)$. (79)

Thus to show that $xR^*y \to \ldots y \ldots$, it suffices to let $F = [z : \ldots z \ldots]$, assume $a = x \vee Fa$ and aRb, and show Fb.

4. $xRy \to xR^*y$. (*Begriffsschrift*, 91)

Proof. Suppose xRy and $\forall a \forall b([(a = x \vee Fa) \wedge aRb] \to Fb)$. Then Fy follows, if we let $a = x$ and $b = y$.

5. $xR^*y \wedge yR^*z \to xR^*z$. (*Begriffsschrift*, 98)

Proof. Suppose xR^*y, yR^*z, and (*) $\forall a \forall b([(a = x \vee Fa) \wedge aRb] \to Fb)$. Show Fz. Since yR^*z, it suffices to show $\forall a \forall b([(a = y \vee Fa) \wedge aRb] \to$

Fb). Suppose $(a = y \lor Fa)$ and aRb. Show Fb. Since xR^*y, by (*) Fy. We may thus suppose Fa. But then by (*) we are done.

6. $xP^*n \to \exists m\, mPn \land \forall m(mPn \to [xP^*m \lor x = m])$.

Proof. Let $F = [z : \exists m\, mPz \land \forall m(mPz \to [xP^*m \lor x = m])]$. Suppose $a = x \lor Fa, aPb$. Show Fb. Since $aPb, \exists m\, mPb$. Suppose mPb. By 2, $m = a$. If $a = x, x = m$, and we are done. So suppose Fa. Then for some $m', m'Pa$, and xP^*m' or $x = m'$. Since $m'Pa = m, m'Pm$. If xP^*m', then $xP^*m'Pm$, whence by 4 and 5, xP^*m; if $x = m', xPm$, whence by 4, xP^*m.

7. $0P^*n \to \neg\, nP^*n$. (83)

Proof. Let $F = [z : \neg\, zP^*z]$. Suppose $a = 0 \lor Fa, aPb$. Show Fb. Suppose bP^*b. By 6, $bP^*a \lor b = a$, whence by 4 and 5, aP^*a, contra Fa. Thus $a = 0, 0P^*0$, and by 6, $\exists m\, mP0$, contra 3.

Defs. $m \leq n$ iff $mP^*n \lor m = n$. Finite n iff $0 \leq n$.

8. $mPn \land 0P^*n \to \forall x(x \leq m \leftrightarrow x \leq n \land x \neq n)$. (83)

Proof. Suppose $mPn, 0P^*n$. If $xP^*m \lor x = m$, then xP^*n, by 4 and 5; and by 7, $x \neq n$. If $x \leq n$ and $x \neq n$, then xP^*n, and by 6, $x \leq m$. ("$0P^*n$" cannot be dropped: if $n = $ Frege's ∞_1, i.e., $\#[x : 0 \leq x]$, then nPn but $x \leq n$ iff $x = n$.)

9. $mPn \land 0P^*n \to \#[x : x \leq m]P\#[x : x \leq n]$. (82)

Proof. Suppose $mPn, 0P^*n$. By 8, $[x : x \leq m] \approx [x : x \leq n \land x \neq n]$; since $n \leq n, \#[x : x \leq m]P\#[x : x \leq n]$.

10. $mPn \to (0 \leq m \land mP\#[x : x \leq m] \to 0 \leq n \land nP\#[x : x \leq n])$. (82)

Proof. Suppose $mPn, 0 \leq m$. By 4 and 5, $0P^*n$. Thus $0 \leq n$. Suppose $mP\#[x : x \leq m]$. By 2, $\#[x : x \leq m] = n$. By 9, $nP\#[x : x \leq n]$.

11. $0P\#[x : x \leq 0]$. (82)

Proof. Let $F = [x : x \leq 0]$. $F0$; but by 6, if $xP^*0, \exists m\, mP0$, contra 3. Thus $\forall x\, \neg(Fx \land x \neq 0)$; and by 1, $\#[x : Fx \land x \neq 0] = 0$, whence $0P\#[x : x \leq 0]$.

12. $0 \leq n \to 0 \leq n \land nP\#[x : x \leq n]$.

Proof. If $0 = n$, done by 11. Supppose $0P^*n$. Let $F = [z : 0 \leq z \land zP\#[x : x \leq z]]$. Suppose $m = 0 \lor Fm$ and mPn. Show Fn. If $m = 0$, by 11, Fm. And then by 10, Fn.

13. Finite $n \to nP\#[x : x \leq n]$. (83)

Proof. By 12.

Notes

1 A similar observation is found in section 13 of Bolzano's *Paradoxes of the Infinite* (Leipzig, 1851). (Footnote by Dedekind.)

2 α states that the successor of a number is a number; β, that 1 is a number and that mathematical induction holds of the numbers; γ, that 1 is not the successor of a number; and δ, that successor is one-one.

3 In "Logic [1897]," in Gottlob Frege, *Posthumous Writings*, ed. H. Hermes, F. Kambartel, and F. Kaulbach (Chicago: University of Chicago Press, 1979), 136. I am grateful to Arnold Koslow for telling me of this quotation.

4 For a more detailed account of this notion, see Parsons's "Structuralist View of Mathematics," cited below.

5 Charles D. Parsons, "The Structuralist View of Mathematics," *Synthese*. In press.

6 We didn't need it for the other half, since we are there entitled to *assume* that there is a system satisfying $\alpha, \beta, \gamma, \delta(N, s, 1)$. *Was sind* proves that this assumption could have been replaced by the assumption that there is an infinite set.

7 Parsons, "The Structuralist View of Mathematics."

8 Is it possible to say what logicism is without using intensional notions like *part* or *content*?

9 *Treatise*, I, III, I, para. 5.

10 "$F \approx G$" abbreviates the second-order formula: $\exists\phi(\forall x[Fx \rightarrow \exists y(Gy \& \phi xy)] \& \forall y[Gy \rightarrow \exists x(Fx \& \phi xy)] \& \forall x\forall x'\forall y\forall y'[\phi xy \& \phi x'y' \rightarrow (x = x' \leftrightarrow y = y')])$.

11 Cf. Paul Benacerraf, "Frege: The Last Logicist," *Midwest Studies in Philosophy VI*, ed. P. French, T. Uehling, and H. Wettstein (Minneapolis: University of Minnesota Press, 1981), 17–35.

12 In Gottlob Frege, *Philosophical and Mathematical Correspondence*, ed. G. Gabriel et al. (Chicago: University of Chicago Press, 1980), 172.

13 On hearing me say what I meant by "Hume's principle," a *very* famous philosopher exclaimed, "But that's just a *definition*!"

14 *Journal of Philosophy* 81 (1984), 138.

15 A less natural example to the same purpose, but one that is less heavily dependent on set theory, is the following. Abbreviate: $(\exists x\exists y[x \neq y \wedge Fx \wedge Fy] \vee \exists x\exists y[x \neq y \wedge Gx \wedge Gy]) \rightarrow \forall x(Fx \leftrightarrow Gx)$ as: F Equ G. Equ is an equivalence relation. The principle: $\forall F\forall G(^\frown F =^\frown G$ iff F Equ $G)$ is evidently satisfiable in all domains containing one or two members. It is, however, satisfiable in no domain containing *three* or more members and is therefore inconsistent with Hume's principle. For suppose that $a \neq b \neq c \neq a$. Define Rx as follows: If $x \neq a, b, c$, then Rx iff for some F, $x =^\frown F$ and $\neg Fx$; but if x is one of a, b, c, then let $Ra, Rb, \neg Rc$ hold if none of a, b, c is $^\frown F$ for some F such that $Fa, Fb, \neg Fc$; otherwise let $Ra, \neg Rb, Rc$ hold if none of a, b, c is $^\frown F$, for some F such that $Fa, \neg Fb, Fc$; otherwise let $\neg Ra, Rb, Rc$ hold if none of a, b, c is $^\frown F$, for some F such that $\neg Fa, Fb, Fc$; otherwise let Ra, Rb, Rc hold. Then $\exists x\exists y(x \neq y \wedge Rx \wedge Ry)$. Let $d = ^\frown R$. If $d =^\frown F$, then by the principle, $\forall x(Rx \leftrightarrow Fx)$. Thus $d \neq a, b, c$. If Rd, then for some F, $d =^\frown F$ and $\neg Fd$. But then $\forall x(Rx \leftrightarrow Fx)$ and Fd. Thus $\neg Rd$. So $\forall F(d =^\frown F \rightarrow Fd)$, whence Rd, contradiction.

16 Cf. Allen Hazen's review of Crispin Wright's *Frege's Conception of Numbers as Objects*, cited below. Hazen's review is in *Australasian Journal of Philosophy* 63 (1985), 251–4.

17 *Frege's Conception of Numbers as Objects* (Aberdeen: Aberdeen University Press, 1983), 153.

18 Ibid.

19 Ibid.

13

Doing what one ought to do

RUTH ANNA PUTNAM

Our teacher, Hilary Putnam's and mine, Hans Reichenbach used to speak of a gap between knowledge and action. When I asked myself how we bridge that gap, I remembered Hume's claim that neither reason nor understanding but only passion leads to action. I want to argue in this essay for the claim that often, not always, 'passions' – emotions, feelings, positive and negative attitudes – of various sorts carry us from knowledge to action. In other cases the gap is bridged by habits, by certain virtues. I shall be concerned in particular with the question of how we bridge the gap between knowledge (moral or otherwise) and *moral* action. I do not mean to suggest that there is a hard and fast line to be drawn between moral concerns and other concerns. Willful inefficiency may amount to injustice toward those who suffer as a result; an attractively served meal may be how one shows appreciation or compassion. Nevertheless there is the somewhat amorphous field of morality. Moral judgments have to do with the good life, right actions, virtuous characters, the sort of communities or societies in which people can live those lives, develop those characters, and act rightly without too much difficulty. Morality applies to human beings. To be sure, the *objects* of our morality are various: Even if one does not want to speak of animal rights, one has to acknowledge that we have duties toward animals; nor are all our duties toward nature simply duties toward future generations of human beings. The primary sense of moral terms, however, is the sense in which they apply to human beings. Though animals have virtues and vices – there are faithful dogs, fiercely protective lionesses, cruel cats, and timid birds – their virtues and vices are simplified versions of ours. As far as we know, the faithful dog does not reflect, is limited in his range of faithful behavior, and experiences fewer conflicts than a human friend. Animals may obey or disobey our commands, but if they disobey it is our fault more than

As always, I was greatly helped by the patient and wise advice of my colleague Owen Flanagan. I was also helped at an early stage of the project by a conversation with T. Scanlon.

theirs: We didn't train them properly. Animals are not properly moral agents; they lack autonomy. Someone might say that we apply moral terms also to God. But nothing I have to say depends on the difficult question of how we are to understand such talk; so I shall ignore this possibility. That leaves us with moral judgments made by and applied to human beings, and with the moral lives to which they are supposed to lead. Although not all moral judgments are commandments, imperatives, or prescriptions, and not all ethical theories regard these kinds of judgments as fundamental, these are the judgments that seem most directly tied to action. I want to consider, therefore, the questions both of how we come to know what we ought to, or must, do and of how knowing what one ought to do becomes doing it.

I

Practical reasoning leads to conclusions of the form

(1) I (you) ought to (must) do A.

Practical reasoning begins with premises of all sorts. It is a mistake to believe that all practical reasoning must rest on evaluative premises; it is also a mistake to believe that all value-judgments are intended to be prescriptive. In short, the fact-value distinction is not the descriptive-prescriptive distinction. I shall argue for this claim for the most part indirectly, that is, by exhibiting some modes of practical reasoning.

It is easy to see that not all value-judgments are prescriptive. Bach's Brandenburg concerti are magnificent, among the best pieces of music ever composed; but that is not to say that a contemporary composer should attempt to write music in the baroque style. Of course, that the concerti are magnificent is a reason for listening to them, but not everything one has a reason to do is something one ought to do or must do; not all reasons for action are prescriptions.

Even moral judgments, when they are not in the form of "ought"-statements or imperatives, may fail to be prescriptive.

(2) The slave-owning signers of the Declaration of Independence were hypocrites.

does not impose any obligation on anyone now living. It may be an expression of shock, of disillusionment, of anger by someone who, for the first time, reflects on the fact that a slaveholder affirmed the equality of all men. One may be moved to moral judgment when one has no intention to influence behavior, or, again, when one has no hope of doing so. It is, however, not difficult to imagine contexts in which (2), though not prescriptive, is intended to influence attitudes and conduct. If a teacher were to remark (2) as part of a history lesson, she would thereby draw attention to the discrepancy between the words of the Declaration and the conduct of, say, Jefferson. Of course, there would be no discrepancy if "all men" were understood to refer to white men only. So the teacher indicates at least that distinctions of color or continent of origin are morally irrelevant. That may suggest that certain other distinctions, of gender or religion, for example, are also morally irrelevant. That a distinction is morally irrelevant is part of what Hilary Putnam calls a moral image of the world,[1] part of the way one sees human beings, and that in turn is part of one's character and influences one's conduct. On this scenario, when the teacher utters (2) she hopes indeed to guide the future conduct of her pupils; but she neither prescribes nor proscribes anything. Alternatively, we may suppose that the egalitarian moral image is taken for granted; the emphasis is on "hypocrite." Describing affirmations of principles inconsistent with one's conduct as hypocritical is to condemn such affirmings; here proscription follows virtually immediately.

Sometimes quite simple descriptions lead naturally and directly to prescriptions. Thus the observation

(3) Your car is almost out of gas.

leads, in normal situations (there are gas stations, you are able to pay for gas) and given normal motivations (you are willing to pay for gas, you don't want to find yourself stranded), directly to

(4) You (I) must stop at the next gas station.

In fact, (3) may lead directly to your driving into the next station; we do not always say to ourselves "I ought to ..." or "I must ... ". When an old person drops her gloves, we pick them up without thinking "I ought ... "; but for the time being I am interested in cases where our thinking issues in a thought of that form. Although passage from (3) to (4) is immediate, arguments leading from description to prescription may be of great complexity; one need only contemplate the thought that led Marx from his knowledge of the misery of industrial workers to "Workers of the world, unite." Equally apt examples come from science, where a long chain of reasoning leads from a hypothesis to the design of an experiment. Having designed the experiment, the scientist may then say to herself that the experiment ought to be carried out. Analogously a former pupil of the teacher in my first example may say to herself that she ought to adopt a minority recruitment program in her company.

The former pupil arrives at her 'prescription' on the basis of some facts about the economic plight of minorities and its relation to personal and institutional racism; but not everyone shares her conclusion.

Her thought is shaped by the moral image of the world that she acquired (at least in part) from her teacher. Scientists design experiments and resolve to perform them because they have an image of the nature of science, of how the virtues of accuracy and intellectual honesty and the ideals of knowledge and clarity and the scientists' position in the culture and their relation to nature hang together.

I have repeatedly spoken of moral images, and I have just adapted Hilary Putnam's description of a moral image of the world to the case of the scientist's image of science. I have suggested that our moral images inform our practical reasoning, that they enable us to move from descriptive premises to prescriptive conclusions. It is time to explore this notion.

Hilary Putnam introduced the notion of a moral image when he wanted to develop internal realism for ethics.

A moral image, in the sense in which I am using the term, is not a declaration that this or that is a virtue, or that this or that is what one ought to do; it is rather a picture of how our virtues and ideals hang together with one another and of what they have to do with the position we are in. It may be as vague as the notions of "sisterhood and brotherhood"; indeed, millions of human beings have found in those metaphors moral images that could organize their moral lives – and this notwithstanding the enormous problem of interpreting them and of deciding what could possibly make them **effective**. (51; Hilary Putnam's bold type)

I do not think that the notion of a moral image is quite as clearly developed as one would like. A moral image may be an ideal; but not every ideal is a moral image. "To describe an ideal as a moral image is to say that it is far more than a characterization of some one trait or some one mode of behavior as virtuous" (61). The Kantian moral image, which is one that Hilary Putnam finds very attractive, is said to be "a vision which includes and organizes a complex system of values" (62). But, though he characterized moral images as pictures or visions, he lists "the system of beliefs which constitutes the tradition of civic republicanism" and "the metaphor of the human 'family'" as other examples of moral images. Still later, he refers to "the statements we make using the language of one or another such moral image" (78), or speaks of moral images as "philosophical anthropology" (57, 62). The notion of a moral image that emerges from this for me is this. A moral image is not a single value-judgment, but it is not a complete morality (a list of virtues, a description of the good life, a set of commandments or moral laws) either; for we are told that "a genuine morality must always reflect a substantial moral image" (61). A morality, I take it, goes beyond a moral image in articulating how that moral image is to be made effective. Still a moral image, or at least a substantial part of one, may be articulated in a set of statements. Such articulation seems to be called for by the fact that

rational criticism of a moral vision is possible. A moral vision may contradict, for example, what we know or think it rational to believe on other grounds, be they logical, metaphysical, or empirical. (86)

Nevertheless, we must take seriously Hilary Putnam's use of expressions like "picture" and "vision." It seems to me, as I believe it seems to him, that we can never completely articulate a moral image. A moral image is a way of seeing the world, in particular other human beings and our relations to them. If one sees women as permanently immature creatures, unable to cope with matters of finance or politics, one may put them on a pedestal but one will not allow them to manage their money and deny them the suffrage. In other words, one's moral image shapes one's appreciation of the facts just as a scientist's sense of relevance and importance shapes her appreciation of the evidence. Beyond that, our moral images are what enables us to move from the facts so described to prescriptive conclusions. One might, for example, grant that women are as competent as men but fail to recognize the relevance of that fact to the economic or political rights of women. On the other hand, one might regard the question of competence beyond a minimal level as irrelevant to questions of economic or political rights.

That a moral image is not simply a set of beliefs should not be surprising. The virtues too are not sets of beliefs. Both moral images and the virtues involve ways of apprehending the world. These can be learned and criticized; but what is learned is not a set of 'designation rules' and criticism does not take the form of refuting a premise by showing that it leads to false conclusions. Rather we are prompted by our virtues to act, or we are led by our moral images to conclude that we ought to act in certain ways and (not always) we do so act. Those actions and the moral emotions that accompany them and their results seem to me to play the role for ethics that experiment and observation-play in science. These are the places where the web of belief – beliefs concerning facts and beliefs concerning values – is anchored in experience, and these experiences may move us to change not only our explicit premises, as Morton White has argued, but our ways of thinking, our moral images.[2] But, Hilary Putnam warns us,

we cannot any longer hope that these kinds of criticism will leave just **one** moral vision intact. Ultimately, there is still one point at which one has to say: "This is where my spade is turned." (86; Hilary Putnam's bold type)

Still, even one's most fundamental moral visions and beliefs may be upset. William James, speaking of habits rather than images but having in mind just such radical changes as I am here contemplating, wrote:

Now life abounds in [new experiences], and sometimes they are such critical and revolutionary experiences that they change a man's whole scale of
values and system of ideas. In such cases, the old order of his habits will be
ruptured: and if the new motives are lasting, new habits will be formed, and
build up in him a new and regenerate "nature."[3]

II

I suggested that images of the world underlie our practical reasoning,
and when that reasoning concerns our moral lives they are properly
moral images. By asking how we come to move from knowledge to
action, I also suggested that the conclusions of such reasoning constitute knowledge. That view has been challenged. In particular, it has
been said that there are two types of 'imperatives', hypothetical (or
technical) imperatives, which can be known, and categorical imperatives, which cannot. Hilary Putnam's concluding argument in *The Many
Faces of Realism* was intended to show that "the hypothetical imperative is in the same situation as the categorical, that rationality is as
difficult a thing to 'explain' in both cases" (80). That rationality is a
difficult thing to explain in both cases is only one of the ways in which
the two types of imperatives turn out to be in the same situation. I shall
now suggest some others.

Hypothetical imperatives are said to be knowable because they rest
on causal connections, on the claim that the action A is a means (an
efficient, or the most efficient means) to some end E; but nothing is
said about the desirability of E. In his response to Morton White,
speaking in particular of epistemic values and norms, Quine states the
view I wish to rebut: "The normative, here as elsewhere in engineering,
becomes descriptive when the terminal parameter is expressed."[4] But
this is not so. Consider:

(5) If you want your friends to trust you, you must be loyal and honest.

This looks like

(6) If you want a bountiful harvest, you must use fertilizer.

I do not deny that (6) is as knowable, as warranted, as is

(7) Other things equal, fertilized soil will bring forth a more bountiful
harvest than unfertilized soil.

(7) may well serve as paradigmatic for the sort of scientific, or factual,
or descriptive means-ends statements that are said to support hypothet-

ical imperatives. But (5) is analogously based on

(8) People who are loyal and honest are generally trusted by their friends.

Loyalty and honesty are notions that are both descriptive and evaluative. Honesty is not just truth telling, it is good or appropriate truth telling. One has grasped the notion of truth telling only when one is able to determine what constitutes "*good* truth telling" in at least some novel situations. I had occasion some years ago to read what physicians have written about truth telling to patients. There is not only the question of how much to tell the patient under what circumstances – one does not want to frighten a person about to undergo major surgery, but one needs to receive *informed* consent – but also the question of how to tell it (gently or bluntly). Finally the words one chooses depend on what one believes the patient will make of them. There was considerable debate because physicians found themselves in a new situation, a situation in which they were supposed to be honest with their patients rather than paternalistically secretive. Loyalty is a virtue, it is one of the more difficult virtues. It is difficult to know what loyalty requires and it is difficult to be loyal. Honesty is only slightly less problematic, and there may be conflicts between loyalty and honesty as well as between loyalties. To tell someone to be honest and loyal is not like telling them to spread fertilizer, whether or not either is put hypothetically or categorically.

I do not, of course, deny the truth of (8) or that it supports (5). Rather, I wish to point out that

(9) Be loyal to your friends and honest.

does not become "descriptive when the terminal parameter is expressed" (as in [5]) because our vocabulary cannot be neatly divided into a descriptive and a prescriptive part.

Someone might reply to my argument by saying that what is important is neither the form nor the content of the practical conclusion but the thought that leads to it. Thus Quine writes that we could say that morality becomes descriptive when the terminal parameter is expressed "if we could view it as aimed at reward in heaven."[5] Since the hypothetical imperative gives advice on how to reach certain ends without raising any questions about the legitimacy of those ends, the thought process seems to follow a familiar pattern. One simply finds out what means lead to the desired end. But matters aren't quite that simple. There are costs associated with those means; there are also risks; one's values and, again, one's moral image may be involved. Success in, say, business may be achieved by a combination of talent and hard work, it may be aided by daring *or* by ruthlessness. Here I am reminding us that the purely 'technical' hypothetical imperative – the manual for fixing the car – is simply one extreme of a continuum near the other end of which one wonders how to guarantee adequate healthcare for all, or how to develop one's artistic talent to the fullest extent. The means that one finally concludes are the best means to that end must cohere with all one's values. It may, of course, be the case that no such means can be found. Then one may either abandon the goal, or change one's values. That is one way in which one may find oneself confronting a moral dilemma, but moral dilemmas are not as pervasive in our moral lives as philosophers sometimes suggest. If the means one has found do cohere with one's values, there is the question whether one is capable of carrying them out. If not, one may abandon one's goal, although in more technical cases – fixing the car – one can transfer the task to another person. The fact that one's values other than the particular end to which one is seeking the means are involved in the thinking that leads to the hypothetical imperative shows, once again, that the hypothetical imperative does not differ interestingly from the categorical.

Finally it may be said that hypothetical imperatives do not require action. That is most clearly seen in the case of the most clearly technical imperatives. Nothing obliges me to cook any dish in the cookbook I received as a wedding gift. If there's never a leak in the fuel line of my car, no one will follow the service manual's directions for replacing it. Only categorical imperatives require action; hypothetical imperatives become categorical if the hypothesis is satisfied. Categorical imperatives, in the Kantian sense, are 'hypotheticals' whose protasis is always true. Of course, Kant held that hypothetical imperatives were known a posteriori while categorical imperatives were known a priori, but the important point was that categorical imperatives were absolutely binding while one could always choose not to fall under a hypothetical imperative. Much has been written in recent years against the notion that moral considerations trump all others. Philippa Foot has expressed her rejection of that notion by saying that moral imperatives are hypothetical.[6] Bernard Williams rejects the "morality system," a system of ethical thought that makes the notion of moral obligation central and inescapable.[7] Of course, Williams does not reject morality in the sense in which I have employed the term, that is, what he calls the ethical life. But he denies, among other things, that the distinction between hypothetical and categorical imperatives marks a difference between ethical and non-ethical obligation. There is, he points out, practical necessity – the conclusion that one must, unconditionally, do something – but practical necessity is not peculiar to ethics.

What is at issue here is, once again, not the form of the practical, action-requiring conclusion but rather what sorts of considerations are relevant to reaching it. To say that moral considerations do not (always) override all others means that moral considerations sometimes do, and should, give way to other considerations.

Most of us, as Philippa Foot points out, spend some money frivolously without feeling the least bit guilty, although we are aware that the money could be spent to alleviate some real suffering, nor do we blame our friends for behaving in the same way. Clearly, it would be sheer hypocrisy to say that we actually conclude in these cases that we ought to forgo the expensive restaurant and send the money thereby saved to our favorite famine relief organization. But it is not as clear to me as it seems to be to Foot and Williams that this is to be welcomed. There are, they would surely agree, many times when one wishes that people were less self-centered, less blindly devoted to some cause, less mindlessly chauvinistic, in other words, when one wishes that moral considerations were, for these people and in these cases, overriding.

It is also true, as both Foot and Williams point out, that not all moral considerations take the form of obligations. Any account of our moral lives – our reasons and reasonings, our reactions and motivations, our deeds and our failures – which focuses only on obligations must be utterly inadequate for a variety of reasons. In particular, as we learned from Williams, any adequate theory must acknowledge that people have projects and ideals that give shape and coherence to their lives, that define who they are. Such projects and ideals make demands that override not only the agent's own lesser, temporary desires, they also drown out many demands that others make on the agent. But just as most people do not give up "everything" for their major goals – one must relax sometimes, one is entitled to have some fun – so one's projects must give way sometimes to the claims of others. One should not pursue one's projects or ideals so singlemindedly that one fails to respond to even the most urgent demands of one's family; but if one is too open to the requests of family, friends, neighbors, and 'good causes', one's own projects will come to nought. Finding a proper balance and maintaining it is a mark of the morally wise agent. I am not sure that we are aided in our search for that balance either by affirming or by denying that moral considerations are overriding. We are better off reminding ourselves that moral considerations come in many guises. Some moral considerations are omni-overriding, some carry little weight, most fall in between, overriding some non-moral considerations and being overridden by others.

The issue of the hypothetical imperative was raised because it is said that hypothetical imperatives are knowable while categorical ones are not because the latter insofar as they are based on reasons are based on evaluative premises. I have now shown that hypothetical imperatives may also be the result of reasoning involving moral considerations and that they may prescribe behavior that requires moral sensitivity and moral effort. It does not follow, however, that hypothetical, or indeed categorical, imperatives are not knowable or not objective. There is moral knowledge, but this is not the place to defend that claim.[8] Here it suffices to point out that skepticism in ethics as elsewhere is the result of believing that there can be no knowledge without foundations but despairing of there being such. Hilary Putnam has taught us that there are no foundations either in science or in ethics but that being without foundation does not condemn us to skepticism or relativism. Instead he offers us internal realism, the view that we cannot say what is true or false independent of any conceptual scheme but that within a given conceptual scheme questions of truth and falsehood are not "up to us." In ethics that means that our moral judgments are shaped by our moral images of the world and by the world. There is no description of the world as it would appear if one had no moral point of view at all. This does not mean simply that we would not engage in moral reflection if we did not care, if there were not things we value, though that too is true. It means that when we engage in moral reflection we do so neither with an empty mind nor with a set of universal or eternal values firmly engraved. The difference I have in mind here is a difference that Dewey marked by contrasting valuing with evaluation, or prizing with appraising. Needs, wants, desires, even whims give rise to valuing; we come to evaluate as we learn we can't satisfy all our desires, as we come to reflect and ultimately to sacrifice some for the sake of others. But all that is for the most part a social rather than an individual enterprise. Individual agents' evaluations employ the categories of their societies and are shaped, but not determined, by the prevalent values and moral images. Still, the emphasis here needs to be as much on "not determined" as on "shaped." Good parents and good teachers teach not only their values but also how to be critical. Moral reformers could not arise if one could not in some sense stand outside one's own tradition, nor could we otherwise understand and learn from other traditions. Appreciating other traditions is easier for us if it is part of our own to respect them and to cherish our own within reason.

III

It is time, finally, to ask how we come to act, in particular how we come to do what we ought to do. Let us begin, however, with cases where the thought 'I ought' does not occur. You tell me that you are thirsty. I say,

"There's iced tea in the refrigerator." Either you get up and get some, or you say, "May I have some, please," and I get up and get you some. Now, certainly, you do not think either that you ought to get up and get yourself some tea or that you ought to ask me to get you some; you just do one or the other. Nor, when I heard you, did I think that I ought to tell you about the tea – though, if I don't tell you (because it slipped my mind, say) I might later think that I should have told you. Even when I get up to bring you the tea, it is unlikely that I have the thought 'I ought...'. This is a simple, mundane case of action prompted by knowledge (that you are thirsty, that there is tea, etc.). What moves you to action is your thirst, your wanting something to drink. What moves me is not so clear; some low-grade fellow feeling or a habit of obliging will suffice.

Your action is a simple case of action prompted by some want, need, desire. In other cases there may be much deliberation (e.g., when fixing a car), and that deliberation may eventuate in the thought that one ought to do such and such (remove that bolt and replace that gadget with a new one); but the move from that thought to doing it is prompted by the same want that prompted the deliberation; no new explanation is called for.

My action in bringing you the tea is also a simple case of virtuous action though, the effort being small and that amount of helpfulness being quite common, it doesn't suffice to certify me as a virtuous or even as a helpful person. In one sense, virtuous actions are simply habitual actions. Certainly the virtuous person is one who generally acts in the virtuous way in question without moral struggle – one might say 'without thinking' except that in complicated cases there may be much deliberation about means. William James was intensely aware of the extent to which our moral lives are governed by habit. Not only did he write, rather disturbingly, "Habit is thus the enormous fly-wheel of society, its most precious conservative agent." He also asserted:

No matter how full a reservoir of *maxims* one may possess, and no matter how good one's *sentiments* may be, if one have not taken advantage of every concrete opportunity to *act*, one's character may remain entirely unaffected for the better.... There is no more contemptible type of human character than that of the nerveless sentimentalist and dreamer, who spends his life in a weltering sea of sensibility and emotion, but who never does a manly concrete deed.[9]

One should act at every opportunity in order to build up the habit; given the habit, less 'passion' is required to carry us from knowledge to action. A generous and compassionate person responds to appeals from

Amnesty International with little reflection and no moral struggle. Her compassion and her habits of giving combine to move her from the knowledge of the plight of political prisoners to the action. An equally compassionate person who has not developed the virtue of generosity may act only after much inner struggle. Or, having sighed sadly, she, a contemptible "nerveless sentimentalist," may throw the appeals letter into the wastebasket.

Habit alone, however, is not virtue. The virtues typically involve wisdom, the ability to appreciate that a certain situation calls for a certain type of action. This is where one's moral image becomes once again relevant, for it shapes what one sees, or what one makes of what one sees. Thousands of just and compassionate men for thousands of years made nothing of the sight of prostitution. Given a Kantian moral image, one sees in prostitution a denial of the very humanity of the women; so one seeks to free women from that bondage and to solve their economic problems by other means. Moreover, given a Kantian moral image, one will develop certain virtues (e.g., conscientiousness) and slight others (e.g., humility) that were fostered by a different moral image.

Having said all this, there remains the fact that sometimes we are faced with a moral problem, find that our moral life doesn't run smoothly. There are, first of all, cases of ordinary temptations, cases where our virtue, whatever virtue is relevant, wasn't quite firm enough from other considerations coming to mind, blocking the smooth running of the habit. (As if one were to begin to think about how one walks: Immediately one begins to falter, and it is difficult then to stop the thought and resume walking.) Think of the temptation to cancel your classes because an old friend has come to town. Here one doesn't have to go through very much thinking, still one reflects and concludes that one must teach one's classes. And then it may happen that one just picks up the phone, calls one's secretary and says, "Please cancel my classes." Here, surely, it is longing to be with the friend, or regret over what would be a lost opportunity that overwhelms one's sense of responsibility. But then, likewise, in the case where one sticks to one's moral resolution it is that sense of responsibility, that caring for one's students (or that caring for one's self-image as a conscientious teacher?) that overwhelms those other feelings.

More interestingly, our moral lives may come to something like a halt. (Not as if one were suddenly thinking about walking but as if one's walk had led one to the edge of an abyss or in front of an impenetrable wall.) Perhaps the projects that have governed our lives or the ideals we have pursued are called into question. (An artist comes to question her talent, a dedicated Communist learns of Stalin's crimes.) Perhaps doing what we have done for years without effort suddenly becomes difficult. (Taking care of a spouse who has suffered a stroke makes demands that marriage in normal circumstances did not.) Sometimes there are the conflicts of duty that philosophers love to talk about, or our virtues pull us in opposite directions. In those cases one must deliberate, one considers the alternatives. One asks what the consequences will be; one wonders whether one could justify to oneself and to others what one proposes to do (especially if things should turn out badly); one questions whether one would or could wish others (everyone?) to act according to one's maxim; one examines oneself, asking whether one is capable of acting that way; one seeks considerations to throw into the balance (other values, other things one cares about). Finally one ends up with a new project, an alternative ideal, new practical 'oughts' and acts on them; or exhausted, one just goes on in the old way; or, rarely, one commits suicide. But I am interested in the first alternative. What prompts those deliberations is more than intellectual curiosity; rather, there is concern, there may be disappointment, even grief, or frustration, perhaps a sense of failure, or anger, or love. Any one of these, and no doubt others, causes us to take note, to reflect, to take a new resolve. Here too, as in the case of overcoming temptation, effort is required to act on that resolve and perhaps, as James suggests, to establish new habits, acquire new virtues. That effort comes from some of the same emotions that prompted the deliberation.

Needless to say, emotions do not always prompt deliberation, they may cause us to rush heedlessly into action. Nor does deliberation always result in a practical ought that is moral. But I want to suggest that we come to deliberate and we come to act on our practical conclusions because we care. It may be simply that we care to be moral, so that we are prompted both to find out what the moral thing to do is and then to do it. Or it may be that we care for a particular person, or for a cause, or for some project of our own; because we care, we are careful of what we do, and so we deliberate. Because we care, we have some strong feelings that enable us to overcome at least some obstacles to carrying out our resolves. So, as Harry Frankfurt has suggested, "there is naturally an intimate connection between what a person cares about and what he will, generally and under certain conditions, think it best for himself to do."[10] Caring, as Frankfurt understands it, is serious, long lasting, akin to love. Being thirsty, or wanting to fix one's car, would not count as caring in Frankfurt's sense. Caring is more closely related to moral questions; indeed, one may say that the moral impinges on non-moral everyday behavior precisely when something we care about conflicts, or seems to conflict, with the everyday routine. Frankfurt is concerned to distinguish questions pertaining to what we

care about from ethical questions; but I am rather inclined to agree
with MacIntyre, who in his comments on Frankfurt's article says:

> To be a mature moral agent is to have educated one's feelings appropriately. It
> is to care the right amount for the right people and things in the right way at
> the right time and place.[11]

If I understand Hilary Putnam's notion of a moral image rightly, a
moral image is a way of seeing our fellow human beings that involves
caring; but who and what we care about and how much depends on the
kind of moral image it happens to be. Or one might say that what we
deeply and persistently care about shapes our moral image. For William
James the beginning of an objective morality lies in people caring for
each other, and it is the belief (but this is not a propositional belief but
a faith, an attitude or sentiment) that we can make a difference that
gives us the energy for what he calls the strenuous moral life.[12] That we
can make a difference will move us only if we care to make a difference.

In the morally difficult cases the question how we bridge the gap
between knowledge and action is the question how we move from 'I
ought to A' to A-ing, where the sense of 'ought' is that discussed by
Bernard Williams in his articles "Internal and External Reasons,"
"*Ought* and Moral Obligation," and "Practical Necessity."[13] There he
points out that this final 'ought' of practical deliberation constitutes for
the agent a reason for A-ing. A-ing will be the best thing she can do to
further her aims, and sometimes – and then we say 'I must' – A-ing
will be the only thing to do.

Williams has packed into the final ought of deliberation already a
motivation to do A. What one ought to do in this sense is relative to
one's projects, one's goals, one's short- or long-range purposes; it is
what one has most reason to do. But we do not always do what we have
most reasons to do. If you want your toothache to stop for good, then
you ought to go to the dentist. Everyone knows that; so any rational
person will go to the dentist. Anyone who is too cowardly to go is to
that extent irrational. But there is moral cowardice as well, and the
person who fails to stand up for her friend or her cause when the
occasion arises cannot be considered irrational – that is not her failing.
Weakness of will in all its manifestations should not, I think, be
confused with irrationality. For it is not a failure of reason, a mistake in
deliberation; I am inclined to think (with Hume?) that it is a failure of
passion; in my example, love for the friend or commitment to the cause
fails to overcome fear. In short, what moves us to deliberation and from
the result of that to action is caring, and insufficient caring (insufficient
to overcome the internal obstacles) prevents the latter move.

In conclusion I want to return to Hilary Putnam's notion of a moral image. Our moral images shape how we see the world and how we think about what we see, because they reflect what we care about. Because our moral images reflect what we care about, our moral deliberations issue in practical oughts that are conclusive reasons for us. Because we begin with caring, the whole process is so to speak charged with the moral energy that will ultimately carry us from knowledge to action. Hilary Putnam's moral image, which includes the Kantian moral image, the democratic egalitarian image, reflects care about all human beings, about their autonomy, their ability to think for themselves about how they want to live, and about their having the opportunity to realize those wants. If we share that moral image, then we shall be moved to the deliberation that leads to knowledge, and from that to action, whenever we hear what James called the "cries of the wounded." That, I think, is the moral point of *The Many Faces of Realism*.

Notes

1 Hilary Putnam, *The Many Faces of Realism* (LaSalle, Ill.: Open Court 1987), pp. 51ff. Hereafter page references to this text will be given in parentheses.
2 Morton White, "Normative Ethics, Normative Epistemology, and Quine's Holism," in Hahn and Schilpp (eds.), *The Philosophy of V. W. Quine* (La Salle, Ill.: 1986).
3 Williams James, *Talks to Teachers on Psychology and to Students on Some of Life's Ideals* (Cambridge, Mass.: Harvard University Press, 1983), p. 53 (first published 1899).
4 W. V. Quine, "Reply to Morton White," in Hahn and Schilpp (eds.), *The Philosophy of W. V. Quine*, p. 665.
5 Ibid.
6 Philippa Foot, "Morality as a System of Hypothetical Imperatives," *Philosophical Review* (1972); reprinted in her *Virtues and Vices* (Berkeley, Calif.: University of California Press, 1978).
7 Bernard Williams, *Ethics and the Limits of Philosophy* (Cambridge, Mass.: Harvard University Press, 1985), p. 178.
8 For a defense, see my "Weaving Seamless Webs," *Philosophy*, 62 (1987), and the last of Hilary Putnam's Carus Lectures.
9 Both quotations from William James, *The Principles of Psychology* (New York: Dover, 1950), pp. 121 and 125 (first published 1890).
10 Harry G. Frankfurt, "The Importance of What We Care About," *Synthese*, 53:2 (1982), p. 257; reprinted in his *The Importance of What We Care About: Philosophical Essays* (Cambridge: Cambridge University Press, 1988).
11 Alasdair MacIntyre, "Comments on Frankfurt," *Synthese*, 53:2 (1982), p. 292.
12 On the first point, see "The Moral Philosopher and the Moral Life," on the second, "The Dilemma of Determinism," both in William James, *The Will to Believe and Other Essays in Popular Philosophy* (New York: Dover, 1956; first published 1897).
13 All in Bernard Williams, *Moral Luck* (Cambridge: Cambridge University Press, 1981).

14

Closing up the corpses
Diseases of sexuality and the emergence of the psychiatric style of reasoning

ARNOLD I. DAVIDSON

In 1982, when I first drafted this essay, I had very clear memories – memories that have hardly diminished even today – of Hilary Putnam's seminars on problems of realism and rationality. Having attended these seminars throughout the mid and late 1970s, I was still coming to terms with their profound influence on how I conceived of the procedures and aims of philosophical argument. Indeed, Hilary's fall seminar of 1976, in which he worked through the set of topics that produced "Realism and Reason," remains for me one of the sustaining examples of how to teach philosophy. But in addition to absorbing his lectures, articles, and books, I know that I was no less deeply affected by Hilary's philosophical sensibility, especially by his insistence that there was no need to experience any intellectual antagonism between philosophical analysis and historical scholarship. His own capacity and desire to think about and interpret historical texts while at the same time thinking through philosophical problems, allowing each activity to contribute to the success of the other, helped me to realize how I wanted to combine philosophy and history in my own work.

My contribution to this volume takes up issues that go back to Putnam's famous 1962 discussion of analytic and a priori truths in "It Ain't Necessarily So." In a series of papers published in the 1970s, Putnam extends and develops this discussion, and his arguments are directly relevant to my own philosophical motivations in writing a history of the concepts and theories of psychiatry. I offer here an extended case study of the way in which the status of statements is relative to a body of knowledge, what I call a "style of reasoning." More specifically, I want to show that some claims cannot even be conceived without the development of a new style of reasoning. Thus the very possibility of conceiving of certain statements as part of the domain of scientific knowledge depends upon the historically specific formation of new concepts, and new forms of reasoning and argumentation. So I hope to begin to demonstrate how the history of concepts is relevant to problems about the epistemological status of scientific statements.

I

In *The Birth of the Clinic*, Michel Foucault charts the emergence and the effects of the conjunction of pathological anatomy and clinical medicine, and he emphasizes the significance of pathological anatomy as a foundation for the description and classification of diseases.[1] At the beginning of the nineteenth century, assertions like that of Bouillaud in his *Philosophie Médicale* were to determine the fate of medicine:

If there is an axiom in medicine it is certainly the proposition that there is no disease without a seat. If one accepted the contrary opinion, one would also have to admit that there existed functions without organs, which is a palpable absurdity. The determination of the seat of disease or their localization is one of the finest conquests of modern medicine.[2]

The history of this fine conquest is replete with surprises and ironies, the complete story of which still remains to be fully recounted. But we can summarize the hopeful, revolutionary enthusiasm of the pathological anatomists with the words of Bichat:

For twenty years, from morning to night, you have taken notes at patients' bedsides on affections of the heart, the lungs and the gastric viscera, and all is confusion for you in the symptoms which, refusing to yield up their meaning, offer you a succession of incoherent phenomena. Open up a few corpses: you will dissipate at once the darkness that observation alone could not dissipate.[3]

And so Foucault concludes that "the great break in the history of Western medicine dates precisely from the moment clinical experience became the anatomo-clinical gaze."[4]

One of the great breaks in the history of Western psychiatry comes precisely during the time when the anatomo-clinical gaze is in steady decline. The story of psychiatry's emergence, in the nineteenth century, as an autonomous medical discipline, and specifically its autonomy from neurology and cerebral pathology, is, in part, the history of this decline. Pathological anatomy could not serve psychiatry as either an explanatory theory for so-called mental diseases or disorders, or as the foundation for the classification and description of these diseases. But the gradual and virtually anonymous disappearance of pathological anatomy in psychiatry is not merely the history of decline. For with this decline came the proliferation of whole new kinds of diseases and disease categories, a revitalization and reworking of nosologies the consequences of which stamp us even today. Foremost among these new disease categories was the class of functional diseases, of which sexual perversion and hysteria were the two most prominent examples. Although the hope that these functional diseases would yield to pathological anatomy was held out long after there was any evidence for this hope, in clinical practice, and later in theory as well, these diseases were fully describable simply as functional deviations of some kind; in the case of sexual perversion, for instance, one was faced with a functional deviation or abnormality of the sexual instinct. Admitting pure functional deviations as diseases was to create entire new species of diseased individuals, and to radically alter our conceptions of ourselves.

In this essay I focus on the diseases of sexual perversion and try to show how the history of this disease category is intertwined with the fall of pathological anatomy. The results of this history determine some of our concepts of mental disease today, as shown, for example, by the third edition of the diagnostic and statistical manual of the American Psychiatric Association. More important, the effects of this history have helped to determine how we now categorize ourselves, have contributed to our current epistemology of the self. We are all potentially perverts. How has this come to be?

II

It is convenient to divide the history of sexual perversion into three stages, each stage depending upon a different understanding of what these diseases were thought to be diseases of. It is perhaps best to think of each stage as characterized by a different mode or form of explanation, the third stage constituting a decisive break with the first two, since it inaugurates an entirely new style of reasoning about perversion. In the first, most short-lived stage, sexual perversion was thought to be a disease of the reproductive or genital organs, a disease whose basis was some anatomical abnormality of these organs. The second stage, although in clinical practice recognizing perversions to be abnormalities of the sexual instinct, insisted that the psychophysiology of the sexual instinct (and so of its diseases as well) would eventually, with advances in knowledge, come to be understood in terms of the neurophysiology and neuroanatomy of the brain. These first two stages of explanation shared a commitment to the anatomo-pathological style of reasoning. The third stage took perversions to be pure functional deviations of the sexual instinct, not reducible to cerebral pathology. Perversions were to be viewed and treated at the level of psychology, not at the grander level of pathological anatomy. The psychiatric style of reasoning emerged clearly and definitively at this third stage.

Of course, this three-stage structural partition does not precisely coincide with historical chronology; the three forms of explanation were often mixed together, sometimes even in the same article. But they are capable of being distinguished and it will help our understanding to so distinguish them. More specifically, the second and third stages are not separated by some exactly datable dividing line. Indeed, these two stages overlap to such an extent that many of the psychiatrists who are most responsible for our current conception of the perversions were also strongly wedded to the dominance of brain pathology. So that although for analytical and historiographical reasons we must carefully separate these last two stages, as a matter of historical account no such neat division will be found.

In the years between 1870 and 1905 psychiatry was caught between two conceptual grids; in one of which it was aligned with neurology, in the other with psychology. Most psychiatric disease categories, including the perversions, were swept along in this battle over what kind of science psychiatry was to be. The fact that the majority of the great European psychiatrists at the end of the nineteenth century were trained as neurologists meant that they paid at least theoretical homage to their mother discipline. But it was not merely biographical considerations that prompted a constant appeal to the neural sciences. During this span of time, no one really knew what it would mean to conceive of diseases like perversion in purely functional terms. It would be like admitting functions without organs, which, as Bouillaud reminds us, was a palpable absurdity. So the hold of pathological anatomy remained to mask the fact that this palpable absurdity was already reality. In fact, the professions of these brain anatomists in almost no way affected the description and classification of the perversions. From very near the beginning of psychiatry's emergence as an academic discipline, functional diseases were a recognized part of clinical experience. Theories about the neuropathology of the brain had no clinical effects; they were part of an almost useless conceptual space. So although we can, and should, distinguish between perversions as functional deviations ultimately reducible to brain disease and perversions as pure functional diseases, if we look at the *descriptions* of those who advocate these second and third modes of explanation, they are practically identical. The real break, the new style of reasoning, is to be located at that point when the sexual instinct and its functional diseases were introduced together. Functional diseases were diseases of something – not an organ, but an instinct.[5]

III

In one of the earliest articles on what we have come to call perversion, probably the earliest article in French, Dr. Michea takes up the case of

Sergeant Bertrand, accused of having violated female cadavers.[6] Although like all of the discussions prior to 1870, Michea is concerned primarily with the question of Bertrand's legal and moral responsibility for his actions, his article is distinguished by the fact that he does consider, in passing, the classification of what he names *les déviations maladives de l'appétit vénérien*. He classifies these deviations into four kinds, in order of their frequency: first, Greek love, the love of an individual for someone of his own sex; second, bestiality; third, the attraction for an inanimate object; and fourth, the attraction for human cadavers.[7] Michea's paper is significant in that he argues that Bertrand suffers not from vampirism or destructive monomania but from some deviation of the venereal appetite, some kind of erotic monomania. Arguments of this type were crucial in providing grounds for isolating diseases of sexuality as distinct morbid entities, and thus not reducing them to mere effects of other, prior disease processes. But for our purposes, the most interesting aspect of Michea's short paper is his discussion and explanation of "Greek love," to which he devotes, by far, the greatest space. (Indeed, Michea claims that there is only one previous case in judicial records of the attraction for human cadavers, the disease from which Bertrand is supposed to suffer.) After arguing that Greek love should be considered an unhealthy deviation of the venereal appetite, Michea wonders what might explain this strange disorder. His explanation relies on the work of Weber, a professor of anatomy and physiology, who has recently described, in great detail, the location and anatomy of the "masculine uterus." Michea points out that Weber's description of the masculine uterus has already been successfully used by Akermann to explain a hermaphrodite.[8] On the basis of this successful application of Weber's anatomical discovery, Michea concludes:

If these anatomical facts are verified, if, above all, one proceeded to discover that the masculine uterus can have sometimes a greater and sometimes a lesser development, one would perhaps be justified in establishing a relation of causality between these facts and the feminine tendencies that characterize the majority of individuals who engage in Greek love.[9]

Nothing could be more natural than to expect these feminine tendencies to have some anatomical basis; and nothing could constitute a more appropriate anatomical basis than a masculine uterus. The uterus, that almost always diseased female organ, was responsible for masculine deviations as well!

Although perhaps extraordinary in some of its details, Michea's form of explanation is not as uncommon as one might have expected. Writing in English in 1888, J. G. Kiernan puts great emphasis on the biological facts of bisexuality and hermaphroditism in the lowest orders of life.[10] Combining these facts with the fact that the human embryo is not originally sexually differentiated, Kiernan proposes to explain sexual perversions according to a "principle of atavism":[11]

The original bisexuality of the ancestors of the race shown in the rudimentary female organs of the male could not fail to occasion functional if not organic reversions when mental or physical manifestations were interfered with by disease or congenital defect.[12]

Or as he puts it later:

Males may be born with female external genitals and vice versa. The lowest animals are bisexual and the various types of hermaphroditism are more or less complete reversions to the ancestral type.[13]

Writing a year later in *Medical and Surgical Reporter*, G. Frank Lydston elaborates on the observations and hypothesis of Kiernan:

It is puzzling to the healthy man and woman, to understand how the practices of the sexual pervert can afford gratification. If considered in the light of reversion of type, however, the subject is much less perplexing. That maldevelopment, or arrested development, of the sexual organs should be associated with sexual perversion is not at all surprising; and the more nearly the individual approximates the type of fetal development which exists prior to the commencement of sexual differentiation, the more marked is the aberrance of sexuality.[14]

Whether it be the increased development of the masculine uterus or the failed development of sexual differentiation, the forty-two years between Michea and Lydston persist in anatomo-pathological explanations of the perversions. The explanatory ideal here is that of physical hermaphroditism. Since it was natural to suppose that all behavioral disorders had an organic basis, and since the behavioral manifestations in question were diseases of sexuality, it seemed inevitable that the sexual organs themselves must be the seat of the perversions. And it was no accident that the vast majority of the clinically reported cases of perversion were cases of "contrary sexual instinct" or homosexuality. Male organs led to male behavior and female organs to female behavior. Investigate the anatomy of the organs and behavioral science would be on a secure foundation. How this explanatory ideal of physical hermaphroditism was to explain the other perversions was never clear. But these other perversions were sufficiently rare in comparison with contrary sexual instinct that they could be theoretically neglected, at least at first, without much worry. This straightforward style of pathological anatomy wished to trace the behavioral abnormalities of perverts back to some gross physical deformity (or deficiency) of the reproductive organs, and in this way a clear and epistemologically satisfying causal link would be established between organs and functions. The anatomy of the body would continue to be explanatorily supreme.

Medical doctors took great solace in this brute physicalism, insisting on the power of their science to explain even the most bizarre acts. Their attitude is clearly expressed by Lydston, whose article was originally delivered as a clinical lecture to the College of Physicians and Surgeons, Chicago, Illinois. Here is a synoptic passage:

> The subject has been until a recent date studied solely from the standpoint of the moralist, and from the indisposition of the scientific physician to study the subject, the unfortunate set of individuals who are characterized by perverted sexuality have been viewed in the light of their moral responsibility rather than *as the victims of a physical and incidentally of a mental defect*. It is certainly much less humiliating to us as atoms of the social fabric to be able to attribute the degradation of these poor unfortunates to a physical cause, than to a wilful viciousness over which they have, or ought to have, volitional control. Even to the moralist there should be much satisfaction in the thought that a large class of sexual perverts are physically abnormal rather than morally leprous...the sexual pervert is generally a physical aberration – a lusus naturae.[15]

Most of the cases of contrary sexual instinct reported in the nineteenth-century medical literature explicitly record the anatomy of the reproductive organs of these unfortunate patients. And to the consternation of the pathological anatomists, the conclusion is virtually always the same – genital organs, normal; no physical malformations of the reproductive organs. Physical hermaphroditism could no more explain homosexuality than it could any of the other perversions. This grossest level of anatomy proved to be, in this arena, a useless explanatory space. Julien Chevalier had gotten the surprising conclusion correct when he wrote of "sexual inversion" in 1885: "It is characterized by the absence of anatomo-pathological lesions of the sexual organs."[16] But if pathological anatomy was to survive this startling claim, it had to retreat. And it quickly found its site of retreat in the brain.

IV

In the second edition of his acclaimed *Mental Pathology and Therapeutics*, Wilhelm Griesinger, holder of the first chair of psychiatry in Germany, and founder of the *Archiv für Psychiatrie und Nervenkrankheiten*, began with the following proclamation:

> The first step towards a knowledge of the symptoms [of insanity] is their locality – to which organ do the indications of the disease belong? What organ must

necessarily and invariably be diseased where there is madness? The answer to these questions is preliminary to all advancement in the study of mental disease.

Physiological and pathological facts show us that this organ can only be the brain; we therefore primarily, and in every case of mental disease, recognize a morbid action of that organ.[17]

Fewer than ten pages later, commenting on the state of knowledge in brain anatomy, Griesinger continues:

Cerebral pathology is, even in the present day, to a great extent in the same state which the pathology of the thoracic organs was in before the days of Laennec. Instead of proceeding in every case from the changes of structure of the organ, and being able to deduce in an exact manner the production of the symptoms from the changes in the tissue, it has very often to deal with symptoms of which it can scarcely give an approximation to the seat, and of whose mode of origin it is completely ignorant. It must keep to the external phenomena, and establish the groups of diseases according to something common and characteristic in the symptoms altogether independently of their anatomical basis.[18]

Griesinger admits that although in many diseases of insanity anatomical changes in the brain "cannot be ocularly demonstrated by pathological anatomy, still, on physiological grounds it is universally admitted."[19] And he frankly acknowledges, at the beginning of his chapter on the forms of mental disease, that "a classification of mental diseases *according to their nature* – that is, according to the anatomical changes of the brain which lie at their foundation – is, at the present time, impossible."[20]

Writing about diseases of sexuality almost twenty years later, Paul Moreau, a prominent French chronicler of aberrations, claims:

Genital excitation, physical or psychical, is the result of a special physiological or pathological excitement, resulting from the localisation or augmentation of a real morbid process to a center of genital functions. But this center, where is it? – In the cortex, the cerebellum, the medulla?

On this point we confess our ignorance and with Esquirol we repeat: we know nothing about it.[21]

Yet again, over twenty-five years later, Kraepelin, in the seventh edition of his textbook for psychiatrists, insists:

The principle requisite in the knowledge of mental diseases is an accurate definition of the separate disease processes. In the solution of this problem one must have, on the one hand, knowledge of the physical changes in the cerebral cortex, and on the other of the mental symptoms associated with them. Until this is known we cannot hope to understand the relationship between mental symptoms of disease and the morbid physical processes underlying them, or indeed the causes of the entire disease process. ... Judging from experience in internal medicine, the safest foundation for a classification of this kind is that offered by pathological anatomy. Unfortunately, however, mental diseases thus far present but very few lesions that have positive distinctive characteristics, and furthermore there is the extreme difficulty of correlating physical and mental morbid processes.[22]

I have reproduced these pronouncements, separated by forty-five years, because they present us with a significant problem: How are we to understand this obsession with brain anatomy coupled as it is with the constant admission of its theoretical and clinical uselessness? A naive hypothesis is that at the end of the nineteenth century, after the work of Broca and others, brain anatomy was just beginning to prove fruitful. Thus, this hypothesis continues, although brain pathology was perhaps not yet helpful in the classification and explanation of mental diseases, these physicians knew that with the slow progress of scientific knowledge it would soon become, both theoretically and clinically, of supreme importance. There was good evidence, so the claim concludes, on which to base an optimistic prediction about the explanatory power of the brain sciences. I have called this hypothesis "naive" because it takes at face value and as the whole story the statements of these neuropsychiatrists. I have no doubt that Griesinger and his descendants would have replied as this hypothesis suggests.[23] But their own avowed replies are not an accurate index of the historical circumstances. At this time in the history of psychiatry only certain kinds of statements about disease processes could count as either true or false; not every such statement was a possible candidate for the status of truth or falsehood.[24] Specifically, explanations of disease states had to be referred to organs; any explanation not of this type was not so much false as not even in the domain of the true and false. An explanation that did not at least attempt to anatomically localize the disease was more a part of theology than of science.[25] Since it was believed that there were distinct diseases of sexuality, and since these diseases could not be explained by defects of the reproductive organs, the only plausible organ that remained to provide an explanation was the brain. The dominance of brain pathology was as much a consequence of a complicated web of epistemic and conceptual conditions as it was of any empirical evidence. Indeed, for these early psychiatrists it does not seem as if anything could have counted as evidence against the proposition that sexual perversions are ultimately traceable to brain disease. Postmortem examinations that demonstrated no pathological lesions, and should have constituted such evidence, were always explained away; the necessary changes in brain structure were undoubtedly "so fine that with ordinary instruments they are not demonstrable postmortem."[26] Whatever evidence was to be amassed had to be placed within the given framework of pathological anatomy. To affirm explicitly that sexual perversions or other mental diseases were functionally autonomous from the brain would have been to pass from basic truth to palpable absurdity, something beyond falsity.[27]

The epistemological stranglehold of pathological anatomy on psychiatry is perhaps best illustrated by Moriz Benedikt's *Anatomical Studies Upon Brains of Criminals.*[28] In this book Benedikt reproduces, in extraordinarily painstaking detail, the results of his investigations of the anatomical structure of the brains of twenty-two criminals. Believing that we think, feel, desire, and act according to the anatomical construction and physiological development of our brain, Benedikt hopes that his dissections of criminals' brains will furnish the "foundation stones of a Natural History of Crime."[29] He considers the brains of various kinds of criminals from different races – some habitual thieves, murderers, a banknote counterfeiter, someone who killed the husband of his priest's concubine at the priest's instigation, and numerous others. Whatever interest there may be in the details of his presentations, his conclusion is remarkable:

THE BRAINS OF CRIMINALS EXHIBIT A DEVIATION FROM THE NORMAL TYPE, AND CRIMINALS ARE TO BE VIEWED AS AN ANTHROPOLOGICAL VARIETY OF THEIR SPECIES, AT LEAST AMONG THE CULTURED RACES.[30]

The idea that criminals are an anthropological variety of their species, because of their atypical brains, is an idea that we today find no more than amusing. But Benedikt found little amusement in his results. Concerned with criminal deviation, and starting from the framework of pathological anatomy, he found the "evidence" necessary for the logical conclusion. We should be concerned less with his evidence than with his style of explanation and his epistemic framework. Benedikt himself was sometimes aware of this framework:

It is self-evident that the observations here collected are the result of the a priori conviction that the constitutional ("eigentliche") criminal is a burdened ("belastetes") individual; that he has the same relation to crime as his next blood kin, the epileptic, and his cousin, the idiot, have to their encephalopathic condition.[31]

It is this a priori conviction that sets the stage for neuropsychiatry. The sexual pervert was no less burdened an individual than the criminal, epileptic, or idiot. I do not know how many anatomical investigations were performed upon the brains of perverts. But we should be more surprised if there were not such dissections than if there were. Given the explicit theoretical conception of perversion common at this time, Benedikt's kind of anatomical investigation would have been the ideal diagnostic and explanatory tool.

Yet I have claimed that pathological anatomy did not substantially influence the clinical description and classification of the perversions. Indeed, the only person to even attempt a classification of the perversions on an anatomical basis was Paul Magnan, a distinguished medical psychologist and a sometime collaborator with Charcot. In a presentation to the Société Médico-Psychologique in 1885, Magnan divided the perversions into four classes, hoping that his anatomical classification would help to reduce the confusion that surrounded these aberrations.[32] Perversions were to be understood, according to him, as (1) spinal, (2) posterior spinal cerebral (nymphomania and satyriasis), (3) anterior spinal cerebral (contrary sexual instinct), and (4) anterior cerebral (erotomania). As ultimately unsatisfactory as it was, Magnan's classification was at least headed in the right direction, assuming, of course, that pathological anatomy was as useful as was always claimed. But even in Magnan's hands this classification was more nominal than real. His explanation for why the different perversions were classified as they were was less than sketchy, and his classifications had, at most, a minimal influence on his presentation of cases. Magnan was better known among his colleagues for his extended description of contrary sexual instinct (*inversion du sens génital*) and for his linking of this perversion with degeneracy; in this respect his views were quite common and his work followed a long line of predecessors, beginning with Westphal.[33] In fact, Falret, commenting on Magnan's 1885 presentation, mentions nothing about his supposed anatomical classification, but rather insists (as did Magnan) on the importance of the hereditary character of the perversions. Although Magnan's classification was adopted by a few other French physicians, it was without much effect.[34] His classification never really caught on, and no one offered any more sophisticated anatomical classifications in its place. Magnan's attempt was offered more out of theoretical necessity than as a result of any genuine evidence or insight. His was a last effort to keep pathological anatomy alive.

V

The best way to understand the nineteenth-century obsession with perversion is to examine the notion of the sexual instinct, for, as I have said, the actual conception of perversion underlying clinical thought was that of a functional disease of this instinct. That is to say, the class of diseases that affected the sexual instinct was precisely the sexual perversions. Of course, the pathological anatomists did not want the notion of a sexual instinct to escape their grasp. Griesinger himself had said that "there is nothing inconsistent in seeking to discover in certain parts of the brain the seat of the sensual instincts."[35] And Krafft-Ebing, in *Psychopathia Sexualis*, asserts that the sexual instinct is a function of the cerebral cortex, although he admits that no definite region of the cortex has yet been proven to be the exclusive seat of this instinct.[36] He speculates that since there is a close relation between the olfactory sense and the sexual instinct, these two centers must be close together in the cerebral cortex. Indeed, he accepts Mackenzie's observations that masturbators are subject to nosebleeds, and that "there are affections of the nose which stubbornly resist all treatment until the concomitant (and causal) genital disease is removed."[37] But besides these rather vague remarks, Krafft-Ebing says nothing that would help one to determine the anatomical foundation of the sexual instinct, or to lead one to believe that it was actually possible to find distinct cerebral lesions associated with the diseases of this instinct.

The appropriate way to understand the sexual instinct is in functional terms, not in anatomical ones. Without such a functional understanding, there would have been no conceptual foundation for classifiying certain phenomena as perversions or diseases of the instinct. And Krafft-Ebing himself, as I shall show, understood the sexual instinct in this functional way; his pathological anatomy here is just so much window dressing. One of the most explicit recognitions of the importance of this functional characterization of the sexual instinct, a characterization shared by all the significant clinical work on perversion, appears in Legrain's *Des anomalies de l'instinct sexuel et en particulier des inversions du sens génital*, published in 1896:

The sexual instinct is a physiological phenomenon in every normal being endowed with life. It is a need of a general order and in consequence it is useless to look for its localisation, as one has done, in any particular part whatever of the organism. Its seat is everywhere and nowhere . . . . This instinct is therefore independent of the structure itself of the external genital organs, which are only instruments in the service of a function, as the stomach is an instrument in the service of the general function of nutrition.[38]

By acknowledging the subservience of the genital organs to the function of the sexual instinct, Legrain makes overt what by 1896 nobody should have doubted. And by claiming that the seat of the sexual instinct was everywhere and nowhere, he told us to look for its diseases everywhere and nowhere. This "everywhere and nowhere" sometimes had a more common name in psychiatric discussions – it went under the name of *personality*. A functional understanding of the instinct allowed one to isolate a set of disorders or diseases that were disturbances of the special functions of the instinct. Moreau (du Tours), in a book that influenced the first edition of Krafft-Ebing's *Psychopathia Sexualis*, argued that the clinical facts forced one to accept, as absolutely demonstrated, the psychic existence of a sixth sense, which he called the genital sense.[39] Although the notion of a genital sense may appear ludicrous, Moreau's characterization was adopted by subsequent French clinicians, and his phrase *sens génital* was preserved, by Charcot among others, as a translation of our "sexual instinct." So Carl Westphal's *conträre Sexualempfindung* became *inversion du sens génital*. The genital sense is just the sexual instinct, masquerading in different words. Its characterization as a sixth sense was a useful analogy. Just as one could become blind or have acute vision or be able to discriminate only a part of the color spectrum, and just as one might go deaf or have abnormally sensitive hearing or be able to hear only certain pitches, so too this sixth sense might be diminished, augmented, or perverted. What Moreau hoped to demonstrate was that this genital sense had special functions, distinct from the functions served by other organs, and that just as with the other senses, this sixth sense could be psychically disturbed without the proper working of other mental functions, either affective or intellectual, being harmed.[40] A demonstration such as Moreau's was essential in isolating diseases of sexuality as distinct disease entities.

The *Oxford English Dictionary* reports that the first modern medical use in English of the concept of perversion occurred in 1842 in Dunglison's *Medical Lexicon*: " 'Perversion', one of the four modifications of function in disease; the three others being augmentation, diminution, and abolition."[41] The notions of perversion and function are inextricably intertwined. Once one offers a functional characterization of the sexual instinct, perversions become a natural class of diseases; and without this characterization there is really no conceptual room for this kind of disease. Whatever words of pathological anatomy he and others offered, it is clear that Krafft-Ebing understood the sexual instinct in a functional way. In his *Textbook on Insanity* Krafft-Ebing is unequivocal in his claim that life presents two instincts, those of self-preservation and sexuality; he insists that abnormal life presents no new instincts, although the instincts of self-preservation and sexuality "may be lessened, increased or manifested with perversion."[42] The

sexual instinct was often compared with the instinct of self-preservation, which manifested itself in appetite. In a section entitled "Disturbances of the Instincts," Krafft-Ebing first discusses the anomalies of
the appetites, which he divides into three different kinds. There are
increases of the appetite (hyperorexia), lessening of the appetite
(anorexia), and perversions of the appetite, such as a "true impulse to
eat spiders, toads, worms, human blood, etc."[43] Such a classification is
exactly what one should expect from a functional understanding of the
instinct. Anomalies of the sexual instinct are similarly classified as
lessened or entirely wanting (anaesthesia), abnormally increased (hyper-
aesthesia), and perverse expression (paraesthesia); in addition there is a
fourth class of anomalies of the sexual instinct, which consists in its
manifestation outside of the period of anatomical and physiological
processes in the reproductive organs (paradoxia).[44] In both his *Textbook
on Insanity* and *Psychopathia Sexualis*, Krafft-Ebing further divides the
perversions into sadism, masochism, fetishism, and contrary sexual
instinct.[45]

In order to be able to determine precisely what phenomena are
functional disturbances or diseases of the sexual instinct, one must also,
of course, specify what the normal or natural function of this instinct
consists in. Without knowing what the normal function of the instinct is,
everything and nothing could count as a functional disturbance. There
would be no principled criterion to include or exclude any behavior
from the disease category of perversion. So one must first believe that
there is a natural function of the sexual instinct and then believe that
this function is quite determinate. One might have thought that questions as momentous as these would have received extensive discussion
during the nineteenth-century heyday of perversion. But, remarkably
enough, no such discussion appears. There is virtually *unargued una-
nimity* both on the fact that this instinct does have a natural function
and on what that function is. Krafft-Ebing's view is representative here:

During the time of the maturation of physiological processes in the reproductive glands, desires arise in the consciousness of the individual, which have for
their purpose the perpetuation of the species (sexual instinct).... With opportunity for the natural satisfaction of the sexual instinct, every expression of it
that does not correspond with the purpose of nature – i.e., propagation –
must be regarded as perverse.[46]

Nineteenth-century psychiatry silently adopted this conception of the
function of the sexual instinct, and it was often taken as so natural as
not to need explicit statement. It is not at all obvious why sadism,
masochism, fetishism, and homosexuality should be treated as species
of the same disease, for they appear to have no essential features in

common.[47] Yet if one takes the natural function of the sexual instinct to be propagation, it becomes possible to see why they were all classified together as perversions. They all manifest the same kind of perverse expression, the same basic kind of functional deviation. Thus this understanding of the instinct permits a *unified* treatment of perversion, allows one to place an apparently heterogeneous group of phenomena under the same natural disease kind.[48] Had anyone denied either that the sexual instinct has a natural function or that this function is procreation, diseases of perversion, as we understand them, would not have entered psychiatric nosology.

I have already indicated that most nineteenth-century clinical reports of perversion were cases of so-called contrary sexual instinct, and I have offered a hypothesis to explain why this may have been so. In the rest of my discussion of the medical literature on perversion I shall concentrate on these cases, other forms of perversion requiring a separate treatment (which I have provided elsewhere). We can conveniently place the origin of contrary sexual instinct, as a medicopsychological diagnostic category, in 1870, with the publication of Carl Westphal's "Die conträre Sexualempfindung" in *Archiv für Psychiatrie und Nervenkrankheiten*. Westphal's attachment to pathological anatomy did not prevent him from giving the first modern definition of homosexuality. He believed that contrary sexual instinct was a congenital perversion of the sexual instinct, and that in this perversion "a woman is physically a woman and psychologically a man and, on the other hand, a man is physically a man and psychologically a woman."[49] I have called this the first modern definition because it presents a purely psychological characterization of homosexuality, and, detatched from Westphal's meager explanatory speculations, it provides us with the clinical conception of this perversion operative in almost all of the subsequent medical literature. Later issues of the *Archiv* contained similar reports of contrary sexual instinct, and some of Krafft-Ebing's most important early work appeared in this journal.

With the publication of Charcot and Magnan's paper in *Archives de Neurologie* in 1882, an epidemic of contrary sexual instinct, equal to that of Germany, was soon to plague France.[50] An Italian case appeared in 1878;[51] and the first case in English, in 1881.[52] The latter case was reported by a German physician and some English-speaking psychiatrists did not consider it "a contribution to the study of this subject by English science."[53] In 1883, Shaw and Ferris, writing in the *Journal of Nervous and Mental Diseases*, summarize all of the German, French, Italian, and English cases, and conclude that there have been eighteen documented cases of contrary sexual instinct, to which they add one more, bringing the grand total to nineteen.[54] Westphal's psychological characterization of homosexuality is, in effect, the psychiatric transformation of a previous, although nonmedical, understanding of this disorder. Karl Heinrich Ulrichs, a Hanoverian lawyer, had achieved some notoriety with his autobiographical description of contrary sexual instinct, published in the middle 1860s. Ulrichs gave the name "urnings" to those who suffered from these desires, and supposed that a woman's soul dwelled in a man's body (*anima muliebris in virili corpore inclusa*).[55] And of course, throughout the 1870s and 1880s, there were the obligatory anatomical claims that these desires were the result of "the brain of a woman in the body of a man and the brain of a man in the body of a woman."[56] These three ideas of same-sex sexual behavior represent three central places where the phenomenon was thought to reside – the soul, the brain, and the psyche or personality. And, although not always in this historical sequence, theology, pathological anatomy, and psychiatry each took its own opportunity to lay claim to a complete explanation of perverse desires.

The significance of a psychological description of homosexuality is amply illustrated by *Psychopathia Sexualis*:

After the attainment of complete sexual development, among the most constant elements of self-consciousness in the individual are the knowledge of representing a definite sexual personality and the consciousness of desire, during the period of physiological activity of the reproductive organs (production of semen and ova), to perform sexual acts corresponding with that sexual personality – acts which, consciously or unconsciously, have a procreative purpose. . . .

With the inception of anatomical and functional development of the generative organs, and the differentiation of form belonging to each sex, which goes hand in hand with it (in the boy as well as in the girl), rudiments of a mental feeling corresponding with the sex are developed.[57]

With this picture of the definite sexual personality in hand, Krafft-Ebing says of contrary sexual instinct:

It is purely a psychical anomaly, for the sexual instinct does in no wise correspond with the primary and secondary sexual characteristics. In spite of the fully differentiated sexual type, in spite of the normally developed and active sexual glands, man is drawn sexually to the man, because he has, consciously or otherwise, the instinct of the female toward him, or vice versa.[58]

The normal sexual instinct expresses itself in a definite personality or character; functional disorders of the instinct will express themselves as psychical anomalies. Since the sexual instinct was thought to partake of both somatic and psychic features, any functional abnormality of the instinct could be expected to manifest itself psychically. In this way, these functional disorders and psychology were very closely connected.

As Moll says, "To understand the homosexual urge we should consider the genital instinct not as a phenomenon apart from the other functions but rather as a psychic function."[59]

During this period of near-frenetic psychiatric classification, many attempts were made to provide detailed classifications of different degrees and kinds of homosexuality. Psychiatrists were not content with single categories, but rather subdivided the perversions into innumerable kinds so that, before long, the psychiatric world was populated by a plethora of strange beings.[60] Krafft-Ebing believed that, "clinically and anthropologically," there were four degrees of development of homosexuality:

1. With the predominant homosexual feeling there are traces of heterosexual sensibility (psychosexual hermaphroditism).
2. Exclusive inclination to the same sex (homosexuality).
3. The whole psychic existence is altered to correspond with the abnormal sexual feeling (effemination and viraginity).
4. The form of the body approaches that which is in harmony with the abnormal sexual feeling. However, there are never actual transitions to hermaphrodites.[61]

It is important to note here that the degrees or kinds of homosexuality are differentiated according to psychic features, namely, the degree of homosexual sensibility or feeling that is present. Only the rarest and most severe form of homosexuality is accompanied by any somatic changes, and even these changes are subordinate to the abnormal sexual feeling.

This psychological/functional understanding of contrary sexual instinct is not limited to the German medical literature of the time. In 1896 Legrain could warn us not to make a mistake about the true sex (*le sexe vrai*) of a "uranist." Even though registered at birth as a man, if in his contacts with men, he has the feelings that men normally have toward women, then he is a woman.[62] Psychological characteristics, expressions of the sexual instinct, are decisive for the categorization of the sexes:

And this psychical differentiation is a fact of principal importance, for in my view in it alone rests the categorization of the sexes; as long as it is not a complete fact, the individual is really sexually neutral, whatever his genital structure.[63]

This priority of the psychological provided some of the conditions necessary for statements such as Kraepelin's:

It [contrary sexual instinct] is more prevalent in certain employments, such as among decorators, waiters, ladies' tailors; also among theatrical people. Moll claims that women comedians are regularly homosexual.[64]

It is clear from what Kraepelin says later that he does not believe that these employments are causally responsible for this perversion of the sexual instinct. Rather, he must believe that once the psychic anomalies of the perversion are manifest, one tends to choose employment that is more appropriate to these psychical abnormalities.[65] With remarks like these, the death of pathological anatomy is secured.

One of the most notable facts about this early psychiatric literature on perversion is that no explanatory framework is proposed to account for purely functional diseases. None of the writers I am familiar with ever suggests that these so-called functional diseases are not true diseases, are not part of the legitimate domain of medical science. Yet, at the same time, there was no already clearly formulated concept of disease under which they could readily fall. Clinical practice came first; explanatory theory lagged far behind. No doubt the circumstances are complicated by the fact that all of the early writers expressed an allegiance to pathological anatomy. But even after pathological anatomy became an obvious explanatory failure, psychiatry did not regroup and address itself to the question of whether these perversions were really diseases. One unequivocal path to take would have been to claim that precisely because no anatomical changes underlay the perversions, they could not be considered diseases, and physicians must leave their regulation to others more qualified. But clinical practice had already constituted the perversions as diseases, and by the time the hold of pathological anatomy was loosened, they were already a recognized part of psychiatric nosology. This precedence of clinical practice to theory is officially endorsed by the American Psychiatric Association, whose *Diagnostic and Statistical Manual* is meant to be theoretically neutral.[66] But such theoretical neutrality is as unprincipled as it is expansive; indeed, its expansiveness is partially a function of its lack of principle. On a straightforward interpretation, it sanctions the view that whatever psychiatrists do in fact treat as diseases are diseases. So what could not become a disease? The American Psychiatric Association recognizes telephone scatologia, among others, as a psychosexual disorder. Moreover, phenomena do not exhibit their disease status to everyone's untutored vision. To count something as a disease is to make a theoretical classification. The hope of reading diseases straight off of nature, independent of theory, is as philosophically naive as it is historically suspect.

One of the first comprehensive attempts to provide an explanatory framework for functional diseases is Morton Prince's 1898 paper, "Habit Neuroses as True Functional Diseases."[67] Prince considers the whole class of diseases for which there are no anatomical changes different in kind from those that occur in health (sexual perversion being one subclass of functional disease). Not surprisingly, his explanations are of a thoroughly psychological nature, relying mainly on the laws of association. Simply put, his theory was that phenomena may become so strongly associated that their occurrence together is automatic, independent of violation. He thought that we may

by a process of education be taught to respond to our environment or to internal stimuli in such a way as to generate painful sensations or undesirable motor effects.... The painful (disagreeable, undesirable) motor and sensory and other phenomena thus developed constitute so-called disease.[68]

He refers to these diseases as habit neuroses, association neuroses, neuro-mimesis, or true functional diseases.[69] Prince's framework bears a striking resemblance to Freud's attempt to "pass over into the field of psychology" to explain that other great functional disease, hysteria. Freud's explanations also rely on the effects of associations in the genesis of mental disorders, and were published in French five years earlier than Prince's paper.[70] Both papers help to culminate the gradual process by which psychiatry became independent of neurology and annexed itself instead to psychology. I have given these two examples (there are others as well) so as not to be accused of claiming that there were no theories of functional diseases. The important point is that theories of this kind were developed after the fact, after the recognition, in standard psychiatric manuals, of whole new disease categories. These new diseases appeared almost full-blown in clinical practice, and silently, anonymously, became part of psychiatric nomenclature. The effect of this quiet, undisturbed recognition was vastly to enlarge psychiatric therapy and intervention. Psychiatry was not to be concerned solely with the extreme forms, the limits, of the human condition, such as madness. Instead, the entire domain of the unnatural and abnormal was to become its province. And one need not have waited until Freud's *Three Essays on the Theory of Sexuality*[71] to realize that this clinical arena was as common as it was "unnatural"; no one was to escape the psychiatric gaze.

VI

In a groundbreaking essay on the traditional philosophical problem of other minds, Stanley Cavell concludes by saying:

We don't know whether the mind is best represented by the phenomenon of pain, or by that of envy, or by working on a jigsaw puzzle, or by a ringing in the ears. A natural fact underlying the philosophical problem of privacy is that the individual will take *certain* among his experiences to represent his own mind – certain particular sins or shames or surprises of joy – and then take his mind (his self) to be unknown so far as *those* experiences are unknown.[72]

Nineteenth-century psychiatry took sexuality to be the way in which the mind is best represented. To know a person's sexuality is to know that person. Sexuality is the expression of the individual shape of the personality. And to know sexuality, to know the person, one must know its anomalies. Krafft-Ebing was quite clear about this point:

These anomalies are very important elementary disturbances, since *upon the nature of sexual sensibility the mental individuality in greater part depends.*[73]

Sexuality individualizes, turns one into a specific kind of human being – a sadist, masochist, homosexual, fetishist. This link between sexuality and individuality explains some of the passion with which psychiatry investigated the perversions. The more details one has about these anomalies, the better one is able to penetrate the covert individuality of the self. The second edition of Laupts's book on homosexuality announces the first thirteen volumes in a "Bibliothèque des Perversions Sexuelles."[74] Here one can read about the perversions of one's choice, gathering as much information as possible about the most profound truths of the individual.

VII

The question I now wish to ask is: Were there any perverts before the later part of the nineteenth century? Strange as it may sound, the answer to this question is, *no*. Perversion and perverts were an invention of psychiatric reasoning and of the psychiatric theories I have surveyed. (I again restrict myself to the case of homosexuality, but a similar history could be recounted for the other perversions.) I do not wish to be misunderstood – intercourse between members of the same sex did not begin, I dare say, in the nineteenth century; but homosexuality, as a disease of the sexual instinct, did. One will not be able to understand the importance of these new diseases of sexuality if one conflates contrary sexual instinct with sodomy. Sodomy was a legal category, defined in terms of certain specifiable behavior; the sodomite was a judicial subject of the law. Homosexuality was a psychic disease of the instinct, of one's sensibility, not to be reduced to merely behavioral terms. Westphal's "conträre Sexualempfindung" is literally a contrary sexual sentiment or sensation, in which the notion of behavior plays, at most, a subsidiary role; the homosexual is a medical patient of psychiatry. Psychiatrists were forever concerned with carefully distinguishing sodomy from homosexuality; Laupts's book reports the views of D. Stefanowski, which are representative of attempts to differentiate the two. Stefanowski gives a point-by-point comparison of pederasty and "uranism," of which the following are some of the more interesting contrasts. In pederasty "the manner of feeling and acting in matters of love remains masculine, the inclination for women exists everywhere," and "the outward appearance always remains masculine; the tasks and habits remain manly"; on the other hand, in uranism "the manner of feeling and acting is completely feminine: it is accompanied by an envy and hatred towards women," and "the outward look sometimes becomes entirely effeminate; the tastes, habits, and pursuits become those of a woman." Moreover, "pederasty can sometimes be restrained and repressed by a vigorous effort of the will," while "uranist passion is completely outside of the domain of the will." Finally, "pederasty as a vice or profession should be repressed and forbidden by the law, male prostitution should be strictly prohibited"; but "uranism, as an innate moral deformity, can never be punished or prosecuted by the law, still its manifestations must necessarily be repressed, in the name of public morality, but one should judge its manifestations as an expression of a diseased state, as a sort of partial mental illness."[75] These passages make clear how distinct homosexuality and sodomy were considered to be. Homosexuality was a disease, a "perversion" strictly speaking, whereas sodomy was a vice, a problem for morality and law, about which medicine had no special knowledge. The crucial distinction in this area of investigation was made by Krafft-Ebing:

Perversion of the sexual instinct . . . is not to be confounded with *perversity* in the sexual act; since the latter may be induced by conditions other than psychopathological. The concrete perverse act, monstrous as it may be, is clinically not decisive. In order to differentiate between disease (perversion) and vice (perversity), one must investigate the whole personality of the individual and the original motive leading to the perverse act. Therein will be found the key to the diagnosis.[76]

Every psychiatrist writing during this period acknowledged the difference between perversion and perversity, even if they also quickly admitted that it often proved difficult to distinguish the two. Only minutely detailed examination could help to determine that a given patient was a genuine pervert, and not merely evil or wicked. Before the later part of the nineteenth century, questions of sexual perversity were not cloaked in silence or secrecy, but were dealt with primarily in treatises of moral philosophy, moral theology, and jurisprudence, and not in medicine. A good example is the work of Immanuel Kant. Besides his three great critiques on epistemology, moral philosophy, and aesthetic judgment, Kant wrote on just about every imaginable topic that was philosophically interesting. His *Anthropology from a Pragmatic Point of View* (1798) contains a discussion of mental illness in which he distinguishes between hypochondria, mania, melancholia, delirium, and other forms of mental derangement.[77] Not a word about sexual perversion appears anywhere in this book, however, even though there are chapters on the cognitive powers, the appetitive powers, temperament, character, and a section on the character of the sexes. But matters of sex did not escape Kant's pen, for if we turn to a book published a year earlier, *The Doctrine of Virtue*, which is Part II of *The Metaphysic of Morals*, we find Kant devoting an entire section to "carnal self-defilement" in his chapter on "Man's Duties to Himself as an Animal Being."[78] Moreover, he explicitly considers whether the sexual power may be used without regard for nature's purpose in the intercourse of the sexes (namely, procreation), and he uses the concept of "unnatural lust" here.[79] So it is not as if Kant was silent on the topic of sexual deviations, as if he was subject to some pre-Victorian reticence. It is rather that the epistemic and conceptual conditions necessary to formulate the notion of *diseases of sexuality* did not yet obtain, and sexual unnaturalness could no more be seen unequivocally through the lens of medicine than could any other fundamentally moral problem. The reassignment in regulating the perversions, from law/morality to medicine, was not simply a new institutional division of labor; it was to signal a fundamental transformation, and the inauguration of whole new ways of conceptualizing ourselves.

Perversion was not a disease that lurked about in nature, waiting for a psychiatrist with especially acute powers of observation to discover it hiding almost everywhere. It was a disease created by a new (functional) understanding of disease, a conceptual shift, a shift in reasoning, that made it possible to interpret various types of activity in medicopsychiatric terms. There was no natural morbid entity to be discovered until clinical psychiatric practice invented one.[80] Perversion was not a disease candidate until it became possible to attribute diseases to the sexual instinct, and there were no possible diseases of the sexual instinct before the nineteenth century; when the notion of diseases of this instinct loses its last remaining grasp upon us, we will rid the world of all of its perverts.[81]

Of course, I do not for a moment deny that nineteenth-century psychiatry took itself to be discovering a real disease, and not inventing one. Many of the books I have discussed include entire chapters attempting to demonstrate the presence of these diseases throughout history. Moreau, for instance, after one such historical excursion, insists that we need no longer ascribe these frightful debaucheries to the anger of God or to the rebellion of Satan against God. We can now regard them from a scientific point of view, in conformity with "modern ideas."[82] This particular reinterpretation of history was part of the "retrospective medicine" that was so prominent during the nineteenth century, and which consisted in the reinterpretation of misunderstood past phenomena according to medical categories.[83] Charcot, to take a more famous instance, was another one of the practitioners of this revisionist medicine, and his *Les Démonaiques dans l'Art*, written with Paul Richer, argues that artistic representations of demonic possession are in fact representations of hysteria.[84] So we need not be at all surprised to find it repeatedly claimed that these sexual perversions can be seen everywhere in history. These claims, however, should not detain us; all we find before the nineteenth century are descriptions of sodomy, as an actual reading of these pre-nineteenth-century descriptions will confirm. Perversion is a thoroughly modern phenomenon.

VIII

I want to discuss very briefly one last problem before drawing some conclusions. One of the concepts most often linked to sexual perversion is that of the degenerate. This concept derives from B. A. Morel and is understood by him to be an unhealthy deviation from the normal type of humanity; one of the essential characteristics of degeneracy is its hereditary transmissibility.[85] The theory of degeneracy was used as a pseudoexplanatory framework for practically every serious psychopathological state dealt with by nineteenth-century psychiatry. Degeneracy functioned as one of the central ties between what Foucault has called the anatomo-politics of the human body and the bio-politics of the population.[86] Everybody from Westphal to Charcot considered sexual perversion to be one instance of this ever present degeneracy. Krafft-Ebing took the functional anomalies of the sexual instinct to be "functional signs of degeneration";[87] Kraepelin, in his grand classificatory scheme of psychopathology, placed contrary sexual instinct under the general category of "constitutional psychopathological states (insanity of degeneracy)."[88] One advantage of regarding perversion as an inherited degenerate state was that, under this hypothesis, it was difficult to doubt that it was a true disease. Since the etiology of perversion was thought to be constitutional, independent of volition and cultivation, the distinction between perversity and perversion was in principle easily drawn. Yet with this clear advantage of allowing, even requiring, psychiatry to treat perversion as a disease came an unfortunate disadvantage "from a social and therapeutic point of view."[89] It was natural to assume that it was impossible to modify or remove a congenital, inherited condition, and so the theory of degeneracy led to "therapeutic nihilism and social hopelessness."[90] As Kraepelin put it, "There can be no thought of treatment of an anomaly like this, which has developed with the development of the personality and has its origin deep within it."[91] How was psychiatric intervention to be justified in a case where, as a matter of theory, there could be little therapeutic efficacy? Since there was no hope in attempting to treat these patients, psychiatry might seem severely limited in how it could exercise its knowledge and power over the perversions. A. von Schrenck-Notzing was perhaps the first to argue in detail that extraneous influences and education were actually the most significant etiological factors in the genesis of the perversions.[92] He treated thirty-two homosexual patients with hypnotic suggestion and found that 70 percent were greatly improved and 34 percent were cured.[93] As he puts it in the preface to his book,

The favorable results obtained in "congenital" urnings by psychical treatment in the hypnotic state placed before me the alternative either to assume that suggestion is capable of influencing congenital abnormalities of the mind or to prove that in the idea of homo-sexuality at present prevalent the hereditary factor is overestimated, to the disadvantage of educational influences.[94]

He chose, without hesitation, the latter alternative, emphasizing that individuals who actually suffered from contrary sexual instinct found the theory of heredity convenient, for they "find in it a very welcome excuse for their peculiarity."[95] Von Schrenck-Notzing said that the aim of his book was to demonstrate that "useful members of society can be made of such perverted individuals," and he hoped that his work would "open to workers in the domain of suggestive therapeutics a new and productive field of activity and humane striving!"[96] Morton Prince also recognized that the educational theory of the perversions offered "hope and possibilities," possibilities of successful therapeutic intervention that brought with them that social hopefulness that has always been so much a part of American psychiatry.[97] But Prince insisted as well that the theory that perversion was acquired or cultivated, owing to the effect of education, unconscious mimicry, external suggestion, example, and so forth, had its own unfortunate disadvantages. On this theory, weren't perversions really vices rather than diseases, perversity instead of true perversion?[98] And if this was so, then there was still a difficulty in justifying psychiatric intervention. How could psychiatry legitimately interfere in purely moral problems; ought it not to be limited to real mental diseases, to the domain of medical science?[99] The matrix of psychiatric power/knowledge would be maximized if one could claim both that sexual perversion was not congenital and that it was a disease. If it was not congenital, then therapeutic intervention could be efficacious; if it was a disease, then therapeutic intervention would be required. This is exactly where Prince relied on his theory of habit neuroses and true functional diseases. He believed that in order to maintain that perversion, although acquired, was nevertheless a disease, one had to demonstrate that intensely cultivated habits could eventually become automatic, independent of volitional control. The pervert was then subject to "real imperative sensations and ideas."[100]

Analogy with what takes place in other fields of the nervous system would make it intelligible that sexual feelings and actions may by constant repetition (cultivation) become associated together and developed into the sort of quasi-independent neural activities, which may then become practically independent of the will – or, in other words, a psychosis.[101]

Prince could then argue that, given this theory, it is up to "counter-education to replace the morbid processes by healthy ones."[102] Under countereducation one could include almost anything one pleased, and so psychiatry was on its way to an unlimited disciplinary regulation of the sexual life. This theory of perversion as an acquired disease induced one to leave completely the domain of pathological anatomy and embed oneself firmly in psychology. Morton Prince, after all, founded both the *Journal of Abnormal Psychology* (1906) and the American Psychopathological Association (1910). The sexual personality was created so much the better to control the body.

IX

It was Immanuel Kant who argued that we can never know the self as it is in itself, but only as it appears to us.[103] Kant thought that he could give a deduction that would exhibit the determinate and unchanging categories through which everything, including our own self, must appear to us. Even if we reject Kant's own deduction, we ought not to reject his basic idea. The categories and conceptualizations of the self determine not only how others view us, but also how each person conceives of him- or herself. And conceptions of ourselves greatly influence how we actually behave. Part of Foucault's "genealogy of subject in Western civilization" must consist in an investigation of the origin of new categories of the self.[104] These categories may come from

320 ARNOLD I. DAVIDSON

the strangest and most diverse places. Ian Hacking has shown that the grand statistical surveys of the early nineteenth century provided many new classifications of the self.[105] It will not be as surprising to be told that psychiatry is another fertile source for new conceptualizations of the self. The concept of perversion, once exclusively a part of special- ized nineteenth-century discussions, became, in the twentieth century, a dominant way of organizing our thought about our own sexuality. People diagnosed as perverts came to think of themselves as diseased, as morbid, an experience that was not possible before the heyday of the pervert that I have described. Westphal believed that contrary sexual instinct was always accompanied by consciousness of the morbidity of the condition.[106] Being classified as a pervert could alter everything from one's self-conception to one's behavior to one's social circum- stances. And even those of us who are not full-fledged perverts have had to reconceive of ourselves; every little deviation of the sexual instinct may be a sign of our impending perversion. We are all possible perverts. It is perversion as a possible way of being, a possible category of the self, that is the legacy of nineteenth-century psychiatry. The notion of perversion has so penetrated our framework of categories that it is now as natural and unquestioned to think of oneself as a pervert as it was once odd and questionable.

Ian Hacking has argued that

the organization of our concepts, and the philosophical difficulties that arise from them, sometimes have to do with their historical origins. When there is a radical transformation of ideas, whether by evolution or by an abrupt mutation, I think that whatever made the transformation possible leaves its mark upon subsequent reasoning.[107]

The problem of perversion is a case in point. All of our subsequent reasoning about perversion is afflicted by the historical origins of the concept. Moreover, we cannot think away the concept of perversion, even if we no longer claim to believe that there is any natural function of the sexual instinct. We are prisoners of the historical space of nineteenth-century psychiatry, "shaped by pre-history, and only arche- ology can display its shape."[108] The archaeology of perversion is a crucial stage in understanding the genealogy of the twentieth-century self. Perhaps there will come a time when we can think to ourselves, "How do I love thee; let me count the ways," and no longer fear our possible perversion.

Acknowledgments

Among Putnam's papers most central to my motivations, see especially, "It Ain't Necessarily So," in *Mathematics, Matter and Method. Philosophical Papers, Volume I*

(Cambridge: Cambridge University Press, 1975); " 'Two Dogmas' Revisited," "There Is at Least One *A Priori* Truth," and "Analyticity and Apriority: Beyond Wittgenstein and Quine," in *Realism and Reason. Philosophical Papers, Volume 3* (Cambridge: Cambridge University Press, 1983).

This essay, first written in 1982, has a long history that I will not recount here. A number of discussions of it have already appeared in print. The most significant of these is Ian Hacking, "Making Up People," in *Reconstructing Individualism: Autonomy, Individuality, and the Self in Western Thought*. Edited by Thomas C. Heller et al. (Stanford: Stanford University Press, 1986). In order fully to assess the implications of the arguments in this essay, it must be placed in the context of two other papers, written subsequent to this one, but already published. These papers are "Sex and the Emergence of Sexuality," in *Critical Inquiry* (Autumn, 1987), and "How to Do the History of Psychoanalysis: A Reading of Freud's *Three Essays on the Theory of Sexuality*," in *The Trial(s) of Psychoanalysis*. Edited by Françoise Meltzer (Chicago: University of Chicago Press, 1987).

I am grateful to Michael Lavin, John McNees, and Alan Stone for comments on an earlier version of this essay. I owe two special debts of gratitude. Conversations with Michel Foucault in 1976 were crucial in helping me to conceptualize these issues. And discussions with Ian Hacking contributed to this paper in a multitude of different ways.

Notes

1 Michel Foucault, *The Birth of the Clinic* (New York: Vintage Books, 1973).
2 Quoted in Foucault, ibid., p. 140.
3 Quoted in Foucault, ibid., p. 146 from Bichat's *Anatomie générale*.
4 Foucault, ibid.
5 See, for example, the brief remarks of Michel Foucault, "The Confession of the Flesh," in *Power/Knowledge* (New York: Pantheon Books, 1980), pp. 221–2.
6 Dr. Michea, "Des déviations maladives de l'appétit vévérien," *Union Médicale*, 17 (juillet 1849). The case of Sergeant Bertrand provoked a number of discussions, of which Michea's is the most instructive.
7 Michea, ibid., p. 339.
8 Ibid.
9 Ibid.
10 J. G. Kiernan, "Sexual Perversion and the Whitechapel Murders," *The Medical Standard*. November 1888, volume 4, number 5, pp. 129–30, and December 1888, volume 4, number 6, pp. 170–2.
11 The phrase "principle of atavism" is used by Morton Prince in his discussion and critique of Kiernan and related views. "Sexual Perversion or Vice? A Pathological and Therapeutic Inquiry," *Journal of Nervous and Mental Diseases*, April 1898. Reprinted in *Psychotherapy and Multiple Personality: Selected Essays* (Cambridge, Mass.: Harvard University Press, 1975), pp. 89–90.
12 Kiernan, op. cit., p. 129.
13 Ibid., p. 130.
14 G. Frank Lydston, "Sexual Perversion, Satyriasis and Nymphomania," *Medical and Surgical Reporter*, September 7, 1889, volume LXI, number 10, pp. 253–8 and September 14, 1889, volume LXI, number 11, pp. 281–5. The quotation is from p. 255.
15 Ibid., p. 253; my emphasis. See also E. Gley, "Les Aberrations de l'instinct sexuel," *Revue Philosophique*, janvier 1884, pp. 88–9.
16 Julien Chevalier, *De l'inversion de l'instinct sexuel au point de vue médico-légal* (Paris: O. Doin, 1885). Chevalier summarizes his conclusions at the end of Chapter VI.
17 Wilhelm Griesinger, *Mental Pathology and Therapeutics* (London: The New Sydenham Society, 1867), p. 1. The first edition was published in German in 1845; the second enlarged edition in 1861.
18 Ibid., p. 8.
19 Ibid., p. 4.

20 Ibid., p. 206, my emphasis.
21 Paul Moreau (de Tours), *Des aberrations du sens génésique* (Paris: Asselin, 1880), p. 146.
22 Eugene Kraepelin, *Clinical Psychiatry: A Textbook for Students and Physicians* (London: Macmillan, 1907), pp. 115–16.
23 Another discussion of cerebral pathology that bears attention is Richard von Krafft-Ebing, *Textbook of Insanity* (Philadelphia: F. A. Davis, 1904). See especially pp. 20–4.
24 See Ian Hacking, "Language, Truth and Reason," in *Rationality and Relativism*. Edited by S. Lukes and M. Hollis (Oxford: Blackwell Books, 1982), and Michel Foucault, "Truth and Power," in *Power/Knowledge*.
25 See Kiernan, op. cit., p. 130, and Griesinger, op. cit., pp. 5–7.
26 Krafft-Ebing, op. cit., p. 21.
27 The same set of problems surrounds Charcot's introduction of the ambiguous notion of "dynamic lesion" in reference to hysteria. See *Diseases of the Nervous System*, volume III (London: The New Sydenham Society, 1889), pp. 12–14. I briefly discuss this notion in "Assault on Freud," *London Review of Books*, vol. 6, no. 12, 1984.
28 Moriz Benedikt, *Anatomical Studies upon Brains of Criminals* (New York: Wm. Wood, 1881). Published in German in 1878.
29 Ibid., pp. v and vii.
30 Ibid., p. 157; emphasis in the original.
31 Ibid., p. 158.
32 Paul Magnan, "Des anomalies, des aberrations et des perversions sexuelles," *Annales Médico-Psychologiques*, septième série, tome premier, 1885, pp. 447–74.
33 J. M. Charcot and P. Magnan, "Inversion du sens génital," *Archives de Neurologie*, volume 3, number 7 (janvier 1882), pp. 53–60, and volume 4, number 12 (novembre 1882), pp. 296–322.
34 See, for example, Paul Sérieux, *Recherches cliniques sur les anomalies de l'instinct sexuel* (Paris: Lecrosnier et Babé, 1888).
35 Griesinger, op cit., p. 41.
36 Richard von Krafft-Ebing, *Psychopathia Sexualis* (New York: Stein & Day, 1965; translation of the twelfth German edition), p. 17. There are significant differences between the first edition of *Psychopathia Sexualis* (1886) and later editions; when referring to the first edition, I shall so indicate.
37 Ibid., pp. 17–21. The quotation is from p. 21. Mackenzie's paper appears in the *Journal of Medical Science*, April 1884.
38 M. P. Legrain, *Des anomalies de l'instinct sexuel et en particulier des inversions du sens génital* (Paris: Carré, 1896), p. 36.
39 Moreau (de Tours), op. cit., p. 2.
40 Ibid., p. 3. Moreau classifies as "perversion génital absolue" bestiality, the profanation of corpses, and rape. He also discusses erotomania, satyriasis, and nymphomania. Remarkably, he has no discussion of contrary sexual instinct.
41 *Oxford English Dictionary* (Oxford: Clarendon Press, 1933), volume 7, p. 739.
42 Krafft-Ebing, *Textbook on Insanity*, p. 79. Krafft-Ebing considers abolition to be the extreme case of diminution.
43 Ibid., pp. 77–81.
44 Ibid., p. 81. This same classification is given in *Psychopathia Sexualis*, p. 34.
45 Krafft-Ebing, *Textbook on Insanity*, pp. 83–6, and *Psychopathia Sexualis*, pp. 34–6. I discuss masochism in "Sex and the Emergence of Sexuality."
46 Krafft-Ebing, *Psychopathia Sexualis*, pp. 16, 52–3. See also *Textbook on Insanity*, p. 81. For other representative statements see Albert Moll, *Perversions of the Sex Instinct* (Newark: Julian Press, 1931), pp. 172, 182; originally published in German in 1891; and Dr. Laupts (pseudonym of G. Saint-Paul). *L'homosexualité et les types homosexuels: Nouvelle édition de Perversion et perversités sexuelles* (Paris: Vigot, 1910).
47 In eighteenth-century medicine, masturbation was considered exclusively as a causal factor, omnipresent of course, in the genesis of disease processes. It was not considered a distinct and autonomous disease. See S. A. Tissot, *L'onanisme, disserta-*

tion sur les maladies produites par la masturbation (Paris: Bechet, 1823). Originally published in Latin in 1758. In the nineteenth century, it came to be thought of as both a distinct morbid entity and a significant causal factor in the genesis of other diseases. For the later understanding, see Moreau (de Tours), op. cit., p.168.

48 It is instructive to compare this conception of perversion with Aquinas's treatment of unnatural vice. St. Thomas believed that there was a distinct kind of lustful vice, "contrary to the natural order of the venereal act as becoming to the human race: and this is called the unnatural vice." He considered onanism, bestiality, sodomy, and the sin of not observing the right manner of copulation all to be unnatural vices. He thought them to be not only distinct from but also worse than incest, adultery, rape, and seduction. See *Summa Theologica*. Question 154, Articles 11 and 12. One must be careful, however, not to assimilate this moral conception of perversion to the nineteenth-century medical conception. For discussion see my "Sex and the Emergence of Sexuality." I am indebted to John McNees for discussion on this point.

49 Carl Westphal, "Die conträre Sexualempfindung," *Archiv für Psychiatrie und Nervenkrankheiten*, Band ii (1870), pp. 73–108.

50 See note 33. A case reported by Legrand du Saulle appears in *Annales médico-psychologiques* in 1876, Tome IV. But this case is not nearly as well documented as those of Charcot and Magnan.

51 Arrigo Tamassia, "Sull'inversione dell'istinto sensuale," *Revista sperimentale di freniatria*, 1878, pp. 97–117.

52 Julius Krueg, "Perverted Sexual Instincts," *Brain*, Volume IV (October 1881), pp. 368–76.

53 J. C. Shaw and G. N. Ferris, "Perverted Sexual Instinct," *Journal of Nervous and Mental Diseases*, Volume X, number 2 (April 1883), p. 198. A useful discussion of the nineteenth-century medical literature can be found in Chevalier, op. cit., Chapter 2.

54 Shaw and Ferris, op. cit. This article is the most comprehensive early article to appear in English.

55 Ibid., p. 100.

56 See Sérieux, op. cit., p. 37 (quoting Magnan), and Kiernan, op. cit., p. 130.

57 Krafft-Ebing, *Psychopathia Sexualis*, p. 186.

58 Ibid., pp. 35–6.

59 Moll, op. cit., p. 171.

60 Michel Foucault, *The History of Sexuality. Volume I: An Introduction* (New York: Pantheon Books, 1978), Chapter 2.

61 Krafft-Ebing, *Textbook on Insanity*, p. 85. By the fourth category Krafft-Ebing seems to have in mind those cases where "the secondary physical sexual characteristics approach that sex to which the individual, according to his instinct, belongs." He refers to these cases as pseudohermaphroditism. See *Psychopathia Sexualis*, p. 36.

62 Legrain, op. cit., p. 51.

63 Ibid., pp. 37–38.

64 Kraepelin, op. cit., p. 510.

65 Ibid., pp. 510–14.

66 American Psychiatric Association, *Diagnostic and Statistical Manual of Mental Disorders, Third Edition* (Washington, D.C.: APA, 1980), pp. 6–8.

67 Morton Prince, "Habit Neuroses as True Functional Diseases," *Boston Medical and Surgical Journal*, volume CXXXIX, number 24 (1898), pp. 589–92. Alfred Binet's "Le Fetichisme dans l'amour," *Revue Philosophique*, volume 24 (1887), must be mentioned as one of the earliest articulations of the associationist point of view. However, his associationism still left room for the notion of congenital morbid states, which he also invoked as part of his explanation of fetishism.

68 Ibid., p. 589.

69 Ibid., p. 590.

70 Sigmund Freud, "Some Points in a Comparative Study of Organic Hysterical Paralyses." *Early Psychoanalytic Writings*. Edited by Philip Rieff (New York: Collier Books, 1963).

71 I have deliberately left aside Freud's views on the perversions. The best brief

discussion of this topic is the entry on perversion in J. Laplanche and J. B. Pontalis, *The Language of Psychoanalysis* (New York: Norton, 1973), pp. 306–9. Also see my essay, "How to Do the History of Psychoanalysis: A Reading of Freud's *Three Essays on the Theory of Sexuality.*"

72 Stanley Cavell, "Knowing and Acknowledging," in *Must We Mean What We Say?* (New York: Charles Scribner's Sons, 1969), p. 265.

73 Krafft-Ebing, *Textbook on Insanity*, p. 81; my emphasis. This is one theme of Foucault's writings on the history of sexuality.

74 Laupts, op. cit.

75 Ibid., pp. 200–1.

76 Krafft-Ebing, *Psychopathia Sexualis*, p. 53.

77 Immanuel Kant, *Anthropology from a Pragmatic Point of View* (The Hague: Martinus Nijhoff, 1974), pp. 82–9.

78 Immanuel Kant, *The Doctrine of Virtue* (Philadelphia: University of Pennsylvania Press, 1964), pp. 87–9.

79 Ibid., p. 89.

80 Charcot was greatly disturbed by critics who claimed that hysteria was an artificial creation, not to be found in nature, but rather learned through imitation by "patients" who visited the Salpêtrière. He vigorously affirmed that the truth is "que la grande attaque dont j'ai formulé les caractères, est bel et bien un type morbide naturel; ce n'est pas un création artificielle; elle appartienent à tous les ages, à tous les pays." J. M. Charcot, *Leçons du Mardi à la Salpètrière. Policlinique 1887–1888*, tome I (Paris: Aux Bureaux du Progrès Médical, 1892), p. 105.

81 Of course, the general doctrine of scientific realism has come under increasingly detailed attack. For some of the most important recent critiques, see Hilary Putnam, *Meaning and the Moral Sciences* (London: Routledge & Kegan Paul, 1978), *Reason, Truth and History* (Cambridge: Cambridge University Press, 1981), and *Realism and Reason* (Cambridge: Cambridge University Press, 1983); Nancy Cartwright, *How the Laws of Physics Lie* (New York: Oxford University Press, 1983); and Ian Hacking, *Representing and Intervening* (Cambridge: Cambridge University Press, 1983).

82 Moreau, op. cit., pp. 67–8.

83 E. Littre, "Un fragment de médicine rétrospective," *Philosophie Positive*, 5 (1869), pp. 103–20.

84 J. M. Charcot and Paul Richer, *Les Démoniaques dans l'Art* (Paris: Delahaye et Lecrosnier, 1887). See especially "Preface," p. vi. Charcot's retrospective medicine is discussed in Jan Goldstein, "The Hysteria Diagnosis and the Politics of Anticlericalism in Late Nineteenth Century France," *Journal of Modern History*, volume 54, number 2 (June 1982).

85 B. A. Morel, *Traité des degenérescences physiques, intellectuelles et morales de l'espèce humaine* (Paris: J. B. Ballière, 1857), pp. 4–5. Morel also uses the notion of a functional lesion (*lésion functionnelle*), p. 53. For some examples of the use of the theory of degeneracy, see Jacques Borel, *Du concept de dégénérescence à la notion d'alcoolisme dans la médicine contemporaine* (Montpellier: Caues et cie, 1968), and Alan Corbin, *Les Filles de noce: Misère sexuelle et prostitution (19ᵉ et 20ᵉ siècles)* (Paris: Aubier Montaigne, 1978).

86 Foucault, *The History of Sexuality*, p. 139.

87 Kraft-Ebing, *Psychopathia Sexualis*, p. 32.

88 Kraepelin, op. cit.

89 Morton Prince, "Sexual perversion or Vice?", p. 85.

90 Ibid. One of the first persons to recognize this consequence of the degeneracy theory of perversion was A. von Schrenck-Notzing, *Therapeutic Suggestion in Psychopathia Sexualis* (Philadelphia: F. A. Davis, 1895) (published in German in 1894). See, for example, p. 145.

91 Quoted by von Schrenck-Notzing, op. cit., p. 145.

92 Ibid.

93 Ibid., p. 304.

94 Ibid., p. v.
95 Ibid., p. 146.
96 Ibid., p. 305.
97 Prince, "Sexual Perversion or Vice?" p. 85.
98 Ibid., p. 95.
99 See Krafft-Ebing's preface to the first edition of *Psychopathia Sexualis*, p. xiv.
100 Prince, "Sexual Perversion or Vice?" p. 95.
101 Ibid.
102 Ibid., p. 96.
103 Immanuel Kant, *Critique of Pure Reason* (New York: St. Martin's Press, 1929), B68–B69.
104 Michel Foucault, "Sexuality and Solitude," *London Review of Books*, volume 3, number 9, 1981, p. 5.
105 Ian Hacking, "Bipower and the Avalanche of Numbers," *Humanities in Society*, vol. 5, no. 3/4, 1982. See also Hacking's "The Invention of Split Personalities," *I & C*, no. 10/11, 1988.
106 Westphal, op. cit. See also Gley, op. cit., pp. 83–4, footnote.
107 Ian Hacking, "How Should We Do the History of Statistics?" *I & C*, Spring 1981, p. 17. See also Hacking's *The Emergence of Probability* (Cambridge: Cambridge University Press, 1975), and his Dawes Hicks Lecture on Philosophy, "Leibniz and Descartes: Proof and Eternal Truths," *Proceedings of the British Academy* (London: Oxford University Press, 1974).
108 Hacking, "Leibniz and Descartes: Proof and Eternal Truths," p. 188.

15

Perception and revolution
The Princess Casamassima and the political imagination

MARTHA NUSSBAUM

I

'She told me you've changed – you've no more the same opinions.'

'The same opinions?'

'About the arrangement of society. You desire no more the assassination of the rich.'

'I never desired any such thing!' said Hyacinth indignantly.

'Oh if you've changed you can confess,' his friend declared in an encouraging tone. 'It's very good for people to be rich. It wouldn't be right for all to be poor.'

'It would be pleasant if all could be rich,' Hyacinth more mildly suggested.

'Yes, but not by stealing and shooting.'

'No, not by stealing and shooting. I never desired that.'

'Ah no doubt she was mistaken. But today you think we must have patience?' the Prince went on as if greatly hoping Hyacinth would allow this valuable conviction to be attributed to him. 'That's also my view.'

'Oh yes, we must have patience,' said his companion, who was now smiling to himself in the dark. (II.319)

Only months before, Hyacinth Robinson had viewed the workers' revolution and the utopian future it projected as goals to be approached with passionate optimism and a violent desire for confrontation. Now we find him in at least verbal agreement with one of the more obtuse and decadent members of the aristocracy: speaking of progress in a mild voice in which we hear no accent of blood, approving of patience and gentleness toward political change, even when this coincides (both comically and tragically) with the exploiter's fondest wish. His smile in the dark acknowledges, wryly, the incongruity. What has happened? And what is it, what can it ever be, this politics of patience, based, as it seems, upon gentleness to human life, on the love of beauty, on the fine-tuned perception of particular things and people, the responsive and responsible activity of feeling?

When I first saw Hilary Putnam, back in that long summer of 1970, he was standing on a platform in Zion, Illinois, calling for the workers' revolution in a voice of infinite gentleness, mildly assenting to killings of the innocent and guilty. That summer the urgency of human need seemed to many to leave no place for any patience; and the violence of the war, which saturated all of life with its ugliness and baseness, seemed to convict any slow liberal response of naïveté at best – at worst, of collaboration with evil. One saw then, too, before one, the shining image of the Marxian "Kingdom of Freedom" on the far side of the cleansing struggle, the rectification on this earth of all crimes that had ever been committed against human dignity, the new world in which all alike, liberated from constraints of class and from alienating labor, would achieve, in peace and leisure, their full humanity. And that image, resonating that night through Putnam's speech, became a part of the call for violence, making the projected war a holy war and sluggish-ness a sin. Later that night in Zion, we watched the film *The Battle of Algiers*, with its compassionate killings, its blood-thirst for the kingdom.

I wondered then, as I now wonder, about the strange juxtaposition, in Putnam's politics at that period, of gentleness with violence, of the loving perception of concrete human lives with the call for abstract killing. In one way these elements seemed to imply one another: For a keen response to suffering seemed then to call forth a rapid and a radical solution. But in another way they seemed, quite obviously, to point in different political directions. Most people who made such revolutionary statements left out the gentleness, and their discourse had a correspondingly greater unity of tone. What was, and is, after all, then, the place of the gentle perceiving heart in the political life? Is the sensibility of a Hyacinth Robinson anything but a liability, when the task is to help?

In recent years Hilary Putnam has criticized the utopian politics of the form of Marxism he formerly endorsed, characterizing it as "a politics which combines hatred with exaggerated optimism."[1] He has also written that "the central *long run* philosophical problem facing people generally is how to maintain a belief in progress without a belief in Utopia."[2] Like Hyacinth Robinson, he has claimed that any viable conception of progress must insist upon the continuity of culture, and on a careful patient conservatism toward the social traditions and the works of art through which human beings express and identify them-selves. He has, like Hyacinth again, spoken of works of art as essential sources of insight and illumination, which could not be taken from human societies without robbing us of a central element in our moral life.[3] He has described a "model for a political stance" that contains three elements: "*socialism* as the guiding principle in the economy;

liberalism as the guiding principle in politics; *conservatism* as the guiding principle in culture"[4] – all of which would find, as we shall see,
many echoes in Hyacinth's own reflections. So I have decided, in
honoring this extraordinary philosopher and wonderful friend, whose
compassion for suffering humanity has been, throughout, a mainspring
of his thought and action, to turn to the one novel in which Henry
James, that apostle of a fine-tuned awareness of particulars, asks about
the relationship between that ideal and his own compassion for suffering humanity. I shall turn, then, to *The Princess Casamassima*, asking
what its idea of progress might be, and what role the perceiving
imagination plays in it; what relationship there might be between
Hyacinth's cultural conservatism and his belief in patience, between his
being a person "on whom nothing is lost" and his inability to stick with
the optimism of revolutionary socialism. Asking, above all, the novel's
tragic and comic question: How can one in fact be a person of
compassion and either kill, or, after all, not kill, the enemies of the
people?

II

My project faces opposition, from two related sources. For it has been
influentially claimed by Irving Howe, in *Politics and the Novel*, that *The
Princess Casamassima* cannot be mined, as I wish to mine it, for
political thought, since it actually shows Henry James's complete indifference to, and incapacity for, political thought.[5] Howe assumes that a
certain propensity for abstraction and a fondness for general statement
are hallmarks of the real political thinker; and, furthermore, that the
proper subject matter of political thought is "a collective mode of
action": a way of seeing action that is not reducible to, or properly
approached in terms of, the actions and desires of particular human
beings. He then observes that in James's novel we notice an "aversion"
to generalizing that amounts to "a deep distrust, indeed a professional
refusal." We find what Howe calls a "trained inexperience in abstract
thought." And, finally, we find the absence of any sense of a "larger
view of politics as a collective mode of action" – the attention of the
novelist being, instead, all turned toward the doings and sufferings of
particular human beings.[6] All this seems, in a sense, accurate enough as
description of the novel. But we might still hold out some hope for our
political interest in James if we consider that perhaps this refusal of the
abstract and the general might spring from a deeper source in James's
thought than the habits of the novelist's trade; that the inability to see

events in collective, rather than personal, terms might spring from a
deep sense of what morality actually requires; and that the propensity
to generalize (present in the novel, as we shall see, in the discourse of
more than one of its socialist characters) might seem from this viewpoint to be a moral and also a political deficiency; that (as I have
elsewhere argued) the best way to regard James might be not so much
the way Howe regards him, as a novelist by trade who, because that was
his trade, expressed in that form (with whatever its limitations) his
moral vision, but as a thinker about human social life whose thought
about life found in the novel its necessary form and fitting expression.

Putnam himself, however, has expressed, concerning Henry James, a
reservation that, while related to Howe's, is both more fundamental
and more carefully expressed.[7] Unlike Howe, Putnam acknowledges
that it is essential to James's moral vision that the perception of
particulars is in a sense prior to general moral rules and principles –
that in this sense the fine-tuned non-abstractness of these novels
appropriately expresses something that was important to James's conception of what human life should be. But Putnam expresses doubts
about the value of this idea as a model, even for the personal life. He
charges that this morality of perceptions, which is also a morality of
tender attention toward particulars, is dangerously lacking in general
rule-guided toughness. A person who deliberates in the way that James
recommends might be all too free from binding obligations, all too
capable of any trade-offs. I have more than once tried to answer this
charge where personal morality is concerned, and to spell out carefully
the dialogue between rules and perceptions that we actually find in
James's morality.[8] But even if we can defend James in that context, we
might still feel that the objection has some force in the political life,
where even moral thinkers who advocate particularism in personal
choice still sometimes claim that we need to be guided by firm and
general rules.[9] Putnam has not connected his own political interest in
art and literature (and in the related new model of progress, conservative with respect to culture) with these criticisms of James's conception
of morality. But the juxtaposition of Putnam's anti-utopian "Note on
Progress," so apparently close to the thought of Hyacinth Robinson,
with "Taking Rules Seriously," so skeptical of James's heroes and
heroines, forces *us* to inquire about the moral and, in this case, political
viability of the Jamesian conception.

It is evident that James himself was prepared to defend his moral
ideal as appropriate for the public as well as the private realm. He
repeatedly speaks of the author's task as not only moral, but also
political. And he once says, concerning the author's work in creating

heroes and heroines of a certain sort, that the goal is

> ... to *create* the record, in default of any other enjoyment of it: to imagine, in a word, the honourable, the producible case. What better example than this of the high and helpful public and as it were, civic use of the imagination? – a faculty for the possible fine employment of which in the interest of morality my esteem grows every hour I live.[10]

So a central task of our reading of *The Princess*, the most overtly public and civic among his many public and civic writings, must be to ask how a James character can (*pace* Howe) express political thought, and also how (*pace* Putnam) we might defend this thought as valuable in our actual political lives.

III

This novel places before us a consciousness of a certain sort, even as it also demands that we be, as readers, just such actively responding consciousnesses. In its intricate sentences and paragraphs it creates the record of such a mind, and it bids us, as we follow their complicated windings, to be ourselves the complexity it shows. This aspect of the novel is given tremendous emphasis, both within its design and in the remarkable Preface, one of James's most extended and justly famous accounts of the role of a certain sort of hero in his conception of the novelist's function. Hyacinth Robinson is a person "on whom nothing was lost" (I.169).[11] James has endowed him, he tells us in the Preface, with a fine sensitive intelligence, with the power to feel intensely everything that befalls him, with, in short, "the power to be finely aware and richly responsible" (I.viii). In contrast to the "coarse and the blind" (viii), for whom what befalls has little import, Robinson will be among "the more deeply wondering ... the really sentient" (viii). James stresses that while "the imputing of intelligence" is here the "very essence" (ix) of the novelist's work, by intelligence he means not simply intellectual keenness, but, rather more, an ability to perceive and also to feel the practical significance of each particular event and person and perplexity. Indeed, the distinction between responding and acting loses its sharpness in the life of such characters, since a great part of what they morally and significantly and assessibly *do* will consist in fitting response to the seen. "I then see their 'doing,' that of the persons just mentioned, as, immensely, their feeling, their feeling as their doing," he concludes (I.xi). And the political scene of the novel will, crucially, be displayed to us through "a consciousness (on the part of the moved and moving creature) subject to fine intensification and wide enlargement" (xii), a consciousness many of whose most appropriate acts are just such feelings and perceptions. It is made clear that this is not simply a useful device for conveying to the reader a rich sense of what happens; it is a device with a distinct moral dimension, through which we get "the value and beauty of the thing" (xiii); we can count on Hyacinth Robinson not only as our storyteller, but also, in some sense, as a fine moral touchstone and guide.

I have written elsewhere about James's moral ideal and the role it plays in his claim that the work of the author and the reader is an exemplary kind of moral conduct.[12] I shall return later to some of the particular features of Hyacinth's moral imagination. But if we are to take James's heroes seriously as models for the political, as well as for the moral, life, we must confront, clearly, a number of troublesome questions. First, we will be asked what political conception this moral norm implies. If it is best for human beings to be "finely aware and richly responsible," doesn't this imply that the best political structure is some sort of aristocracy or oligarchy? (And if it does, might this not give us reason to be skeptical of the moral norm itself?) This question is implicitly raised by many of James's novels, with their concentration on the vibrant sentience of people who just happen also to be leisured gentlemen and ladies, with these novels' suggestion that the essence of the moral life resides in the sort of exchange that might take place at a house-party. *The Princess* shows us that James does not shirk this question, but anxiously confronts it. So one primary task of any reading of this novel would be to see what comes of that confrontation.

Next, we will have to turn from the question of political structure to the question of the political imagination and to the question raised by Putnam and Howe. To cast it in political terms, doesn't all this agonized feeling and subtle perceiving have both too much complexity and nuance and also too little rule-governed toughness? Don't we need something straighter, harder, more direct, more general, when it is social choice that is in question? Again, this is a question that James by no means shirks;[13] and he gives us an interesting array of political actors against whom, by contrast, the claims of Hyacinth's imagination can be assessed. As we consider them, we will also need to consider the political significance of Hyacinth's attachment to art and to the continuity of culture; for these attachments are presented as essential elements in his moral outlook, integrally connected to his way of seeing and feeling. And they have, clearly, political consequences of a problematic kind. Do we, then, want political actors who share those attachments?

Finally, we cannot avoid confronting the most intractable question, the question that bears in upon us with embarrassing force from the moment that we hear his name: Isn't such a character really too gentle for this world? Too soft, too little, too like a flower, too naturally, incapable of violence and of crudely vigorous response, to engage in the political life, which seems much of the time to be nothing if not crude and violent? Isn't such a character, dedicated to tender care for the particulars, just the wrong sort of person for, and rather ludicrous in, that dark and corrupt environment? The delicacy that in the personal life, that in the work of the novelist, may be an asset looks in politics like a fatal liability. Such a person can do no good for anyone; he can only be crushed, or bent to the will of the oppressor. James will not permit us not to confront this question. From the names alone, we know that Hyacinth is a delicate plant to Paul Muniment's fortified stronghold. Is not a politics of perception, then, nothing more than a weak or foolish politics?

IV

If we take our moral norm from the movements of thought and feeling represented, and created in us, by James's sentences, must we then be aristocrats? It could seem so. For if that sort of finely responsive thinking has, as the novels frequently suggest, certain necessary conditions, such as the absence of mindless grinding labor, a certain level of education, and perhaps a certain amount of leisure, and if that sort of thinking is really the only sort we can trust for good decision making, then it might seem that we will be urged to leave decision making to a privileged few, and to let them take care, Platonically, of the interests of those who are too dull to see clearly on their own. In many of James's novels this issue is simply not addressed, for we see there only the upper-middle and upper classes, usually in conditions removed from work, even when we know (as in the case of Adam Verver, Lambert Strether, Mervyn Densher) that work has been a substantial part of their existence. But the issue is confronted head on in *The Princess*, with its working-class hero.

In order to see how James confronts the issue we must first distinguish, as many who depict James as an aristocratic conservative do not, between two sorts of defenses of aristocracy – or, better put, between a defense of aristocracy and a defense of a general political perfectionism. On the one hand, there is the traditional aristocratic view, of which James sometimes stands accused: the view that only the members of a certain class have, by nature, the refinement of mind that is essential to good governing, and that they, therefore, should govern for everyone. On the other hand, we have a perfectionist view that insists that not all human lives are equally complete, equally flourishing – even where moral development itself is concerned – and that this is so, in great part, because the central human capabilities have, for their development, material and educational necessary conditions that are not, as things are in most actual societies, available to all. The latter (Aristotelian) view is not a conservative view.[14] If we combine it, as Aristotle does, with the claim that it is the essential task of politics to make people, everyone in the city, capable of living well in the most important human ways, it generates a radical demand for social and educational change, with the aim of bringing to all human beings[15] the conditions of *eudaimonia* and practical wisdom. *The Princess*, I believe, shows us that James's view is the Aristotelian view, and not the conservative/aristocratic view.

The novel shows to us clearly, recommends to us as an important social insight, that thinking, imagining, and even desiring are very much affected by the material circumstances of life – by nutrition, by the squalor or spaciousness, the beauty or ugliness, of one's surroundings, by education, by the stability and quality of one's family ties. The worst things about poverty and squalor, as this book presents them, is that they corrupt the capabilities of thinking, feeling, and desiring. Hyacinth tells the Princess that "centuries of poverty, of ill-paid toil, of bad insufficient food and wretched housing hadn't a favourable effect on the higher faculties.... In his own low walk of life, people had really not the faculty of thought; their minds had been simplified – reduced to two or three elements" (I.245–6).

This sentiment is, of course, not one that is easy for compassionate, privileged, somewhat radical people to swallow. We as readers are expected to share the Princess's discomfort, as "she turned about, she twisted herself vaguely as if she wished to protest" (I.246). And yet the novel makes perfectly clear how far removed its own position is from the endorsement of hereditary aristocracy, by insisting repeatedly that it is material conditions, conditions that can be changed, that make the difference in thought. Once Hyacinth almost forgets this; but he is brought up short by Muniment, who, for all his moral defectiveness when it comes to perceiving and feeling, still is permitted here to state the truth as the novel presents it:

The low tone of our fellow mortals is a result of bad conditions; it's the conditions I want to alter. When those who have no start to speak of have a good one it's fair to infer they'll go further. I want to try them, you know. (II.216)

Hyacinth assents to the diagnosis. And when, later, he finally ventures out, curious Princess on his arm, to confront for the first time the most squalid conditions in the London slums, he understands that even the desire for amelioration can be undercut by misery:

He was aware the people were direfully wretched – more aware, it often seemed to him, than they themselves were; so frequently was he struck with their brutal insensibility, a grossness proof against the taste of better things and against any desire for them. (II.262)

One may not like this. I find that my privileged students, at this point, wishing to be, as they take it, more compassionate, tend to protest, saying, for example, "But what about Tolstoy's peasants?" But the view that goodness and fine thought have no material conditions is a view inseparable, in Tolstoy, from a Christian conception of the soul as both impervious to material conditions and awaiting another world's reward. The novel does not endorse that conception of the soul. Indeed the otherworldly promises of Christianity are unambiguously portrayed, in James's novel, as accomplices of a callous and repressive aristocracy. (The Prince says that the absence in England of "the true faith" is what explains the excessive demands of the English poor for social change: With faith, one is willing to wait longer [II.312].) James would presumably claim that Tolstoy's sentimentalizing account of the poor is both false about the relation between the spirit and its material conditions and itself an obstacle to social progress. The more truly compassionate view, he could plausibly claim, is the one that shows the full ugliness of poverty without shrinking, and shows its cost not only to the body but also to the soul. The humanistic writings of the young Marx about what full human functioning requires, and about the worker's alienation from all but the most animal use of his human faculties, correspond in their harshness to the perceptions of Hyacinth Robinson.[16] And the aim of those writings – as, I claim, of this one – was surely to arouse a less self-serving and a more radical kind of compassion toward workers, by measuring clearly the distance between their current lives and the full flourishing of which we think human beings capable.

The novel shows us as the most miserable in soul those whose physical conditions are horrendous. But it does not stop, clearly, at this point. It shows even the life of skilled laborers like Hyacinth to be, in part, a life inimical to the full exercise of practical reason. Here labor itself does not seem to be at fault: The trade of the bookbinders is shown, in the novel, as one in which much high humanity can be lovingly expressed. The workers at the bindery, and also the other skilled laborers who frequent the political meetings at the Sun and Moon café, are shown as decent fellows, capable of discontent, capable of visions, of friendship, of political deliberation. But they lack education; and their minds have not been influenced by the experience of high complex creation, either artistic or intellectual. Because nobody led them to read or otherwise perceive works in which thought is rigorous and sentiment refined, their own political discourse is usually muddy and gross. They strive for the good "blindly, obstructedly, in a kind of eternal dirty intellectual fog" (I.340). They continually repeat themselves; they substitute "iterations" for arguments. One of them "had always the same refrain; 'Well now are we just starving or ain't we just starving? I should like the v'ice of the company on that question.'" Others "remarked to satiety that if it was not done today it would have to be done tomorrow" (I.339). It comes as no surprise to the reader of James that there is in this novel no sentimentalizing of simplicity. Life, both personal and political, is a tough, complex business, requiring, at its best, much refinement of feeling and much clarity of thought. There is no use pretending that this thought and feeling spring up spontaneously, without education, or that political discourse without them is discourse at its best and most human.

Again, I think James is right here, both right and more truly compassionate than an author who would sentimentalize simplicity, or pretend that complexity has no requirements. James's view is as far from Tolstoy's as a social view can be, both on the issue of simplicity of soul and concerning the art we need to shape the soul. It is, however, very close, here again, to the views of the young Marx, who imagines that the worker's newfound leisure will be used for the full education of the mind, by contact with great works of art and literature.

How has Hyacinth escaped? For if we can understand how, in spite of these facts, a working-class man can be a hero of a Henry James novel, we will have more insight into the background conditions for James's norm. Clearly Hyacinth has been brought up in conditions that meet adequate minimum standards of nutrition and health care. He is healthy and strong; and though Lomax Place is drab, it is not squalid, as we clearly see from his horrified reactions elsewhere. The availability of decent medical care is something James goes out of his way to document. When Pinnie is ill, Hyacinth calls in a famous expensive doctor, only to be told by this doctor that the treatment their usual local doctor had already given has been admirable. We also learn that Hyacinth has been raised stably and with love, by both Pinnie and Vetch; this, again, is given emphasis by juxtaposition to the casual domestic violence and drunkenness of the Henning establishment. (In that case, we are given some clear hints about a set of social problems that are often connected to poverty and that demand urgent attention.)

Hyacinth's work, furthermore, is not alienating work, work to which the worker feels external. He affirms himself in his bookbinding, identifies himself with what he produces, takes pride in his creations as expressions of his thought and feeling. And his work leaves him enough leisure to pursue social relations and entertainment. (Much of the novel's activity takes place on Sundays.)

And Hyacinth has been educated. Pinnie and Vetch have given every encouragement to his desire for learning, so that, in spite of class barriers, his resourceful mind has managed to go through quite a lot of great literature (we hear casual allusions to Dumas, Balzac, Musset, Tennyson), to attend the theater frequently, to listen to music, at least of the theatrical sort, to master French and some Italian, and to learn enough about the history of art so that he knows how to situate and appreciate what he sees when he later sees it. It is clear that Hyacinth is a remarkably well-motivated and able pupil. We are not led to believe that everyone could be a successful autodidact in this way. But Vetch, too, is one, and wiser than any aristocrat. And we feel that being brought up with a sense that this is what is absolutely expected of one's dignity has done far more than has native energy, important as that is, to propel Hyacinth on his way. So we are left with the thought that if education were not only demanded of all but also held out to all (by the family, by society generally) as their appropriate birthright and the appropriate completion of the humanity they each have, an essential first step would have been taken. It's hardly a sufficient step; Sholto is educated without being intelligent, and the Princess's idle desire for new emotional intensities leads her to abuse the educated intelligence she possesses. But it is, in this world, something.

And this brings me to one last feature in Hyacinth's biography. His most unusual feature, if we contrast him with the novel's other working-class characters, is that he has been brought up to believe that he is really a gentleman – therefore, one of whom clarity of thought and refinement of sentiment are demanded, one of the ones about whom great works of art are written, one for whom there is no excuse if he does not live up to the standard held out in those works. Both the responsibilities and the opportunities of being a certain sort of human being are vividly conveyed to him in the myth of his origin on which he is lovingly brought up. And allegiance to a high image of himself is, throughout, an essential part of what keeps him straining to miss nothing, to be just and fine and gentle and lucid. By contrast, the other workers expect little of themselves, seeing their possibilities always in the images of members of their class held out to them by the disdainful aristocrats who control their cultural life. (Only Millicent Henning, with her boundless energy and her "large, free nature," manages to escape self-stereotyping and to live out her own unique part with a joyful exuberance that is no less wonderful, in its own way, than Hyacinth's subtle responsiveness.)

In this way James shows us another invidious feature of English class distinctions: that they cripple people's sense of the possible by tying images of high humanity to images of class membership. The life of Rosy Muniment is twisted by her inability to imagine beauty in other than an aristocratic garb; even the loving Pinnie associates freedom and nobility with images of aristocracy. And Hyacinth, too, is, finally, caught. He cannot imagine a constructive political solution because he thinks of the moral goal, always, in connection with the idea of becoming like one of the privileged ones. This is perhaps why, before the poor, his thought yields to "a sense of the inevitable and insurmountable" (II.262). James, however, shows us – through the limitations of his characters, Hyacinth among them – that what would be absolutely essential to any "ameliorating influence" (II.170) in education would be images of high humanity with which the pupil of whatever class might identify. It is one of his great achievements here to show us how Hyacinth both does and does not escape the traps set by a class-divided society for the thought and desire of a person of his class: escapes, to the extent that he finds ways of believing in his own dignity and projecting it into society, trusting the resources of his imagination; does not escape, to the extent that his image of himself as dignified is so closely linked to his fantasy of himself as a nobleman's child. Certain parts of French literature give Hyacinth a start beyond this point. For in Paris he proves able to imagine his proletarian revolutionary grandfather speaking to him, as in a novel of his own creation, with "a gaiety which even political madness could never quench," and with a French prose "delightful and sociable in accent and phrase" (II.122). This "vague yet vivid personage" (II.122) is the projected hero of a new literature for humanity. Hyacinth himself is, for us, another.

What, politically, does this give us? Seeing, as we must, through Hyacinth's eyes, we can see this none too clearly. But insofar as we are invited to think critically about him, we are invited also to imagine for ourselves the possibilities. We seem, in fact, to have a case made out for all three elements in Putnam's "model for a political stance." First, for socialism in the economy: For we are clearly shown that the provision to all of the basic needs of life, including food, housing, recreational space, decent health care, and education, is an essential part of any society that would have any chance of transcending the wrongs with which this novel confronts us.

"Liberalism as the guiding principle in politics": This too is, I believe, in the novel. For James shows us a conception of the human being according to which our essential dignity resides in the free and responsive activity of thought and the free creative use of language. And he displays revolutionary socialism, insofar as it impinges on the liberties of thought and speech, as a prison for the spirit as pernicious as the prison of poverty. The frequency of images of the prison, and the denial of freedom, in connection with both socialism and the repressed condition of the poor, leaves no doubt of this intent. The novel's strong claims for the moral value of the literary imagination are inseparable from a demand for the artist's freedom of expression, for freedom of expression generally. The tyrannical attitude of the revolutionary leader Hoffendahl, who "treated all things, persons, institutions, ideas, as so many notes in his great symphonic massacre" (II.55), is contrasted throughout with the humanity of the artist's loving perception, an "ameliorating influence" (II.170) that could not survive under that sort of socialism. The contrast indicates that the latter had better not be put under the direction of the former.

The novel advocates liberalism, too, in its mistrust of revolutionary violence and its preference for patient, slow change; this theme we shall examine shortly. It advocates liberalism, finally, in that, while it certainly does insist that not all ways of life are equally valuable, it insists as well that we do not want a politics that coerces diverse individuals into identical paths, or prevents their diverse self-expression in choices of profession, friends, entertainments. With Vetch we see as remarkably dreary the socialistic vision of Poupin, "where the human family would sit in groups at little tables, according to affinities, drinking coffee (not tea, *par exemple!*) and listening to the music of the spheres. Mr. Vetch neither prefigured nor desired this organized beatitude; he was fond of his cup of tea" (I.96). Here James confronts us with a telling point about many socialist (and many conservative) visions of the good: that they consist, all too often, of the enforcement as a general law for everyone of some elite's arbitrary preference. Because the Frenchman Poupin prefers coffee, everyone will have to have coffee. Vetch, wisely, wants to protect, albeit within a general vision of good human functioning, a substantial amount of space for the freedom of private choice.

"Conservatism as the guiding principle in culture": James suggests, as we have seen, the importance of creating new heroes, new identifications, of criticizing the old. He does not recommend nostalgic traditionalism, clearly. He also causes us to think about the need to devise ways of public access to the finest works of art, to humanistic education generally. But preservation, for all, of cultural traditions is, with these qualifications, a central emphasis of the novel. We shall shortly return to those arguments as we ask what sort of political agent a Henry James hero can be.

In short, there is, it seems to me, a political program, or at least a political stance, in this novel, and one that the Britain of the pre-Thatcher years was going a long way toward executing, with its combination of socialist economic policies in health and nutrition with the protection of liberal freedoms, with its policies of free public access to museums and galleries, with its public parks and musical performances, with its schemes, however vexed with difficulty, of public education.

V

We still have not answered Howe and Putnam. We still have not shown that the sort of consciousness James puts before us as exemplary *is* actually exemplary in the political life. Isn't a Henry James hero after all, as Putnam suggests, *too much* concerned with particulars and not enough with principle? Too much with the finely concrete and not enough with moral abstractions? To answer Howe we need to ask the same question. For what we want to show is that the absence of generality of thought and expression in Hyacinth Robinson – and in the novelist's consciousness as well – is not neglect or incapacity, but the deliberate creation of a different, and plausible, norm.

We have begun to say something of what, as an actor on the political scene, "our hero" is. (And since I have elsewhere discussed in detail the moral approach of Hyacinth's close relatives in *The Golden Bowl* and *The Ambassadors*,[17] I shall be brief.) Above all, Hyacinth is "a youth on whom nothing was lost." The "stage of his inner consciousness" (I.169–70) is peopled with rich impressions, as, "precociously attentive" (I.19) and "all-observant" (I.76), he responds, almost without conscious effort, to all that presents itself to his faculties, "seeing indescribable differences" (I.167) in things:

For this unfortunate but remarkably-organized youth every displeasure or gratification of the visual sense coloured his whole mind, and ... nothing in life had such an interest or such a price for him as his impressions and reflections. They came from everything he touched, they made him vibrate, kept him thrilled and throbbing, for most of his waking consciousness, and they constituted as yet the principal events and stages of his career ... Everything in the field of observation suggested this or that; everything struck him, penetrated, stirred; he had in a word more news of life, as he might have called it, than he knew what to do with – felt sometimes as he could have imagined an overwhelmed man of business to whom the post brought too many letters. The man of business indeed could keep a secretary, but what secretary could have cleared up for Hyacinth some of the strange communications of life? (I.159)

We see, here as elsewhere, not only a lively responsiveness of the physical senses; we see also that he *reflects* and *feels* intensely; reflects intensely even when reflection leads to bewilderment, and feels intensely even when feeling has its "price." This combination of a capacity to be bewildered, *not* to simplify, with a willingness to be "penetrated" emotionally – all this, James makes clear, both in the text and in the Preface, is what makes him, in fact, a perceiver, on whom nothing is lost. For if you are going to see life as it is, you have to be willing to be perplexed, to see its mystery and complexity; consoling simplification brings dullness of vision. And, as Godfrey Sholto tells the Princess, "There are mysteries you can't see into unless you happen to have a little decent human feeling" – so if he is going to see he will have to "vibrate," in his heart, for what he sees. His feelings, as the Preface insists, are a large part of his morally assessible "doings," and in Hyacinth's relation to the world around him we "have then at once a case of feeling, of ever so many possible feelings, stretched across the scene like an attached thread on which the pearls of interest are strung" (I.xii).

James makes it very clear that Hyacinth's perceiving is inseparable from a keen sense of ethical value, and from an active love of human beings. The Preface tells us that his responsiveness is a responsiveness to value. And from the beginning of the novel Hyacinth "wants to be very good" (I.52); he "strove to cultivate justice in his own conduct ... catching every aspect and feeling every value" (II.7). The values he feels include, primarily, ethical values. And this means that his encounter with human misery brings him torment (I.viii): his ability was "fairly founded on" the "knowledge of suffering." It is made clear that the ability to perceive particular lives and contexts with clarity, and to imagine, as he constantly does, the motivations and experiences of others, is combined with a general desire for goodness and justice; and that it is this combination that makes Hyacinth a fine ethical and political agent.

But the nature of his fineness can even more clearly be seen from the novel's contrasts, as Hyacinth's richly peopled and concrete mind is set up against minds whose moral grossness is the consequence of an obtuseness of vision, a refusal to see and feel concretely any particular unique life. And it is James's contention, in the peopling of this novel, that most actual political thought and agency suffer from this obtuseness. Eustache Poupin is an honest, well-intentioned man, apparently generous and benign. And yet, from the moment when we are told of the coarse, flat sentimentality of his socialist image of utopia – in which "all the nations of the earth would abolish their frontiers and armies and custom-houses, and embrace on both cheeks and cover the earth with boulevards" – we know that the mind that is hooked on this image of "organized beatitude" has a dull eye for the actual lives of individuals. His eventual betrayal of Hyacinth is, from that moment, prepared. The grander direction of the revolutionary movement is shown as even more coarsely lacking in the ability to see and feel for people one by one – as the brief account of the mind of the revered leader Hoffendahl scathingly shows:

Humanity, in his scheme, was classified and subdivided with a truly German thoroughness and altogether of course from the point of view of the revolution... He treated all things, persons, institutions, ideas, as so many notes in his great symphonic massacre. (II.55)

But it is in the brilliant portrait of Paul Muniment, charismatic future leader of the socialist bureaucracy, that James gives us his most penetrating indictment of political generalizing. For Muniment's relation to Hyacinth is, or so it seems, a relation of personal friendship. To Hyacinth, this relation requires trying to see the good in Muniment's thoughts and actions, even when they seem impossibly remote from his own responses; and for Muniment, this *should* mean, or so we with Hyacinth expect, the effort, at least in this one case, to achieve an emotionally rich particular response and vision. Through the narrative of the failure of their friendship, in tragic bewilderment on one side and high obtuseness on the other, James most pointedly shows us his case for a political discourse based on perception, and his indictment of the abstracting tendency.

From the beginning, we know that Muniment is coarse: "A delicate tact that was not his main characteristic" (I.124), and his face "offered our quick youth the image of a rank of bristling bayonets." And Hyacinth finds for Muniment's remoteness from concrete human life images such that, if we are familiar with James's iconography of guilty innocence (of the kind of remoteness from the real that allows one to do terrible things with a sublime sense of one's own purity), we sufficiently get the tip: images of loftiness, of "singleness of vision" (II.218), description of a "touch of a kind at once very firm and very soft yet strangely cold" (II.212). Determined to love him still, and, loving him, to see the good in his betrayal, Hyacinth gets himself for a moment to carry, in his imagination, the "weight" of

the sense of such a sublime consistency. Hyacinth felt that he himself could never have risen so high. He was competent to take the stiff engagement to Hoffendahl and was equally competent to keep it; but he couldn't have had the same fortitude for another, couldn't have detached himself from personal prejudice so effectually as to put forward in that manner for the terrible 'job' a little chap he to all appearance really liked. (II.136)

And shortly after this we understand how Muniment has risen so high. For we are permitted – perhaps through Hyacinth's empathetic efforts to understand him – a glimpse of the way the world looks through Muniment's eyes:

On behalf of others he never sounded the pathetic note – he thought that sort of thing unbusinesslike; and the most that he did in the way of expatiation on the woes of humanity was occasionally to allude to certain statistics, certain 'returns', in regard to the remuneration of industries, applications for employment and the discharge of hands. In such matters as these he was deeply versed, moving ever in a dry statistical and scientific air in which it cost Hyacinth an effort of respiration to accompany him. (II.137)

Above all, we learn, as we go on, of Muniment's "absence of passion, his fresh-coloured coolness, his easy exact knowledge, the way he kept himself clean (save for fine chemical stains on his hands) in circumstances of foul contact" (II.137). And emotionless and dedicated to having "as little" emotion "as possible" (II.291), he keeps himself clean to the end, but for the fine stain of his friend's life (scientifically and chemically recorded) upon his efficient hands.

This is political discourse. We cannot deny (thinking back, once again to the revolutionary parties of the sixties) that we recognize its note and know the people. We can't deny either that in a certain conventional sense Hyacinth's contrasted discourse and thought are personal and not political. He can't rise that high, breathe in that air. He cannot help seeing each individual person in all his or her individuality, in all his or her tangled web of relations to others and to himself, in all of his or her history; and his imagination, holding him close to the tangled world, will not permit him the lofty cleanliness of mathematical abstraction. But James's point is that this commitment to the personal *is* political: that it is in rising so high that politics becomes capable of atrocity, ceases to breathe the human air; that the stance of the perceiver is superior not only on account of what is *can* see, be touched by, and therefore do (all the things to which Muniment is blind and which he therefore cannot include in any vision for a nation), but also on account of what it *cannot* do, is prevented from doing. James connects the delicate emotion-laden perception of particulars (Hyacinth's sort, infused with ethical aspiration and the desire for human justice) with gentleness and kindness, the ability to cut off emotion and to rise high above the people with the possibility of terrible acts. The claim seems to be that if you really vividly experience a concrete human life, imagine what it's like to live that life, and at the same time permit yourself the full range of emotional response to that concrete life, you will (if you have at all a good moral start) be unable to do certain things to that person. Vividness leads to tenderness, imagination to compassion. The patient effort to see moderates the coarseness of which political horror is made. (We recall, in this connection, the tendency of Nazi functionaries to speak of Jews as "cargo," or as certain quantities of merchandise, to be packed, transported, quantified. Allowing themselves the sight of a particular human being was for them, as for Muniment here, a jeopardy.)

One scene in the novel makes this point with particular clarity. Hyacinth and Lady Aurora Langrish meet after both have been abandoned by the Princess. They sit "looking at each other in an odd, an occult community of suffering" (II.354). It now would be very natural that they might get angry together, express rage or hatred, even wish or plan some revenge. But this is not what happens:

A tacit confession passed and repassed, and each understood the situation of the other. They wouldn't speak of it – it was very definite they would never do that; for there was something in their common consciousness that was inconsistent with the grossness of accusation. (II.354)

Here, as so often in James's novels, we find a refusal to retaliate, a refusal to hate, linked with the perceiver's fine consciousness of the particulars of the situation. The connection is made by responsiveness, by love. Hyacinth and Aurora love the Princess, love her in a perceiving way, seeing her in all her tangled complexity. To complain about her would be, then, too blindly self-proclaiming, too crudely unloving and self-absorbed. Focusing on *her*, they lay down their revenge. (The most persistent complainer and accuser in the novel is Rosy Muniment, wrapped in a fog of envy, unable to see beyond her own injured condition. And the socialists too are, all too frequently, as Hyacinth sees, motivated by the spirit of envy, which takes them away from the vision of what is before them.) Clarity leads, it seems, to gentleness. To see as the novelist sees is to see more humanely.

If this is plausible, then Howe's criticism misses the mark; for instead of showing himself incapable of political thought, James is offering us a searching critique of most actual political thought, and arguing that the sort of thought we usually call personal promises a politics richer in humanity. Lionel Trilling, whom Howe dismissively criticizes, saw all of this more deeply.[18] And as for Putnam's worry that the perceiver will be capable of anything, we see here, I think, a convincing argument that it is rather the person who goes by the general that we should worry about; that the perceiver (if adequately steered by an education that includes, we insist again, moral vision and good moral principles) will be most deeply and firmly bound to human values in choosing political action.

VI

But we still have not described the whole of James's case for the politics of perception. For we still have not discussed one of this novel's central political insights, namely, the tension between the love of art and high culture and the politics of the workers' revolution. As Trilling has movingly shown,[19] Hyacinth's growing disenchantment with the motivations and goals of the revolution is closely linked to his love for art and culture, his desire to conserve this "fabric of beauty and power" (II.125) that he sees and, seeing, loves. Architecture, literature, and painting are for him "the richest expression of the life of man" (II.265), "splendours" that "took the form sometimes, to his imagination, of a vast vague dazzling presence, an irradiation of light from objects undefined" (II.217). This love of art, seen as a beauty and a mystery, is a great part of Hyacinth's tragedy, since it is his (true) belief that the revolution intends to destroy the continuity of culture, that Hoffendahl would with equanimity "cut the ceilings of the Veronese into strips" (II.146) that precipitates his abandonment of revolutionary goals. But what *are*, more specifically, the motivations and the political consequences of this conservatism?

In the first place, we have to say that Hyacinth's love of art is a natural consequence of his perceiver's approach to the world, and one that reinforces, in him, that approach. Hyacinth learned his habits of vision from books; and these habits make him, in turn, a better lover of books and other artworks. To love high art, literary or visual, one must stay close to the sensuous and the concrete; and if one combines Hyacinth's closeness with his dedication to the seeing of value, a deep response to great works of art is, James suggests, the natural result. Loving art, furthermore, makes him love more intensely, and with a generous love, the world and its concrete inhabitants, including, indeed, himself. As he walked along the Seine,

a sudden sense overtook him, making his heart falter to anguish – a sense of everything that might hold one to the world, of the sweetness of not dying, the fascination of great cities, the charm of travel and discovery, the generosity of admiration. (II.141)

And, seeing in himself this connection between art and a generous love of the world, he comes to believe, as well, that art must be kept because it is, for all human beings, an incentive to life and to good life:

'I think there can't be too many pictures and statues and works of art,' Hyacinth broke out. 'The more the better, whether people are hungry or not. In the way of ameliorating influences are not those the most definite?' 'A piece of bread and butter's more to the purpose, if your stomach's empty,' the Princess declared. (II.170)

This is a difficult exchange for us, with our political interests and our sympathy with some aspects of Marx's vision. It might be taken to suggest, on James's part, a lack of concern with hunger and a callous preference for elite values. It also might be taken to negate the insight we earlier found in the novel: that perception and responsiveness have material necessary conditions. Both, I think, would be mistaken readings. What is being said is that politics must not address the problems of human life entirely from the bottom up, so to speak, thinking of the spirit only at a time when the needs of the body have been completely satisfied. The revolution wishes to destroy the treasures of art in order to get everyone materially satisfied. Hyacinth's argument is that any real solution to the problems of hunger and misery must take place in the context of an ongoing sense of life's richness and value and full humanity. That food has point only as food for something, and if the sense of this something is lost, feeding will be a feeding of animals. If in the process of concerning ourselves for hunger, we allow life to be emptied of that which holds people to the world, that which inspires love of life and of humanity itself, then we will have, in the end, at best well-fed pigs. James is clearly opposed to the role played by organized religion in getting people to place a certain sort of spiritual promise ahead of their material needs. His placement of those arguments in the Prince's mouth discredits them utterly. We should not accept a promise of comfort in the next world as a substitute for social change in this one. But James does hold that a more worldly development of spirit is an essential part of giving life, including material life, a human meaning, and that art and what we might call a general education in the humanities, are an essential part of that development.

Another argument for Hyacinth's cultural view is found in his reflection about the connection between cultural continuity and a population's sense of its own identities, individual as well as collective. The revolution seems sometimes to him like a flood that will "ris(e) over the world" and "sweep all the traditions of the past before it" (II.262). This means pulling down "things with which the yearnings and tears of generations have been mixed" (II.145–6). It is clear that for Hyacinth it is not only the beauty and humane value of art, it is, as well, its historical depth as record of what has given a people its identity that makes him so fear its desecration. And his fear that under the revolution his trade of bookbinding will no longer win esteem (II.263) is a fear not only for the loss of beauty, but also for the loss of history and the historically constituted self. Once again, this is not an uncritical defense of tradition, nor is it the restriction of humanistic education to works drawn from the history of one's own culture. We are already aware of Hyacinth's keen interest in a new literature of the working class; and his imagination is stirred by many different images of humanity, distant as well as near. But he reminds us, simply, that *one* important function of humanistic education is to learn about one's own history, and that this historical understanding is essential to self-understanding.

There is a further point in Hyacinth's concern with culture that helps us, beyond what we have said already, to understand his new respect for patience in the political life. This is, that fine works of art, loved and studied, show, both in their content and in the facts of their production, some of the deeply rooted conflicts and tragic tensions out of which human history is woven: the connection of beauty with ugliness, of high goal with someone's suffering and misery, of good with evil intentions. Hyacinth sees that the treasures he admires are "rescued" and "redeemed" from the people's misery and toil; that they issue from a civilization that supported this misery. His attention to them is full of critical reflection; in no sense is this a nostalgic traditionalism. (Indeed, it seems wrong to use Putnam's language of cultural *conservatism*, and I have not used it here.) And the art itself, he sees, expresses "yearnings and tears": In its very content it shows him (as this novel shows us) the complex tangle of human motivations, the frequent connection, as James wrote in another preface, of "bliss and bale, of the things that help with the things that hurt," of "somebody's right and ease" with "somebody's pain and wrong"[20] – in short, the pervasiveness of tensions among the goods that, with imperfect attention and defective circumstances, human agents pursue.

James frequently insists that a central function of literary art is to show us the tensions that make us flawed objects with respect to our highest aims, the tragic tensions in our love and attention, as well, to the objects that claim us. And he reminds us that a knowledge of these flaws is an essential prerequisite of any genuine altruism – for, as Charlotte Stant says, "If we may perish by cracks in things we don't know, we can never then give each other anything." Denial of these difficulties breeds an innocence that is, in its exaggerated optimism, frequently intolerant and even cruel to what actually exists. Knowledge of difficulty breeds a tenderness to the flawed object, toward also oneself, seen as flawed.

Here James makes the point a political one. Great art plays a central role in our political lives because, showing us the tangled nature of our loves and commitments, showing us ourselves as flawed crystals, it moderates the optimistic hatred of the actual that makes for a great deal of political violence, moderates the ferocious hopefulness that simply marches over the complicated delicacies of the human heart. As Putnam writes, politics needs, what Marxism as he sees it lacks, a realistic moral psychology, an understanding of the humanly possible. It needs, too, an understanding of the plurality of human values and the often tragic tensions among them.

With this understanding goes a political attitude that is not more *tolerant* of evils, but is, perhaps, more inclined to mercy, less to anger, seeing how pervasive the obstacles to goodness are, how deeply rooted, how much a part of oneself as well as others. This politics tends to diverge from the strict and merited punishment toward humane patience, from cruel retaliation toward a slow gentle fostering of what good there may be. It is a politics of patient consistent labor for hard-won slow progress, a politics aimed (as Seneca once wrote, reproving political anger) "not at ending evils, but at preventing their victory" (*De Ira* II.10). We need art to keep difficulties before us, keeping us from excessive crudeness of hope.

The Princess Casamassima is itself just such a reminder of the difficult. For in its tragic conclusion, Hyacinth's sense of obligation to his promise (and to the cause of workers, which he has agreed to represent) and his newer obligation to perception of the fine collide, leaving him, as he sees it, no exit but a bullet through the heart. His new awareness of art makes him more, not less, responsive to the workers' misery; he can abandon neither side.[21] Muniment's "sublime consistency" will, we know, always keep him safe from tragedy, enabling him to deny any claim that would be too difficult to see and to feel. The Princess, too, will in her way survive, for "the Princess Casamassima had a clear faculty of completely ignoring things of which she wished to take no account; it was not in the least the air of contempt, but thoughtful, tranquil, convenient absence, after which she came back to the point where she wished to be" (I.211). The high view of difficulty brings with it a terrible vulnerability, both to Hyacinth and to us, since his "emotions, (his) stirred intelligence, (his) moral consciousness, become thus, by sufficiently charmed perusal, our very own adventure" (I.xv). Seeing and feeling his tragedy, keeping his difficulty all before us, we see something that is true, for us, of the condition of goodness in the world.

Visiting Cambridge, Massachusetts, in 1941, W. H. Auden wrote a poem of reflection about the relationship between the political attitude that makes and is made by war and the habits of mind that are encouraged by the novels of Henry James, at whose grave the poet/speaker stands. This is a part of that reflection:

> Now more than ever, when torches and snare-drum
> Excite the squat women of the saurian brain
>   Till a milling mob of fears
> Breaks in insultingly on anywhere, when in our dreams
> Pigs play on the organs and the blue sky runs shrieking
>   As the Crack of Doom appears,
>
> Are the good ghosts needed with the white magic
> Of their subtle loves. War has no ambiguities
>   Like a marriage; the result
> Required of its *affaire fatale* is simple and sad,
> The physical removal of all human objects
>   That conceal the Difficult.
>
> Then remember me that I may remember
> The test we have to learn to shudder for is not
>   An historical event,
> That neither the low democracy of a nightmare nor
> An army's primitive tidiness may deceive me
>   About our predicament,
>
> That catastrophic situation which neither
> Victory nor defeat can annul; to be
>   Deaf yet determined to sing,
> To be lame and blind yet burning for the Great Good Place,
> To be radically corrupt yet mournfully attracted
>   By the real Distinguished Thing.
>
> And shall I not specially bless you as, vexed with
> My little inferior questions, today I stand
>   Beside the bed where you rest
> Who opened such passionate arms to your *Bon* when It ran
> Towards you with Its overwhelming reasons pleading
>   All beautifully in Its breast?[22]

In certain ways, I believe, Auden distorts James's moral vision – in particular, by placing the accent on a "radical corruption" of the heart, rather than, what James more often emphasizes, on the difficulty of doing justice, in a tangled world, to all our loves and commitments, the difficulty even of seeing truly all we ought to see, feeling all that we ought to feel. But the essential point is wonderfully made: that war is, from the Jamesian viewpoint, the easy crude cowardly way with the problems of the moral and political life, whereas a patient, lucid confrontation with difficulty is the way of true courage. War doesn't confront, doesn't *see*, our humanity; it simply breaks in on it. It appears to be strong, vigorous, passionate; but it avoids passionate engagement with the reality, the complexity of each thing. The James novel, on the other hand, confronts those complexities and ambiguities, opening its arms, passionately and tenderly, to humanity's hopes and conflicts as to a child, with all the love, patience, and gentle interest in the difficult that this parental relation entails.

Now we see more fully why Hyacinth smiles when the Prince attributes to him a sentiment that agrees, verbally, with the Prince's own: "We must have patience." (Or, as the Prince earlier expresses it more freely in Italian, "Che vuole? Ci vuol' pazienza." "What do you want? These things require patience.") The Prince means by this that the poor should stop making trouble, should go get involved in otherworldly religion, should await the discretion and the almsgiving charity of their betters. Hyacinth does not mean this. He remains committed to the people to the end, though unable in his tragic situation to undertake a practicable strategy for their material and spiritual betterment. He does not want the people to depend upon characters like the Prince. And yet, he says, "We must have patience." For tragically, and with bewilderment, smiling in the dark, he is groping toward the thought that a genuine and lasting political solution must be achieved by a non-violent patient effort to change hearts and minds – an effort of the imagination, of persuasion, an effort, we might say, of writing and reading. This is not to say that such a politics would never find revolutionary strategies justified, for we know that Hyacinth admires the French Revolution. But such strategies will always be subordinated to the deeper and larger end of changing the heart; and all too often they do not serve, but actually impede, such changes. The revolution projected in the novel, for example, simply covers the depth of the problem. Hyacinth smiles, in the dark, at the irony and the difficulty of his verbal coincidence with the forces of reaction, at the difficulty of getting respectable lovers of the people to take this seriously as a response, at the difficulty of convincing sensitive readers of life that what looks like a capitulation is actually the truest courage. And perhaps this smile in the dark is also the novelist's smile at the fact that intelligent readers will no doubt mistake his own advocacy of patience for reaction, his defense of perception for an aversion to political ideas.

VII

But still, isn't he simply too weak? James repeatedly brings us back to his littleness, his physical fragility, his delicacy, his vulnerability. How can "our little hero" (II.155), "our slight hero" (I.261) survive, after all, in politics? Isn't he bound to be simply walked over, even wiped out, by the "superior brutality" (I.338) of the Muniments of this world? Auden's poem, too, draws attention to this question; for its portrait of James embracing his vision of humanity is almost pathetic in the exposed and childlike character of the love it describes, pathetic by contrast to the violence that will, we feel, surely prove able to eclipse it. Isn't there in this novel a recipe for the impotence and even for the suicide of good?

James does not make this issue easy, for in many ways he does invite us to criticize Hyacinth Robinson. This imperfection in his hero (even beyond the general imperfection of human life) is an important part, we have suggested, of his design. For if he showed Hyacinth as escaping altogether through effort and imagination the constraints of his class-divided society he would undercut the case he makes for the link between perception and social conditions. Thus Hyacinth has the fault that comes of having, as images of dignity and worth, only images of aristocracy: He is far too trusting when it comes to the Princess, far too ready, generally, to see in the elegant a non-existent moral worth. His failure to find a viable course of action is to some extent explained by these failings. And James complicates our question still further by placing together with Hyacinth, at the heart of the novel, a character altogether different, healthier, stronger, less refined, less credulous, but nonetheless still generous and compassionate and loving. Millicent Henning is, we might say, to Hyacinth what Bob Assingham is to Fanny: Her simple, rule-governed morality and her genuine kindness of heart sustain him in an essential way. We are led to think that a healthy political community would be made up not only of Hyacinths, but, perhaps, from an affectionate partnership between these two sorts of spirits.[23]

But in the end we are brought back to "our hero," whom we love with all his difficulties. And here we must once again reply that it is not in the least evident that Hyacinth is, in the novel, a weak character. To say that he is weak is not to take seriously the inversion that James proposes in our usual judgments of weakness and of strength. We are asked to recognize that in patient lucidity and non-violent slow effort are more strength altogether than in bristling bayonets, a courage to and for humanity rather than a flight from it into the sublime air. As Hyacinth turns the saying on its head, "One might as well perish for a lamb as for a sheep" (I.145) – for in being a lamb one exposes oneself for the sake of others, and shows in this a superior courage of imagination. Things that at first naturally strike us as ridiculous – for example, the name "Hyacinth Robinson," which would not get many votes in an election ("Muniment" perhaps would, suggesting a tough defense policy) – are, at the novel's end, to strike use as not only finer but also as braver than the tough things, just as it is braver to be a plant, as a man, than a fortification. For a real man *not* to dare to be a flower: *that*, we must see, is the cowardly thing. Lady Aurora Langrish, who patiently helps people one by one, is, in this same way, seen to be a far more courageous revolutionary than the radicals, who play games of violence without looking any one human life in the face.[24]

VIII

There is, then, a revolution called for in this novel. Not the revolution its characters envisage at the start, but one both more achievable and more radical. Not the revolution that consists in hating and then in killing, but the revolution in the heart that consists in learning to see and to love, without disgust, imperfect human beings. It is the demand that we not rest content, as social beings, with half-baked abstract discourse and crude perceptions, with what James elsewhere calls "the rule of the cheap and easy," but that, in public and private, we create our lives with one another with as much subtlety, responsivenes, delicacy, and imagination as are involved in the creation of a work of literary art, dismantling our anger, fostering our gentleness. That, as a politics of perception requires, we work with patient commitment to bring to human beings the material conditions of this life of the spirit, and, at the same time, the spiritual and educational conditions of a loving relation to the world and to one another. Novels like this one create that revolution as a record, and also generate it, as an act, in the hearts of its readers, who exemplify for some brief hours the record and who may come to feel, thereafter, a marked discontent with the crudeness of everyday discourse and action and feeling, a marked desire for the finer, the more truly compassionate, thing. As James said, "What better use than this of the high and helpful public and, as it were, civic use of the imagination?"

"And suppose the readers don't feel this. That nothing happens and it all goes its way as before."

"What do you want? These things need patience."

(Smiling, perhaps, in our darkness.)

Notes

1 Hilary Putnam, "A Note on 'Progress,'" *Erkenntnis* 11 (1977), 1–4, on p. 1.
2 *Ibid.*
3 Putnam, "Literature, Science, and Reflection," in Putnam, *Meaning and the Moral Sciences* (London, 1979), 83–96, also "A Note," 3–4.
4 Putnam, "A Note," 4.

5 Irving Howe, *Politics and the Novel* (New York, 1957). The chapter on James is reprinted in *Henry James: A Collection of Critical Essays*, ed. L. Edel (Englewood Cliffs, N.J., 1963), 156–71. Page numbers are cited from that edition.

6 Howe, pp. 165–7.

7 Putnam, "Taking Rules Seriously: A Response to Martha Nussbaum," *New Literary History* 15 (1983), 193–200. Putnam's article was a response to Nussbaum, "Flawed Crystals: James's *The Golden Bowl* and Literature as Moral Philosophy," *New Literary History* 15 (1983), 25–50.

8 Nussbaum, "Reply to Richard Wollheim, Patrick Gardiner, and Hilary Putnam," *New Literary History* 15 (1983), 201–8; Nussbaum, "The Discernment of Perception: An Aristotelian Conception of Private and Public Rationality," *Boston Area Colloquium for Ancient Philosophy* 1 (1985), 151–201; Nussbaum, " 'Finely Aware and Richly Responsible': Literature and the Moral Imagination," in *Literature and the Question of Philosophy*, ed. A. Cascardi (Baltimore: Johns Hopkins University Press, 1987), 169–91.

9 On this, see Nussbaum, "The Discernment," in a longer version forthcoming in Nussbaum, *Love's Knowledge: Essays on Philosophy and Literature* (Oxford, 1990).

10 H. James, Preface to "The Lesson of the Master," in James, *The Art of the Novel* (New York, 1907), 222–3. See also the discussion of this passage in Nussbaum, " 'Finely Aware.' "

11 All page references to the novel are to *The Novels and Tales of Henry James: New York Edition* (New York: Charles Scribner's Sons, 1907–9). Volumes 5 and 6 of the set contain *The Princess Casamassima*, Volumes I and II. The Preface to *The Princess* will be cited in that pagination and not as it appears in *The Art of the Novel*.

12 In " 'Finely Aware.' "

13 Compare the question of the imaginary interlocutor in the Preface to "The Lesson of the Master": "Where on earth, where round about us at this hour," has James found "such super subtle fry?" (*The Art of the Novel*, 221).

14 See Nussbaum, "Nature, Function, and Capability: Aristotle on Political Distribution," *Oxford Studies in Ancient Philosophy*, Supplementary Volume 1988.

15 On the question of exactly who is included in Aristotle's own distributive project, see "Nature, Function, and Capability." For discussions of the contemporary implications of Aristotle's view, see Nussbaum, "Aristotelian Social Democracy," forthcoming in G. Mara and H. Richardson (eds.), *Liberalism and the Good* (New York: Routledge, Chapman, and Hall, 1990).

16 See, for example, the following passage from *Economic and Philosophical Manuscripts of 1844*, written in response to Marx's reading of Aristotle: "It is obvious that the *human eye* gratifies itself in a way different from the crude, non-human eye; the human *ear* from the crude ear, etc.... The sense caught up in crude practical need has only a restricted sense. For the starving man, it is not the human form of food that exists, but only its abstract being as food; it could just as well be there in its crudest form, and it would be impossible to say wherein this feeding-activity differs from that of *animals*." Trans. M. Milligan, in *The Marx-Engels Reader*, ed. Robert C. Tucker (New York, 1978), 88–9.

17 Nussbaum, "Flawed Crystals"; " 'Finely Aware' "; and "Perceptive Equilibrium: Literary Theory and Ethical Theory" (on *The Ambassadors*), in *The Future of Literary Theory*, ed. Ralph Cohen (New York: Routledge, Chapman, and Hall, 1989), 58–85, and also in Nussbaum, *Love's Knowledge*.

18 Lionel Trilling, "*The Princess Casamassima*," in *The Liberal Imagination* (New York, 1950), 58–92.

19 Ibid.

20 Preface to *What Maisie Knew*, in *The Art of the Novel*, 143.

21 See the fine discussion of this in Trilling.

22 W. H. Auden, "At the Grave of Henry James," in *Collected Poems* (London, 1979).

23 See my discussion of the Assinghams in " 'Finely Aware.' "

24 See the related reflections in Isaiah Berlin, "On the Pursuit of the Ideal," *New York Review of Books*, March 17, 1988.

16

Human rights, population aging, and intergenerational equity

NORMAN DANIELS

1. The aging of populations and welfare rights

The aging of society forces major changes in the institutions responsible for social well-being. As the 'age profile' of a society – the proportion of the population in each age group – changes, social needs change.[1] As society ages, proportionally fewer children need education, fewer young adults need job training, but more elderly need employment, income support, and health care, including long-term care. Changing needs find political expression. Strong voices press for reforms of the institutions that meet these needs. At the same time, advocates for existing institutions and their beneficiaries resist change. The result is a heightened sense that the old and the young are in conflict, competing for a critical but scarce resource, public funds that meet basic human needs.

Underlying this common perception of the competition between the old and the young, underlying the call for "intergenerational equity" being voiced in some industrialized societies, there lurk two challenging "new" problems of distributive justice.[2] First, what is a just or fair distribution of social resources among the different *age groups* competing for them? The approach I shall sketch to this problem, the prudential lifespan account, involves our imagining that we can prudently allocate a lifetime fair share of a particular resource, such as income support or health care, over the whole lifespan. Then, what counts as a prudent allocation between stages of a life will be our guide to what counts as a just distribution between age groups. But an institution that solves the age group problem must also solve the second problem, the problem of *equity between birth cohorts*: What is fair treatment of different cohorts as they age and pass through transfer and savings schemes that solve the age group problem? In this essay I shall

A version of this chapter was delivered as a paper at the United Nations Expert Group Conference on Population and Human Rights, Geneva, April 1989, and it will appear in a United Nations report on that conference. I draw at many points in this essay on ideas contained in my *Am I My Parents' Keeper?: An Essay On Justice Between the Young and the Old* (New York: Oxford University Press, 1988), and I thank the publisher for permission to do so.

distinguish these two problems and suggest how they can be simultaneously solved for schemes that transfer such goods as income support
and health care over the lifespan. As we shall see, somewhat different
issues arise in industrialized and developing countries.

Solving the age group and birth cohort problems is necessary if we
are to understand the human rights implications of the aging of society.
Articles 23–26 of the United Nations Universal Declaration of Human
Rights (1948) affirm that people have what I shall call *welfare* rights –
rights to decent jobs, to rest and leisure, to a standard of living
adequate to assure health and well-being, and to education. In a
general and abstract way these Articles assert that nations have obligations to ensure that certain basic human interests and needs are met.

Just what governments are required to do and just what individuals
are entitled to claim in light of these rights – that is, just what the
content of these rights really is – depends fundamentally on the kinds
of needs that must be met and on their distribution in the society. In a
rural, agricultural society, the needs of the small number of elderly may
be met through part-time employment and family support. The rights of
these elderly to a decent standard of living may thus be met through
traditional employment patterns and the discharge of familial obligations, without any governmental intervention.[3] But industrialization and
urbanization, combined with a major demographic shift that produces
many elderly, may mean that the basic economic needs of the elderly
are no longer met. New social transfer mechanisms must be forthcoming or the welfare rights of the elderly will be violated.

Similarly, what a government is obliged to do to meet the health care
rights of its citizens depends on the profile of medical needs in that
society and on the resources that can be made available to meet those
needs. In the same way, what individuals are entitled to claim by way of
medical services depends on what counts as a fair distribution of
medical services, given those needs and the limitations on resources
available to meet them. For example, when there are very few aged
people with partial disabilities, and when there are typically many
children per aged parent, including adult daughters not in the work-
force, and when medical technology can rarely prolong the lives of the
frail elderly, then their "right to long-term health care" (which seems to
be implied by Article 25 of the United Nations Declaration) seems to
be satisfied by the discharge of family obligations. But as all these
conditions change, social resources for long-term care, including personal services at home, become an important way of meeting health
care needs and discharging health care rights.[4]

The problem is not as simple as these examples suggest. As the
profile of needs changes with societal aging, new disputes arise about

the priorities for meeting these needs. These are especially difficult problems to solve. The needs of the elderly for employment opportunities and income support compete with the needs of younger workers for the same goods. The rights of the young and the old to a decent standard of living are in conflict under conditions of limited resources. Similarly, the old and the young both need health care. If resources are scarce and not all needs can be met, we still have a serious problem of distributive justice. This is not a case in which the basic needs of one group are not being met while another group enjoys special privileges or affluence. In that case, we can justify redistribution by appealing to the greater urgency of the needs of the worse-off group. Indeed, that is when an appeal to their welfare rights seems most compelling. But what do we do when the competition between the old and the young is for life-extending health care, or for income support necessary to meet other basic needs? Here claims of comparable importance, based on appeals to the same rights, conflict. To resolve such disputes about the content of welfare rights we must determine what counts as a fair distribution of social resources among the different age groups and birth cohorts competing for them.[5]

These examples also point to another implication of societal aging for human welfare rights. Demographic changes combine with other economic and social forces to raise complex questions about *who is responsible* for guaranteeing these rights. Under some conditions, these rights may be protected largely through private, non-governmental systems of support. But under other conditions, formerly limited to the industrialized countries, but now quite general throughout the world, coordinated public action is required to guarantee welfare rights. The aging of society further advances the need for public responsibility. Nevertheless, it remains a complex question how to mesh public obligations with private or familial obligations and systems of support. For example, heated debate in the United States still focuses on the degree to which "traditional family values" will be undermined by enlarging government programs for long-term care. In developing countries, the problems are even more complex, as we shall later see.

In what follows, I shall first distinguish the age group and birth cohort problems and sketch my approaches to them. Then I shall return to consider further the implications of societal aging for human welfare rights in both industrialized and developing countries.

2. Age groups and birth cohorts

In the United States, the call for "intergenerational equity" has been confusing. Some complain that we have spent too much on the old and too little on the young in recent years (see Preston 1984; Longman 1987), in effect removing many elderly from poverty while pushing many children into it. They refer to this as "intergenerational inequity." Others argue that the current young will never benefit as generously from Social Security as the current elderly, and they refer to this as "intergenerational inequity." There are really distinct issues of distributive justice here. The first complaint is one about justice between *age groups*. The second complaint is about equity in the treatment of different *birth cohorts*.

It is easy to confuse these notions. The term "generation" is ambiguous. We can speak of the perennial struggle between the generations, meaning the conflict between the old and the young, or we may speak about the generation of the 1960s, meaning a particular birth cohort. The notions are also easily confused because, at a given time, people in a given age group, say the elderly (those over sixty-five), are also members of a particular birth cohort (those born prior to 1925).

Nevertheless, age groups and birth cohorts are different notions and give rise to distinct problems of distributive justice. Over time, an age group includes a succession of birth cohorts. Twenty years ago, the elderly included only pre-1925 birth cohorts. Today, they include all pre-1925 cohorts. Age groups do *not* age. Over time, new and different birth cohorts simply move into an age group. In contrast, birth cohorts *do* age. They pass through the stages of life, and so, at different times, fall into different age groups.

A birth cohort is a distinct group of people with a distinctive history and composition. The question, "What is a just distribution of social goods between birth cohorts?" thus carries with it the assumption that we are focused on the differences between distinct groups of people. For example, special questions of fairness may arise because of particular facts about the socioeconomic history and composition of particular birth cohorts. The notion of an age group abstracts from the distinctiveness of birth cohorts and considers people solely by reference to their place in the lifespan. Consequently, our question about justice between age groups also abstracts from the particular differences between the current elderly and the current young that arise because of the distinctive features of the birth cohorts that happen to make up those age groups. We are concerned with a common problem about justice between the old and the young that persists through the flux of aging birth cohorts.[6]

Age groups and birth cohorts are not only conceptually distinct, but distinct issues of justice concern them. Insisting, for example, that different cohorts should be treated equitably or fairly does not tell us just what transfers society ought to guarantee between the young and the old. Knowing that what we do for one cohort must be equitable compared to what is done for another does not help us to learn what we should do for either as they age. Answering the age group question properly, however, may teach us what to do for each birth cohort over time.

Another point suggests that these problems are distinct. The question about age groups is centrally connected to certain other issues of justice in a way that the question about birth cohorts is not. For example, worries about age bias and age discrimination abstract from any consideration about birth cohorts. In asking whether people over sixty-five should be required to retire, or whether they should be denied access to life-extending medical services such as dialysis, as they are in Great Britain (Aaron and Schwartz 1984), we are not asking a question that in any way turns on differences between birth cohorts. We are asking a question about the treatment of different age groups. Similarly, other moral issues, such as questions about filial obligations, are raised about the young and the old in general. These issues too abstract from questions about particular birth cohorts.

In what follows, we must address two problems of "intergenerational equity." The age group problem asks, What is a fair distribution of resources between the old and the young? The birth cohort problem asks, What is fair treatment for different birth cohorts as they pass through institutions that distribute goods over the lifespan? The justice of transfer schemes, such as health care and social security systems, depends on answers to both questions. Though there has been some tendency in industrialized countries to be most alarmed about the birth cohort problem, since the solvency of social welfare systems is a matter of concern, I will begin with the age group problem. We must, in any case, solve it since every birth cohort has an interest in knowing how resources should be distributed across the lifespan.

3. The prudential lifespan account

What is a just distribution of resources between the young and the old? The key to answering this question lies in the humbling fact that we all age. In contrast, we do not change sex or race. The relevance of these banal observations needs some explanation.

If we treat blacks and whites or men and women differently, then we produce an inequality between persons, and such inequalities raise questions about justice. For example, if we hire and fire on the basis of race or sex rather than talents and skills, then we create inequalities that are objectionable on grounds of justice. (Article 2 of the UN Declaration on Human Rights bears on this issue.) If we treat the old and the young differently, however, we may or may not produce an inequality between persons. If we treat them differently just occasionally and arbitrarily, then we will be treating different persons unequally. But if we treat the young one way as a matter of policy and the old another, *and we do so over their whole lives*, then we treat all persons the same way. No inequality between persons is produced since each person is treated both ways. Thus the banal fact that we age means age is different from race or sex for purposes of distributive justice.

My account of justice between age groups builds on this basic point: Unequal treatment at different stages of life may be *exactly what we want* from institutions that operate over a lifetime. Since our needs vary at different stages of our lives, we want institutions to be responsive to these changes. For example, in many industrialized countries, we defer income from our working lives to our post-work retirement period through some combination of individual savings and employee or government pension or social security plan. In many such schemes there are no *vested* savings, but a direct transfer from the working young to the retired old. Viewed at a moment, it appears that "we" young workers are taxed to benefit "them," the old. If the system is stable over the lifespan, it appears that our needs for income vary through the different stages of life, and we have designed a system that treats us appropriately – differently – at different ages.

The same point holds for health care. When we reach age sixty-five in the United States, we consume health care resources at about 3.5 times the rate (in dollars) that we do prior to age sixty-five. But we pay, as young working people, a combined health care insurance premium – through private premiums, through employee contributions, and through social security taxes – that covers not just our actuarially fair costs but the health care costs of the elderly and of children as well. Age groups are treated differently. The old pay less and get more, the young pay more and get less. If this system continues as we age, others will pay "inflated premiums" that will cover our h:gher costs when we are elderly. In effect the system allows us to defer the use of resources from stages in our lives when we need them less into ones in which we need them more. In general, budgeting these transfers prudently enables us to take from some parts of our lives in order to make our lives as a whole better.

We have learned two important lessons about the unequal treatment of different age groups. First, treating the young and old differently does not mean that persons are treated unequally over their lifespan. Second, unequal treatment of the young and old may have effects that benefit everyone. These two points provide the central intuition behind what I call the prudential lifespan account of justice between age groups: Prudent allocation among stages of our lives is our guide to what is just between the young and the old.

The lifespan account involves a fundamental shift of perspective. We must not look at the problem as one of justice between distinct groups in competition with each other, for example, between working adults who pay high premiums and the frail elderly who consume so many services. Rather, we must see that each group *represents* a stage of our lives. We must view the prudent allocation of resources through the stages of life as our guide to justice between groups. From the perspective of stable institutions operating over time, unequal treatment of people by age appears to be budgeting within a life. If we are concerned with net benefits within a life, we can appeal to a standard principle of individual rational choice: It is rational and prudent that a person take from one stage of his life to give to another in order to make his life as a whole better. If the transfers made by an income support or health care system are prudent, they improve individual well-being. Different individuals in such schemes are *each* made better off, even when the transfers involve unequal treatment of the young and the old. This means that neither old nor young have grounds for complaint that the system is unfair.

The contrast of age with race or sex should now be clear. Differential treatment of people by age, when part of a prudent lifetime plan, involves treating people equally and benefiting them over their whole lives. There are no losers. Differential treatment by sex or race always creates inequalities, benefiting some at the expense of others. Losers will have legitimate complaints about unfairness or injustice.

Because it will help to have an example in mind, I will first develop the prudential lifespan account for the case of health care. Some elements of the problem of social allocation can be brought out by considering an individual – let us call her Prudence – who is trying to design a lifetime health care insurance package for herself. Prudence is willing to spend only a certain amount of her lifetime resources insuring herself against health care risks – health care, however important, is not the only good in her life. She quite realistically accepts the fact that the benefits she can buy with that lifetime premium will not meet every conceivable medical need she will have. Therefore, she must be willing to trade coverage for some needs at certain stages of her life for coverage at others. Prudence also believes that she should give equal consideration to her interests at all points in her life. Unfortunately, if she knows how old she is and thinks about things only from the perspective of what she considers important at that point in her life, then she risks biasing the design of her insurance package, for example, by underestimating the importance of things she will need much later in life. To compensate for this bias, she may pretend that she does not know how old she is and will have to live through all the trade-offs she imposes at each stage of her life.

Just as the individual, Prudence, sets a reasonable limit on her lifetime insurance premium, prudent planners acting on behalf of society in general are limited by what counts as a "fair share" of health care (I return to this concept shortly). Their problem is to find the distributive principle that allocates this fair share over the whole lifespan. Their goal is a distribution that people in each age group would think is fair because they would all agree it makes their lives as a whole better than alternatives. To ensure that our planners avoid biasing the design in favor of their own age group, we shall force them to pretend that they do not know how old they are, and we require that they accept a distribution only if they are willing to live with what it does to them at each stage of their lives. Each stage of their own lives thus stands in as proxy for an age group, and they will age from conception to death in the system of trade-offs to which they agree. (For a more detailed statement of these and some other qualifications on the concept of "prudent deliberation" appropriate for solving the age group problem, see Daniels 1988, Chapter 3.)[7]

The notion of a "lifetime fair share" of health care requires clarification. This share is not simply a dollar allotment per person. It consists of entitlements to services that are contingent on our having certain medical needs. I must say more about which contingent entitlements form a fair share.

I have argued elsewhere (Daniels 1985) that a central, unifying function of health care is to maintain and restore functioning that is typical or normal for our species. Health care derives its moral importance from the following fact: Normal functioning has a central effect on the opportunity open to an individual. It helps guarantee individuals a fair chance to enjoy the normal opportunity range for their society. The *normal opportunity range* for a given society is the array of life plans reasonable persons in it are likely to construct for themselves. An individual's fair share of the normal opportunity range is the array of life plans he may reasonably choose, given his talents and skills. Disease and disability shrink that share from what is fair; health care protects it. Health care lets a person enjoy that portion of the normal range to which his full range of skills and talents would give him access, assuming these two are not impaired by special social disadvantages. The suggestion that emerges from this account is that we should use impairment of the normal opportunity range as a fairly crude measure of the relative moral importance of health care needs at the macro level.

Some general theories of justice, most notably Rawls's (1971), provide foundations for a principle protecting fair equality of opportunity, and equality of opportunity underlies Articles 21, 23, and 26 of the UN Declaration of Human Rights. If such a principle is indeed a requirement of an acceptable general theory of justice, then I believe we have a natural way to extend such general theories to govern the distribution of health care. We should include health care institutions among those basic institutions of a society that are governed by the fair equality of opportunity principle.[8]

Because we have obligations to assure people fair equality of opportunity, we have social obligations to provide health care services that protect and restore normal functioning. This account implies that there should be no financial, geographical, or discriminatory barriers to a level of care that promotes normal functioning, given reasonable or necessary limits on resources. We can guide hard public policy choices about which services are more important to provide by considering their relative impact on the normal opportunity range. Rights to health care are thus *system relative*: Entitlements to services can only be specified within a system that works to protect opportunity as well as possible, given limited resources.

Our prudent planners solve the age group problem if they can clarify what the right to health care means for each age group. To do this, they must agree to a principle for allocating their lifetime fair share to each stage of life. Remember, these planners do not know how old they are. This means that it is especially important for them to make sure social arrangements give them a chance to enjoy their fair share of the normal range of opportunities open to them at each stage of life. This protection of opportunity at each stage of life is particularly important, since they are planning for their whole lives and must keep in mind the importance of being able to revise their views about what is valuable in life as they age. But impairments of normal functioning by disease and disability clearly restrict the portion of the normal opportunity range open to individuals at any stage of their lives. Consequently, health care services should be rationed throughout a life in a way that respects the importance of the age-relative normal opportunity range. In effect, all specific allocation decisions must be constrained by this principle. (I shall return to consider its implications for health care rights in developed and developing countries shortly.)

This approach to solving the age group problem is quite general and will help us think about other welfare rights as well. For example, Article 25 includes rights to income support during periods of unemployment, including retirement in old age. The young and the old seem to be in competition here just as much as in the case of health care. The prudential lifespan account asks us to think about how planners who do not know their age would allocate a lifetime fair share of such entitlements to each stage of life. Here, too, the lifetime fair share is not some lump sum in dollars, but a range of contingent entitlements to support. These entitlements are specified relative to what justice in general permits in the way of economic inequalities between persons.

Prudent planners, operating under the constraints I have sketched before, would have to reason as follows. They cannot expand their lifetime income share by allocating it in certain ways, for example by setting aside income early in life and investing it heavily in their own human capital or otherwise. Such investment strategies are already accommodated within the notion of a lifetime fair income share, or so I am supposing when I imagine them budgeting a fixed but fair lifetime share.[9] These planners do not know how old they are, and they must allow for the fact that their preferences or views about what is good in life will change over the lifespan. The prudent course of action would be to allocate their fair share in such a way that standard of living would remain roughly equal over the lifespan (call this the Standard of Living Preservation Principle). They would want institutions to facilitate income transfers over the lifespan in such a way that the individual, at each stage of life, has available an adequate income to pursue whatever plan of life he or she may have at that stage of life. Of course, "adequate" is here relative to the individual's fair income share, as determined by the acceptable inequalities in the society. This principle has implications for income support in old age, and I shall return to them later.

The general rights to education described in Article 26 also must be refined to solve the age group problem. We are used to thinking of education as a process early in life, one that helps set the trajectory for the quality of later life. But as more and more people live longer lives in the context of rapidly changing technologies, and as societies age, we must think anew about the role of education throughout the lifespan. Education, like health care, is important to protecting fair equality of opportunity, and prudent planners would probably want the education system to be designed so that it protects the normal opportunity range at each stage of life.

In Section 6, I shall discuss in somewhat greater detail how we must think about welfare rights given the aging of society in developed and developing countries. But first I want to describe quite briefly how we should address the problem of equity between birth cohorts. The solution to this problem also places constraints on the specific entitlements that can be granted through a system of welfare rights under different conditions.

4. Equity between birth cohorts

In the United States, many people have pointed to the fact that benefit ratios – the overall ratio of benefits to contributions – have been falling for successive cohorts entering the Social Security system, and there is considerable concern that these ratios will continue to fall. A special instance of the problem of equity between birth cohorts is this: What inequalities in benefit ratios are fair or equitable? More generally, what inequalities in the treatment of different cohorts are just or fair as these cohorts pass through institutions intended to meet the requirements of justice between age groups?

Each birth cohort has an interest in securing institutions that solve the *age group* problem effectively. This is true because each cohort ages and has an interest in solving the age group problem. But institutions or transfer schemes that solve the age group problem operate under considerable uncertainty. There is uncertainty about population and economic growth rates, as well as about technological change, which further affects productivity. Errors are likely to abound, and inequalities in benefit ratios between cohorts will arise as a result. But institutions that can solve the age group problem must remain stable over time. They must weather the political struggle that will result from unjustifiable or unacceptable inequalities in benefit ratios. Such institutions will be able to survive the struggle among coexisting birth cohorts only if each feels it has a stake in preserving them. Each will feel it has such a stake only if it believes these institutions work to its benefit within the limits of fairness.

The practical target for this commitment we can take to be *approximate equality* in benefit ratios. Nevertheless, uncertainty obtains. Productivity can increase – or decrease – under certain economic conditions. How should the benefits of increasing productivity be shared? Some argue that the concept of *desert* should play a role here. Rewards or entitlements should be proportional to contributions one – or one's cohort – has made. But this would imply that benefit ratios should depend on disentangling the many sources of change that contribute to rising or falling economic fortune. It is hard to see how a stable system could incorporate such factors in its scheme of benefits.

We might try to cut through some of the complex issues raised by the concept of desert by appealing to the interest each cohort has in providing for stable institutions that solve the age group problem. Cohorts must cooperate to achieve such stability. But cooperation will require some *sharing of risks* across cohorts. In general, the burdens of economic declines and of living through unfavorable retiree/employee ratios must be shared, as must the benefits of economic growth and favorable retiree/employee ratios. This suggests again that approximate equality in benefit ratios should be the practical target of public policy, if not a hard and fast rule. This may mean, for example, that transfer schemes may have to build cushions of reserves, which are not spent on the current elderly, if cohorts that will retire under less favorable conditions are to enjoy equity of treatment. In systems like the United States, building such reserves creates considerable political tension, for the reserve funds are targets of convenience for those who want to use these resources for other purposes.

My solution to the birth cohort problem, that we should strive for approximate equality of benefit ratios since that will help ensure stability, is open to an important objection. The objection is that birth cohorts cannot be trusted to abide by a transfer scheme that ideally solves the age group problem through intercohort transfers, because, as they age, they may use their increasing political power to revise the scheme in favor of their old age, benefiting heavily at both ends of the lifespan. Thomson (1989) suggests that a particular cohort has been greedy in just these ways in New Zealand, and that similar distortions have occurred in transfer schemes elsewhere. His argument is compatible with the view that this behavior is just the result of the special circumstances or opportunities that faced a particular cohort. But a stronger version of this objection might claim that the pattern is general or inevitable. For example, some public choice theorists (e.g., Epstein 1988) have argued that large-scale, state-managed transfer schemes are sitting ducks for the self-interested behavior of aging cohorts, as their political power increases.

My solution of the birth cohort problem rests on the claim that each cohort has an interest in providing itself with a stable solution of the age group problem. The objection I just noted says that sometimes or even generally, given the opportunity, self-interest will drive a cohort to undermine a fair scheme, leading it to take unfair advantage of the less powerful cohort that follows it.

We should notice that not all cohorts behave in this way. More important, it is not obvious what the alternative is. If we avoid schemes that depend on intercohort transfers of the sort that take place in the U.S. Social Security system, then we still have to answer the question: How can social institutions facilitate adequate types and rates of savings? That is, we are back to the age group problem, but we must now solve it by relying only on the resources of one cohort. Moreover, we are ruling out an important advantage offered by a system that involves intercohort transfers, namely, that it tends to share risks more widely over time. We cannot take advantage of the fact that an equitable form of risk sharing would be much more desirable than the results of "privatizing" the age group problem for each cohort.

Avoiding schemes that involve intercohort transfers in order to avoid unequal benefit ratios does not mean that different cohorts will fare equally well once each is solely responsible for its own well-being over the lifespan. In fact, inequalities will abound because of uneven economic growth rates. It is not at all obvious that inequalities of benefit ratios in intercohort schemes will generate more intolerable forms and degrees of inequality than the inequalities that result when each cohort must depend on its own resources and good luck. Cooperation may be a better strategy than "go it alone," and the problem becomes one of institutional design and of securing a long-term commitment to schemes that are fair.

The ideal solution I am sketching to both age group and birth cohort problems, then, is not merely utopian. It can serve as a basis for moral and political criticism of attempts by particular cohorts to undermine just transfer schemes. There is more than one way to learn from history. Rather than learn that no cohort can trust another, we should seek to make more explicit the principles around which cohorts can seek the benefits of cooperation.

5. Welfare rights and family obligations

My account thus far has skirted a very important issue concerning societal aging and welfare rights, namely, whose responsibility it is to assure that welfare rights of the elderly are met. Specifically, how is this responsibility to be divided between government and individuals or families? The position I take is that these welfare rights are ultimately the responsibility of society to assure through government authority, but this ultimate responsibility does not preclude dividing the burden of meeting these rights in various ways among families and the government, depending on important facts about the given society. I can here only touch briefly on several related points.

There are obvious reasons why the ultimate responsibility for assuring these welfare rights of the elderly must be societal. Many elderly will have no families who can be assigned specific responsibility. The economic policies and social structures that affect employment, health status, and health services are all beyond the immediate control or responsibility of individuals or families. Even if the burden of providing economic or personal support falls on families for the care of some elderly, it is society that must coordinate (through incentives or sanctions) that individual behavior, and supplement it where necessary.

This general point about societal responsibility is sometimes lost in the controversy – and rhetoric – about who should bear the costs of meeting the needs of the elderly. In the United States, for example, recent appeals in the political arena to return to "traditional family values" provided a background for some (unsuccessful) state initiatives to make adult children legally responsible for some of the costs being incurred by state governments for nursing home care of the elderly. This appeal to filial or family obligations warrants making several points.

First, in a culturally diverse nation like the United States, there is no shared cultural tradition that picks out just one, well-defined set of filial obligations. The attempt to elevate some mythical set of traditional values into a shared tradition should be avoided, for it is an unsound basis for public policy. It risks failing to respect the cultural diversity that exists in the United States and in many larger nations. In some countries, where a set of filial obligations is widely recognized as a shared heritage, public appeal to such tradition may be less objectionable, but it still risks doing an injustice to some minorities.

Second, even where there is a widely shared tradition of family support for the elderly, it may be very difficult to extrapolate from the obligations that held under past demographic, social, and economic patterns to the obligations it would be appropriate to consider binding under current conditions. After all, very few adult children had to support frail elderly parents in past generations; many do now and more will in the future. And support provided in traditional agricultural settings, where the elderly controlled the land, is not necessarily the same thing as support provided under quite different social and economic conditions in urban settings today. Even a well-defined tradition may not tell us just what is a comparable burden today.

Third, even in culturally diverse, yet highly developed, societies like the United States, a substantial proportion of support services and care for the partially disabled elderly is provided by families (up to 80 percent according to some estimates). It is unlikely that any purely public system of social support could provide an adequate substitute for the quantity and quality of care provided by families. So the real task for public policy is to *facilitate* family support wherever possible, by providing incentives and supports for families that offer such care. It is quite inappropriate for governments to insist that the obligations to provide such care are really individual and, at the same time, to avoid providing a climate in which such obligations can be met without undue strains on moral commitment. Of course, changes in family structure and geographical mobility mean that many elderly have no adult children who are in a position to help them at all. As society ages, in both developed and developing countries, some supplementary system of public supports will have to be provided.

In developing countries the challenge to protect the welfare rights of the growing numbers of elderly is very great because resources for social transfer schemes are hard to come by. Many commentators have noted that government policy may have to make up for inadequate social transfer schemes by developing varied incentives to continue the provision of family support. Policies that focus on employment and housing may be crucial in maintaining the family and community networks capable of meeting the welfare needs of the elderly under rapidly changing economic and social conditions (Binstock et al. 1982). Even where the focus of public effort must remain on creatively encouraging private and family transfers of support, the ultimate responsibility for assuring welfare rights remains a societal one.

These remarks suggest that public policies can successfully assure welfare rights to aging societies in a variety of ways, dividing the burden in various ways between public and private systems of support, depending on local economic conditions and cultural traditions. Thus we again see that the actual content of welfare rights will be quite system-relative. In some contexts, entitlements to care will mainly be correlated with family obligations to provide support; in others, entitlements will be to public systems of support. There does not seem to be any one model that best assures these rights in all existing conditions.

6. Current controversies and welfare rights

Because the aging of society alters the content and distribution of welfare needs, it has important implications for welfare rights. Conflict about these implications has surfaced as concerns about "intergenerational equity," especially in some developed countries with extensive social welfare systems. I have argued that we can clarify the content of these welfare rights if we can solve two distinct problems of distributive justice, the problem of justice between age groups and the problem of equity between birth cohorts. To solve the age group problem, we must imagine prudent planners (who do not know how old they are) budgeting a lifetime "fair share" of an important good, such as health care or income support, among the stages of life. What is prudent between stages will count as what is fair between age groups. Distinct birth cohorts will be treated equitably if they receive approximately equal benefit ratios as they pass through institutions that solve the age group problem appropriately. Finally, depending on complex facts about a given society, there may be various ways to distribute the burdens of meeting welfare rights among families, employers, and governmental programs, though the ultimate responsibility for assuring these rights is societal, not individual.

I would like to develop a few implications of this general approach to problems of intergenerational equity by considering several issues of current controversy. Though these controversies have arisen first in developed countries where the aging process is well advanced, they have implications for welfare rights in developing countries as well. Specifically, I shall consider the following questions that concern the design of health care and income support systems: (1) Are rights to long-term care of comparable importance to rights to acute care? (2) Is rationing of high-technology medicine by age a violation of welfare rights? (3) Do current levels of income support benefits, including early retirement incentives, mean that the welfare rights of future generations will be compromised?

Long-term care

Are rights to long-term care of comparable importance to rights to acute care?

Because the likelihood of needing long-term care increases with age, the aging of society raises urgent questions about the long-term care systems in many developed countries. Some experts suggest that long-term care "may well be the major health and social issue of the next four decades, polarizing society over the next 20 to 40 years" (Vogel and Palmer 1982: v). By 2040, there is likely to be a fivefold increase in the number of people aged eighty-five and over in the United States and other European countries, and similar increases in the numbers of very old who are nursing home residents or functionally dependent on the community (Soldo and Manton 1985: 286). These trends are present in many developing countries as well.

The problem will not be that of merely expanding a basically adequate system. The system in the United States, for example, is by no means adequate to handle current needs. Criticisms of the U.S. long-term care system focus on the following central faults:

1. It is difficult for poor patients who need high levels of care, especially Medicaid recipients, to find nursing home placements.
2. The cost of nursing home care and the eligibility requirements for Medicaid reimbursements drive spouses into poverty, often reducing their ability to maintain independence.
3. There is premature institutionalization of many individuals, who could be sustained in less restrictive settings if services were available.
4. There are many unmet needs for personal care and social support services for frail elderly people trying to maintain independent living arrangements.
5. Care in institutions for the elderly is often not aimed at rehabilitation, even though some would be possible.
6. Families providing long-term care are given few services aimed at relieving their burdens.

Two issues are central to explanations of these problems in long-term care systems. First, there is confusion about the moral importance of long-term care services, that is, about their relative importance compared to acute medical services. Second, there is controversy about how to mesh public obligations to provide long-term care with the belief that families are responsible for caring for their elders. The prudential lifespan account gives a unified view of both issues.

The moral importance of personal medical services derives not from their glamour or prestige but from the purpose and function, which is to maintain or restore or compensate for the losses of normal functioning. Keeping people normal in these ways is of importance because it affects an individual's share of the normal opportunity range at each stage of life. The moral importance of long-term care services also derives from their general purpose and function, which is identical to that of medical services. Their importance for purposes of distributive justice is also measured by their impact on the normal opportunity range at each stage of life. Since the disabilities that require long-term care affect such a substantial portion of the elderly population in the very late stages of life, it is imprudent to design a system that ignores them and meets only the acute care crises of the elderly. That long-term care should be so seriously neglected in the United States and some other developed countries is morally indefensible and constitutes a violation of welfare rights of the elderly.

Many advocates of increased home care services, including personal care and social support services, have emphasized the importance of independent living. They have sometimes cited a principle calling for care in the "least restrictive environment" (cf. Callahan and Wallack 1981). Similarly, others have talked about the loss of dignity that accompanies premature or inappropriate institutionalization. The underlying issue, however, is the loss of opportunity range, which has a direct effect on autonomy and dignity, as well as on self-respect. The moral issues here thus go beyond comparing the costs of institutionalized and home-based services.

In improving the long-term care system, however, attention should be paid to building on the high level of home care already provided by families. Providing support for families that give such care, through economic incentives and through facilities that give temporary relief from the burdens of providing care, will improve circumstances both for the recipients of the care and for the providers; that is, it will improve that at two stages of life, not just one. The prudent planners of a health care system should, therefore, assist in family provision of care wherever possible.

There are lessons to be learned here for use in developing countries. These countries can avoid the bias that exists in many developed countries in favor of high-technology acute care and against long-term care services. A properly designed health care system will better protect the welfare rights of the elderly if it gives appropriate importance to long-term care, which may be of greater value than the provision of high-cost, high-technology interventions that marginally extend the lives of the dying elderly. Of course, some level of institutional care will have to be provided for those elderly who have no other alternatives. A number of commentators have emphasized the importance of facilitating the care of the elderly by paying attention to housing and other community policies that allow families to preserve support relationships in non-traditional settings (cf. Lawton 1982).

Rationing by age

Is rationing by age a violation of the health care rights of the elderly?

In the United States, there is much concern that the increasing numbers of elderly will intensify the already acute problem of health care costs that rise at rates much higher than the rate of inflation. Much of this rate of increase is due to the rapid dissemination of high-cost medical technologies, many of which are aimed at conditions prevalent among the elderly. In this context, there is a growing discussion about the need to ration beneficial medical treatments. In the United States, the greatest threat to health care rights will come from the temptation to use ability to pay as a criterion for rationing, but there is a growing discussion of the relevance of age as a basis for rationing some high-cost medical technologies. Callahan (1987) has drawn considerable critical comment on his proposal that we consider rationing life-extending medical services explicitly by age. Less hypothetically, there is evidence that the British National Health Service already uses age as a basis for rationing some expensive technologies such as renal dialysis (Aaron and Schwartz 1984).

Some critics of rationing by age consider it morally impermissible in exactly the way that rationing by race or sex would be. They consider age, as opposed to medical suitability, a "morally irrelevant" basis for distributing medical services. Others (see Callahan 1987) argue that rationing by age is permissible because the elderly have a duty to step aside and sacrifice for the young or that it is fair for the elderly, who have had the opportunity to live a long time, to improve the chances of the young, who have had less opportunity to live (see Veatch 1988).

The prudent lifespan approach to the age group problem provides a way to resolve this dispute (see Daniels 1988, Chapter 5). A policy will be fair to different age groups if prudent planners who did not know how old they were would choose it as a way of allocating a fair share of lifetime health care among the stages of life. Under certain conditions of resource scarcity, the following might happen: Provision of expensive or scarce life-extending services to those who have reached normal life expectancy can be accomplished only by reducing access by the young to those resources. That is, saving these resources by giving ourselves claim to them in our old age is possible only if we give ourselves reduced access to them in earlier stages of life. An important effect of this form of saving is that we increase our chance of living a longer-than-normal lifespan at the cost of reducing our chances of reaching a normal lifespan. Under some conditions, it would be prudent for planners to agree to ration such technologies by age, making them more available to the young than to the elderly. If that is true, then such a rationing policy would be fair to each person. Each person would have maximized the chances of reaching a normal life expectancy, and so would benefit from the rationing. All people would be treated equally – judging from the perspective of a whole life. This argument turns on no prior moral assumption that life at one age is more valuable than life at another; nor does it turn on prior moral views about the duties of the elderly to the young, or vice versa.

It is important to understand that this argument is not an endorsement of rationing by age as a general strategy for reducing health care costs. Rationing by age would not be the preferred strategy except under special circumstances of resource scarcity. Also, such rationing would have to be constrained by other considerations of justice. For example, the criteria for rationing and its rationale would have to be public, and people would have to consent to such a scheme through some democratic means. Under a broad range of circumstances, it seems quite likely that other criteria for rationing medical services would seem preferable to rationing by age. When it would be prudent to ration by age, however, age would become a morally relevant basis for distribution. In general, however, it is likely that there are better strategies for rationing health care than rationing by age – ones that would be judged preferable by the prudential lifespan account.

Income support policy

Do current levels of income support benefits, including early-retirement incentives, mean that the welfare rights of future generations will be compromised?

Some of the loudest complaints about intergenerational equity come from critics of social security policies in developed nations. The complaint is that relatively high levels of benefits enjoyed by current elderly cohorts cannot be sustained as the aging of society proceeds and the ratio of employed to retired workers is reduced. The complaint is that current cohorts of workers will never be able to enjoy comparable benefits ratios when they retire. In the United States, some of the shrillest proponents of intergenerational equity call for dismantling the Social Security system and forcing each cohort to rely on its own resources for income support in old age.

The approach I have sketched to the birth cohort problem has important implications for this issue. In general, we need to secure stable solutions to the age group problem, ones that will earn the support of successive cohorts. This suggests that approximate equality in benefit ratios should be a target for public policy. Several strategies are available for adjusting benefits so that this target is achievable despite demographic shifts such as the aging of society. One strategy is to build a cushion of unexpended benefits while the ratio of workers to retirees is still relatively high. This strategy has been adopted in some recent financing reforms of the U.S. Social Security system, although there is always a risk that these benefits will be a target of convenience for politicians seeking to reduce budget deficits.

A second strategy is more basic, for it involves rethinking some of the policies toward retirement that have dominated developed welfare systems in recent decades. Many current policies provide considerable incentives for older workers to withdraw from the work force well before any disability actually makes such withdrawal necessary. It is also difficult for older workers to find flexible, part-time employment that can reduce the need for drawing on income support benefits. Underlying these incentives and policies are both economic and moral considerations. Pushing older workers out of the work force in periods of unemployment, when large numbers of young people are seeking employment opportunities, may have seemed an acceptable way to ration jobs by age, or it may have seemed an appropriate way to make room for better-educated and potentially more productive workers in technologically advancing economies. These economic considerations may have been reinforced by the view that the elderly want to enjoy more leisure time. The question now arises as to whether these underlying considerations should be reassessed.

Health status for the elderly remains quite good well into the mid-seventies. Millions of elderly who would be happier with some form of meaningful work, at least on a part-time basis, find themselves facing forced withdrawal from the work force. At the same time, many European economies actually face a shortage of workers in the next few decades. Under these conditions, it may well be wise to consider revising the existing benefits and incentives that lead workers to withdraw from the work force early. The new shape of a life, with many vigorous and healthy years extending well beyond standard retirement age, means that we may be in the grip of an antiquated conception of the typical course of life.

In the United States, compulsory retirement ages have been raised or eliminated, at least for large categories of employment, and this may encourage some reassessment of the employability of older workers. It may not be enough, however, simply to eliminate legal or quasi-legal barriers to the employment of willing, elderly workers. Rather, we may have to encourage the emergence of flexible employment practices that accommodate the needs of older workers. Such practices may become an increasingly important way of assuring the welfare rights of an aging population.

Developing countries may have a chance to avoid what is now appearing to be mistakes in the design of income support systems in some developed countries. Given the scarcity of resources in developing countries, a policy that recognized the growing absolute numbers of healthy, employable elderly people would be highly advisable. Such policies may make it possible to target income support for the elderly so that it meets the needs of those without family or work-based support.

The new shape of a life

Increased life expectancy, especially for the elderly, combined with the demographic shift to an older society, changes the typical *shape* of a life. We can no longer look at the problems of the old as exceptional. Each of us individually faces the prospect of planning for life through its expanded late stages. But collectively society must adjust institutions and policies to accommodate this new shape. Here quantity changes to quality: When enough lives have the new shape, there is a critical mass of people who have a common interest in making the later stages of life meaningful and productive. The social task – and this involves issues of distributive justice and welfare rights – is to provide an adequate framework of opportunities and means through which diverse individuals can pursue their own views of the good life. The prudential lifespan perspective can help us to understand some of the distributive issues that are involved.

One issue that has been discussed frequently by gerontologists is the standard expectation that the elderly, even the energetic and active majority of the elderly, will face the later stages of life without meaningful work. For many people, including the elderly, being productive or pursuing meaningful work is a central element of well-being – one clearly singled out by Article 23 of the UN Declaration of Human Rights. Work is much more important than as a mere means to income. Protecting equality of opportunity in the later stages of life will require that we develop flexible policies regarding employment of the elderly, as well as many community programs using volunteers. This argument for the importance of such policies goes well beyond reducing the economic dependence of the elderly on transfers from the young. It also goes beyond the importance of reducing the rate at which society must save for the later stages of life although this is an important issue.

Society must further face the educational implications of the fact that life has a new shape. People must be educated to think prospectively about what an additional fifteen or twenty years beyond age sixty-five should include. We shall have to undertake extensive adult education so that people can actively prepare for the projects and plans an extended life makes possible. The new shape of life makes it more important to provide people with the means and opportunity to revise their plans for life relatively late in life. We must also explore new housing and community living arrangements that harness the cooperative energy of the increased numbers of the elderly. Many of our attitudes toward education, work, family, and living arrangements are tied quite directly to the old shape of a life. It would be imprudent not to revise these attitudes and the institutions that arise from them. Not revising them would lead to unjust, that is, imprudent, distributions of resources between the old and the young. Not revising them would threaten the welfare rights articulated in the UN Declaration.

7. Conclusion

I have offered a rather abstract and general description of two problems of distributive justice highlighted by the aging of society. Solving them gives us a way to clarify the content of welfare rights and to resolve disputes about intergenerational equity. It would be easy in this essay to lose sight of the most important aspect of my approach: I offer a unifying vision. We all pass through institutions that distribute goods over our lifespan. If these institutions are prudently designed, *each* of us benefits throughout life. It is only prudent to treat ourselves differently at different stages of life, as our needs change. What is prudent with respect to different stages of a life determines what is fair between age groups. Prudence here guides justice. If as policymakers, planners, and the general public we can all keep our eyes on this unifying vision, and if we can ignore the divisive talk about competition between age groups and birth cohorts, then our target will be policies that benefit us through our whole lives. Establishing such policies would mean doing justice to the old and the young. It would mean giving clear content to our welfare rights.

Notes

1 See Russell (1982) for a detailed study of the effects of the Baby Boom generation as this demographic bulge has passed through schools, entered the work force, and faces retirement.

2 These problems are not really *new*. Since every society has some system of transfers of wealth, power, and other goods between age groups and birth cohorts, its practices embody, at least implicitly, a solution to the age group and birth cohort problems. Stable, traditional institutions camouflage the existence of these long-standing solutions to the age group and birth cohort problems. We do not see the problems because nothing unusual seems to be happening. But changing economic, social, and demographic conditions force us to face these problems anew.

3 Of course, traditional agriculture societies varied considerably in the degree to which, and the arrangements by which, they met the needs of the elderly; I am not advocating

a myth of the premodern Golden Age of the family. See Daniels (1988), Chapter 2, and Laslett (1972, 1976).

4 I am not implying that family support no longer is an important way of meeting personal care needs of the frail elderly in industrialized societies. Families provide about 80 percent of such support in the United States (Frankfather et al. 1981).

5 Throughout this discussion, I am avoiding, as much as possible, philosophical questions about whether these welfare rights are themselves basic or are derived from other, more basic moral notions; my point about their content arises in any case. See Daniels (1985) for an argument that health care rights derive from basic notions in a theory of distributive justice, namely, from a principle protecting equality of opportunity.

6 This is *not* to say that in general (e.g., in the social sciences) we can talk about the old and the young in abstraction from the different experiences these groups have that derive from differences between cohorts. The "experience of old age," for example, will vary from birth cohort to birth cohort, depending on facts about each cohort's education and prior history. See Featherman (1983).

7 I argue in Daniels (1988) that considerations of prudence require even further restrictions on the knowledge of the deliberators, making them even less like the standard "fully informed consumer" of economic theory. For example, they should judge their well-being by reference to all-purpose goods, like income and opportunity, rather than through the very specific lens of the "plan of life" they happen to have at a given stage of life; otherwise the design of the lifetime allocation may be biased by a conception of what is good that just happens to be held at a given point in life. See also Rawls (1971, 1982, 1988).

8 This requires modifications of Rawls's equal opportunity principle, however. Cf. Daniels, *Just Health Care*, Chapter 3.

9 At the level of resources it is a zero sum game, although the resource can be allocated in ways that can be estimated to make their lives go better or worse overall.

References

Aaron, H. J. (1966). "The Social Insurance Paradox." *Canadian Journal of Economics and Political Science*. 32(August): 371–7. Cited in Aaron 1982:76.

(1982). *Economic Effects of Social Security*. Washington, D.C.: Brookings Institution.

Aaron, H. [J.], and Schwartz, W. (1984). *The Painful Prescription*. Washington, D.C.: Brookings Institution.

American Association for International Aging (1985). *Aging Populations in Developing Nations*. Washington, D.C.: United States Agency for International Development.

Andrews, G. R., Esterman, A. J., and Braunack-Mayer, A. J., and Rungie, C. M. (1986). *Aging in the Western Pacific*. Manila: World Health Organization.

Binstock, R. H., Chow, Wing-Sun, and Schulz, J. H., eds. (1982). *International Perspectives on Aging: Population and Policy Challenges*. Policy Development Studies Number 7. New York: United Nations Fund for Population Activities.

Boskin, M. J., ed. (1978). *The Crisis in Social Security: Problems and Prospects*. 2nd ed. San Francisco: Institute for Contemporary Studies.

Boskin, M. J., Kotlikoff, L. J., Puffert, D. J., and Shoven, J. B. (1986). "Social Security: A Financial Appraisal across and within Generations." Unpublished.

Boskin, M. J., and Shoven, J. B. (1984). "Concepts and Measures of Earnings Replacement During Retirement." Working paper no. 1360. National Bureau of Economic Research.

(1986). "Poverty Among the Elderly: Where Are the Holes in the Safety Net?" National Bureau of Economic Research.

Callahan, Daniel (1987). *Setting Limits: Medical Goals in an Aging Society*, New York: Simon & Schuster.

Callahan, J. J., and Wallack, S. S., eds. (1981). *Reforming the Long-Term-Care System*. Lexington, Mass.: Heath.

Daniels, N. (1985). *Just Health Care*. Cambridge: Cambridge University Press.

(1988). *Am I My Parents' Keeper?: An Essay on Justice Between the Young and the Old*. New York: Oxford University Press.

Epstein, R. A. (1988). "Justice Across the Generations." Conference on Intergenerational Justice, University of Texas, Austin.

Featherman, D. L. (1983). "The Life-Span Perspective in Social Science Research." In P. B. Blates and O. G. Brim, Jr. (eds.), *Life-Span Development and Behavior*. Volume 5, pp. 1–59. New York: Academic Press.

Frankfather, D. L., Smith, M. J., and Caro, F. G. (1981). *Family Care of the Elderly*. Lexington, Mass.: Lexington Books.

Gibson, R. M., and Fisher, C. R. (1979). "Age Differences in Health Care Spending, Fiscal Year 1977." *Social Security Bulletin*. 42:1:3–16.

Heisel, Marsel A. (1985). "Aging in the Context of Population Policies in Developing Countries." *Population Bulletin of the United Nations*, no. 17-1984. Department of Internatinal Economic and Social Affairs.

Kreps, J. (1971). *Lifetime Allocation of Work and Income: Essays in the Economics of Aging*. Durham, N.C.: Duke University Press.

Laslett, P., ed. (1972). *Household and Family in Past Time*. Cambridge: Cambridge University Press.

(1976). "Societal Development and Aging." In R. H. Binstock and E. Shanas (eds.), *Handbook of Aging and the Social Sciences*. New York: Van Nostrand Reinhold, pp. 87–116.

Lawton, M. Powell (1982). "Environments and Living Arrangements." In Binstock et al. 1982: 159–92.

Leimer, D. R., and Petri, P. A. (1981). "Cohort Specific Effects of Social Security Policy." *National Tax Journal* 34 (March): 9–28. Cited in Aaron 1982:74.

Longman, P. (1987). *Born to Pay: The New Policies of Aging in America*. Boston, Mass.: Houghton Mifflin.

Moffitt, R. (1982). "Trends in Social Security Wealth by Cohort." Paper prepared for the National Bureau of Economic Research Conference on

Income and Wealth, Madison, Wisconsin, May 14–15, 1982, cited in Aaron 1982:6.

Neugarten, B. (1974). "Age Groups in American Society and the Rise of the Young-Old." *Annals of the American Academy of Political and Social Science*. 415:189–98.

Parsons, D. O., and Munro, D. R. (1978). "Intergenerational Transfers in Social Security." In Boskin 1978: 65–86.

Preston, S. H. (1984). "Children and the Elderly: Divergent Paths for America's Dependents." *Demography* 21:4:435–57.

Rawls, J. (1971). *A Theory of Justice*. Cambridge, Mass.: Harvard University Press.

(1982). "Social Unity and the Primary Goods." In A. K. Sen and B. Williams (eds.), *Utilitarianism and Beyond*. Cambridge: Cambridge University Press, pp. 159–85.

(1988). "The Priority of Right and Ideas of the Good." *Philosophy and Public Affairs* 17:4:251–76.

Russell, L. (1982). *The Baby Boom Generation and the Economy*. Washington, D.C.: Brookings Institution.

Soldo, G. J., and Manton, K. G. (1985). "Changes in the Health Status and Service Needs of the Oldest Old: Current Patterns and Future Trends." *Milban Memorial Fund Quarterly* 63:2:286–323.

Spengler, J., and Kreps, J. (1963). "Equity and Social Credit for the Retired." In J. Kreps (ed.), *Employment, Income, and Retirement Problems of the Aged*. Durham, N.C.: Duke University Press, pp. 198–229.

Thomson, David (1989). "The Welfare State and Intergenerational Conflict: Winners and Losers." In C. Conrad, P. Johnson, and D. Thomson (eds.), *Workers Versus Pensioners: Intergeneration Justice in an Ageing World*. New York: Academic Press.

United Nations Universal Declaration of Human Rights (1948).

United States Department of Commerce, Bureau of the Census (1988). *Aging in the Third World*. International Population Reports Series P-95, No. 79. Washington, D.C.: Government Printing Office.

Veatch, Robert M. "Justice and the Economics of Terminal Illness." *Hastings Center Report*, 18:4(August–Sept.): 34-40.

Vogel, R. J., and Palmer, H. C. (eds.) (1982). *Long-Term Care: Perspectives from Research and Demonstrations*. Washington, D.C.: Health Care Financing Administration, U.S. Department of Health and Human Services.